Comprehensive Law Practice

Comprehensive Law Practice

Law as a Healing Profession

Susan Swaim Daicoff

PROFESSOR OF LAW
FLORIDA COASTAL SCHOOL OF LAW

CAROLINA ACADEMIC PRESS
Durham, North Carolina

Library of Congress Cataloging-in-Publication Data

Daicoff, Susan Swaim.
 Comprehensive law practice : law as a healing profession / Susan Daicoff.
     p. cm.
 Includes bibliographical references and index.
 ISBN 978-1-59460-880-3 (alk. paper)
 1. Dispute resolution (Law)--United States. 2. Practice of law--United States. I. Title.
 KF9084.D35 2011
 347.73'9--dc23
                              2011018881

Carolina Academic Press
700 Kent Street
Durham, North Carolina 27701
Telephone (919) 489-7486
Fax (919) 493-5668
www.cap-press.com

Printed in the United States of America

This book is dedicated to my mother, Mary Jane Daicoff, the most brilliant woman and best teacher I know, who knows something about everything, whose unending curiosity inspires me, and who always encourages me to synthesize — and to my father, George R. Daicoff, Sr., whose shining example as a cardiovascular surgeon, lecturer, and professor impressed me and who always reminds me of the importance of doing good, healing people, and enjoying what you do. Their incredible talents as lecturers, investigators, and professors are present in all that I do.

Because my father always starts every lecture he gives with a joke, I'll start with this one, which he gave me just for this purpose:

Pearly Gates

On their way to get married, a young couple was involved in a fatal car accident. The couple found themselves sitting outside the pearly gates waiting for St. Peter to process them into heaven. While waiting they began to wonder; could they possibly get married in heaven? When St. Peter arrived, they asked him if they could get married in heaven. St. Peter said, "I don't know. This is the first time anyone has asked. Let me go find out." And he left.

The couple sat and waited for an answer ... for a couple of months.

While they waited, they discussed the pros and cons. If they were allowed to get married in heaven, should they get married, what with the eternal aspect of it all? "What if it doesn't work? Are we stuck in heaven together forever?" they wondered.

Another month passed. St. Peter finally returned, looking somewhat bedraggled. "Yes," he informed the couple, "You can get married in heaven." "Great!" said the couple. "But we were just wondering; what if things don't work out? Could we also get a divorce in heaven?"

St. Peter, red-faced with anger, slammed his clipboard on the ground. "What's wrong?" asked the frightened couple.

"Oh, COME ON!!!" St. Peter shouted. "It took me three months to find a priest up here! Do you have ANY idea how long it'll take to find a lawyer?"

Of course my father knows the purpose of this book is, in part, to change this perception of lawyers, which makes the joke here even more ironic. I hope this book will serve as part of the change of lawyers, the legal system, and society.

Susan Daicoff, July, 2011

Contents

Acknowledgments

Enormous gratitude is due to the support of my children, Arizona and Graylin, who carried books and materials, looked up things, sat through endless lectures, and separated proofsheets and their father, Robert N. Baskin, Jr., who provided countless forms of support, encouragement, faith, and love and urged me to, as the football coaches say, "leave nothing on the field!"

Thanks are due to Florida Coastal School of Law, who graciously funded and supported my research and writing, my course, and this book. Thanks are due to the three hundred or so students who have taken my Comprehensive Law Practice course; whether or not they "bought" all the ideas, they have greatly influenced and helped me write this. Thanks are due to Deans Peter Goplerud and Don Lively for supporting innovation, Dennis Stone for the idea of "ubuntu," Stephen Durden for encouragement, Jim Cataland for collaborative teaching, and all my colleagues at FCSL.

Thanks are due to my friends, family, and extended family for their encouragement and willing ears.

Enormous thanks are due to Professor David B. Wexler and the late Professor Bruce J. Winick, who co-founded therapeutic jurisprudence (which is arguably the hub of the wheel of the comprehensive law movement vectors) and included me in the "fold," were kind enough always to encourage and include anyone working in this field, allowed me to try out the working title, "comprehensive law," never engaged in turf wars, created quite a "community" of like-minded professionals, and have mentored me since our first meeting. It is one thing to create an idea that becomes a discipline; it is quite another to graciously nurture its growth and create a "community," as they have done.

Great appreciation is due to all of my comrades in this venture for their vision and encouragement—you are too many to name and I appreciate you all, but particularly want to thank: J. Kim Wright, Larry Krieger, Marjorie Silver, Len Riskin, Michael Perlin, Robert Schopp, Thomas Barton, Peggy Hora, John McShane, Rick Halpert, Arnie Herz, Ruth Rickard, Joanne Fahey, Maureen Holland, Pauline Tesler, Stuart Webb, Dennis Coyne, David Hobler, Linda Morton, Janet Weinstein, Ellen Waldman, Barbara Babb, Norma Trusch, Bill Van Zyverden, David Hoffman, David Link, Daniel Bowling, Stuart Levine, the late William Weston (who once told me I was doing "God's work"), Bill Valentine, Helene Dublisky, Helena Haapio, Steven Keeva, Bill Schma, Michael Jones, Stella Rabaut, Nickolas Alexander, Nicole Habl, Larry Richard, Clint Bowers for his mentorship, John Braithwaite and David Hall for their inspiring examples, my new friends in Australia, Arie Frieberg, Michael King, and all of the "nonadversarialites," Erica Fox for her vision and example, Cheryl Niro for her inspiring example, and Forrest "Woody" Mosten. I have been inspired to innovate by observing many, including Deborah Rhode, Carrie Menkel-Meadow, and Janet Reno. I am also grateful for the able research assistance, encouragement, and ideas of Adriann S. Garland, Joshua Kesselman, and two great "comprehensive" lawyer couples: Elizabeth Roach & Andrew Wentzell and Kristen Herbst Grossman & A.J. Grossman, III. Thanks are due to the gracious and able Clare Raulerson for her excellent assistance and tireless efforts to assist me in everything, for her encouragement, and for reminding me to "slow down!"

Two apologies: First, I am certain that I have left off this list, in complete inadvertence, many, many people important to me and to the movement. I apologize in advance for those omissions and hope you will forgive my memory loss. Second, I am also painfully aware of the shortcomings and omissions in this book. It became impossible for me to keep up with and include all of the wonderful comprehensive law movement resources available, particularly as their number has exploded in recent years. Please forgive those omissions as well; they are not intentional in any way.

Finally, I have wanted to write something like this since 1991, when I finished graduate school with a masters' degree in clinical psychology, after having worked as a corporate, securities, and tax lawyer for several years. At the time, I had no idea it would be this extensive. There wasn't that much to write about and the profession wasn't dealing well with the integration of psychology into law. Thankfully, the last twenty years have seen many needed changes in our great profession. This book, therefore, represents a lifelong achievement for me, as it integrates my two careers, law and psychology, "does good," improves my profession, and addresses problems I have struggled with since becoming a lawyer in 1984.

Susan Swaim Daicoff, July, 2011

Introduction

All Systems Fail

The legal profession, if not the world, is in crisis. Reportedly, the Chinese character for "crisis" denotes danger and opportunity, simultaneously. If crisis brings opportunity, then the profession is at a turning point. The legal profession is dangerously close to obsolescence for all but the most wealthy individuals, corporate, and institutional clients. It is estimated that 85% of Americans cannot afford a lawyer, resulting in unequal access to justice. However, the number of lawyers has doubled in the United States since about 1970, which influx has led to increased economic pressure and competition among lawyers.

The adversarial court system has failed. It is no longer functioning as a primary and efficient dispute resolution system, as 98% of all litigated cases settle without trial. Negotiation, settlement, mediation, and other forms of alternative dispute resolution, mandatory or not, are growing and legal personnel are experimenting with new models for resolving legal problems, such as collaborative law. In those rare civil cases that actually go to trial, the process frequently takes two years to resolve, resulting in calls for more accountability from lawyers. Lawyers are being asked to justify their fees and value. The corrections system has failed, as the United States has one of the highest per capita incarceration rates in the world and a high recidivism rate. Judges and court personnel are experimenting with alternative court models, such as problem solving courts, and alternative disposition systems, such as restorative justice.

One in five lawyers is suffering from clinically significant levels of depression, anxiety, psychopathology, alcoholism, or substance abuse. Many lawyers are desperate for work that matters, makes sense, makes a difference, is moral, is valuable and valued, and produces sustainable outcomes. The current economic crisis has pushed unemployment among lawyers to unprecedented levels, leading to more competition and demand for new forms of legal work, while law school admissions levels remain steady or continue to slowly rise. Legal education, operating on Langdell's century-old model, has become increasingly irrelevant and unrelated to the skills required for and the demands of modern law practice, thus, new graduates are less prepared than ever to face practice conditions and capably serve clients. Clearly, it is time for a change.[1]

---

1. *See generally* RICHARD SUSSKIND, THE END OF LAWYERS? RETHINKING THE NATURE OF LEGAL SERVICES (Oxford University Press, 2008) (arguing for the obsolescence of traditional lawyering and calling for a sea change in the legal profession).

Traditional Adversarialism Wanes

I have been researching and writing about the legal profession since the early 1990s, when I became interested, as a lawyer enrolled in a graduate program for clinical psychology, in lawyer distress, dissatisfaction, wellbeing, and ethical decisionmaking. That research led me to survey 40 years of empirical research on lawyers. I concluded that there were about eight distinct traits that distinguished lawyers from nonlawyers, psychologically and decisionmaking preference-wise. In the mid-1990s, I argued that these "lawyer traits" were adaptive to the modern practice of law, which at the time demanded that lawyers be unemotional, rational, objective, amoral, zealous, and partisan advocates and representatives of their clients.

However, a number of developments in the law and in the world since then have eroded that model, leading the profession to where it is today—on the brink (or in the midst) of change. I am not convinced that the traditional adversarial model of law and lawyering was optimal, anyway, but recent developments have placed even greater stress on it, forcing change forward.

In response to the pressures on the legal profession, many proposed solutions. These solutions ranged from stress management, to mediation, to sheer innovations in the law. In the 1970s and 1980s (and, in some cases, as early as the 1930s), seeds were sown for a new legal profession by a number of insightful pioneers, trailblazers, and innovators. By 1990, many of these individuals had begun formulating and experimenting with new ways of practicing and adjudicating law and resolving legal disputes. Just a few of these (this is by no means an exhaustive list and I apologize for omissions) are: Professors David Wexler, Bruce Winick, Edward Dauer, Thomas Barton, Marjorie Silver, Michael King, John Braithwaite, Howard Zehr, Baruch Bush, David Hall, and Leonard Riskin; author Steven Keeva; judges Peggy Hora and William Schma; attorneys Stuart Webb, Bill Van Zyverden, John McShane, Pauline Tesler, J. Kim Wright, Rick Halpert, David Hoffman, Forrest Mosten, and Arnie Herz; and many more.

A Movement Emerges

In the late 1990s, at one of the many therapeutic jurisprudence conferences organized by Professors Wexler and Winick to which I was invited, I asked these founders whether they thought collaborative law, therapeutic jurisprudence, preventive law, restorative justice, and other emerging disciplines might be part of a larger movement in the law. Their response was to challenge me; if so, they said, then articulate the common ground among all these developments that bind them together, that unify them and distinguish them from the traditional adversarial justice system. So I tried. What I found was that all of these developments shared at least two common features. The first was what Pauline Tesler calls "rights plus," meaning, reaching beyond bare legal rights to incorporate the parties' needs, desires, goals, mental status, wellbeing, relationships, and future functioning into the resolution of the legal problem. Second, they all seek to optimize the outcomes of legal matters as measured by their impact on human wellbeing (meaning emotions, psychological functioning, and relationships involved in legal matters), while still resolving the particular legal matter. While many share other features in common as well, these are the only two features that appear to be common to all of the disciplines in the "comprehensive law movement" that are also not present in traditional forms of law, lawyering, and dispute resolution. For example, many forms of comprehensive law practice are non-adversarial, eschew protracted, scorched-earth litigation in favor of consensual, collaborative, community-based methods and processes affording voice and participation for all, solve legal problems creatively and holistically by teams of lawyers and clients working together as equal partners, and avoid having lawyers function as dispassionate expert legal technicians who "know best." Excited by the forward-moving innovation I saw in these disciplines, I thought of them as "vectors" of a movement. I called the overall movement the "comprehensive law movement," simply as a working title for the synthesis of these important developments.

As the various disciplines of the comprehensive law movement eked into the legal consciousness from 1990 to now, they hit a chord. Many recognized the need for the reforms being proposed and more reforms, innovations, research, scholarship, and interest among legal educators, lawyers, mediators, and judges emerged. By the end of the 1990s, these innovators and many others interested in these disciplines were connecting with each other (often through the tireless work of Professors David Wexler and Bruce Winick, founders of therapeutic jurisprudence). They shared information and ideas at various conferences, realizing that their observations were similar and their objectives were related.

The next decade saw growth, experimentation, and collaboration; by the mid-2000s, it became clear that these efforts did indeed herald an overall movement, one that touches all areas of the law and transcends the scope of each individual discipline. From 2006 to 2010, no less than five books were published recognizing the scope of the changes being wrought in the legal profession; Julie MacFarlane in Canada, Marjorie Silver, Susan Brooks and Robert Madden, Michael King and his associates in Australia, and J. Kim Wright have all authored books on this greater "movement" (these books are listed at the end of this Introduction). Ambitious research and scholarship agendas, frequent national and international conferences, and the persistent efforts of hundreds of committed individuals in the law have all contributed to the growing weight of this movement towards positive change.

Comprehensive Law Practice

This book begins with the premise that the time is ripe for a "new model" for lawyering, adjudicating, and dispute resolution to fully emerge, one which might even become the dominant model for the future. It then attempts to begin to outline how this "new lawyer" might approach clients, witnesses, other parties, lawyers, judges, mediators, cases, and matters (whether transactional or litigative). It proposes that these approaches may be a useful addition to all lawyers' toolkits, including those lawyers who prefer not to practice "comprehensively."[2] Continuing the "toolkit" analogy, if what lawyers have been using in the legal profession to date have been hammers and nails, with an occasional saw, the comprehensive law movement adds screwdrivers, chisels, and drills to the lawyer's toolbelt. Staying competitive in today's challenging market for legal services may well require additional, new, and innovative tools, such as those afforded by the comprehensive law movement.

---

2. Credit for this excellent idea is due to attorney (and my former student) Jeffrey D. Devonchik, *see* http://www.shblaw.com/devonchik.htm (last visited July 11, 2010).

The tools or approaches introduced here are creative problem solving, therapeutic jurisprudence, problem solving courts, restorative justice, collaborative law, holistic justice, preventive law, procedural justice, and transformative mediation. They all share the vision that law can have positive social and psychological consequences for those involved in legal matters. Together, they form an overall movement towards law as a healing profession. Here, they are often individually referred to as "vectors" of the comprehensive law movement, denoting their forward movement into the future and their parallel but related status.

This book briefly describes the conditions propelling the emergence of this movement, explores the overall philosophical and behavioral shifts inherent in practicing law "comprehensively," and then develops each discipline (or vector) within the movement in more detail, in a separate chapter. It concludes with an attempt to synthesize all of these approaches, or tools, in a comprehensive approach to law, legal problems, and legal disputes.

This book can be read alone as an introduction to the vectors of the comprehensive law movement or can be used as a practice guide to accompany existing anthologies on the subject (listed below in this Introduction). The purpose of this book is to introduce the reader to the vectors of the comprehensive law movement and begin to explore the skills required to apply the vectors in a practical manner. Actual practice of the vectors will, however, require reading and training beyond this book; each chapter suggests resources for this additional study.

Acknowledgments, Adaptations, and Reprints

Many portions of this book were adapted from, and excerpt or reprint portions of, previously published works by the author and are here used by permission. These are:

1. Susan Daicoff, *Resolution Without Litigation: Are Courtrooms Battlegrounds for Losers?* GPSOLO 44–50 (October/November 2003) (republished as a book chapter, Susan Daicoff, *The Comprehensive Law Movement: An Emerging Approach to Legal Problems*, in PETER WAHLGREN, ED., A PROACTIVE APPROACH, 49 SCANDINAVIAN STUDIES IN LAW 109–129 (2006)) (incorporated in its entirety in Chapter 3);

2. Susan Daicoff, *Growing Pains: The Integration vs. Specialization Question for Therapeutic Jurisprudence and Other Comprehensive Law Approaches*, 30 T. JEFFERSON L. REV. 551 (2008) (used in its entirety in Chapters 1–4) © Professor Susan Daicoff, reprinted with permission. This article was originally published with Thomas Jefferson Law Review, available at 30 T. JEFFERSON L. REV. 551 (2008);

3. Susan Daicoff, *Collaborative Law*, 20 U. FLA. J. L. & PUB. POL'Y 113 (2009) (reprinted in Chapter 12);

4. Susan Daicoff, *Lawyer Personality Traits and Their Relationship to Various Approaches to Lawyering*, in MARJORIE A. SILVER, ED., THE AFFECTIVE ASSISTANCE OF COUNSEL (Carolina Academic Press, 2007) (adapted for use in Chapter 4);

5. Susan Daicoff, *Law as a Healing Profession: The "Comprehensive Law Movement,"* 6 PEPPERDINE DISP. RESOL. J. 1 (2006) (incorporated in its entirety and adapted for use in Chapters 1–3; expanded upon in Chapters 4–16 hereof);

6. Susan Daicoff, Lawyer, Know Thyself: A Psychological Analysis of Personality Strengths and Weaknesses (American Psychological Association Books, 2004) (this book summarizes Chapters 1–6 and incorporates Chapter 7 in its entirety) Copyright © 2004 by the American Psychological Association. Reproduced or adapted with permission. The use of this information does not imply endorsement by the publisher;

7. Susan Daicoff & David B. Wexler, Chapter 26: Therapeutic Jurisprudence, in Comprehensive Handbook of Psychology: Volume 11: Forensic Psychology (Alan M. Goldstein, ed., John Wiley & Sons, Inc. 2003) (adapted for use in Chapters 5–7) Copyright © 2003, John Wiley & Sons, Inc. Reprinted with permission of John Wiley & Sons, Inc.;

8. Susan Daicoff, Afterword: The Role of Therapeutic Jurisprudence Within the Comprehensive Law Movement, in Dennis P. Stolle, David B. Wexler, & Bruce J. Winick, Eds., Practicing Therapeutic Jurisprudence (Carolina Academic Press, 2000) (incorporated in its entirety);

9. Susan Daicoff, Making Law Therapeutic for Lawyers: Therapeutic Jurisprudence, Preventive Law, and the Psychology of Lawyers, 5 Psych., Pub. Pol'y. & Law 811 (1999) (incorporated in its entirety into Chapters 1–3 and 4) Copyright © 1999 by the American Psychological Association. Adapted with permission. The use of this information does not imply endorsement by the publisher;

10. Susan Daicoff, Lawyer, Know Thyself: A Review of Empirical Research on Attorney Attributes Bearing on Professionalism, 46 Am. U. L. Rev. 1337 (1997) (incorporated and adapted for use in Chapter 1);

11. Susan Daicoff, Asking Leopards to Change Their Spots: Can Lawyers Change? A Critique of Solutions to Professionalism by Reference to Empirically-Derived Attributes, 11 Geo. J. Legal Ethics 547 (1998) (incorporated and adapted for use in Chapter 1);

12. Susan Daicoff, (Oxymoron?) Ethical Decision-Making by Attorneys: An Empirical Study, 48 Fla. L. Rev. 197 (1996) (incorporated into Chapter 1);

13. Susan Daicoff, Lawyer, Be Thyself: An Empirical Investigation of the Relationship Between the Ethic of Care, the Feeling Decisionmaking Preference, and Lawyer Wellbeing, 16 Va. J. Soc. Pol'y & L. 87 (2008) (incorporated into Chapter 1);

14. Susan Daicoff, Sorry Seems to Be the Hardest Word: Apology, Forgiveness, Reconciliation, & Therapeutic Jurisprudence, Case Western Reserve University School of Law symposium article (manuscript) (adapted and excerpted in Chapter 11);

15. Susan Daicoff, Preventive Law Essay (reprinted in Chapter 6);

16. Susan Daicoff, Comprehensive Law: Transformative Responses by the Legal Profession, in Candice C. Carter, Ed., Conflict Transformation and Peace Education: Transformations Across Disciplines (Palgrave MacMillan, 2010) (incorporated in its entirety throughout the book and excerpted in the Resources section of each Chapter);

17. Manuscript of The Future of the Legal Profession, accepted for publication in Monash University Law Review (in press) (ideas incorporated throughout the book, particularly in Chapters 1–3 and 16); and

18. Susan Daicoff, *On Butlers, Architects, and Lawyers: The Professionalism of "The Remains of the Day" and "The Fountainhead,"* 17 J. L. Bus. & Ethics 23 (2011) (excerpted in Chapter 1).

In addition, various previously published articles and books in the comprehensive law field have been excerpted for various chapters; those works are also used by permission and credited, where used.

Use of This Book

This book can be used as a reader by itself, as a course book for a course on comprehensive law practice, or as an adjunctive book in a skills-oriented law school class. While it is designed to be of use to practicing lawyers, judges, mediators, law students, law professors, or any other legal professionals, it is most likely helpful for practicing lawyers who represent clients and judges seeking reform. It introduces the comprehensive law movement and its vectors to the reader; it is an overview and not a complete guide for training oneself to practice in any one discipline within the movement. In its attempt to summarize the vectors, it may oversimplify them or appear to distort them, to the seasoned comprehensive law practitioner.

It is also specifically designed to be a practical, skills-oriented companion to any one of the following, listed books. For example, one might read one or more of these books for more detail on the included subjects and use this book to begin to apply those concepts in simulated practice settings. (Where relevant, the Resources section of each Chapter will list the related portions of the following books by Brooks & Madden, Silver, Stolle, et al., Wright, King, et al., and Macfarlane, to aid in such coordination.)

Companion books are:[3]

Susan L. Brooks & Robert G. Madden, Relationship-Centered Lawyering: Social Science Theory for Transforming Legal Practice (Carolina Academic Press, 2010) (including TJ, PL, TJ/PL, PJ, TM, & RJ).

Marjorie A. Silver, The Affective Assistance of Counsel (Carolina Academic Press, 2007) (including CL, TJ, & PSCs).

Dennis P. Stolle, David B. Wexler, & Bruce J. Winick, Eds., Practicing Therapeutic Jurisprudence: Law as a Helping Profession (Carolina Academic Press, 2000) (including TJ, PL, TJ/PL, PJ, & CL).

J. Kim Wright, Lawyers As Peacemakers: Practicing Holistic, Problem-Solving Law (American Bar Association, 2010) (including all of the vectors).

Michael King, Arie Frieberg, Becky Batagol, & Ross Hyams, Non-Adversarial Justice (The Federation Press, 2009) (Australian publication including all of the vectors).

Julie Macfarlane, The New Lawyer: How Settlement Is Transforming the Practice of Law (UBC Press, 2008) (Law & Society Series) (Canadian publication exploring

---

3. *Note*: While this book was not designed as a companion to it, when listing books that synthesize the vectors of the movement, it is important to note the synthesis of vectors in Thomas D. Barton, Preventive Law and Problem Solving: Lawyering for the Future (Vandenplas Publishing, 2009) (integrating PL, CPS, & TJ).

in depth the lawyering approach underpinning the movement and including CL, RJ, TJ, & PSCs).

The assignments at the end of each chapter are designed to assist the reader in applying the concepts described above, in the practice of law.

A sample course description for a course based on this book might be as follows:

Comprehensive Law Practice is designed to teach the theory, practice, and skills of law as a helping or healing profession. It explicitly uses psychology and social science to assess the consequences of law and legal procedures on people, their relationships, and their communities in an effort to make law have a positive effect. It explores approximately nine emerging innovations in law, legal process, and dispute resolution based on these ideas, covering civil, criminal, family, and all substantive areas of the law. If you have found yourself thinking during the course of your career in the law, "there must be a better way," then perhaps this course is for you.

Comprehensive
Law Practice

Chapter 1

The Legal Profession, Lawyers, and Professional Roles and Values

Just prior to the emergence of the disciplines or vectors making up the comprehensive law movement, a "tripartite crisis" faced the legal profession:[1] a decline in professionalism, a decline in public opinion of attorneys, and high levels of psychological distress (like alcoholism and depression) among lawyers.[2] In 2006, I argued that:

> Since at least 1980, commentators within the legal profession have bemoaned the state of the profession. Commentary on our lack of professionalism, rampant immorality, malfeasance, malpractice, client neglect, overly aggressive natures, greed, and unethical behavior, as well as the lack of attorney discipline and oversight, has been prolific. Individuals inside and outside the legal profession alike have been dissatisfied with the law, the American legal system, and lawyers. The situation has been described as a professionalism crisis. Society's opinion of lawyers is depressingly low. The public sees lawyers as makers of conflict and dissension rather than as positive forces in people's lives or work. Alcoholism, depression, and other psychological problems exist in the legal profession at least twice as frequently as they appear in the general population. These problems comprise a "tripartite crisis" in the legal profession, consisting of deprofessionalism, low public opinion of lawyers, and lawyer distress and dissatisfaction.

---

1. Susan Daicoff, *Lawyer, Know Thyself: A Review of Empirical Research on Attorney Attributes Bearing on Professionalism*, 46 Am. U.L.Rev. 1337 (1997) [hereinafter Daicoff, *Review*].

2. Susan Daicoff, *Asking Leopards To Change Their Spots: Can Lawyers Change? A Critique of Solutions to Professionalism by Reference to Empirically-Derived Attributes*, 11 Geo. J. Legal Ethics 547 (1998); Susan Daicoff, Lawyer, Know Thyself: A Psychological Analysis of Personality Strengths and Weaknesses (American Psychological Association Books, 2004) [hereinafter Daicoff, Know Thyself]. Much of this Chapter 1 has been summarized from ideas contained in Daicoff, Know Thyself, *supra* this note. Copyright © 2004 by the American Psychological Association. Reproduced or adapted with permission. The use of this information does not imply endorsement by the publisher. This chapter is also based on material in and/or adapted from the following, by the author: *Lawyer, Be Thyself: An Empirical Investigation of the Relationship Between the Ethic of Care, the Feeling Decisionmaking Preference, and Lawyer Wellbeing*, 16 Va. J. Soc. Pol'y & L. 87 (2008) (reporting on the results of an empirical study of these characteristics); *Lawyer Personality Traits and their Relationship to Various Approaches to Lawyering*, in Marjorie A. Silver, Ed., The Affective Assistance of Counsel (Carolina Academic Press, 2007); *Making Law Therapeutic for Lawyers: Therapeutic Jurisprudence, Preventive Law, and the Psychology of Lawyers*, 5 Psych., Pub. Pol'y. & Law 811 (1999) (arguing that TJ and PL can enhance lawyer wellbeing) (Copyright © 1999 by the American Psychological Association. Adapted with permission. The use of this information does not imply endorsement by the publisher.); *Asking Leopards to Change Their Spots*, 11 Geo. J. Legal Ethics (1998) (concluding that the typical lawyer traits are helpful and adaptive in the traditional practice of law);

In response to this tripartite crisis, many well-seasoned practicing lawyers have sought alternative forms of law practice, often saying something like, "If I can't find another way to practice law, one that I find satisfying and fulfilling, then I am quitting law entirely." .... Many of the vectors emerged because of lawyers', clients', and society's deep dissatisfaction with existing models for handling legal matters.[3]

This chapter will begin by examining the empirical support for the existence of the "tripartite crisis," then move to possible causes and conditions therefor, and conclude with examining certain values and preferences. These values and preferences can assist lawyers in customizing their legal career to maximize their satisfaction and effectiveness.

Professionalism and
Public Opinion of Attorneys

Very little data exists to document the "decline in professionalism" portrayed by commentators in the latter part of the 20th century, in the legal profession. In fact, per capita disciplinary actions against attorneys did not increase over a decade in the late 20th century. However, public opinion did suffer. The following figures present the dismal results of public opinion polls regarding lawyers during the early 1990s—generally, the public held negative opinions of attorneys, often did not feel that lawyers had the sufficient ethics to serve the public, and did not feel that lawyers' honesty and ethical standards were high compared to other professions. More people liked their own medical doctor than liked their own attorney, debunking the myth that, like Congresspersons, people "hate lawyers but like their own."

Daicoff, *Review, supra* note 1 (reporting on the results of 40 years of empirical research on lawyer personality); and *Oxymoron? Ethical Decisionmaking by Attorneys*, 48 U. F. L. Rev. (1996) (reporting on the results of an empirical study of attorneys' decisionmaking in various professional ethical dilemma situations).

3. Excerpt from Susan Daicoff, *Law as a Healing Profession: The "Comprehensive Law Movement,"* 6 Pepperdine Disp. Resol. J. 1 (2006).

**Figure 1. American Bar Association Survey (1993) —
Peter D. Hart Research Associates[4]**

Respondents Who Believe Attorneys	Percentage of Respondents
Are Caring and Compassionate	19%
Are Honest and Ethical	22%
Are a Constructive Part of the Community	36%
Make Too Much Money	63%
Are Greedy	59%
Charge Excessive Fees	55%
Lack the Necessary Ethics to Serve the Public	48%
Are Not Honest or Ethical	40%
Who Liked Their Own Physician	78%
Who Disliked Their Own Physician	7%
Who Liked Own Attorney	45%
Who Disliked Own Attorney	16%

Figure 2. Public Opinion Poll — Various Professions (1991)[5]

Respondents Who Believed These Groups Have "High Honesty or Ethical Standards"	Percentage of Respondents
Pharmacists	62%
Doctors, College Teachers, Clergy, Dentists, & Engineers	50%
Funeral Directors, Bankers, & Journalists	35%
Newspaper Reporters	24%
Lawyers	**22%**
Building Contractors	20%
Realtors	16%
Advertisers	12%
Car Salesmen	6%

Lawyer and Law Student Distress

Lawyers experience alcoholism, depression, and other forms of psychological distress and job dissatisfaction at a rate of about 20%, or one in five, which is about twice the levels found in the general population.[6]

---

4. Peter D. Hart Research Associates, Inc., A Survey of Attitudes Nationwide Toward Lawyers and the Legal System (1993).

5. Gary A. Hengstler, *Vox Populi: The Public Perception of Lawyers: ABA Poll*, A.B.A. J., Sept. 1993, at 60, 63–64 (reporting on the poor public opinion of attorneys).

6. Daicoff, Know Thyself, *supra* note 2.

Figure 3. Compilation of Several Studies: Lawyer Distress, a Constant 20%?[7]

Condition	Percentage of Lawyers Reporting	Percentage of the General Population Believed to Have
Depression	19%	3–9%
Alcoholism	18%	9%
General Psychological Distress	18%	2.27%
Job Dissatisfaction	27.5%	not available

Figure 4. Psychological Distress among Lawyers, 1995–96[8]

Condition	Male Lawyers	Female Lawyers	Estimate in the General Population
Global Distress	18%	10%	2.27%
Anxiety	30%	27%	2.27%
Depression	28%	20%	2.27%
Paranoid Ideation	25%	19%	2.27%
Interpersonal Sensitivity	21%	16%	2.27%
Social Isolation & Alienation	20%	15%	2.27%
Obsessive-Compulsiveness	13%	9%	2.27%
Hostility	7%	11%	2.27%

---

7. G. Andrew H. Benjamin et al., *The Prevalence of Depression, Alcohol Abuse, and Cocaine Abuse Among United States Lawyers*, 13 Int'l J. L. & Psychiatry 233 (1990) (depression); G. Andrew H. Benjamin, Alfred Kaszniak, Bruce Sales, & Stephen B. Shanfield, *The Role of Legal Education in Producing Psychological Distress Among Law Students*, 11 Am. B. Found. Res. J. 225 (1986) (depression, anxiety, hostility, phobic anxiety, obsessive-compulsive behavior, isolation and paranoid ideation); Barbara S. McCann, Joan Russo, & G. Andrew H. Benjamin, *Hostility, Social Support, and Perceptions of Work*, 2 J. Occup. Health Psychol. 175, 175, 178, and 180 (1997) (job dissatisfaction); G. Andrew H. Benjamin, Bruce Sales, & Elaine Darling, *Comprehensive Lawyer Assistance Programs: Justification and Model*, 16 Law & Psychol. Rev. 113 (1992) (depression among lawyers in Washington, Wisconsin and Florida); Stephen B. Shanfield & G. Andrew Benjamin, *Psychiatric Distress in Law Students*, 35 J. Legal Educ. 65, 68–69 (1985); Connie J.A. Beck, Bruce D. Sales & G. Andrew H. Benjamin, *Lawyer Distress: Alcohol Related Concerns Among a Sample of Practicing Lawyers*, 10 J.L. & Health 1, 5, 18, 50–58 (1995–1996) (lawyer distress) [hereinafter collectively referred to as the "Benjamin, et al. Studies"].

8. Beck, et al., *supra* note 7.

Figure 5. Depression among Law Students and Lawyers[9]

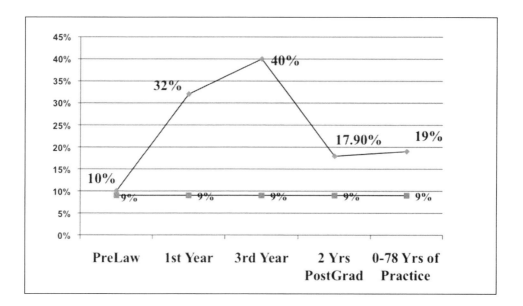

Figure 6. Career Satisfaction among Lawyers[10]

Attorneys' Satisfaction with the Practice of Law	Percent of Attorneys Reporting
Very Satisfied	21.2%
Somewhat Satisfied	51.2%
Somewhat Dissatisfied	20.6%
Very Dissatisfied	6.9%

---

9. Benjamin, et al. Studies, *supra* note 7. The straight line at 9% represents the estimated prevalence of depression in adults in Western, civilized countries. I often refer to this as the "ski slope" graph due to the steep increase in depression among law students in the first year of law school. Krieger and Sheldon have linked this phenomenon empirically to an increased focus on external and extrinsic rewards (grades, class rank, reputation) rather than on intrinsic satisfactions; Kennon M. Sheldon & Lawrence S. Krieger, *Does Legal Education have Undermining Effects on Law Students? Evaluating Changes in Motivation, Values, and Well-Being*, 22 BEHAV. SCI. LAW 261–286 (2004).

10. A.B.A. Young Lawyers Division Survey, The State of the Legal Profession: 1990 (1991) [hereinafter "1990 ABA/YLD Report"] (reporting results of National Survey of Career Satisfaction/Dissatisfaction Waves I and II conducted by the Young Lawyers Division in 1984 and 1990 which surveyed attorneys of all ages); A.B.A. Young Lawyers Division, The State of the Legal Profession: 1990 — Executive Summary (1992) (summarizing results of National Survey of Career Satisfaction/Dissatisfaction Waves I and II conducted by the Young Lawyers Division in 1984 and 1990); A.B.A., The Report of At The Breaking Point: A National Conference on The Emerging Crisis in the Quality of Lawyers' Health and Lives — Its Impact on Law Firms and Client Services (Apr. 5–6, 1991) (presenting results of the ABA's 1984 and 1990 surveys of lawyer dissatisfaction and burnout and including reasons for the problem such as too much work, lack of communication between lawyers and with clients, isolation in the firm, lack of mentoring and training).

Figure 7. Increasing Job Dissatisfaction among Lawyers, 1984–1995[11]

American Bar Association Young Lawyers' Division Survey Year	Percent of Lawyers Reporting Being "Somewhat Dissatisfied" with Their Work	Percent of Lawyers Reporting Being "Very Dissatisfied" with Their Work
1984	12%	3%
1990	14%	5%
1995	17%	7%

Reasons for this unduly high level of psychological distress within the legal profession are unclear. Most commentators have pointed to the long hours, the pressures of private practice, competition in the profession, and deprofessionalism. However, until 2001, the empirical research linked lawyer distress not to these factors, but instead only to feelings of hostility, marital distress, job dissatisfaction, and a lack of social support.[12]

Intrinsic and Extrinsic Values

In 2001, in a groundbreaking empirical study, Lawrence Krieger and Kennon Sheldon discovered that law student distress is associated with certain shifts in one's value system during law school. Specifically, law students were more likely to be distressed as they became progressively less oriented toward personal "growth/self acceptance, intimacy/emotional connection and community/societal contribution." Distress also increased as students became less likely to act for intrinsic or inherent satisfaction and "more oriented toward appearance/attractiveness" and "money/luxuries, popularity/fame" as well as more motivated to please others.[13] As law students focused less on intrinsic satisfactions and more on extrinsic rewards, they were more likely to experience a decline in their emotional wellbeing.[14] This suggests that lawyers who focus on external rewards such as money, prestige, Martindale-Hubbell ratings, and even win-loss records, may be at risk for developing distress. It also suggests that lawyers, as early as law school, would be wise to identify and preserve their own individual "intrinsic values," as they navigate the challenges of law school and the profession.

What are intrinsic values? They can easily differ from individual lawyer to individual lawyer. For some, they may be doing one's personal best, upholding constitutional rights, ensuring that due process is received, making cogent and persuasive oral or written arguments, crafting an appellate brief, helping one's clients out of legal trouble, or helping

---

11. See studies cited in n. 10, *supra.*

12. Connie J.A. Beck, Bruce D. Sales & G. Andrew H. Benjamin, *Lawyer Distress: Alcohol Related Concerns Among a Sample of Practicing Lawyers*, 10 J.L. & HEALTH 1, 5, 18, 50–58 (1995–1996) (linking lawyer distress to hostility, anger and marital dissatisfaction).

13. Kennon M. Sheldon & Lawrence S. Krieger, *Does Legal Education have Undermining Effects on Law Students? Evaluating Changes in Motivation, Values, and Well-Being*, 22 BEHAV. SCI. LAW 261–286 (2004) (studying the emotional wellbeing of Florida State University law students and comparing it to that of advanced undergraduate students at the University of Missouri).

14. *Id.* This values shift and decline in wellbeing occurred as early as the first year of law school.

one's clients become successful in business. Think of what you would do even if you weren't being compensated for it, e.g., what you find intrinsically, inherently satisfying; the answer may shed light on some of your intrinsic values.[15]

What are extrinsic values, those that have been empirically associated with a decline in wellbeing among law students? Extrinsic rewards in law school might include grades, class rank, being invited to join law review due to one's grades, Order of the Coif, awards, honors, judicial clerkships, clerkships at prestigious law firms, and even the approval and approbation of one's classmates and professors. In practice, extrinsic values might include money, status, cars, houses, boats, Martindale-Hubbell ratings, prestige of one's law firm, awards, honors, and the esteem of others, such as judges and one's colleagues. Intrinsic rewards in law school might include setting a personal goal or benchmark and achieving it (not in competition with others), organizing complex information into a simple and understandable format, engaging in oral advocacy, writing, being an excellent mediator and dispute resolver, listening to and advising clients, helping others, or working with others in a team setting. In law practice, intrinsic rewards might include the same values (illustrating that one's values need not change from law school to practice), as well as some others, such as: making a difference in society or in the legal profession, solving others' problems effectively and satisfactorily, and preserving others' legal or constitutional rights.

The "Lawyer Personality"

Empirical research suggests that there are a number of traits or preferences that distinguish lawyers from nonlawyers, even as early as in childhood. These traits are summarized in the following table. One can see that some of these traits, such as an emphasis on achievement, were present in lawyers even when they were children, according to the research.

---

15. For example, David Hall, former dean of Northeastern University School of Law, argues for a spiritual base in the practice of law in his 2005 book, DAVID HALL, THE SPIRITUAL REVITALIZATION OF THE LEGAL PROFESSION: A SEARCH FOR SACRED RIVERS (Lewiston, NY: Edwin Mellen Press, 2005).

Figure 8. How Lawyers Differ From Non-Lawyers[16]

As Children	As Pre-Law Students	In Law School	In Practice
Emphasis on scholastic achievement			Psychological need for achievement over other needs, such as affiliation with others or power over others
Preference for leadership	Psychological need for dominance, attention, and leadership	Report becoming more aggressive and ambitious when under stress	Emphasis on extroversion and sociability
Active approach to life	Are less subordinate and deferent, more authoritarian	Prefer competitive peer relationships, do not rely on peers for support	Desire to be competitive, masculine, argumentative, aggressive, & dominant
Low interest in emotions and others' feelings	Low interest in emotions, interpersonal concerns, and others' feelings	Increased focus on "rights" (justice, rationality) in decisionmaking, over ethic of care	Low interest in people, emotional concerns, and interpersonal matters; prefer "Thinking" and conventional, rule- and rights-based morality in decisionmaking
	Higher socioeconomic status, materialistic motives for choosing law	Increased focus on extrinsic rewards over intrinsic satisfactions; decreased interest in public interest work	Focus on the economic bottom line, when evaluating settlement options in litigation
	Normal levels of depression	Elevated levels of depression	Elevated levels of psychological distress and alcoholism

These lawyer-specific traits coalesce into eight traits, as follows:

Figure 9. The Lawyer Personality — "Eight Traits"[17]

Drive to Achieve	1. Need for achievement; tendency to become ambitious under stress 2. Competitiveness; pessimism 3. Materialism; emphasis on extrinsic rewards and the economic bottom line
Interpersonal Relating Style	4. Preference for "Thinking" as a decisionmaking style, as measured by the Myers-Briggs Type Indicator 5. A "rights" orientation to decisionmaking, as opposed to the "ethic of care" 6. Interpersonal insensitivity 7. Dominance 8. Tendency to become aggressive under stress

---

16. Synthesized from many empirical studies cited in Daicoff, Know Thyself, *supra* note 2.

17. *Id.*

Fig. 10 depicts these traits graphically:

Figure 10. The "Lawyer Personality"

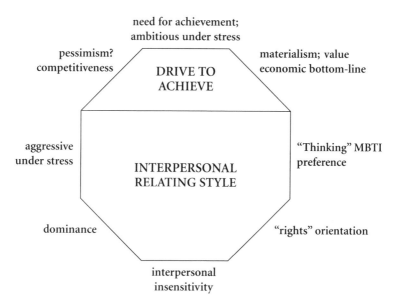

To summarize, lawyers tend to be competitive, prefer dominance in social settings, focus on the economic bottom line rather than noneconomic factors when making decisions, need and be motivated by achievement, become more aggressive and ambitious when placed under stress in law school, be somewhat insensitive to interpersonal and emotional concerns, be pragmatic and be seen as materialistic, and prefer a "rights orientation" and "Thinking" approach to ethical and moral decisionmaking. Law school indirectly rewards pessimism, as higher-grade achieving law students have been found to be more pessimistic in outlook than their lower-grade achieving peers. There is even a study of the testosterone levels of lawyers that found that, while lawyers across the board did not have levels higher than that of other white collar workers, when one separated out the trial lawyers as a group, the results differed. Male and female trial lawyers as a group had higher testosterone levels than did lawyers and white collar workers in general, suggesting even a biological basis for aggressiveness, dominance, and competitiveness in some sectors of the legal profession.

Most of these traits are adaptive to the practice of law; one can easily see how these traits would be useful in litigation and client representation. For example, to the extent that the practice of law is competitive, economic bottom-line oriented, aggressive, and focused on winning and uses logical, rational analysis of issues, these traits are quite suited to it. However, not all lawyers share these traits and not all legal matters or clients require these characteristics. The "lawyer traits" do, however, help lawyers identify and understand areas in which their natural proclivities may differ from those of their clients.

As the decisionmaking preference research is the most plentiful and the most relevant to how lawyers make strategic choices, it deserves a closer look.

Decisionmaking Preferences as Measured by the Myers-Briggs Type Indicator

The following chart demonstrates that, while most males in the general population prefer Thinking and most females prefer Feeling, as a decisionmaking preference, the overwhelming majority of both male and female attorneys makes decisions via a "Thinking" strategy, as measured by the Myers-Briggs Type Indicator, a popular preference test.

Figure 11. Decisionmaking Preferences of Lawyers Compared to the General Population, as Measured by the Myers-Briggs Type Indicator[18]

	Thinking Preference	Feeling Preference
Male Lawyers	81%	19%
Female Lawyers	66%	34%
Males in General	60%	40%
Females in General	35%	65%

Feelers prefer "harmonizing, building relationships, pleasing people, making decisions on the basis of [their own] … personal likes and dislikes, and being attentive to the personal needs of others" and like to avoid conflict and criticism.[19] The opposite of Feeling is Thinking; Thinkers prefer "logical analysis, principles, cool and impersonal reasoning and cost/benefit analyses" and are "more tolerant of conflict and criticism." Psychologist and lawyer Lawrence Richard, one of the leading researchers on the Myers-Briggs type of lawyers, says that the dimensions of Thinking and Feeling both represent:

> rational, valid decisionmaking methods. Both involve thought, and neither process is related to emotions.…
>
> Those who prefer to make decisions on the basis of Thinking prefer to come to closure in a logical, orderly manner. They can readily discern inaccuracies and are often critical. They can easily hurt others' feelings without knowing it. They are excellent problem-solvers. They review the cause and effect of potential actions before deciding. Thinkers are often accused of being cold and somewhat calculating because their decisions do not reflect their own personal values. They focus on discovering truth, and they seek justice.
>
> Those who prefer to make decisions on the basis of Feeling apply their own personal values to make choices. They seek harmony and, therefore, are sensitive to the effect of their decisions on others. They need, and are adept at giving, praise. They are interested in the person behind the idea or the job. They seek to do what is right for themselves and other people and are interested in mercy.[20]

---

18. Lawrence R. Richard, *Psychological Type and Job Satisfaction Among Practicing Lawyers in the United States*, 29 Cap. U. L. Rev. 979 (2002) (detailing the results of perhaps the most comprehensive study of the Myers-Briggs type of lawyers in the United States) [hereinafter Richard, 2002]; and Lawrence R. Richard, Psychological Type and Work Satisfaction Among Practicing Lawyers in the United States (1994) (unpublished Ph.D. dissertation, Temple University) (on file with author) [hereinafter Richard, 1994] (reporting on the relationship of the Thinking vs. Feeling preference for decisionmaking to attorney work satisfaction).

19. Daicoff, *Review, supra* note 1, at 1394.

20. Susan J. Bell & Lawrence R. Richard, Anatomy of a Lawyer: Personality and Long-Term Career Satisfaction, in Full Disclosure: Do You Really Want to Be a Lawyer? 149, 152 (Susan J. Bell ed., 2d ed. 1992). Richard also notes that the Thinking/Feeling scale is important for

Empirical research indicates that the great majority, about 78%, of lawyers prefer the "Thinking" mode of decisionmaking as measured by the Myers-Briggs Type Indicator.[21] Not only are individuals with a "Feeling" preference in the minority in the legal profession,[22] but evidence shows that they also are more likely to drop out of law school,[23] are likely to have lower law school grades, and may be more prone to experience job dissatisfaction as lawyers.[24] However, Feelers may also find "niches" within the legal profession that suit their preferences and values, such as perhaps positions as a guardian ad litem, family law magistrate, or child and family enforcement officer.

Feeling-type individuals are very likely to be attracted to comprehensive law approaches, because they encourage the lawyer to focus on interpersonal harmony, do what is right for others, avoid conflict and harm to others, and incorporate therapeutic, humanistic, or sanative values into his or her work. These approaches allow a Feeling-oriented lawyer to infuse his or her own personal morals and values into his or her work, assuming that the lawyer values enhanced mental wellbeing and improved interpersonal relationships.[25]

To the extent that Feeling-oriented lawyers and law students are likely to drop out of law, or are simply dissatisfied with their work, the comprehensive law approaches offer great promise and hope. They offer an appealing alternative to traditional law practice that actually utilizes the lawyer's Feeling preference as an asset to his or her professional life, rather than marginalizing it as a detrimental or neutral feature. Finally, the Thinking/Feeling dimensions may assist lawyers and law students in identifying their preferences and thus, their intrinsic values, so they can better retain those values throughout law school and in the legal profession.

---

predicting lawyer satisfaction, stating, "... those with a preference for Feeling are swimming against the tide." *Id.* at 153. *See also* Richard, 2002 and Richard, 1994, both *supra* note 18.

21. The Myers-Briggs Type Indicator is a counseling instrument used to categorize individuals into one of 16 "types," based on their preferences on four continua: Extraversion/Introversion; Sensing/Intuiting; Thinking/Feeling; and Judging/Perceiving. It was developed by Katharine Briggs and Isabel Myers and is widely used in corporate and academic settings to help people better understand the preferred approaches to life of themselves and others. There are a number of published studies of the Myers-Briggs "types" preferred by lawyers and law students. These are collected in Richard, 2002 and Richard, 1994, both *supra* note 18. *See also* Paul Van R. Miller, *Personality Differences and Student Survival in Law School*, 19 J. Legal Educ. 460–67 (1967); Vernellia R. Randall, *Increasing Retention and Improving Performance: Practical Advice on Using Cooperative Learning in Law Schools*, 16 T.M. Cooley L. Rev 201 (1999); Eric Y. Drogin, *Jurisprudent Therapy and Competency*, 28 Law & Psychol. Rev. 41 (2004); Mary H. Mccauley & Frank L. Natter, Psychological (Myers-Briggs) Type Differences In Education (1974).

22. Daicoff, *Review, supra* note 1, at 1391–92.

23. Paul Van R. Miller, *Personality Differences and Student Survival in Law School*, 19 J. Legal Educ. 460–67 (1967) (finding that almost twice as many "Feeling" types dropped out of law school as compared to "Thinking" types).

24. Richard, 2002 & Richard, 1994, *supra* note 18, and Bell & Richard, *supra* note 20 (Thinkers more plentiful in law; Thinking lawyers more satisfied with their jobs than Feeling lawyers).

25. For example, the vectors of restorative justice and collaborative law explicitly focus on interpersonal and relational harmony, while transformative mediation may indirectly foster it as well. All three tend to avoid interpersonal conflict. Holistic justice explicitly encourages lawyers to follow their own values in determining whether to take a case and what courses of action to take in representing the client. Creative problem solving and therapeutic jurisprudence allow the lawyer to feel as if he or she is "doing good," to the extent that good is defined as optimizing one's total life situation or maximizing others' psychological wellbeing, respectively.

Ethic of Care and the Rights Orientation

Carol Gilligan, a Harvard professor, developed another continuum of decisionmaking styles with an "ethic of care" at one end and a "rights" orientation at the other.[26] While these preferences initially sound similar to the Feeling/Thinking differences outlined above, empirical research shows that Feeling and the care orientation are not synonymous. Individuals who make decisions from a care perspective focus on contextual factors and harm to people; seek to avoid harm, maintain and restore relationships, and protect others from hurt; and decide by assessing the relative harm to and vulnerabilities of the parties. They value interpersonal harmony, maintaining relationships, individuals' feelings and needs, and preventing harm.[27]

Individuals who make decisions from a rights orientation weigh conflicting rights and duties; seek fairness, justice, and equality; and maintain and apply rules, standards, and role obligations to arrive at clear, absolute answers. They value individuality, independence, justice, fairness, objectivity, principles, and freedom from the interference of others.[28] The description of a rights-oriented approach even sounds like the Thinking style fostered in law school; not surprisingly, a rights orientation is more prevalent among lawyers and law students.[29] One set of researchers found that those students who espoused an ethic of care at the beginning of law school had shifted to a rights orientation as early as the end of the first year.[30] The following chart displays the results of a small study of New York lawyers in the early 1990s:

Figure 12. Moral Orientation of Lawyers (Gilligan-Based Categories)[31]

	Rights Orientation	"Balanced"	Ethic of Care
Male Lawyers	50%	33%	17%
Female Lawyers	35%	43%	22%

This study by Erica Weissman also linked the ethic of care to certain forms of job dissatisfaction among female lawyers only. Again, lawyers with an ethic of care orientation towards decisionmaking may find themselves in the minority in the legal profession; for them, comprehensive law approaches may dovetail nicely with their natural inclination to include contextual factors, relationships, and emotions in their decisionmaking processes.

---

26. CAROL GILLIGAN, IN A DIFFERENT VOICE: PSYCHOLOGICAL THEORY AND WOMEN'S DEVELOPMENT (1982). The ethic of care typically emphasizes interpersonal concerns and is believed to be more prevalent among women. Unsatisfied with the appropriateness of Lawrence Kohlberg's theory of moral development to women, Gilligan and others performed research that found that women more often make decisions from an "ethic of care" while men more often decide on the basis of a "rights" orientation. *See also* Carol Gilligan, *Moral Orientation and Moral Development* in E. F. KITTAY & D. T. MEYERS (EDS.), WOMEN AND MORAL THEORY (New Jersey: Rowman & Littlefield, 1987) and Judith White & Chris Manolis, *Individual Differences in Ethical Reasoning Among Law Students*, 25 SOC. BEHAV. & PERSONALITY 19, 33 (1997) (briefly describing the history of the debate between Kohlberg and Gilligan).

27. Sandra Janoff, *The Influences of Legal Education on Moral Reasoning*, 76 MINN. L. REV. 193, 219–22 (1991).

28. *Id.*

29. Janoff, *supra* note 27; Erica Weissman, Gender-Role Issues in Attorney Career Satisfaction, at 74–76 (1994) (unpublished Ph.D. dissertation, Yeshiva University) (on file with author).

30. Janoff, *supra* note 27.

31. Weissman, *supra* note 29.

Finally, the care/rights dichotomy may also assist lawyers and law students in identifying their preferences and thereby their intrinsic values, so they may better retain those intrinsic values during law school and in the legal profession.

Multiple Intelligences

Multiple intelligence ("MI") theory, developed by Howard Gardner, may also help lawyers and law students identify their preferences. One's preferred modes of intelligence, of eight types, can be assessed via a paper and pencil test. The eight types are musical, mathematical/logical, linguistic/language, intrapersonal/self, interpersonal/social, spatial, naturalistic, and body movement/kinesthetic.[32] The following is an excerpt from an article by Joyce Martin, an Australian lawyer and lecturer.[33] It echoes many of the themes encountered so far and links MI theory to understanding one's craft as a lawyer:

> Mathematical intelligence refers not only to the ability to perform mathematical operations but includes the abilities of being able to think logically and rationally, to proceed in an organised and sequential manner and to understand how technology works and can be brought to bear when solving problems. While logic, rationality and organisational skills are integral to the practice of law, these elements are frequently overemphasised in the training and practice of lawyers....
>
> Interpersonal intelligence is exhibited as not only a sensitivity and understanding of the needs, wants, desires and motivations of others, but also the ability to apply repertoire of appropriate responses to these. While law has been defined by Cottrell as the epitome of a practical craft for the systematic control of social relations, solicitors, as a class, have come to suffer a major image problem being seen as cold, aloof, greedy and insensitive. This image can only be reversed by individual practitioners not only feeling, but demonstrating greater respect for the needs of clients and their opinions, greater willingness to apply the skills of negotiation and mediation and developing a manner which is approachable and humane.
>
> While interpersonal intelligence focuses outward, intrapersonal intelligence looks inward in an effort to understand and appraise one's own needs, drives, motives and achievements in meeting these. Researchers like Mary Ann Glendon claim that while lawyers have never wielded more political and economic power, they are reporting a declining sense of control over their own lives, a high incidence of clinical depression and family breakdown and suicide. Conservative estimates are that one in six lawyers is a problem drinker....
>
> According to Gardner, we can tell when we are positively exercising any intelligence by how we feel. If we feel excited, challenged and ultimately invigorated, we are in positive territory. If we feel self-actualised at the end of our efforts, we have realised the purpose of intelligences. However, if we feel drained, stressed or minimised, we are either using the wrong intelligences toward the right ends or the right intelligences toward the wrong ends....

---

32. One short, free online test can be found at http://literacyworks.org/mi/assessment/findyourstrengths.html (last visited July 11, 2010).

33. Joyce Martin, Lecturer, Australian Catholic University, *Multiple Intelligences, Sex and the Practice of Law* (manuscript provided to the author in 2001).

Gardner provides evidence that what Daniel Goleman (1995) popularized as EQ, or emotional intelligence, is comprised of two separate intelligences, interpersonal intelligence, which is the capacity to notice, distinguish, and respond to the emotions of others, and intrapersonal intelligence, which applies these skills to one's own feelings, needs, desires, motivations, and the ability to meet them [citations omitted].[34]

Professional Role Preferences

Finally, in addition to a lawyer's personality, decisionmaking preferences, and intrinsic values, he or she is also likely to have a preference as to his or her professional approach to working with clients. The remainder of this Chapter is adapted from two articles of the author on the professional roles of lawyers.[35] Some lawyers frame the question as follows:

.... whether they should (1) act as instruments of their clients' will, carrying out their clients' wishes without questioning or examining the morality or desirability of those particular wishes or whether they should (2) act as independent moral agents, bringing their own personal moral values into the lawyer-client representation and counseling.

Of course, these two approaches — the "amoral professional role" and "moral lawyering," respectively — are the extremes. Many lawyers undoubtedly practice in a way that falls somewhere between these two poles of the professionalism continuum. At least one commentator, Professor Rob Atkinson, has identified more than two polar "ends" of a "continuum."[36] He sets forth a "taxonomy" of approaches to lawyering and advocates for lawyers to adopt an eclectic approach to professional roles, perhaps utilizing different approaches in different situations or with different clients. Atkinson suggests that there are at least three approaches to the professional role of the lawyer, which are all ethical and can serve as role models for lawyer behavior.[37]

Atkinson identifies the amoral professional role, where lawyers are instruments of their clients' wills, as "Type I" lawyering, describing this lawyer as the "full advocate or hired gun, who goes full bore for any client or cause." He describes his "Type III lawyer" as the "moral individualist or lawyer vigilante, who goes full bore, but only for virtuous clients and causes, personally and perhaps idiosyncratically defined" and as a "true believer."[38] These lawyers represent only cases or causes they believe in; they always infuse their personal values and morals into the legal representation. However, Atkinson goes on to describe a type of lawyering falling somewhere in between the polar extremes, which he calls "Type II," the "wise counselor." Type II is explored a bit more fully, below.

---

34. *Id.*

35. This text accompanying notes 35–81, *infra*, is an excerpt from Susan Daicoff, *On Butlers, Architects, and Lawyers: The Professionalism of "The Remains of the Day" and "The Fountainhead,"* 17 J. L. Bus. & Ethics 23 (2011), edited and used by permission, combined with material published by the author in her 2004 book, Daicoff, Know Thyself, *supra* note 2.

36. A continuum implies a two dimensional, linear model; some approaches may represent points that do not fall neatly on a line between two extremes but are more properly seen as part of a three-dimensional model.

37. Rob Atkinson, *A Dissenter's Commentary on the Professionalism Crusade*, 74 Tex. L. Rev. 259, 303–320 (1995) (arguing for three approaches to the professional role of the lawyer as opposed to a monolithic standard of neutral partisanship or zealous advocacy).

38. *Id.* at 312.

Grouping various conceptions of the lawyer's professional role into three categories surely blurs significant distinctions between them and yet many do share enough common features with each other that they can be located generally in the same neighborhood on the continuum. These broad categories of lawyer professional roles are expanded on, below.

Type I or the Amoral Professional Role

At the one extreme, lawyers might represent clients blindly and unquestioningly, pursuing their clients' ends zealously and to the fullest extent allowable by law, regardless of the lawyers' personal feelings about the morality, desirability, beneficence, or utility of those ends. In this model, it is simply irrelevant whether the lawyer's personal feelings, morals, values, beliefs, etc. conflict with the particular goals of the client. This approach has been called the amoral professional role,[39] instrumentalism,[40] utilitarianism,[41] the technocratic lawyer,[42] neutral partisanship,[43] and the confusingly named client-centered approach[44] or client orientation.[45] In this approach, the lawyer functions as a technician who carries out the goals and ends of legal representation dictated by the client. The only constraints on the lawyer's behavior are the client's wishes, substantive law, and the code of legal ethics.[46] The lawyer's own personal morals do not form a constraint on his or her behavior nor do they constrain the client's decisions and behavior. The amoral role allows lawyers to ignore their own personal values and morals which conflict with the client's wishes and instead engage in any behavior as long as it achieves the client's stated goals. It is often justified by reference to a lawyer's duty to be a "zealous advocate" for his or her clients.

---

39. Fred C. Zacharias, *Reconciling Professionalism and Client Interests,* 36 Wm. & Mary L. Rev. 1303, 1326 (1995) (arguing that ethics codes are silent or ambiguous in various ethical dilemmas, and that lawyers' natural incentives lead them to choose "partisanship," or blindly zealous advocacy, over "objectivity," or an approach that includes the lawyers' personal values and considers what is best for all involved in the situation, not simply what is best for the client, and arguing that the amoral role "avoids the need to confront what might be difficult moral choices for lawyers and their clients"). *See also* Stephen L. Pepper, *The Lawyer's Amoral Role: A Defense, A Problem, and Some Possibilities,* 1986 Am. B. Found. Res. J. 613, 624 (1986).

40. Daniel R. Coquillette, *Professionalism: The Deep Theory,* 72 N. C. L. Rev. 1271, 1273 (1994).

41. Heidi Li Feldman, *Codes and Virtues: Can Good Lawyers Be Good Ethical Deliberators?* 69 S. Cal. L. Rev. 885, 908 (1996).

42. *Id.* at 886–87 (describing the dichotomy between the amoral role and moral accountability as the difference between "the technocratic lawyer" and "honorable legal analysis").

43. Deborah L. Rhode, *Institutionalizing Ethics,* 44 Case Wes. Res. L. Rev. 665, 667 (1994) ("neutral partisanship").

44. It is confusingly named because it is *not* the same as the client-centered approach espoused by Robert Bastress and associated with psychologist Carl Rogers, which Bastress describes as putting "the attorney in the role of an open, accepting helper and leav[ing] both priority-setting and decision-making to the client. The lawyer helps the client determine what is best for him in light of his own priorities"; it requires the lawyer to engage in reflective, empathic listening to the client to form a "helping relationship" in which the lawyer is "demonstrably sincere, empathic, nonjudgmental, and honest" and focused on the client's problems, goals, and feelings. Robert M. Bastress, *Client Centered Counseling and Moral Accountability For Lawyers,* 10 J. Legal Prof. 97, 98–9 (1985).

45. Zacharias, *supra* note 39, at 1314–16.

46. Pepper, *supra* note 39, at 613. This [excerpt] ... will refer to the concept as the amoral role or amoral professional role. *See also* Andrew Kaufman, *A Commentary on Pepper's "The Lawyer's Amoral Ethical Role,"* 1986 Am. B. Found. Res. J. 651, 652 (1986) and David Luban, *The Lysistratian Prerogative: A Response to Stephen Pepper,* 1986 Am. B. Found. Res. J. 637, 639 & 667 (1986) (*citing* Model Code of Professional Responsibility EC 7-1 (1980)).

Both Richard Matasar and Stephen Pepper have argued that the dissonance between one's personal values and one's work on behalf of clients may cause discomfort or even psychic pain for the attorney.[47] Thus, the amoral role may assist attorneys in carrying out the functions of their work, without undue angst or pain.

Pepper provides a vivid analogy that beautifully illustrates the concept. He explains that the lawyer in this role acts like a car mechanic, who has been engaged to fix a car. The mechanic does not ask the customer about the morality of the uses to which the car will be put, once it is fixed.[48] For example, it would be ludicrous to imagine the car mechanic saying to the client, "You mean, you are going to take this car, as soon as I fix it, drive across the country and abandon your wife, taking this jointly-owned car with you at a time when your wife is nine months pregnant and needs the car to get to the hospital? Well, in that case I refuse to repair your vehicle!" It is an extreme but memorable analogy to the amoral professional role.

Andrew Kaufman explains that one reason lawyers have a moral dilemma in their work, unlike car mechanics, is that they often know the intended uses of their legal efforts, whereas the mechanic simply does not normally have access to this information.[49] If the mechanic knew, for example, the car owner's intentions, then the mechanic would have a moral problem. Kaufman argues that it is the lawyer's knowledge that creates the moral dilemma and the inability to simply say that one is a value-neutral "technician."[50]

Type III or Moral Lawyering

At the other end of the spectrum is an approach often called objectivity,[51] honorable legal analysis,[52] moral lawyering,[53] or Atkinson's Type III "true believer." This approach advocates that lawyers can and should consider their own personal beliefs, values, morals, standards, and feelings in their representation of clients. In this model, lawyers should ask whether the client's goals and ends are inconsistent with their own personal values. If so, then perhaps the lawyer might discuss with the client the moral advisability of his or her proposed course of action. In extreme cases, where the lawyer's values are irreconcilably divergent from the client's goals, then the lawyer would refuse or withdraw from representation of the client in the particular matter.

For example, suppose a corporate lawyer is also an environmentalist in his or her personal and political beliefs; he or she might refuse to represent corporations whose environmental policies he or she did not agree with, even though the matter requir-

---

47. Richard Matasar says this conflict results in unavoidable "pain." Richard A. Matasar, *The Pain of Moral Lawyering,* 75 Iowa L. Rev. 975, 986 (1990) (actually he promises "gut-wrenching, sleepless nights"). Stephen Pepper, one of the main advocates for the amoral professional role, admits that the lawyer adopting this role will not be "comfortable." Pepper, *supra* note 39, at 635.

48. Pepper, *supra* note 39, at 624.

49. Kaufman, *supra* note 46, at 652.

50. *Id. See also* Luban, *supra* note 46, at 639.

51. Zacharias, *supra* note 39, at 1306–09.

52. Feldman, *supra* note 41, at 887.

53. *See* generally Matasar, *supra* note 47. In this [excerpt] … it will be referred to as moral lawyering, to highlight the distinction from the "amoral" role. The idea of lawyering with an "ethic of care" (as opposed to a "rights" or "justice" orientation) is easy to confuse as similar to or consistent with moral lawyering, though they are not identical.

ing legal representation does not involve environmental concerns (it might be a corporate merger or employment dispute). Another example might be a general practice lawyer who does not approve of divorce for personal reasons; he or she might refuse to represent a client seeking a divorce though he or she is competent to handle the matter.

Moral lawyering usually contemplates several courses of action for the lawyer. First, in initial interviews with a new client, the moral lawyer will likely discuss with the client those non-legal concerns raised by the client's request for legal services. The lawyer and client will enter into an open, usually collaborative, discussion of the non-legal advantages and disadvantages of the client's request. They might evaluate whether the proposed action would be moral, right, just, fair, ethical, therapeutic, beneficial to the client and to others, psychologically satisfying or optimal, or harmony-building, etc.[54] If the client and lawyer engage in this discussion and mutually agree on a course of action for the lawyer to take as the client's representative, then the handling of the case goes forward. If, however, the client and lawyer disagree over the proper course of action, then the lawyer has several options. He or she may continue the representation having voiced his or her objections or concerns, refuse to take certain actions on behalf of the client, or withdraw entirely from representation and refer the client to another lawyer.[55]

Certainly, this approach ultimately can reduce lawyers' income, as lawyers often will refuse particular causes, clients, or courses of action.[56] However, advocates of this approach argue for its benefits; for example, Fred Zacharias[57] asserts that it will "reduce immoral actions by attorneys, minimize public perception of attorneys as amoral or immoral, and eliminate lawyers' conflicts between their advocate roles and their own values and morals, which would result in happier lawyers."[58]

The philosophy behind moral lawyering is usually traced to the Aristotelian concept that one's character flows from one's actions, even if those actions are taken in a profes-

---

54. In fact, even the main advocate of the amoral role, Stephen Pepper, admits that "moral dialogue" with the client is a way to resolve the inevitable conflicts between the client's goals and the lawyer's morality, Pepper, *supra* note 39, at 630–32, and that "conscientious objection" may have to be exercised (albeit rarely) by the lawyer, when the conflicts remain unresolved. *Id.* at 632–3.

55. Examples are Zacharias, *supra* note 39, and Robert M. Bastress, *Client Centered Counseling and moral Accountability for Lawyers,* 10 J. LEGAL PROF. 97 (1985) (arguing that lawyers need to become more client-centered in the Rogerian sense as well as morally accountable in their representation of clients and arguing for lawyering which requires the lawyer to discuss his or her personal morals and beliefs with the client and to refuse to take actions which are inconsistent with these morals and beliefs—"moral accountability"), *cf.* Bruce A. Green, *The Role of Personal Values in Professional Decisionmaking,* 11 GEORGETOWN JOURNAL OF LEGAL ETHICS 19 (Fall, 1997) (suggesting that lawyers' personal values often must be excluded in professional decisionmaking and, therefore, lawyers are not always able to be accountable to their consciences in all aspects of their professional lives).

56. Carrie Menkel-Meadow, *Review Essay, What's Gender Got to Do with It?: The Politics and Morality of an Ethic of Care,* 22 N.Y.U. REV. L. & SOC. CHANGE 265 (1996); *see also* Carrie Menkel-Meadow, *Is Altruism Possible in Lawyering?,* 8 GA. ST. U. L. REV. 385, 414 n. 100 (1992) (arguing that lawyers should become more altruistic and also noting that once a client is accepted, zealous advocacy is required by the Model Rules).

57. Zacharias, *supra* note 39, at 1323–24, 1349.

58. *Id.*; Susan Daicoff, *Asking Leopards to Change Their Spots,* 11 GEO. J. LEGAL ETHICS, at 575, *citing* Bastress, *supra* note 55, at 118–19 (happier lawyers would result from eliminating the conflict between one's work and one's beliefs—this is consistent with the Aristotelian concept that one's self-esteem depends on how estimable one's actions are in one's own opinion).

sional capacity on behalf of someone else.[59] In other words, this is the idea that: "I am what I do," or "All that I do, reflects on me." Because this lawyer believes that a lawyer's actions on behalf of a client affect the lawyer's character, an amoral professional stance may not be possible or desirable.

Type IIIA or Lawyering with an Ethic of Care

A related concept is the idea of lawyering with an ethic of care.[60] This approach to lawyering developed from the ideas of Professor Carol Gilligan, who developed a moral decisionmaking model in response to the deficiencies she perceived in Professor Lawrence Kohlberg's six-stage theory of moral decisionmaking, which she found gender biased and unreflective of the morality of women.[61] Gilligan argued that Kohlberg's scheme did not adequately measure women's decisionmaking and indeed often scored it as less developed than men's.[62] She asserts that the "ethic of care" is an approach to decisionmaking that "values interpersonal harmony, maintaining relationships, people's feelings and needs, and preventing harm."[63] Gilligan presents the care ethic as one end of a continuum; the other end is called the "rights orientation."[64] [*This is the same ethic of care/rights continuum described earlier in this Chapter.*]

Perhaps not surprisingly, empirical research on law students in 1991 found that the ethic of care tended to disappear during the first year of law school, while the rights orientation either increased or became more ingrained.[65] Most of the shift was attributable to female law students shifting from an ethic of care to a rights orientation, in law school; many male law students, who more often espoused the rights orientation at the outset, became more firmly planted in that preference.[66] I've asserted that this research suggests that legal education tends to "silence the ethic of care."[67]

Despite this finding that law school deemphasizes the care ethic and other data suggesting that the ethic of care may be underrepresented in the legal profession,[68] Profes-

---

59. Robert F. Cochran, Jr. et al., *Symposium: Client Counseling and Moral Responsibility*, 30 Pepp. L. Rev. 591, 598 (2003).

60. Carol Gilligan et al., Contributions of Women's Sex Bias in Moral Development Theory and Research, Final Report to National Institute of Education, cited in Lawrence Kohlberg, The Psychology of Moral Development: Essays on Moral Development (Volume II) 344 (1984).

61. *Id.*

62. *Id.*

63. Daicoff, *Review, supra* note 1, at 1400.

64. Lawrence J. Landwehr, *Lawyers as Social Progressives or Reactionaries: The Law and Order Cognitive Orientation of Lawyers*, 7 Law & Psychol. Rev. 39, 40 n.2 (1982) (Stage 4 values fixed rules, authority, and the maintenance of social order; the rights orientation also emphasizes rights, rules, standards, fairness, and justice, along with other concepts).

65. Janoff, *supra* note 27, at 219–233, 238 (finding that law students' [particularly women law students'] moral decisionmaking style shifted from an ethic of care to a rights perspective as early as after the first year of law school).

66. *Id.* at 229–30 (students who displayed a rights orientation at the beginning of the first year of law school generally had an even stronger rights orientation by the end of the first year).

67. Daicoff, *Review, supra* note 1, at 1401, citing Janoff, *supra* note 27 (finding that law students who entered law school with an ethic of care tended to lose that ethic of care, and shift to a rights orientation, by the end of the first year of law school).

68. Weissman, *supra* note 29.

sors David Wexler and Carrie Menkel-Meadow have argued that lawyering with an ethic of care is an appropriate and desirable alternative to the amoral professional role.[69] They believe that certain lawyer-client relationships and certain forms of lawyering may be enhanced by a care-oriented approach, particularly where the relational, emotional, and psychological needs and concerns of the parties are paramount.

Type II or the "Wise Counselor"

Atkinson's Type II lawyer is the wise counselor, or the lawyer who brings a consideration of public and moral values into the representation of clients, via open dialogue with the client, but ultimately is guided by the client's decisions as to the ends of representation. His Type II is probably close to Yale University Law School Dean Anthony Kronman's ideal of the sage lawyer exercising "practical wisdom"[70] and the concept of lawyer as Aristotelian "friend."[71] An Aristotelian friend is not the kind of friend who tells you what you want to hear, but a kind of true friend who tells you when you are off course, off the mark, about to do something foolish, or not at your best.

The Type II lawyer embodies the very spirit of the scheme established by the current American Bar Association Model Rules 2.1, 1.2, and 1.3. Model Rule 2.1 explicitly blesses the attorney's role as a candid counselor and permits the lawyer to refer to extralegal concerns such as moral, economic, social, and political factors and cost and effects on other people in rendering advice. The Official Comments to Model Rule 2.1 encourage lawyers to render advice to the client even if the advice will be "unpalatable to the client,"[72] encourage lawyers to refer to relevant moral and ethical considerations in giving advice, since they "impinge upon most legal questions and may decisively influence how the law will be applied,"[73] and state that lawyers may initiate advice, unasked, to the client.[74] However, Model Rule 1.2 then reminds the lawyer that the ultimate decision regarding the substance and objectives of the legal representation belongs to the client, while decisions about means and processes used, particularly regarding "technical, legal and tactical mat-

---

69. Carrie Menkel-Meadow, *Review Essay, What's Gender Got to Do With It?: The Politics and Morality of an Ethic of Care*, 22 N.Y.U. Rev. L. & Soc. Change 265, 279–84 (1996) (supporting lawyering with an ethic of care); David B. Wexler, *Not Such A Party Pooper: An Attempt to Accommodate (Many of) Professor Quinn's Concerns About Therapeutic Jurisprudence Criminal Defense Lawyering*, 48 B.C. L. Rev. 597, 599 (2007) (also advocating for lawyering with an ethic of care, in the context of lawyering from a therapeutic jurisprudence perspective). *See also* Vernellia R. Randall, *The Myers-Briggs Type Indicator, First Year Law Students and Performance*, 26 Cumb. L. Rev. 63, 91, n.138 (1995) (proposing a greater emphasis on "Feeling" in legal education).

70. Anthony Kronman, The Lost Lawyer: Failing Ideals of the Legal Profession (1993).

71. Thomas L. Shaffer & Robert F. Cochran, *"Technical" Defenses: Ethics, Morals, and the Lawyer As Friend*, 14 Clinical L. Rev. 337 (Fall, 2007) (discussing the idea of lawyer as Aristotelian "friend").

72. Comment 1 to Model Rule 2.1 of the 2008 American Bar Association Model Rules of Professional Conduct (as amended) [hereinafter, "Model Rules"], in Susan R. Martyn, Lawrence J. Fox, & W. Bradley Wendel, The Law Governing Lawyers: National Rules, Standards, Statutes, and State Lawyer Codes 57 (2009–2010) [hereinafter Martyn, et al.].

73. Comment 2 to Model Rule 2.1, in Martyn, et al., *supra* note 72, at 57.

74. Comment 3 to Model Rule 2.1, in Martyn, et al., *supra* note 72, at 57. ABA Model Rule 2.1 states: "In representing a client, a lawyer *shall* exercise independent professional judgment and render candid advice. In rendering advice, a lawyer *may* refer not only to law but to *other considerations such as moral, economic, social and political factors* that may be relevant to the client's situation (italics added)." *Id.*

ters,"[75] belong to the lawyer.[76] The Type II lawyer is naturally likely to be sensitive to these extralegal factors, bring them to the client's attention, initiate a discussion with the client about the effect of these factors on the client's ultimate decision, and then finally abide by the client's decision about the goals and ends of the legal representation. The ethical rule framework allows the Type II lawyer to integrate his or her personal morals, values, and beliefs into his or her representation of clients (or, at the least, not ignore or trample on them) while simultaneously upholding the ideals of zealous advocacy and client autonomy.

Zealous Advocacy and the Ethics Code

Interestingly, my experience with presenting these ends of the spectrum to law students usually results in a response like, "But professor, we are required by the ethics code to be zealous advocates. Anything other than zealous advocacy will subject us to malpractice liability or disciplinary action. As lawyers, we will not be allowed to question the morality of our client's goals or wishes, since our job is solely to be zealous advocates and represent the client to the nth degree. To do anything else would be malpractice." This is a *myth* that some law schools implicitly engender in law students, who then carry this perception into practice and unquestioningly adopt an amoral professional role. Adopting it is not objectionable; it is the students' perception that there is *no other lawful alternative available* to them that is problematic.

This pervasive myth is not entirely consistent with some portions of the model legal ethics rules promulgated by the American Bar Association. The current American Bar Association's Model Rules of Professional Behavior reference "zeal in advocacy" only in one comment to one Model Rule.[77] Model Rule 1.1 imposes a duty of diligence and promptness in representing a client, but this does not mean that every advantage must be pursued in furtherance of the client's cause. Comment 1 to Model Rule 1.3 refers to "zeal in advocacy" but then states that not every advantage must be pursued; the lawyer has discretion in this area. However, the ultimate decision as to the overall goal of legal representation belongs to the client, according to Model Rule 1.2.

While the ultimate decision is the client's, the lawyer is explicitly permitted and even encouraged to counsel with the client about extralegal factors bearing on the legal representation, in the lawyer's role as counselor of the client, in order to assist the client's decisionmaking. Model Rule 2.1 states:

> In representing a client, a lawyer *shall* exercise independent professional judgment and render candid advice. In rendering advice, a lawyer *may* refer not only to law but to *other considerations such as moral, economic, social and political factors* that may be relevant to the client's situation (italics added).[78]

and thereby seems to encourage a diverse approach to professionalism. It appears to explicitly bless moral lawyering (or wise counseling) and discourage a monolithic adherence to neutral partisanship, where the lawyer acts only as a "zealous advocate."

One possible explanation for the primacy of zealous advocacy in the culture of the legal profession is the fact that zealous advocacy was the main topic of one of the origi-

---

75. Comment 2 to Model Rule 1.2, in MARTYN, ET AL., *supra* note 72, at 57.
76. Model Rule 1.2 and Comments 1–2 thereto, in MARTYN, ET AL., *supra* note 72, at 14–15.
77. Comment 1 to Model Rule 1.3 in MARTYN, ET AL., *supra* note 72, at 16.
78. Model Rule 2.1 (titled: "Advisor") in MARTYN, ET AL., *supra* note 72, at 57.

nal 1908 Canons of Professional Ethics.[79] Canon 7 of this earlier Model Code stated that "a lawyer should represent a client zealously within the bounds of the law."[80] However, like current Model Rule 2.1, an Ethical Consideration of the 1983 Model Code also explicitly encouraged lawyers to engage in a moral analysis of the client's proposed actions. Even early on, an approach like moral lawyering was contemplated.[81]

The era of "zealous advocacy" as one of the thirteen Canons, or fundamental values of the legal profession, appears to have passed. This emphasis is no longer as strong in the legal ethics code as it was in the pre-1983 ABA Model Code. Yet the modern culture of the legal profession maintains the myth of "zealous advocacy" as a mandate, perhaps because many of the senior partners in today's private firms (and tenured law professors in today's law schools) learned legal ethics during this pre-1983 era. This myth pervades even into law school, among students who have not yet entered the practice of law, while the formal ethics codes explicitly envision a more diverse approach to the lawyer's professional role.

---

79. The history of the Model Rules, Model Code, and Canons is explained in MARTYN, ET AL., *supra* note 72, at 1–5. The current (2002 and 2003, as amended) Model Rules replaced the 1983 Model Rules, which in turn replaced the earlier (1908) Canons of Professional Ethics. The Canons originally appeared in 1908 and were supplemented by the ABA's "Model Code of Professional Responsibility" in 1969.

80. Canon 7 of the ABA Model Code of Professional Responsibility (1983), in MARTYN, ET AL., *supra* note 72, at 150.

81. Its advice is couched in a bit stronger language than the current Model Rule (emphasis {in italics} and underlining added):

EC 7-8 INFORMING CLIENT OF RELEVANT CONSIDERATIONS; WITHDRAWAL FROM EMPLOYMENT

A lawyer should exert his best efforts to insure that decisions of his client are made only after the client has been informed of relevant considerations. A lawyer ought to *initiate* this decisionmaking process if the client does not do so. *Advice of a lawyer to his client need not be confined to purely legal considerations.* A lawyer should advise his client of the possible effect of each legal alternative. *A lawyer should bring to bear upon this decisionmaking process the fullness of his experience as well as his objective viewpoint.* In assisting his client to reach a proper decision, it is *often desirable for a lawyer to point out those factors* which may lead to a decision that is *morally just* as well as *legally permissible.* He may emphasize the possibility of *harsh consequences that might result from assertion of legally permissible positions.* In the *final* analysis, however, the lawyer should always remember that the decision whether to forego legally available objectives or methods *because of non-legal factors is ultimately for the client and not for himself.* In the event that the client in a *non-adjudicatory matter* insists upon a course of conduct that is *contrary to the judgment and advice of the lawyer but not prohibited by Disciplinary Rules, the lawyer may withdraw from the employment.*

In the Model Code, an Ethical Consideration is only aspirational and is not mandatory. Most states have gradually abandoned the Model Code in favor of the Model Rules, which contain no such blessing of moral lawyering. The current Model Rules explicitly remind the lawyer that the ultimate decision is the client's and not the lawyer's and allow the lawyer to withdraw from representation only in non-adjudicatory matters, where the lawyer's judgment and the client's conflict. However, Michael Distelhorst, who has documented the history of legal ethics codes and rules since 1830, asserts that legal ethics has consistently swung between two poles—from a formulation of aspirations and ideals of ethics and professionalism, to an emphasis on minimum rules to which lawyers must conform or be sanctioned. Currently, most jurisdictions have adopted the Model Rules, which embody the latter approach (the minimal standards), but Professor Distelhorst asserts that the pendulum may be moving back towards a more aspirational or ideal approach. The old Model Code reflects both: the Ethical Considerations set out the ideals to which lawyers should aspire and the Disciplinary Rules set out the minimum rules to which lawyers must conform. Therefore, to dismiss this EC as merely aspirational or a current minority view simply ignores both the bulk of the history of legal ethics and its probable future direction. Personal communication with Professor Michael Distelhorst, Capital University Law School, March, 2007.

It may be useful, before entering the active practice of law with all of its competing pressures, to identify which of these approaches one sees oneself embodying, professionally. One's intrinsic values may also be a guide to assist in determining which approach is the best fit.

Intrinsic Values and Comprehensive Law "Vectors"

The disciplines within, or "vectors," of the comprehensive law movement explicitly allow lawyers to infuse a set of values into their law practice that may provide intrinsic rewards.[82] For example, the therapeutically-oriented lawyer may feel inherent satisfaction from legal work if he or she values "doing good" for others and defines "good" as enhancing others' psychological wellbeing. A family lawyer might obtain inherent satisfaction from doing legal work that preserves and fosters harmonious relationships between divorcing spouses, knowing that those relationships will lead to a better life and better mental health for the children of the divorce. A criminal lawyer using restorative justice might experience satisfaction in seeing victims of crime achieve "closure" by coming to terms with the crime and its effects, in seeing victims and offenders receive apologies and forgiveness, respectively, and in seeing offenders experience "therapeutic shame" that effectively motivates them towards permanent change and nonrecidivism. Preventive lawyers may experience satisfaction in knowing their legal efforts helped avoid the economic and temporal waste of a lawsuit. Lawyers and judges using procedural justice may appreciate the enhanced satisfaction their clients and litigants gain from a legal process that allows for voice and participation. Lawyers, judges, and other legal personnel involved in drug treatment courts have reported personal satisfaction from the success of the court's graduates in staying free from drugs and crime.[83]

Law as a healing profession has great transformational potential. It could begin to address the "tripartite crisis" in the legal profession of deprofessionalism, low public opinion of lawyers, and lawyer distress.[84] It could make the legal system a more inspiring, humane, and hospitable place for clients, lawyers, judges, and society as a whole.

---

82. Susan Daicoff, *Lawyer Personality Traits and Their Relationship to Various Approaches to Lawyering,* in MARJORIE A. SILVER, ED., THE AFFECTIVE ASSISTANCE OF COUNSEL 79–107 (Carolina Academic Press, 2007).

83. *See* Deborah Chase & Hon. Peggy Fulton Hora, *Special Issue: Substance Abuse and Addiction in Family Courts — The Best Seat in the House: The Court Assignment and Judicial Satisfaction,* 47 FAM. CT. REV. 209 (April, 2009) (reporting the results of an empirical survey on greater judicial satisfaction in problem solving, therapeutic courts). *See also* Deborah J. Chase & Peggy Fulton Hora, *The Implications of Therapeutic Jurisprudence for Judicial Satisfaction,* 37 COURT REVIEW 12 (May, 2000) (reporting the results of an empirical study on the positive effects on judges of judging from a therapeutic jurisprudence perspective).

84. Susan Daicoff, *Lawyer, Know Thyself: A Review of Empirical Research on Attorney Attributes Bearing on Professionalism,* 46 AM. U. L. REV. 1337 (1997) (describing and documenting this "tripartite crisis").

Resources

For more detail on empirical studies of lawyers and their traits, see Susan Daicoff, Lawyer, Know Thyself: A Psychological Analysis of Personality Strengths and Weaknesses (American Psychological Association Books, 2004).

There are many important works in this area; a few are:

Julie Macfarlane, The New Lawyer: How Settlement Is Transforming the Practice of Law (UBC Press, 2008) (Law & Society Series) (exploring in detail the current state of the legal profession, changing professional roles of the lawyer, and lawyering).

Marjorie A. Silver, The Affective Assistance of Counsel. (Carolina Academic Press, 2007) (exploring how lawyers approach clients, comprehensively).

Richard Susskind, The End of Lawyers? Rethinking the Nature of Legal Services (Oxford University Press, 2008) (asserting the obsolescence of traditional lawyering and calling for a sea change in the legal profession).

Lawrence R. Richard, *Psychological Type and Job Satisfaction Among Practicing Lawyers in the United States*, 29 Cap. U. L. Rev. 979 (2002).

Kurt M. Saunders & Linda Levine, *Learning to Think Like a Lawyer*, 29 U.S.F. L. Rev. 121 (1994).

Patrick Schiltz, *On Being a Happy, Healthy and Ethical Member of an Unhappy, Unhealthy Profession*, 52(4) Vand. L. Rev. 872 (1999).

Kennon M. Sheldon & Lawrence S. Krieger, *Does Legal Education Have Undermining Effects on Law Students? Evaluating Changes in Motivation, Values, and Well-Being*, 22 Behav. Sci. Law 261–286 (2004).

Elizabeth Dvorkin, Jack Himmelstein, & Howard Lesnick, Becoming A Lawyer: A Humanistic Perspective on Legal Education and Professionalism (West, 1981).

This chapter is based on and/or adapted from the following, by the author:

Lawyer, Be Thyself: An Empirical Investigation of the Relationship Between the Ethic of Care, the Feeling Decisionmaking Preference, and Lawyer Wellbeing, 16 Va. J. Soc. Pol'y & L. 87 (2008) (reporting on the results of an empirical study of these characteristics).

Lawyer Personality Traits and their Relationship to Various Approaches to Lawyering, in Marjorie A. Silver, Ed., The Affective Assistance of Counsel (Carolina Academic Press, 2007).

Making Law Therapeutic For Lawyers: Therapeutic Jurisprudence, Preventive Law, and the Psychology of Lawyers, 5 Psych., Pub. Pol'y. & Law 811 (1999) (arguing that TJ and PL can enhance lawyer wellbeing).

Asking Leopards to Change Their Spots, 11 Geo. J. Legal Ethics (1998) (concluding that the typical lawyer traits are helpful and adaptive in the traditional practice of law).

Lawyer, Know Thyself, 46 Am. U. L. Rev. 1337 (1997) (reporting on the results of 40 years of empirical research on lawyer personality).

Oxymoron? Ethical Decisionmaking by Attorneys, 48 Fla. L. Rev. (1996) (reporting on the results of an empirical study of attorneys' decisionmaking in various professional ethical dilemma situations).

Coordination: Also read Silver (Chapter 3), Wright (Chapter 4), and all of Macfarlane.

Chapter Assignments

Exercise 1-1

Watch the following two movies. Answer the following questions in one typed page, single spaced.

Erin Brockovich *(Columbia Pictures, 2000)*

a. Identify and describe the various types of "professional role" displayed by Erin Brockovich (played by Julia Roberts), Ed Masry (played by Albert Finney), and the female co-counsel in the large firm associated by Masry on the case (the one with "ugly shoes" and a stilted manner) as they interact with other lawyers and with the clients.

b. Identify the pros and cons of each of these three approaches to the professional role of an attorney.

c. Identify which role you believe you would adopt, as you work with clients as a lawyer.

A Civil Action *(Touchstone/Paramount Pictures, 1998)*

d. How does Jan Schlictmann (the attorney played by John Travolta in the movie) define success at the beginning of the movie?

e. During the trial?

f. At the end?

g. Why does his definition of success change from the beginning to the end of the movie?

Exercise 1-2

Complete the following self-inventory. You may want to refer to your work on this assignment as you engage in the active practice of law.

"Lab 1": Self-Inventory and Self-Awareness Exercises

(*Published in* Susan Daicoff, *Lawyer Personality Traits and their Relationship to Various Approaches to Lawyering,* in MARJORIE A. SILVER, ED., THE AFFECTIVE ASSISTANCE OF COUNSEL (Carolina Academic Press, 2007) *and here used by permission.*)

I. Self-Inventory

This is designed to assist you to identify your personality traits, your decisionmaking preferences, and your values.

A. Decisionmaking Styles:

Identify which you prefer, on a scale of 1 to 10:

1. <u>**Thinking vs. Feeling as a decisionmaking preference**</u> (you may navigate to www.keirsey.com (last visited July 11, 2010) to take an online test for a fee to determine your preference, or simply choose from the following definitions).

    THINKERS: value justice, rationality, truth, & objectivity; decisions don't reflect own personal values; can be cold & calculating; good problem-solvers.

    FEELERS: value harmony, interpersonal relationships, praise & mercy; apply their own personal values to make decisions; seek to do what's right for self & others; sensitive to the effect of decisions on others.

    1   2   3   4   5   6   7   8   9   10
    Thinking...Feeling

2. <u>**Rights/justice orientation vs. ethic of care as a moral decisionmaking preference**</u> (can be assessed with the Moral Orientation Scale available from Professor Sharon Weinberg at New York University or choose from the following definitions):

    RIGHTS/JUSTICE: weighs conflicting rights & duties; seeks fairness, justice, & equality; maintains & applies rules, standards, & role obligations to arrive at clear, absolute answers.

    CARE: contextual; focuses on harm to people; seeks to avoid harm, maintain & restore relationships & protect others from hurt; decides by assessing relative harm to & vulnerabilities of parties.

    1   2   3   4   5   6   7   8   9   10
    Rights...Ethic of Care

3. <u>**Multiple Intelligences Preferences:**</u>

    Visit http://literacyworks.org/mi/assessment/findyourstrengths.html (last visited July 11, 2010) and report your results here (list at least your top three preferences and the strength, i.e., values or numbers, of those preferences):

    1. _____value: _____

    2. _____value: _____

    3. _____value: _____

B. Values Sort:

Read the following values, activities, or pursuits. Rank the top 15 in order of their importance to you (1–15). Feel free to add some that are not on this list.

___ Competitive — I like to win

___ Spending time with family

___ Spending time with friends

___ Inner peace

___ Greater connection to my community

___ Spending time with my children

___ Being respected and admired in my profession

___ Being good at what I do

___ Excelling, achieving scholastically

___ Healthy body, physical fitness

___ Creativity

___ Being visionary

___ Art

___ Music

___ Sports

___ Current events; following politics

___ Hobbies (describe: _____)

___ Marriage

___ Parenting

___ Children

___ Family

___ Extended family

___ Personal growth and awareness

___ Spirituality

___ Relationship with God

___ Harmony between people

___ Environmental concerns

___ Championing a cause

___ Leading others

___ Friends

___ Knowledge, education, formal learning

___ Greater professional ability, experience, and acumen

___ Making money

___ Being financially secure

___ Nature, being in nature

___ Animals

___ Charitable activities, giving to others, helping others

___ Others (describe): _____

_____

_____

_____

C. Values Clarification:

Write your own eulogy in three sentences, based on the following three questions:[85]

1. What do you want your closest person (spouse, partner, best friend) to say about you?

2. What do you want your professional colleagues to say about you?

3. What do you want your dependents (clients, children, others whom you lead or who look up to you) to say about you?

II. Professional Inventory

A. Professional Roles:

On a scale of 1 (not like this) to 10 (this describes me perfectly), rate your level of agreement with the following lawyering styles:

1. Neutral partisanship/zealous advocacy: I am comfortable detaching my own personal values from the particular client or cause that I am representing. I am able to view my legal representation as a good in itself, regardless of the ultimate goals of my client. My client is the ultimate arbiter of his or her goals; those goals are in a sense none of my business. My job is to provide the most excellent legal representation that I can, designed to help my client achieve his or her goals. Part of my job is to give my client my professional advice about the legal aspects of his or her problem.

1   2   3   4   5   6   7   8   9   10
disagree strongly   agree strongly

----

85. This exercise is credited to Professor Lawrence S. Krieger of Florida State University College of Law, the leading expert in law student wellbeing in the United States.

*2. **The wise counselor:*** I believe that I should clearly pursue my client's aims and goals, however, I also believe that part of my role is to point out to the client extralegal concerns (moral, ethical, relational, emotional, psychological, etc.) that are raised by his or her wishes. The client is the final decisionmaker, however, and my job is simply to provide all the options and point out the consequences.

1   2   3   4   5   6   7   8   9   10
disagree strongly   agree strongly

*3. **Moral lawyering:*** I am unable to divorce my personal values, morals, and beliefs from my work as a lawyer. I am most comfortable and satisfied when I am representing clients and causes I truly believe in. I am interested in working with my client as equal partners to determine what his or her best interests are and what his or her goals should be. I believe part of my job as a lawyer is to give my client my honest opinion on nonlegal matters that affect the legal matter at hand.

1   2   3   4   5   6   7   8   9   10
disagree strongly   agree strongly

*4. **Caring lawyering:*** I believe that the lawyer and client should work together as equal members of a team. They should engage in an open, honest discussion of their individual beliefs and values to define the purpose of the legal representation. I believe the lawyer should do more listening than talking. It is important to avoid harm to people and to their relationships, when resolving legal problems.

1   2   3   4   5   6   7   8   9   10
disagree strongly   agree strongly

*5. **If none of these is appealing, write your own:***

B. Personal Definition of Professional Success:

Complete the following sentences:

A good attorney is one who _____

_____

_____

_____

_____

A successful attorney is one who _____

_____

_____

_____

_____

I know I am a successful attorney when I _____

_____

_____

_____

_____

I expect to be most satisfied professionally, in my work as an attorney, when I _____

_____

_____

_____

_____

C. Expected Professional Strengths and Weaknesses:

As you have worked through the foregoing exercises, you have identified your personal characteristics, preferences, and values.

1. What are your best qualities? What are your strongest characteristics that are your greatest assets in your work as an attorney?

List (or type "x" next to the following):

Examples:

Intellectual power

Verbal persuasion

Leadership skills

Written word

Insight into human dynamics and motivations

Compassion for others

Ability to detach emotionally, compartmentalize

Ability to be rational, cool-headed in conflict or in the heat of battle

Ability to be fair and impartial with two disputing parties

Others:

2. What are your weak spots? What aspects of yourself do you think cause you the most trouble as an attorney? What is your "Achilles heel"?

List (or type "x" next to the following):

Examples:

Too compassionate

Can't detach emotionally

Can't be impartial or rational about certain clients and types of cases

Have a hard time listening to others' viewpoints

Are very confident in your ability to know what's right and wrong

Stubborn

Hardheaded

Afraid of conflict

Others:

3. What explicit or conscious biases do you have that might cause you to subtly skew your advice or cause you to treat certain matters or clients differently?

4. What kind of clients or causes would you prefer to avoid?

5. Which clients or causes would you most like to represent?

6. What kinds of clients or situations push your buttons, meaning irritate you to the point of total frustration?

7. What kinds of clients or situations invite your overinvolvement, meaning tread on your weaknesses to the point that you become overinvested in the situation or "in over your head?"

8. What do you normally do when you are extremely frustrated, irritated, angry, worried, or overly stressed with a person or situation? (i.e., what are your usual reactions and coping strategies?)

Chapter 2

Philosophical Underpinnings, Precursors, and Propellers for Change[1]

Comprehensive Law Movement

Beginning in the last decade of the 20th century, partially in response to the tripartite crisis and other concerns explored in the previous chapter, a new movement in law emerged—a movement towards taking an explicitly comprehensive, integrated, humanistic, interdisciplinary, restorative, and often therapeutic approach to law and lawyering. The "comprehensive law movement" is the synthesis of a number of new disciplines within law and legal practice that have been rapidly gaining visibility, acceptance, and popularity in the last two decades, representing a number of emerging, alternative forms of law practice, dispute resolution, and criminal justice. The converging main "vectors" of this movement are collaborative law,[2] creative problem solving,[3] holistic

---

1. This Chapter is reprinted and adapted from the author's 2006 article, Susan Daicoff, *Law as a Healing Profession: The "Comprehensive Law Movement,"* 6 Pepperdine Disp. Resol. L. J. 1 (2006). Where it incorporates other publications of the author, it is so indicated.

2. *See e.g.,* Pauline H. Tesler, Collaborative Law: Achieving Effective Resolution in Divorce Without Litigation (2001) (introducing the concepts and methods of collaborative law as founded by Minnesota divorce attorney Stuart Webb and advanced by California divorce attorney Pauline Tesler). Some of the ideas expressed in this Chapter, namely, the "vectors" of the "comprehensive law movement," were previously published by the author in shorter forms in various book chapters and magazine articles: Susan Swaim Daicoff, Lawyer Know Thyself: A Psychological Analysis of Personality Strengths and Weaknesses (2004) [hereinafter Daicoff, Know Thyself] (final chapter devoted to the movement) Copyright © 2004 by the American Psychological Association. Reproduced or adapted with permission. The use of this information does not imply endorsement by the publisher; Susan Daicoff, *Afterword: The Role of Therapeutic Jurisprudence Within the Comprehensive Law Movement,* in Dennis P. Stolle, David B. Wexler, & Bruce J. Winick, Eds., Practicing Therapeutic Jurisprudence (Carolina Academic Press 2000) [hereinafter Daicoff, *Afterword*] (describing the comprehensive law movement and its relationship to therapeutic jurisprudence generally); Susan Daicoff, *Resolution Without Litigation: Are Courtrooms Battlegrounds for Losers?,* GPSolo, Oct./Nov. 2003, at 44 (summarizing the vectors of the comprehensive law movement).

3. *See, e.g.,* James M. Cooper, *Toward a New Architecture: Creative Problem Solving and the Evolution of Law,* 34(2) Cal. W. L. Rev. 297 (1998) (advocating creative problem solving skills in the practice of law, legal education and other professional fields); Janeen Kerper, *Creative Problem Solving vs. The Case Method: A Marvelous Adventure in Which Winnie-the-Pooh Meets Mrs. Palsgraf,* 34(2) Cal. W. L. Rev. 351 (1998) (introducing the emergence of creative problem solving as a legal discipline in response to the need for change in legal education); and Thomas D. Barton, *Conceiving the Lawyer as Creative Problem Solver,* 34(2) Cal. W. L. Rev. 267 (1998) (discussing a symposium issue to educate creative problem solvers). One issue of the California Western Law Review (volume 34, issue 2)

justice,[4] preventive law,[5] problem solving courts,[6] procedural justice,[7] restorative justice,[8] therapeutic jurisprudence,[9] and transformative mediation.[10] These are briefly described in Chapter 3 and each is explored in detail in its own Chapter, *infra*.

Figure 1. The Vectors of the Comprehensive Law Movement

1. Collaborative Law
2. Creative Problem Solving
3. Holistic Justice
4. Preventive Law
5. Problem Solving Courts
6. Procedural Justice
7. Restorative Justice
8. Therapeutic Jurisprudence
9. Therapeutically Oriented Preventive Law
10. Transformative Mediation

Related Disciplines or Vectors

1. Affective Lawyering
2. Balance in Legal Education/Humanizing Legal Education
3. Mindfulness Meditation
4. Rebellious Lawyering

---

in 1998 was devoted to creative problem solving. California Western Law School houses the McGill Center for Creative Problem Solving, which sponsors a number of national and international programs implementing CPS, as well as several law school courses on CPS.

4. Holistic justice is primarily a grass-roots movement among practicing attorneys in the United States and abroad. Many holistic lawyers are profiled at www.cuttingedgelaw.com (last visited June 29, 2011).

5. *See, e.g.,* Robert M. Hardaway, Preventive Law: Materials on a Nonadversarial Legal Process (1997) (the "textbook" for preventive law; now in its second edition). Preventive law is also known as "proactive law," principally so in Finland, under the guidance and leadership of corporate attorney Helena Haapio.

6. *E.g.,* drug treatment courts, mental health courts, domestic violence courts, and other specialized courts. These courts were formalized in 2000 by the adoption of a joint resolution of the Conferences of Chief Justices and Chief Court Administrators explicitly supporting the development of problem solving courts. CCJ Resolution 22, COSCA Resolution 4, http://dcpi.ncjrs.org/pdf/Chief%20Justice%20Resolution.doc (last visited July 11, 2010).

7. This is a social science concept based on social scientist Tom Tyler's research on the factors creating satisfaction in litigants involved in legal processes. This work has informed, and altered in some cases, thoughts on how legal and judicial processes should proceed. *See* Tom R. Tyler, *The Psychological Consequences of Judicial Procedures: Implications for Civil Commitment Hearings,* in David B. Wexler & Bruce J. Winick, Law in a Therapeutic Key: Developments in Therapeutic Jurisprudence 3 (1996) [hereinafter Wexler & Winick, Key].

8. Restorative justice is one of the largest "vectors" and is associated with restorative criminal justice programs across the United States and in Canada, the United Kingdom, Australia, and New Zealand. Numerous articles and books have been written on RJ; one principal resource in the U.S. is the Center for Restorative Justice at the University of Minnesota, directed by RJ leader and professor Mark Umbreit (website: http://www.cehd.umn.edu/ssw/rjp (last visited July 11, 2010)).

9. Therapeutic jurisprudence is also one of the largest "vectors," if not the largest. It is represented by numerous books and hundreds of law review articles that apply TJ to all areas of the law. Its founders, law professors David Wexler and Bruce Winick, maintain an extensive set of resources at its website, www.therapeuticjurisprudence.org or http://www.law.arizona.edu/depts/upr-intj (last visited July 11, 2010).

10. Transformative mediation is associated with law professor R. Baruch Bush and is explicated in his book co-authored with communications professor Joseph Folger, The Promise of Mediation (Jossey-Bass, 1994). The vectors are listed in alphabetical order, not in order of importance, size, or seniority.

As early as 1997, several of these emerging disciplines had begun to merge, integrate, coalesce, or link, based on similarities in their overall purposes and goals. One of the first scholars to identify this was University of California—Santa Barbara sociology professor Thomas Scheff, who observed in 1997 that: "[i]n recent years, an alternative approach to law, a worldwide movement, has been building momentum. This movement has two vectors, restorative justice and therapeutic jurisprudence ..."[11] The term "vectors" reflects the forward movement of the disciplines into the future and their convergence toward common goals. In 1988, encouraged by Professors Wexler and Winick, I began building on Professor Scheff's insight by examining other potential "vectors" and exploring what their unifying characteristics might be. By 2000, I began using the "comprehensive law movement" as a working title for the movement, now comprised of nine or so vectors.[12] Many conferences and publications since 2000 have acknowledged the link between some of these disciplines, including four books by Stolle, Wexler, and Winick; Silver; Barton; and Brooks and Madden, respectively. Three more books, by Julie MacFarlane in 2006, by Michael King and others in 2009, and by J. Kim Wright in 2010, respectively, have been published synthesizing most of these vectors into an overall movement towards innovation in the legal profession. MacFarlane calls for the "new lawyer," King et al. call it "non-adversarial justice," and Wright writes about "lawyers as peacemakers."[13]

---

11. Thomas J. Scheff, *Community Conferences: Shame and Anger in Therapeutic Jurisprudence*, 67(1) Rev. Jur. U.P.R. 97, 97 (1998).

12. Steven Keeva, *Once More, With Healing: Ex-Law Dean Heads Center Dedicated to Alternative Approaches to Practice*, 90 A.B.A.J. 74 (2004). Admittedly, the title is a rudimentary and nondescript one. However, there are multiple mentions of the term, "comprehensive law movement," in the text of law review articles (37); it has been cited in over one hundred law review articles and journals. Some of these are, *e.g.*, Captain Evan R. Seamone, *The Veterans' Lawyer as Counselor: Using Therapeutic Jurisprudence to Enhance Client Counseling for Combat Veterans with Posttraumatic Stress Disorder*, 202 Mil. L. Rev. 185 (2009); Forrest S. Mosten, *Lawyer as Peacemaker: Building a Successful Law Practice without Ever Going to Court*, 43 Fam. L. Q. 489 (2009); Robin Wellford Slocum, *The Dilemma of the Vengeful Client: A Prescriptive Framework for Cooling the Flames of Anger*, 92 Marq. L. Rev. 481 (2009); Raymond H. Brescia, *Beyond Balls and Strikes: Towards a Problem-Solving Ethic in Foreclosure Proceedings*, 59 Case Western Res. L. Rev. 305 (2009); Michal Alberstein, *The Jurisprudence of Mediation: Between Formalism, Feminism, and Identity Conversations*, 11 Cardozo J. Conflict Resol. 1 (2009); Michael S. King, *Critique and Comment Restorative Justice, Therapeutic Jurisprudence and the Rise of Emotionally Intelligent*, 32 Melb. U. L. Rev. 1096 (2008); Omer Shapira, *Joining Forces in Search for Answers: The Use of Therapeutic Jurisprudence in the Realm of Mediation Ethics*, 8 Pepperdine Disp. Resol. L. J. 243 (2008); Leonard L. Riskin, *The Contemplative Lawyer: On the Potential Contributions of Mindfulness Meditation to Law Students, Lawyers, and Their Clients*, 7 Harv. Negot. L. Rev. 1 (2002); Douglas Codiga, *ADR Reflections on the Potential Growth of Mindfulness Meditation in the Law*, 7 Harv. Negot. L. Rev. (2002); Pauline H. Tesler, *Collaborative Family Law*, 4 Pepp. Disp. Resol. L.J. 317 (2004); Marjorie A. Silver, *Lawyering and Its Discontents: Reclaiming Meaning in the Practice of Law*, 19 Touro L. Rev. 773 (2004); James L. Nolan, Jr., *Redefining Criminal Courts: Problem-Solving and the Meaning of Justice*, 40 Am. Crim. L. Rev. 1541 (2003); J. Kim Wright & Dolly M. Garlo, *Law as a Healing Profession*, 63 Or. St. B. Bull. 9 (2003); 39 Trial 12 (2003); Carole L. Mostow, *Holistic Lawyers Hope to Transform Conflict Resolution*, 12 No. 4 Prof. Law. 24 (2000).

13. These are: J. Kim Wright, Lawyers As Peacemakers: Practicing Holistic, Problem-Solving Law (American Bar Association, 2010) (by an American lawyer, mediator, collaborative lawyer, author, and journalist documenting the comprehensive law movement); Michael King, Arie Frieberg, Becky Batagol, & Ross Hyams, Non-Adversarial Justice (The Federation Press, 2009) (by Australian law professors, documenting the comprehensive law movement); Julie Macfarlane, The New Lawyer: How Settlement Is Transforming the Practice of Law (UBC Press, 2008) (Law & Society Series) (by a Canadian law professor and author documenting the comprehensive law movement). Other important synthesizing books are: Susan L. Brooks & Robert G. Madden, Relationship-Centered Lawyering: Social Science Theory for Transforming Legal Practice (Carolina Academic Press, 2010) (collecting many of the vectors in the same work); Marjorie A.

The similarities of the vectors coalesce into two common features, thus unifying them as a "movement." First, each explicitly recognizes and values law's potential as an agent of positive interpersonal and individual change and seeks to bring about a positive result (such as healing, wholeness, harmony, or optimal human functioning) as part of the resolution of legal matters. Second, each integrates and values extralegal concerns—factors beyond strict legal rights and duties—into law and legal practice. These "rights plus"[14] factors include: needs, resources, goals, morals, values, beliefs, psychological matters, personal wellbeing, human development and growth, interpersonal relations, and community wellbeing....

This Chapter will explore what led up to the emergence of the comprehensive law movement and why it developed now. It will then examine some philosophical concepts underlying the movement and current events propelling it forward.

Philosophical Shifts in Society

Several philosophical shifts have occurred in recent decades, perhaps paving the way for the emergence of comprehensive law approaches within the legal profession. Some of these are global and societal in nature and not limited to law. Others exist entirely within the legal profession....[15]

First, the globalization of the world, hastened by technological advances and worldwide environmental concerns, has made the world smaller. Other cultures and countries have become more accessible and "real." Environmental problems have made us more dependent upon other countries and have forced us to collaborate with them in order to solve imminent global environmental concerns that threaten our way of life. For example, once we realized that toxic dumping in the United States creates a hole in the ozone layer over another country that in turn affects our supply of a particular good produced elsewhere, we began to realize that we were not and could not remain isolated from the rest of the world. In turn, we have gained an awareness that "we are all in this together" and that cooperation is necessary in order for us to thrive and prosper in the future. Also, in the last decade of the 20th century, partly as a result of the end of the Cold War, there may have been a decline in the prominence of a polarized, adversarial, "us and them" mentality in which we viewed other people, other countries, and other cultures as enemies to be feared and avoided.[16] We found ourselves collabo-

---

SILVER, THE AFFECTIVE ASSISTANCE OF COUNSEL. (Carolina Academic Press, 2007) (focusing on how to practice law comprehensively); DENNIS P. STOLLE, DAVID B. WEXLER, & BRUCE J. WINICK, EDS., PRACTICING THERAPEUTIC JURISPRUDENCE: LAW AS A HELPING PROFESSION (Carolina Academic Press, 2000) (collecting many of the vectors in the same work, extending earlier efforts by Wexler & Winick); and THOMAS D. BARTON, PREVENTIVE LAW & PROBLEM SOLVING (2009) (integrating TJ, CPS, and PL). An early, very influential work is STEVEN KEEVA, TRANSFORMING PRACTICES: FINDING JOY AND SATISFACTION IN THE LEGAL LIFE (New York: McGraw-Hill, 1999; republished in 2010) (detailing how the practice of law can be transformed into a more satisfying, helping, healing profession by narrating the story of many trailblazing attorneys in the United States; it has profoundly influenced many in the comprehensive law movement).

14. Term attributed to Pauline H. Tesler, collaborative law co-founder and San Francisco attorney, see TESLER, *supra* note 2.

15. This discussion, in 2011, now seems somewhat dated, with the great changes that have occurred since the mid-2000s. These changes are discussed at pages 43–45, *infra*.

16. This particular shift, however, appeared to have reversed, at least in part, as a result of the events of September 11, 2001.

rating with countries and people we formerly viewed as hostile and intractable. These developments, then, may have contributed to a growing societal awareness of our "connectedness" to, and an openmindedness towards, all people, all countries, and all cultures in the world.

Second, some assert that our society has witnessed the decline of a philosophy focused on individual rights, logic, and reason and the concomitant rise of a counterbalancing ethos, focused on compassion, care, relationships, and connectedness.[17] Perhaps our societal values have begun to shift and change as a result of growing diversity in our power structure, governments, corporations, schools, and other institutions. The ethics and values of previously disempowered individuals may have begun to seep into our collective consciousness.[18] The increasing influence of a "feminine ethic" or "ethic of care" may have led to a greater emphasis on interpersonal relationships, emotional wellbeing, and interpersonal harmony.[19]

For example, in 1988, Anne Wilson Schaef and Diane Fassel argued that our entire society is undergoing a paradigm shift, from the predominance of what they call the "White Male System/Reactive Female System," which values logic, rationality, objectivity, superiority, individuality, detachment, and correctness, to the rise of an alternative system, the "Emerging Female System."[20] They described this paradigm shift as a move from a closed, static, objective worldview to one valuing wholeness, reconciliation, vulnerability, holism, health, cooperation, ecology, spirituality, and transformation. They describe it as a shift from positivism, empiricism, and the certainty of right answers to the uncertainty of the unknown.[21] They track this paradigm shift from science to business, education, religion, and medicine and note the contribution of feminist thought and alternative perspectives to the shift.[22]

Post-Enlightenment Values

Law professor Thomas Barton brilliantly puts this philosophical shift in historical perspective when he identifies that our society is moving into a "Post-Enlightenment" phase, complete with a new set of values. He explains that the current American legal system has idealized Enlightenment values such as personal freedom, independence, autonomy, will, and individual liberty for years, but these values are now giving way to a Post-Enlightenment period, in which "the concepts of separation—both intellectual and social—

---

17. ANNE WILSON SCHAEF, WHEN SOCIETY BECOMES AN ADDICT 5–18 (1987) (controversially describing the rights-based philosophy as the "White Male System" and noting that it is the same as her Addictive System, using the addictions model of human behavior); ANNE WILSON SCHAEF & DIANE FASSEL, THE ADDICTIVE ORGANIZATION 33–46 (1988) (tracking this paradigm shift through the work of (among many others) Thomas Kuhn in 1970, Marilyn Ferguson in 1980, Morris Berman in 1984, and Carol Gilligan in 1979).

18. *See* AMY HILSMAN KASTELY ET AL., CONTRACTING LAW (Carolina Academic Press 2000).

19. Carrie Menkel-Meadow, *Review Essay, What's Gender Got to Do with It?: The Politics and Morality of an Ethic of Care*, 22 N.Y.U. REV. L. & SOC. CHANGE 265 (1996) [hereinafter, Menkel-Meadow, 1996]. *See also* Carrie Menkel-Meadow, *Is Altruism Possible In Lawyering?*, 8 GA. ST. U. L. REV. 385, 414 n. 100 (1992) (arguing that lawyers should become more altruistic).

20. Schaef and Fassel, *supra* note 17.

21. ANNE WILSON SCHAEF, WHEN SOCIETY BECOMES AN ADDICT 8–9 (1987) (quoting Morris Berman's insight that this shift is towards "participatory consciousness").

22. *Id.*

are eroding in favor of the long-subordinated notions of [human] connection."[23] Professor Barton points to an "emerging culture of connectedness" as evidence of the rise of Post-Enlightenment values such as belongingness, loyalty, community, cultural identity, and people's relationships to each other and to their communities. For example, Professor Barton notes a growing concern in the law for issues of inequality of power in human relationships (e.g., domestic violence law) and stronger recognition and protection of one's cultural identity or membership in a particular ethnic group (e.g., Native American law, recognition of specific cultural beliefs as exonerating or mitigating factors, and legal respect for cultural differences). These developments evidence the growth of Post-Enlightenment values.

Professor Barton goes on to argue that law based on Enlightenment values functions well when a decision as to right or wrong, black or white, must be made. However, it is ineffective in other situations, because it does not easily accommodate or honor the fact that the parties may have an ongoing relationship with each other or with their communities. Professor Barton says:

> … in a given case the law may oscillate between either separationist functions or connectedness values. This is because the desired outcomes often involve both protection and the building of a stronger relationship. In many instances of domestic violence, for example, the victim certainly wants and needs protection. The victim, however, may not want or may not be able to afford for the underlying relationship to be terminated. Instead, the victim desires the underlying relationship to be made more healthy and respectful. Yet this is precisely the sort of solution for which the Enlightenment legal process is poorly equipped.… Cases involving communities which are hostile to racial, ethnic, or sexual orientation minorities, cases involving unruly children, and even cases involving noisy neighbors may present the same challenges — to build stronger relationships among the parties while simultaneously stopping whatever immediately threatening behaviors escalated the problem to the legal domain. The fundamental need is for an integrative solution that works with, rather than ignores, the given social context.[24]

Perhaps in response to the shortcomings of Enlightenment law, various alternative ways of handling legal problems have developed, such as creative problem solving, transformative mediation, victim-offender mediation in criminal law, community-based sentencing of criminals, teen court, and collaborative approaches to divorce and child custody matters. All of these approaches, which are part of the comprehensive law movement, explicitly honor people's relationships with each other instead of focusing solely on individual rights. Because they seek to maintain and preserve those connected relationships instead of sacrificing or destroying them in the name of individuality and separateness, they are consistent with Professor Barton's Post-Enlightenment values.

---

23. Thomas D. Barton, *Troublesome Connections: The Law and Post-Enlightenment Culture*, 47 EMORY L. J. 163, 163–64 (1998). Barton explains that Enlightenment values are associated with the Enlightenment period, which has predominated for the past 300 or so years, and with 18th century writers such as Voltaire, Kant, Montesquieu, and Bentham. Interestingly, the period before the Enlightenment is typically thought of as the Renaissance, which is associated with humanism and humanistic values (the pendulum swings, yet again!). And, interestingly, a group of lawyers associated with one of the vectors of the comprehensive law movement, holistic justice, formed a lawyer group, website, and support mechanism named Renaissance Lawyer (http://www.renaissancelawyer.com) (visited July 11, 2010).

24. *Id.* at 214–15.

Jurisprudential Propellers

For years, legal realism was the predominant jurisprudential school of thought in the United States. The pessimism of legal realism and its critical legal studies offspring may have created a longing for solutions and hope. The certainty of realism's predecessors, natural law and legal positivism, probably fostered a reassuring sense of order, predictability, and rationality in the law, but this predictability disintegrated in the last 40 or 50 years. Cynicism and discouragement may have grown, when legal realism emerged in the 1930s to debunk the neat universe of legal positivism and point out that law, as made by legislators and judges, was much more capricious and biased than positivism made it appear. Realism may have helped us lose faith in the justice meted out by the legal system.[25]

After realism, jurisprudential thought Balkanized[26] into various movements that understand law from the lens of a particular viewpoint, including critical legal studies, feminist theory, and the "law and" movements.[27] Most of these newer schools of thought expand upon the basic concept of legal realism by viewing law as a product of deep and pervasive societal biases.

All of these schools of thought, however, leave us with a terrific explication of a problem but without a solution. If law is indeed arbitrary and capricious, what then? What approach does one then take to practicing law, judging cases, or making law? Further, once we accept that law and our legal system are not necessarily rational or logical, the question becomes "why use it at all?" In fact, some sectors of American society have abandoned formal legal courts, either resorting to self-help methods, private judges, mediation, or private courts to settle their legal problems. Therapeutic jurisprudence in particular and the comprehensive law movement in general may have developed in response to the lack of hope and direction we are left with, once we accept the major premise of legal realism and these newer schools of thought. The idea of recognizing law's potential to have a positive impact on people's lives and of creating alternative means of resolving legal problems may provide hope during a time when the reliability, utility, or rationality of law and legal procedures are in question.

Viewing law as a healing profession is a natural outgrowth of feminist jurisprudence. Focusing on the healing, restorative, curative functions of law is entirely consistent with feminine and feminist values,[28] which have mainstreamed into current legal thought

---

25. David M. Hunsaker, *Law, Humanism and Communication: Suggestions for Limited Curricular Reform*, 30 J. Legal Educ. 417, 419 (1979–80) (describing the relationship between legal realism, legal positivism, and Langdell's case method approach to legal education). Originally, natural law predominated, with its idea that laws were simply reflections of preexisting, divine laws that existed independent of man. Then, legal positivism emerged, with its idea that laws were simply black and white rules that conformed to rules of logic and analysis; if one could find the proper rule or exception, and precedent, one could generate the proper rule of law to fit any particular legal problem. Cases were viewed as "the embodiment of legal principles." *Id.* In contrast, realism suggested that judges and juries decided legal cases based on their moods, their biases, their predilections, and a million other unspoken criteria. Cases were viewed as "in fact the rationalizations for values choices made by judges." *Id.*

26. I am indebted to Professor Ellen Waldman of Thomas Jefferson School of Law for this outline of the development of the newer jurisprudential schools of thought and for the term, "Balkanized."

27. *See e.g.,* law and economics, law and literature, law and psychology, law and sociology, law and socioeconomics.

28. For example, a more "feminine" approach to establishing criminal culpability for someone who is mentally disordered is taken by Lady Wooton, as quoted in Ralph Reisner et al., Law and the Mental Health System 589–91 (3d ed. 1999). There, she argues for bifurcating guilt and sentencing and then explains that the distinction between hospitalization and incarceration becomes un-

through feminist jurisprudence. The comprehensive law movement is also a natural product of the law and psychology movement, which looks at law, lawyering, and legal processes from a psychological perspective. Once one begins to examine the psychological aspects of law, or even the psychological aspects of legal problems or clients, the therapeutic potential of law and legal processes becomes apparent. It is natural, then, to propose ways to maximize this potential and minimize any detrimental psychological effects. This is precisely what one of the most vibrant vectors of the movement, therapeutic jurisprudence, seeks to do.

. . . .

[Finally, the comprehensive law movement is a response to the "tripartite crisis" described earlier.] Academic commentators have responded to this tripartite crisis by proposing solutions such as more pro bono and public service, returning to the roots of our profession as counselors and advisors, viewing law as a "calling" rather than as a business, and taking different approaches to lawyering, such as lawyering with an "ethic of care"[29] and "moral lawyering."[30] Despite the lack of an explicit link between these proposals and the emergence of the vectors of the comprehensive law movement, it is clear that the approaches embodied in the comprehensive law movement are consistent with the call of these commentators for value-laden approaches.[31]

Parallel Developments in Psychology

In addition, the comprehensive law movement may reflect a parallel progression within social science and science in general, from a more analytical, scientific approach to a more humanistic, relativistic, and individualized approach. In social science, for example, psychology has undergone several phases, beginning with the analytic approach of Sigmund Freud and Carl Jung and psychodynamic theory. It then progressed from this past-oriented and sometimes elusive approach to a more scientific, logical, tangible, almost mechanical approach, in B. F. Skinner's behaviorism. Then, in response perhaps to the black-and-whiteness of behaviorism, Carl Rogers's humanistic psychology emerged, with its focus on optimizing human potential, on client-centered, individualized treatment, and on the interpersonal relationships involved in therapy.

Similarly, law was first seen as a somewhat undisciplined liberal "art," until Christopher Langdell of Harvard proposed a more "scientific" approach to law through the study of cases. Since then, law has been viewed as something that can be studied via a rational, logical approach. Now, like psychology, law may be moving into a more humanistic mode, focused more on human wellbeing and interpersonal relationships.

---

necessary. Her idea is that the offender simply serves a custodial sentence, with the line between prisons and mental health treatment being blurred. Barbara Wooton, *Book Review of A. Goldstein, The Insanity Defense*, 77 YALE L.J. 1019, 1028–32 (1968), *quoted by* Reisner et al., *supra*, at 589–91.

29. Menkel-Meadow, 1996, *supra* note 19.

30. Robert M. Bastress, *Client Centered Counseling and Moral Accountability for Lawyers*, 10 J. LEGAL PROF. 97, 97–99 (1985).

31. *See* Marc W. Patry, David B. Wexler, Dennis P. Stolle, & Alan J. Tomkins, *Better Legal Counseling Through Empirical Research: Identifying Psycholegal Soft Spots and Strategies*, 34 CAL. W. L. REV. 439, 441 (1998) (suggesting a strong possibility for therapeutic jurisprudence to incorporate an ethic of care in preventive law).

Humanism and Law in the 1970s;
Neo-Humanism in the 2000s

Finally, the comprehensive law movement may reflect a resurgence of a humanistic movement in law that occurred in the 1960s and 1970s. This earlier humanism-in-law effort may have gone "underground" during the materialistic and prosperous 1980s, but be resurfacing today in a sort of "neo-humanism" evidenced by the popularity of the vectors of the comprehensive law movement.

In 1980, Chief Justice Warren Burger called for lawyers to return to their roles as healers, foreshadowing the comprehensive law movement by a decade or more. He said:

> [Lawyers] must be legal architects, engineers, builders, and from time to time, inventors as well. We have served, and must continue to see our role, as problem-solvers, harmonizers, and peacemakers, the healers—not the promoters— of conflict.[32]

As early as 1955, Dean Griswold argued for "the inclusion of human relations and communications training in the law school curriculum."[33] He pointed out that:

> [L]awyers deal with people. They deal with people far more than they do with appellate courts. They deal with clients; they deal with witnesses; they deal with persons against whom demands are made; they carry on negotiations; they are constantly endeavoring to come to agreements of one sort or another with people, to persuade people, sometimes when they are reluctant to be persuaded. Lawyers are constantly dealing with people who are under stress or strain of one sort or another.[34]

Robert Redmount in 1968 charged that legal education emphasized "a cohering framework and system of rules and reason ... in which the data of experience are subordinate."[35] He argued for explicitly using psychology in law school to teach law students greater psychological sophistication and asserted that "continuing social change and the lack of good attunement to personal and social experience jeopardize law's standing and competence to deal effectively with social and personal problems."[36]

Shaffer and Redmount in 1975 condemned legal education for lacking "mental, moral, emotional, and social development and therefore ... not serv[ing] ... the best interests of society, or for that matter, the best interests of the legal profession. It lacks humanistic concern ..."[37] Hunsaker in 1979 agreed and said: "[w]hile the law school may develop skills in analysis, issue spotting, fact-principle discrimination, and logical deduction, it has ne-

---

32. Warren E. Burger, *The Decline of Professionalism*, 61 TENN. L. REV. 1, 5 (1993) *citing* Warren E. Burger, *The Role of the Law School in the Teaching of Legal Ethics and Professional Responsibility*, 29 CLEV. ST. L. REV. 377, 378 (1980).

33. Hunsaker, *supra* note 25, at 421 *citing* Dean Griswold, 37 CHICAGO B. RECORD 199, 203 (1956), *cited in* Howard Sacks, *Human Relations Training for Law Students and Lawyers*, 11 J. LEGAL EDUC. 316, 317 (1959).

34. Hunsaker, *supra* note 25, at 421.

35. Robert S. Redmount, *Humanistic Law Through Legal Education*, 1 CONN. L. REV. 201, 210 (1968) (emphasizing the value of human experience in law, which is pragmatic to the individual) [hereinafter Redmount I].

36. *Id.* at 211.

37. Hunsaker, *supra* note 25, at 419–20, *quoting* THOMAS L. SHAFFER & ROBERT S. REDMOUNT, LAWYERS, LAW STUDENTS AND PEOPLE, chapter 2, at 24 (1977).

glected and ignored the teaching of *humanistic* values and the development of human relations skills [*emphasis in original*]."[38] These authors went on to advocate additional communication skills training, human relations training, and infusion of social science knowledge in legal education.[39]

These pleas were echoed in a 1978 book by clinical psychiatrist Andrew Watson. In this book, Watson integrated law and psychology and advocated a psychological approach to legal counseling.[40] A number of articles and commentary were published from 1965 to 1980, proposing a greater emphasis in the law on psychological knowledge, human experience, interpersonal skills, and humanistic values.[41] These efforts culminated in a 1981 book by lawyers and law professors Dvorkin, Himmelstein, and Lesnick titled "Becoming a Lawyer: A Humanistic Perspective on Legal Education and Professionalism."[42]

Most of this early humanism-in-law commentary noted that law and legal education focused almost exclusively on logical, rational analysis of cases and legal problems. Perhaps this was originally appropriate, as Charles Reich in 1965 noted that, before the 1960s, lawyers usually concerned themselves chiefly with what law dealt with: commerce and business. However, he argued that the role of law in society in the 1960s began to change, as law became a "primary instrument ... for fundamental social change."[43] Law began to permeate every activity. Social problems, such as poverty, civil unrest, unemployment, and mental illness, increasingly became legal problems. As law became more and more intertwined with social and human problems, Reich says, law had to look to social science for assistance and become "the queen of the humanities."[44] Lawyers and legal education needed to focus on developing interpersonal skills, psychological sophistication, and a more humanistic orientation.[45]

However, the ideas espoused in this earlier psychology in law movement did not entirely become mainstream in legal education, nor did they appear in law practice. What did occur was a greater emphasis on clinical training and clinical programs, including lawyering skills training, in law school. Interviewing, counseling and negotiating courses

---

38. Hunsaker, *supra* note 25, at 419.

39. *See generally* Charles A. Reich, *Toward the Humanistic Study of Law,* 74 YALE L. J. 1402 (1965) (advocating for greater emphasis on social science, interdisciplinary approaches, and moral and psychological knowledge in legal education); Hunsaker, *supra* note 25; and Redmount I, *supra* note 35 (all arguing for curricular reform in law school).

40. ANDREW S. WATSON, THE LAWYER IN THE INTERVIEWING & COUNSELING PROCESS (Bobbs-Merrill 1975).

41. *See* Peter D'Errico, Stephen Arons, & Janet Rifkin, *Humanistic Legal Studies at the University of Massachusetts at Amherst,* 28 J. LEGAL EDUC. 18 (1976–77) (predicting a sustained national interest in humanist analysis in the law in spite of pressure for formal legal techniques); Robert S. Redmount, *Humanistic Law Through Legal Counseling,* 2 CONN. L. REV. 98 (1969–70) [Redmount II]; Redmount I, *supra* note 35; Reich, *supra* note 39; and Hunsaker, *supra* note 25 (proposing greater emphasis on interpersonal skills, communications skills, and people skills training in legal education). Other individuals associated with this earlier humanism and law movement include Paul Brest (now dean of Stanford Law School), Columbia University law professor Peter Straus, Charlie Halpert (former dean at CUNY-Queens), Professor Howard Lesnick, and Jack Himmelstein.

42. ELIZABETH DVORKIN, JACK HIMMELSTEIN, & HOWARD LESNICK, BECOMING A LAWYER: A HUMANISTIC PERSPECTIVE ON LEGAL EDUCATION AND PROFESSIONALISM (1981). This book was in fact specifically influenced by Carl Rogers' work on humanistic psychology, thus strengthening the link between various movements in psychology and law. For a critique of this book, *see* Walter Gellhorn, *"Humanistic Perspective": A Critique,* 32 J. LEGAL EDUC. 99 (1982).

43. Reich, *supra* note 39, at 1407.

44. *Id.* at 1408.

45. Hunsaker, *supra* note 25, at 420.

and clinical opportunities are now available and encouraged in practically every American law school. Thus, this earlier humanistic movement did have an effect. However, the hoped-for wholesale infusion of psychology into legal training and law practice did not occur.

However, the integration of law and psychology, or humanism and law, may have emerged in the 1990s in the vectors of the comprehensive law movement. The approaches to law and lawyering embodied by the various vectors of the comprehensive law movement are consistent with the humanistic approach advocated in the 1981 book, *Becoming a Lawyer*,[46] yet they did not develop as a direct result of this early humanistic movement. Instead, they developed mostly from the practicing bar and from a different law and psychology movement known as therapeutic jurisprudence. If these earlier law professors' efforts to bring humanistic psychology into law have had an effect, the effect appears to have been indirect: skipping over legal education, skipping over a few decades, and emerging now from the "trenches." Marjorie Silver's 2006 book, *The Affective Assistance of Counsel*, continues this humanism-in-lawyering effort.

Dean Emeritus Edward Dauer, who is one of the leaders of preventive law, suggests that perhaps the idealism of this earlier humanism-in-the-law movement crumbled under the strain of the Vietnam War and Watergate, two events that fostered massive cynicism towards law and lawyers.[47] The cynicism and disappointment felt by society after these two events may have quashed burgeoning idealism in the 1960s and 1970s and then paved the way for the materialism and self-centeredness found in the profession (and society) in the 1980s. If so, the comprehensive law movement may reflect a concrete response to growing societal disillusionment with the materialism and cynicism of the 1980s.

Legal and World Forces

There are a number of forces, in the law and in the greater society, moving the comprehensive law movement forward.[48] In the legal profession, these include:

1. growing demographic and psychological diversity in the legal profession, resulting in lawyers who demand work consonant with their values and incorporative of psychology and relationships;

2. failing court systems & clogged dockets, which lead to increased use of out-of-court settlement, mediation, and alternative dispute resolution (even mandated);

3. unequal access to justice and a two-tiered justice system, which lead to a stratified profession with fewer elite BigLaw firms (first tier), more lawyers in small practices or public service (second tier), more "one-shotter clients," more in-house counsel, and more minorities and women in the second tier; and

4. client, lawyer, and societal dissatisfaction with the legal system, causing demand for: cost-effective legal services that are consonant with lawyers' own values and

---

46. Elizabeth Dvorkin, Jack Himmelstein, & Howard Lesnick, Becoming a Lawyer: A Humanistic Perspective on Legal Education and Professionalism (1981).

47. Personal communication (e-mail) with Edward Dauer, Dean Emeritus at Denver University College of Law, August 5, 2002.

48. Many of these developments are summarized from and explored in Richard Susskind, The End of Lawyers? Rethinking the Nature of Legal Services (Oxford University Press, 2008).

incorporative of psychology, relationships, emotions, and values; more client autonomy, voice, and participation in legal processes and in the lawyer-client relationship; and more accountability of lawyers to their clients to justify their fees or offer fixed fees.

In the world, these include:

1. a nonhierarchical, non-command-and-control corporate culture emphasizing collaboration, transparency, humility-based leadership, and team-oriented decisionmaking and problem solving;

2. the technology explosion, with instant global connectivity and access to information, causing changes in how law is practiced (e.g., outsourcing);

3. global awareness of interdependence and the need for collaboration and cooperation;

4. environmental awareness and a growing desire for sustainable, green methods and processes, leading to a desire to make legal services cost-effective and conducive to sustainable outcomes and processes (or, at least, not destructive of sustainable processes);

5. a shift from left-brained dominance to more right-brained emphasis, resulting in an increased focus on the human element, relationships, emotions, collaboration, connectivity, creativity, holistic analyses of matters and problems, problem solving, and multidisciplinary practice (e.g., apology and forgiveness are receiving increased attention);

6. the current economic crisis with shocking unemployment rates, causing a need to create new demands and markets for legal services and lawyers (clients are demanding fixed, lower fees; there are more pro se litigants; there is greater demand for online legal knowledge and forms); and

7. the Millennial generation coming of age with its increased emphasis on collaboration, innovation, civic mindedness, and technology.[49]

In 2009, I argued that:[50]

Scientists point to the exponential advances made in technology to argue that the world is on the verge of massive and rapid change;[51] parallel shifts in philosophy may be part of the precursor movements preparing for this change. Some call this

---

49. Howe & Strauss, Generations: The History of America's Future, 1584 to 2069 (1991); Howe & Strauss, Millennials Rising: The Next Great Generation (2000) (both books defining and establishing the existence of this generation, within generational theory). *See* Susan K. McClellan, 15 Clinical L. Rev. 255 (2009); Melissa H. Weresh, 61 S. C. L. Rev. 337 (2009); and Melody Finnemore, 66-Nov. Or. St. B. Bull. 9 (2005) (describing the characteristics, preferences, and needs of Millennials in the legal profession).

50. The following two paragraphs are excerpted from the author's essay, Susan Daicoff, *Collaborative Law*, 20 U. Fla. J. L. & Pub. Pol'y 113 (2009).

51. *See e.g.,* Damien Broderick, The Spike: How Our Lives are Being Transformed by Rapidly Advancing Technologies 24–25 (2001), quoting Dr. Vernor Vinge's address to the Vision-21 Symposium, sponsored by NASA Lewis Research Center and the Ohio Aerospace Institute, March 30–31, 1993, and quoting Gregory S. Paul & Earl Cox, Beyond Humanity: Cyberevolution and Future Minds (1997).

new attitude "Post-Enlightenment,"[52] while others attribute the shift in emphasis to postmodernism.[53]

In short, a number of philosophical shifts and world developments in the last century and the 1990s have paved the way for the comprehensive law movement in the 21st century. Perhaps we have become sated with our own thirst for individual freedom, with our promotion of personal good at the expense of others, and with our worship of individual rights. Maximizing our legal rights and our clients' has not brought us emotional wellbeing, harmony, peace, joy, or even satisfaction. Many litigation-experienced clients and lawyers are seeking a better way to resolve legal disputes, handle legal matters, and practice law.

This search has led to experimentation with: more mediation; shifting the lawyer's role from warrior to conflict resolver, wise counselor, and Aristotelian "wise" friend; a more egalitarian lawyer-client relationship; less gamesmanship and more open disclosure in litigation; and a shift from a rights focus to an emphasis on interests and needs.

Challenges and Obstacles

Despite these fundamental shifts and forces propelling the movement forward, there are a number of obstacles to its growth and implementation. Some existing structures that serve to impede its progress include:

1. the perception that the ethics code permits only zealous advocacy, in the law;

2. the typical "lawyer personality," which is unattuned to emotions, relationships, and similar factors and motivated towards the appearance of dominance;

3. the reluctance of lawyers to settle cases early, as it cuts off their ability to earn legal fees;

4. the ossification of legal education in a state of irrelevance to the skills required by modern law practice;

5. the current emphasis of legal education on extrinsic rewards, litigation, and "thinking like a lawyer";

6. the current climate of private law firms, with an emphasis on billable hours and economic bottom line;

7. lawyers' and judges' perceptions of the mandate towards zealous advocacy as a bar to practicing law comprehensively; and

8. the dominance in society of what Deborah Tannen calls the "Argument Culture" and a concomitant tendency to blame someone else for anything that goes wrong, leading to adversarial litigiousness.

---

52. Thomas D. Barton, *Troublesome Connections: The Law and Post-Enlightenment Culture*, 47 Emory L.J. 163, 163–64 (1998).

53. *See, e.g.*, Brian D. McLaren, A New Kind of Christian 81, 144–145 (2001) (attributing to postmodernism a shift away from judgments of right and wrong towards a focus on connectedness, adding "maybe postmodern is postanalytical and postcritical").

For example, the current emphasis of legal education is often on grades, class rank, awards,[54] and "thinking like a lawyer."[55] Change in legal education can be glacial in speed. The legal profession emphasizes the economic bottom line (particularly with the recent decline in the economy), billable hours, and zealous advocacy. Lawyer personalities often display a preference for "Thinking," low interest in interpersonal matters, a mask of dominance over an internal feeling of awkwardness and insecurity,[56] and discomfort with emotional or relational matters. Comprehensive law practice may be seen as too paternalistic, too simplistic, or it may be mis-practiced or mis-applied; the law's traditional emphasis on legal rights may trump comprehensive concerns; and, finally, many lawyers may need retraining to practice law this way or it may not fit with their intrinsic values or preferences.

Most of these challenges can be overcome, however. For example, comprehensive law practice can be demonstrated and recast simply as a "best practice" in the law, as many have suggested that "this is what good lawyers already do." It can be assessed whether comprehensive law approaches actually reduce clients' dissatisfaction with the legal system, judges' dissatisfaction with the recidivism they see among the parties before them, and some lawyers' dissatisfaction with their work, as well as improve the lives of the individuals involved with the law. The public can be educated about the availability of the comprehensive law approaches. Lawyers and judges can seek explicit ethics opinions, as they experiment with new approaches to legal matters and disputes.

Assumptions Underlying Comprehensive Law Practice

Before delving into the comprehensive law "vectors," it is useful to examine various assumptions often underlying this form of practice. In many cases, these assumptions are the antithesis of adversarialism and modern, traditional law practice. For example, collaboration, cooperation, and interdependence are often valued and pursued. Shows of ego, force, and strength are either avoided or sparingly used and, if used, are used for a purpose and not for the feeling of self-gratification or dominance such behavior often brings. Teamwork and group purpose are valued. Underlying needs are explored, in dispute resolution, rather than taking positions at face value. Win/win solutions are sought and creativity is valued. J. Kim Wright's 2010 book, *Lawyers as Peacemakers*, nicely documents and explains many of the attitudinal shifts necessary or helpful to practice law comprehensively.[57]

---

54. Kennon M. Sheldon & Lawrence S. Krieger, *Does Legal Education Have Undermining Effects on Law Students? Evaluating Changes in Motivation, Values, and Well-Being*, 22 Behav. Sci. Law 261–286 (2004); Lawrence S. Krieger, *Institutional Denial About the Dark Side of Law School, and Fresh Empirical Guidance for Constructively Breaking the Silence*, 52 J. Legal Educ. 112, 122–23 (March/June, 2002) (reporting the results of an empirical study linking intrinsic values to law student wellbeing); and Lawrence S. Krieger, *Psychological Insights: Why Our Students and Graduates Suffer, and What We Might Do About It*, 1 J. Ass'n Leg. Writing Directors 259, 262 (2002).

55. Kurt M. Saunders & Linda Levine, *Learning to Think Like a Lawyer*, 29 U.S.F. L. Rev. 121 (1994).

56. Stephen Reich, *California Psychological Inventory: Profile of a Sample of First-Year Law Students*, 39 Psychol. Rep. 871–874 (1976).

57. J. Kim Wright, Lawyers as Peacemakers: Practicing Holistic, Problem-Solving Law (American Bar Association, 2010).

In American corporate culture, some management experts document a shift from a command-and-control hierarchical model of corporate organization to one in which transparency, accountability, and consensus are valued, among leaders.[58] They also speak of "disappearing attitudes;" these are attitudes which have become obsolete in modern, forward-looking corporate culture, such as: (1) what's in it for me?; and (2) how does it make me look?[59] I thought in 2009 that:

> Corporate America has recently recognized the importance of "emotional intelligence" ("EQ"), referring primarily to excellent self-management skills, relational skills, and teambuilding and collaborative skills and trainings and books have emerged to teach these concepts to high-level corporate managers.[60] The idea is that excellent corporate management, ultimately leading to maximized profits for the organization, requires a high level of sophistication and expertise in these areas.[61] Graduate business schools include EQ in their curricula; law schools have begun to implement "leadership" programs in their curricula, including some of these concepts.[62] The importance of cooperation, collaboration, and community values is echoed in these efforts, again.[63]

---

58. *See, e.g.,* JIM COLLINS, FROM GOOD TO GREAT: WHY SOME COMPANIES MAKE THE LEAP … AND OTHERS DON'T (2001); PATRICK LENCIONI, THE FIVE DYSFUNCTIONS OF A TEAM: A LEADERSHIP FABLE (2002) (both describing the modern shift in corporate management from hierarchical, command-and-control to team- and humility-based leadership that is present in those Fortune 500 corporations that have prospered).

59. Credited to Rick Inatome, Chief Executive Officer of The Infilaw System and Managing Director at Sterling Partners.

60. JIM COLLINS, FROM GOOD TO GREAT: WHY SOME COMPANIES MAKE THE LEAP … AND OTHERS DON'T (2001); PATRICK LENCIONI, THE FIVE DYSFUNCTIONS OF A TEAM: A LEADERSHIP FABLE (2002); JAMES M. KOUZES & BARRY Z. POSNER, THE LEADERSHIP CHALLENGE (2002); and DANIEL GOLEMAN, EMOTIONAL INTELLIGENCE: WHY IT CAN MATTER MORE THAN IQ (2005). While recent research indicates that "emotional intelligence" as a concept may have been altered from its original definition and concept, *see* John D. Mayer, Peter Salovey, & David R. Caruso, *Emotional Intelligence: New Ability or Eclectic Traits?,* 63 AMERICAN PSYCHOLOGIST 503, 504–05 (2008), these efforts in corporate management circles are likely to affect clients' expectations of lawyers, if the clients are inured to making decisions and working in teams under popular concepts of "EQ."

61. *Id. See also* DANIEL GOLEMAN, ANNIE MCKEE & RICHARD E. BOYATZIS, PRIMAL LEADERSHIP (2002).

62. Examples include Ohio State University (leadership program in the law school) and Santa Clara University (Leadership for Lawyers law school course, taught by Professor Robert Cullen and Dean Don Polden).

63. Susan Daicoff, *Collaborative Law: A New Tool for the Lawyer's Toolkit,* 20 U. FLA. J. L. & PUB. POL'Y 113 (2009).

Chapter 3

Overview of the Movement, the Vectors, and Their Common Ground

Vector Definitions

A brief definition of each of the vectors of the comprehensive law movement follows [*this is an excerpt from the author's GPSolo article*]:[1]

Therapeutic jurisprudence is one of the most well-known vectors, with the broadest applications. Since around 1990, it has focused on the therapeutic or countertherapeutic consequences of the law and legal procedures on the individuals involved, including the clients, their families, friends, lawyers, judges, and community. It attempts to reform law and legal processes in order to promote the psychological well-being of the people they affect. Its website explains that TJ "concentrates on the law's impact on emotional life and psychological well-being. It is a perspective that regards the law (rules of law, legal procedures, and roles of legal actors) itself as a social force that often produces therapeutic or anti-therapeutic consequences. It does not suggest that therapeutic concerns are more important than other consequences or factors, but it does suggest that the law's role as a potential therapeutic agent should be recognized...." TJ has been applied to almost every area of law, including mental health law, family law, employment law, health law, elder law, appellate practice, criminal law, criminal sentencing, litigation, and estate planning. It has been applied to police work and become very popular with judges. Its founders are David Wexler, Professor of Law at University of Arizona and University of Puerto Rico and the late Bruce Winick, Professor of Law at University of Miami. Its website is: http://www.law.arizona.edu/depts/upr-intj/ (last visited July 11, 2010) and it has a listserv and an extensive bibliography.

Preventive law has been around for many years. Like preventive medicine, it explicitly seeks to intervene in legal matters before disputes arise and advocates proactive intervention to head off litigation and other conflicts. It emphasizes the lawyer-client relationship, relationships in general, and planning. In recent years, its lawyering techniques were integrated with TJ concepts in order to describe "how to" practice TJ-oriented law, thus re-

---

1. Susan Daicoff, *Resolution Without Litigation: Are Courtrooms Battlegrounds for Losers?* GPSolo 44–50 (October/November 2003) (republished as a book chapter, Susan Daicoff, *The Comprehensive Law Movement: An Emerging Approach to Legal Problems*, in Peter Wahlgren, Ed., A Proactive Approach, 49 Scandinavian Studies in Law 109–129 (2006)). This Chapter also includes material drawn from Susan Daicoff, *Law as a Healing Profession: The "Comprehensive Law Movement,"* 6 Pepperdine Disp. Resol. J. 1 (2006).

sulting in therapeutically-oriented preventive law. Its founder was the late Louis Brown and it is associated with Professor and Dean Emeritus Edward Dauer at the University of Denver College of Law. California Western School of Law houses the National Center for Preventive Law and it has its own textbook, reporter, and website: http://www.preventive lawyer.org/main/default.asp (last visited July 11, 2010).

Procedural justice refers to Tom Tyler's research finding that, in judicial processes, litigants' satisfaction depends more on (1) being treated with respect and dignity, (2) being heard and having an opportunity to speak and participate, and (3) how trustworthy the authorities appear and behave, than it does on the actual outcome (e.g., winning vs. losing) of the legal matter. It is being used to re-engineer dispute resolution processes (litigative and nonlitigative) to incorporate these three important features.

Creative problem solving is a broad approach to lawyering that is explicitly humanistic, interdisciplinary, creative, and preventive. Its website explains that "clients and society are increasingly asking lawyers to approach problems [not always as fighters, but] more creatively." CPS seeks to prevent legal problems if possible and creatively solve those that exist. It "focuses both on using the traditional analytical process more creatively and on using nontraditional problem solving processes, drawn from business, psychology, economics, neuroscience, and sociology." CPS is associated with the McGill Center for Creative Problem Solving at California Western School of Law (website: http://www.cwsl.edu/main/ default.asp?nav=creative_problem_solving.asp&body=creative_problem_solving/home.asp (last visited July 11, 2010)), which sponsors a number of law school courses on CPS, national and international projects, and periodic conferences. The merging of the vectors is clear in CPS's use of preventive law and transformative mediation.

Holistic justice is a grass-roots movement among practicing lawyers which "acknowledge[s] the need for a humane legal process with the highest level of satisfaction for all participants; honor[s] and respect[s] the dignity and integrity of each individual; promote[s] peaceful advocacy and holistic legal principles; value[s] responsibility, connection and inclusion; encourage[s] compassion, reconciliation, forgiveness and healing; practice[s] deep listening, understand[s] and recognize[s] the importance of voice; contributes[s] to peace building at all levels of society; recognize[s] the opportunity in conflict; draw[s] upon ancient intuitive wisdom of diverse cultures and traditions; and [encourages the lawyer to] enjoy the practice of law" (from its former website: http://iahl.org (last visited July 11, 2010)). It is explicitly interdisciplinary, allows the lawyer to incorporate his or her own morals and values into client representation, and seeks to "do the right thing" for the lawyer, clients, and others involved. Like holistic medicine, it takes a broader view of legal problems and possible solutions. It was promoted by the International Alliance of Holistic Lawyers, whose founder was practicing lawyer William Van Zyverden in Vermont.

Collaborative law is a nonlitigative, collaborative process employed mainly in divorce and family law, where the spouses, their respective attorneys, and neutral experts resolve the issues outside of court in a four (or more) party process. No litigation is usually instituted until settlement is reached. The attorneys are contractually forbidden from representing their clients in court should the agreement process break down. Basically, it puts the divorcing spouses with their respective attorneys into a collaborative series of discussions designed to resolve the issues without litigation. Because the attorneys must withdraw if the process breaks down, the attorneys' financial interests are the same as the clients' — to reach settlement. This contrasts with the usual process, where the lawyers "win" whether the clients settle or not, since they simply litigate if negotiations break down. There is a strong psychological component to the lawyer-client relationship in that emotions, needs, transference, etc. are openly acknowledged and dealt with in order to maximize results of the 4-way conferences. Interdisciplinary models use a "team" of mental health, financial, and other professionals as well. Collaborative law can be appropriate for other areas, such as employment law. Leading trainers include practicing attorneys Pauline Tesler (Bay Area, California) (http://www.lawtsf.com/teslerpro.html (last visited July 11, 2010)) and Stuart G. Webb (Minnesota) (http://www.divorcenet.com/Members/swebb (last visited July 11, 2010)). See also www.collaborativelaw.org (last visited July 11, 2010).

Transformative mediation is a form of alternative dispute resolution set forth in Bush and Folger's 1994 book, *The Promise of Mediation.* TM views conflict as a destabilizing "crisis in human interaction" rather than a violation of rights or conflict of individual interests. Its three-person mediations seek to restore balance between self and other, transform conflict into a positive, constructive process, and encourage parties to do two things: (1) regain their sense of strength and self-confidence (the "empowerment" shift) and (2) expand their responsiveness to each other (the "recognition" shift, much like empathy, or the ability to stand in the other's shoes). By focusing on these goals, the parties are moved towards increased personal development and enhanced personal and interpersonal skills. Baruch Bush is a law professor at Hofstra University School of Law and Joseph Folger is a communications professor at Temple University. The Institute for the Study of Conflict Transformation, Inc. is found at http://www.hofstralawit.org/transformativemediation (last visited July 11, 2010).

Restorative justice refers to a movement employed most often with juvenile offenders in the U.S., although it is more widely used in Australia, Canada, and the United Kingdom, in which criminal justice and criminal sentencing are done by the community, victim, and offender in a collaborative process. It may be as simple as post-sentencing victim-offender mediation or as complicated as sentencing that is done in a community conference with all parties present. It emphasizes relationships between the offender, victim, and community instead of a top-down, hierarchical system of imposing punishment. The website for The Center for Restorative Justice & Peacemaking at the University of Minnesota School of Social Work explains that "[t]hrough restorative justice, victims, communities, and offenders are placed in active roles to work together to … Empower victims in their search for closure; Impress upon offenders the real human impact of their behavior; Promote restitution to victims and communities. Dialogue and negotiation are central to restorative justice, and problem solving for the future is seen as more important than simply establishing blame for past behavior. Balance is sought between the legitimate needs of the victim, the community, and the offender that enhances community protection, competency development in the offender, and direct accountability of the offender to the victim and victimized community." One of its leaders is Mark Umbreit, who is a social work professor at the University of Minnesota (see http://ssw.che.umn.edu/rjp/ (last visited July 11, 2011)).

The **problem solving court movement** resulted from judges' enthusiastic application of TJ to the adjudication process. Frustrated with recidivism and repeat performances, judges developed specialized, multidisciplinary "problem solving" courts focused on resolving the interpersonal issues underlying the legal problems instead of punishing defendants or assigning fault. They take a long-term, relational, interdisciplinary, healing approach to judging. In the criminal setting, judges create collaborative and ongoing relationships with offenders and helping professionals and supervise the offenders' rehabilitation efforts. Examples are drug treatment courts, mental health courts, domestic violence courts, and unified family courts. Drug treatment courts are reporting impressive drops in recidivism as a result of their changed focus and approach. The nonadversarial nature of these courts is consistent with the approach to civil matters taken by vectors like collaborative law and transformative mediation.

Potential Related Vectors

A number of other "movements" in the law have been suggested as related to the comprehensive law movement. These are: law and spirituality; mindfulness meditation; the humanizing legal education movement; the religious lawyering movement (interjecting religious values into law practice); the movement to resurrect secular humanist values in law; the politics of meaning; the efforts of the Contemplative Mind & Society Institute, including the Yale Law School meditation project sponsored by the Fetzer Institute; and affective lawyering and rebellious lawyering, both important in the domestic violence context. These relationships should be explored in the future.

The movement can be depicted visually as in Figure 1, below:

Figure 1. Vectors of the Comprehensive Law Movement

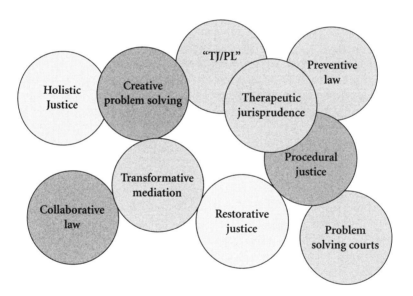

Common Ground

While intuitively the vectors of the comprehensive law movement may appear similar, it is important to examine the precise ways in which they resemble each other, as well as the ways in which they differ. Professor Bruce Winick, one of the two founders of therapeutic jurisprudence,[2] described the vectors beautifully when he said they are like members of an extended family. He explained that some have red hair, some have brown hair

---

2. David B. Wexler & Bruce J. Winick, Essays in Therapeutic Jurisprudence (1991).

and brown eyes, some have blue eyes, but when you put them all together for a group photo, a striking family resemblance is evident in each member. Yet, each member has his or her own distinctive features that are peculiar to that member only.[3] The beauty of the movement is evident not only in the features that unify the vectors, but also in their distinct and individual differences; they remain separate and vibrant movements of their own, while sharing common ground.

Law schools traditionally teach students to sift through facts and issues to eliminate "irrelevant" concerns and focus only on what is "relevant" to the rule of law.[4] The emotional and interpersonal dynamics of a matter are deemed irrelevant to the pure legal analysis learned in the first year of law school. Sometime during the third year of law school or first few years of practice, lawyers are left to their own to rediscover their ability to evaluate these dynamics and somehow incorporate that assessment into their work as lawyers, but this process (if it occurs) happens haphazardly and without direction. It may not happen at all. For example, empirical research on lawyers indicates that, compared to nonlawyers, lawyers tend to evaluate settlement options by focusing solely on monetary value (the "economic bottom-line"), while nonlawyers tend to be much more influenced by nonmonetary, psychological factors in their decisions to accept a settlement offer in a lawsuit.[5] This suggests that instead of incorporating nonlegal factors into our professional decisions, lawyers focus instead on pure legal analysis (who wins or loses) and the economic bottom line (how much in damages will the winner receive).[6]

Certainly, in law school, emotional and interpersonal concerns are strongly de-emphasized, if not blatantly ignored. Empirical research indicates that law school fosters two shifts in values that echo this de-emphasis. First, during law school, law students tend to either intensify their rights orientations or move from a care ethic to a rights orientation.[7]

The second shift that occurs during law school is away from an emphasis on "growth/self-acceptance, intimacy/emotional connection, and community/societal contribution," which have been called "'intrinsic' values," and towards an emphasis on "appearance/attractiveness," "money/luxuries, popularity/fame, and beauty/attractiveness," which have been called "'extrinsic' value[s]."[8]

Both shifts appear among law students as early as the first year of law school. In both shifts, a movement away from valuing interpersonal harmony, connectedness, and emotional wellbeing is evident.[9] These concerns and issues are traditionally ignored, if not actively silenced, in law school and law practice. While "good," traditional lawyers may implicitly or unconsciously take these concerns into account in their representation of clients,

---

3. Personal communication with Bruce J. Winick, Redondo Beach, CA, March, 1997.

4. Janeen Kerper, *Creative Problem Solving vs. The Case Method: A Marvelous Adventure in Which Winnie-the-Pooh Meets Mrs. Palsgraf*, 34 CAL. W. L. REV. 351, 369 (1998).

5. Russell Korobkin & Chris Guthrie, *Psychology, Economics, and Settlement: A New Look at the Role of the Lawyer*, 76 TEX. L. REV. 77 (1997).

6. *Id.*

7. CAROL GILLIGAN, IN A DIFFERENT VOICE: PSYCHOLOGICAL THEORY AND WOMEN'S DEVELOPMENT (1982).

8. Lawrence S. Krieger, *Psychological Insights: Why Our Students and Graduates Suffer, and What We Might Do About It*, 1 J. ASS'N LEG. WRITING DIRS. 259 (2002) and Lawrence S. Krieger, *Institutional Denial About the Dark Side of Law School, and Fresh Empirical Guidance for Constructively Breaking the Silence*, 52 J. LEGAL EDUC. 112 (March/June 2002).

9. SUSAN SWAIM DAICOFF, LAWYER KNOW THYSELF: A PSYCHOLOGICAL ANALYSIS OF PERSONALITY STRENGTHS AND WEAKNESSES (2004).

the comprehensive law movement differs from traditional lawyering in that it *explicitly* values interpersonal, emotional, psychological, and relational concerns.[10] The next two sections explore the two unifying features in more detail.

Optimizing Human Wellbeing

First, the vectors of the comprehensive law movement seek legal solutions that make things better, or at least not worse, for the people involved in the legal matter. They explicitly or implicitly attempt to optimize the psychological and emotional wellbeing of the individuals involved. All of the vectors seek to resolve the legal dispute or matter in a way that prevents harm to, preserves, or enhances individuals' interpersonal relationships, psychological wellbeing, opportunities for personal growth, mental health, or satisfaction with the process and outcome of the matter.[11]

While the vectors may initially focus on the wellbeing of the individual client at hand, they often seek to preserve or enhance the wellbeing of all of the individuals involved in the matter. They intuitively understand the well-known social science finding that positive relationships and good connections with one's family, friends, colleagues, peers, and community lead to enhanced psychological wellbeing and functioning[12] and, as a result, they often work to preserve, maintain, restore, or create good interpersonal relationships.

Because of the emotional devastation that can result from traditional adversarial litigation, many of the vectors explicitly seek nonlitigious solutions to legal problems.[13] Some vectors are explicitly therapeutic to the individuals involved[14] and some are indirectly therapeutic.[15] Many utilize collaborative methods in solving legal problems;[16] however, some explicitly acknowledge that litigation, uncompromising positions, and legal force can themselves be healing and they use these methods in achieving their goals.[17]

Social scientists might call this feature "optimizing human functioning." They might define the vectors' goal as "satisfaction with the legal process" or "good mental health." Jurisprudents might call the goal therapeutic or curative. Others might describe the goal as a search for healing or restoration. Native American tradition might call the goal "harmony" and then define harmony as three-part wholeness, meaning harmony within oneself (intrapersonal harmony), harmony between self and a Supreme Being, if one so believes (vertical harmony), and harmony between self and others (horizontal or inter-

---

10. *Id.*

11. This focus echoes the overall values embedded in the paradigm shifts and jurisprudential precursors to the movement discussed elsewhere in this Chapter, *infra*, such as connectedness, interpersonal harmony, and human wellbeing.

12. *See* Richard Sheehy & John J. Horan, *Effects of Stress Inoculation Training for First-Year Law Students* (August 2000) (paper presented at annual meeting of the American Psychological Association), available at http://horan.asu.edu/d-rs-apa-y2k.htm (visited July 11, 1010).

13. E.g., preventive law, creative problem solving, collaborative law, procedural justice, and holistic justice.

14. Explicit: e.g., therapeutic jurisprudence, transformative mediation, and drug treatment courts.

15. Implicit: restorative justice.

16. *See e.g.*, Tesler, *supra* note 1.

17. *See e.g.*, Susan Daicoff, *Afterword: The Role of Therapeutic Jurisprudence Within the Comprehensive Law Movement, in* Practicing Therapeutic Jurisprudence 465 (Dennis P. Stolle, David B. Wexler & Bruce J. Winick eds., 2000) [hereinafter Daicoff, Afterword].

personal harmony).[18] Whatever moniker is used, the concept is focused first on people and second on leaving people in the best possible internal, psychological, emotional, moral, relational, and spiritual state at the conclusion of their legal matter.

"Rights Plus": Considering Extra-Legal Factors

The second unifying feature is that all of the vectors take into consideration, when assessing or resolving a legal problem, more than just the strict legal rights, liabilities, obligations, duties, and entitlements presented. While law school teaches us to focus only on the law and what facts are relevant to the legal tests used in courts, the comprehensive law approaches explicitly go above and beyond the law to incorporate a consideration of one or more extra-legal factors. The factors considered include: the social, psychological, and emotional consequences of various courses of action, the communities in which the individuals involved exist, and the parties' emotions, feelings, needs, resources, goals, psychological health, relationships, values, morals, and financial concerns.[19] Pauline Tesler, one of the founders of the collaborative law movement, calls this feature "rights plus."[20]

Every traditional lawyer probably takes his or her client's financial concerns into account, so that at least one extra-legal factor is usually considered beyond the client's legal rights or duties.[21] In fact, focusing on the economic bottom line is rather characteristic of attorneys, as compared to non-attorneys.[22] Unlike a more traditional approach, however, the comprehensive law approaches also consider the psychological, social, emotional, and relational consequences of various legal courses of action.

These two main areas of common ground appear to be the unifying characteristics of the otherwise somewhat diverse vectors of the movement. Other features are shared by some but not all of the vectors, such as: nonlitigative or collaborative approaches to dispute resolution, a focus on spirituality and faith, explicitly therapeutic goals, interdisciplinary approaches, shared equal power instead of a hierarchical top-down power structure, a focus on interpersonal relationships, and a focus on process rather than outcome.

Organizational Chart of the Movement

The vectors of the comprehensive law movement range from infinitely theoretical to highly concrete. Professor David Wexler, one of the founders of therapeutic jurisprudence, has noted that the most theoretical vectors can be thought of as "lenses" through

---

18. Definition attributed to Dean Emeritus David Link, formerly of Notre Dame Law School and former president of the International Centre for Healing and the Law (formed under the auspices of the Fetzer Institute).

19. Daicoff, Afterword, *supra* note 17, at 470–71.

20. This term was coined by Pauline Tesler, one of the co-founders of the collaborative law movement and a collaborative divorce lawyer in the San Francisco area. Interview with Pauline H. Tesler, Esq., of Tesler, Sandmann and Fishman, Dublin, Ireland (July 8, 1999).

21. Most lawyers are likely to be finely attuned to the economics of a case, *see* Korobkin & Guthrie, *supra* note 5 (empirical study finding that lawyers evaluated settlement options solely on the basis of economic return, while non-lawyers were swayed by noneconomic concerns such as fault, remorse, and the price of the wrongdoing driver's car).

22. *Id.*

which an attorney can view a particular legal problem.[23] These lenses help the attorney evaluate the problem as well as potential solutions. The more concrete and tangible vectors provide specific "processes" by which an attorney can resolve civil or criminal cases. The process-type vectors provide a particular method for resolving civil or criminal lawsuits, while the lens-type vectors dictate how an attorney might approach a case. For example, every legal process can be viewed from a therapeutic jurisprudence perspective (Is this process therapeutic or not? How could it be made so?), a procedural justice view (How will this process affect the participants psychologically?), or a creative problem solving approach (Does this process allow for the broadest, most creative approach to solving the problem?).

Using this lens/process analysis, one can analyze the comprehensive law movement's contribution to the legal profession. For example, before the comprehensive law movement, the law used a practically monolithic "lens" through which to view legal problems. This lens focused on legal rights, duties, and obligations and was generally adversarial, looking towards a binary outcome when resolving legal disputes or matters: win or lose. It usually led lawyers to one "process" for dispute resolution: litigation and other adversarial judicial processes. While negotiation and settlement prior to litigation were always an option, the spectre of litigation always looms in the background during these processes. With the rise of mediation and other alternative dispute resolution means, other processes have become more popular in the last forty years, adding to the lawyer's toolkit. However, the "lens" for lawyers seeking to utilize mediation and other alternative dispute resolution processes has not always been clarified, from a theoretical basis. Therefore, lawyers steeped in an adversarial, binary, win/lose tradition can find themselves navigating their clients through mediation and arbitration often without a specific theory, goal, perspective, or philosophy other than the traditional, win/lose lens above.[24]

Traditional "lens" (adversarial, win/lose) —————> led to

—————> traditional "processes" (litigation, negotiation, or settlement)

Nontraditional "processes" were then added: mediation, arbitration, private adjudication, and other alternative dispute resolution methods

The comprehensive law movement further expands the lawyer's toolkit by affording him or her an array of lenses through which to view a client's legal problem. It adds at least five lenses; the lawyer can seek a solution which is: therapeutic, procedurally just, preventative, holistic, religious or spiritual, and/or creative problem solving-oriented. Each of these lenses focuses on concerns beyond legal rights.

"Lenses" added: therapeutic jurisprudence, preventive law, procedural justice, holistic justice, creative problem solving, religious/spiritual —————>

In addition, the comprehensive law movement adds at least five more concrete processes for resolving legal matters to the lawyer's toolkit. While these also may contain a theoretical basis, they differ from the lenses above because they provide specific actions to be taken to resolve the legal problem. They are: problem solving courts, preventive law, collaborative law, restorative justice, and transformative mediation.

---

23. Personal communication with David B. Wexler, John Lyons Professor of Law and Psychology, University of Arizona College of Law and University of Puerto Rico School of Law, during 1999–2000.

24. This explains, in part, the popularity of the "win/win" perspective endorsed by ROGER FISHER, BRUCE M. PATTON & WILLIAM L. URY, GETTING TO YES: NEGOTIATING AGREEMENT WITHOUT GIVING IN (Houghton Mifflin, 1981).

—————————> *"Processes" added: problem solving courts, preventive law, collaborative law, restorative justice, and transformative mediation*

The new organizational chart of the law can be seen as depicted in Figure 2, below:

Figure 2. "Organizational Chart" of the Movement

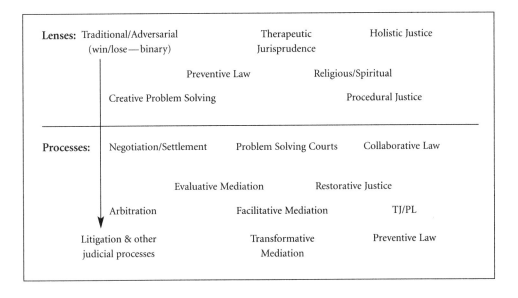

"*Lenses*":

    1. traditional (adversarial, win/lose)
    2. therapeutic jurisprudence
    3. preventive law
    4. procedural justice
    5. holistic justice
    6. creative problem solving
    7. religious/spiritual
    —————————>

"*Processes*":

    1. litigation
    2. negotiation or settlement
    3. mediation
    4. arbitration
    5. private adjudication and other alternative dispute resolution methods
    6. problem solving courts
    7. preventive law (e.g., audits, checkups, rewinds) and TJ/PL
    8. collaborative law
    9. restorative justice
    10. transformative mediation

Any lens or combination of lenses can be used to view the legal problem and any process or combination of processes can be utilized by a lawyer looking through any lens, to resolve it.

Parallel Developments

While many of the vectors of the comprehensive law movement have been developed by practicing lawyers and judges, some parallel developments have emerged in legal education, primarily through the work of various like-minded law professors. These academic developments are related to the comprehensive law movement because of their emphasis on humanism, values, and enhanced interpersonal and intrapersonal sensitivity. They also assist law students to develop or preserve core skills and attributes necessary to effectively practice law comprehensively.

The Humanizing Movement

Energized by the leadership and enthusiasm of law professor Lawrence Krieger,[25] a group of law professors banded together to make law school and legal education a more humane environment. Aware of common complaints about the competitive and intimidating nature of the law school environment[26] and painfully aware of the empirical data demonstrating that law students are "normal" before they enter law school but rapidly develop depression and other psychiatric distress thereafter, which does not abate after graduation,[27] these professors began sharing information, teaching techniques, and research on how to humanize legal education.[28] While the thrust of this movement has focused on humanizing the experience of law school for law students, its values are consistent with comprehensive law's intention of humanizing legal process for participants. The humanizing movement also encourages law students to identify, evaluate, and maintain their own personal morals, values, beliefs, and standards during law school. This exploration of values may prepare or propel some students to practice law comprehensively rather than traditionally.

Mindfulness Meditation

Law professor Leonard Riskin, author and legal commentator Steven Keeva, and others have written about the importance of the lawyer's mental state to the efficacy of his or her work.[29] One strategy that many attorneys and law students are experimenting with,

---

25. Clinical law professor at Florida State University Law School. This group ultimately formed the "Balance in Legal Education" Section of the Association of American Law Schools, *see, e.g.,* http://humanizingideas.law.fsu.edu/default.asp (last visited July 11, 2010).

26. Lawrence S. Krieger, Psychological Insights: *Why Our Students and Graduates Suffer, and What We Might Do About It,* 1 J. Ass'n Leg. Writing Directors 259, 262 (2002).

27. Connie J. A. Beck & Bruce D. Sales, *Lawyer Distress: Alcohol-Related Problems and Other Psychological Concerns Among a Sample of Practicing Lawyers,* 10 J.L. & Health 1, 2 (1996).

28. Their first formal program was presented at the 2001 annual Association of American Law Schools conference, as "Humanizing Legal Education," jointly sponsored by the Sections on Clinical Legal Education, Law & Mental Disability, and Law & Religion, in San Francisco, CA, January 2001; at www.law.fsu.edu/academic_programs/humanizing_lawschool.html (last visited July 11, 2010) (quoting website, "Humanizing legal education is an initiative shared by legal educators seeking to maximize the overall health, well being, and career satisfaction of law students and lawyers."); listserve at www.law.fsu.edu/academic_programs/humanizing_lawschool/listserve.html (last visited July 11, 2010).

29. Leonard L. Riskin, *The Contemplative Lawyer: On the Potential Contributions of Mindfulness Mediation to Law Students, Lawyers, and Their Clients,* 7 Harv. Negot. L. Rev. 1 (2002); Douglas A. Codiga, *Reflection on the Potential Growth of Mindfulness Mediation in the Law,* 7 Harv. Negot. L. Rev.

to improve their professional efficacy, is "mindfulness meditation." Some have incorporated the principles and insights of mindfulness meditation into their preparation for professional practice. These concepts have been introduced to law students through such avenues as the Yale Law School Project for Meditation and the Law and programs sponsored by the Fetzer Institute.[30] Being more aware of and able to manage and monitor one's mental state, emotions, and reactions can assist lawyers in their daily work, particularly if they are practicing comprehensive law, due to its emphasis on the ability to identify and cope with the emotions and mental states of others.

Law and Spirituality

Law and religion is a familiar topic, but some recent commentary has focused on the concept that one's spiritual beliefs, values, and practices are relevant to law, legal education, and law practice.[31] Specifically, they are important for preparing one's mental state or legal work, maintaining one's mental health, the professional choices one makes as a lawyer, and the way in which one interacts with clients. Lawyers who have personal spiritual practices or who are explicitly faith-based themselves may be drawn to comprehensive law practice, due to the easy interface of the goals of comprehensive law with their personal values....

Expert's Comment on the Movement's Growth

J. Kim Wright, lawyer/journalist, restorative justice and collaborative law expert, author of the 2010 book published by the American Bar Association, "Lawyers as Peacemakers," and founder of www.cuttingedgelaw.com, writes:

---

109 (2002); *see also* STEVEN KEEVA, TRANSFORMING PRACTICES, FINDING JOY AND SATISFACTION IN THE LEGAL LIFE (Contemporary Books 1999).

30. *See* Steven W. Keeva, *Practicing From the Inside Out*, 7 HARV. NEGOT. L. REV. 97 (2002); Codiga, *supra* note 29.

31. *See* Calvin G. C. Pang, *Eyeing the Circle: Finding a Place for Spirituality in Law School Clinic*, 35 WILLIAMETTE L. REV. 241 (1999); Charles Senger, *Spirituality in Law School*, 81 MICH. B.J. 44 (Dec. 2002). Professor Calvin Pang, who infuses spirituality into his law school clinical courses, has written at length about how to incorporate spirituality into a clinical course and the benefits of doing so. Pang 1999, *supra* this note; Calvin G. C. Pang, 1995-JUN HAW. B. J. 28; and Calvin G. C. Pang, 1993-SEP HAW. B. J. 24. Professor Charles Senger teaches a law school course devoted entirely to law and spirituality; he presented a talk on his course at the second international conference on therapeutic jurisprudence, May 2001, in Cincinnati, Ohio. In that panel on law and spirituality, Professor Pang of the University of Hawaii Law School spoke, as well as Professor Daisy Floyd of Texas Tech. In 2003, Professor Tim Floyd of Texas Tech noted the importance of concepts such as forgiveness, prayer, and priority-setting to lawyers seeking to incorporate their spiritual values into their law practices. According to Professor Floyd, small groups of practicing lawyers discussing law and spirituality have sprung up around the country. Talk given by Professor Tim Floyd of Texas Tech University School of Law, April 7, 2003, at Touro College, Jacob D. Fuchsberg Law Center, Huntington, New York, at the symposium titled: "Lawyering and Its Discontents: Reclaiming Meaning in the Practice of Law." Practicing lawyer Arnie Herz has, on occasion, introduced a client to nonreligious, nondenominational spiritual practices because he thought it would improve the client's mental state and assist the client in visualizing a positive future for himself of herself after the legal dispute's resolution. Talk given by Arnie Herz at Florida Coastal School of Law, Jacksonville, Florida, on October 22, 2003.

The growth of the comprehensive law movement isn't easily measured. It isn't a section of the ABA (although the ADR section is one of the largest at 19,000 members). It isn't a single discipline but rather a wide range of cross-disciplines. Add to that, it is a relatively new movement. There are some measurements that may be helpful.

Since the first problem solving court in Miami in 1989, thousands of other courts have emerged. Focused on holistic solutions to social and individual problems, the courts address homelessness, domestic violence, drug and alcohol addictions, mental health, and even problems raised by returning veterans. There are thousands of such courts around the United States. The National Association of State Courts provides resources for developing more courts.

Collaborative law is now an international phenomenon with practicing lawyers in some thirty countries. Several years ago, it was estimated that 10,000 lawyers had been trained in collaborative law and since then, the counters have lost track of the growth.

Restorative justice intertwines with the problem solving courts. In addition, 18 state departments of correction provide various forms of restorative justice as an institutional service.

Aside from these measures, there are some qualitative differences that are related to the comprehensive law movement. Attend almost any law conference and you will find workshops on positive psychology, self awareness, non-violent communication: all skills and topics related to the underlying core of the comprehensive law movement.[32]

Resources

J. Kim Wright, Lawyers As Peacemakers: Practicing Holistic, Problem-Solving Law (American Bar Association, 2010) (American lawyer, mediator, collaborative lawyer, author, and journalist documenting the comprehensive law movement).

Michael King, Arie Frieberg, Becky Batagol, & Ross Hyams, Non-Adversarial Justice (The Federation Press, 2009) (Australian law professors documenting the comprehensive law movement).

Julie Macfarlane, The New Lawyer: How Settlement Is Transforming the Practice of Law (UBC Press, 2008) (Law & Society Series) (Canadian law professor documenting the comprehensive law movement).

Susan L. Brooks & Robert G. Madden, Relationship-Centered Lawyering: Social Science Theory for Transforming Legal Practice (Carolina Academic Press, 2010) (collecting many of the vectors in the same work).

Marjorie A. Silver, The Affective Assistance of Counsel (Durham, NC: Carolina Academic Press, 2007) (focusing on how to practice law comprehensively).

Dennis P. Stolle, David B. Wexler, & Bruce J. Winick, Eds., Practicing Therapeutic Jurisprudence: Law as a Helping Profession (Carolina Academic Press, 2000)

---

32. Personal email response to the author from J. Kim Wright, May, 2010.

(collecting many of the vectors in the same work, extending earlier efforts by Wexler & Winick; Afterword explores the comprehensive law movement).

Steven Keeva, Transforming Practices: Finding Joy And Satisfaction In The Legal Life (McGraw-Hill, 1999; republished in 2010) (This groundbreaking book details how the practice of law can be transformed into a more satisfying, helping, healing profession by narrating the story of many trailblazing attorneys in the United States; it has profoundly influenced many in the comprehensive law movement.).

Thomas D. Barton, *Troublesome Connections: The Law and Post-Enlightenment Culture*, 47 Emory L.J. 163 (1998).

Susan Daicoff, *Growing Pains: The Integration vs. Specialization Question for Therapeutic Jurisprudence and Other Comprehensive Law Approaches*, 30 Thom. Jeff. L. Rev. 551 (2008).

Susan Daicoff, *Law as a Healing Profession: The "Comprehensive Law Movement,"* 6 Pepperdine Disp. Resol. L. J. 1 (2006) (introducing the comprehensive law movement and its philosophical underpinnings).

Susan Daicoff, Lawyer Know Thyself: A Psychological Analysis of Personality Strengths and Weaknesses (American Psychological Association Books, 2004) (This book reports on and synthesizes forty years of empirical research on the personality traits, preferences, decisionmaking styles, and characteristics of lawyers, and then relates these findings to the state of the legal profession. The final chapter discusses the comprehensive law movement.)

Websites

Daicoff, S. Article on the Comprehensive Law Movement: http://papers.ssrn.com/sol3/papers.cfm?abstract_id=875449#PaperDownload (last visited July 11, 2010).

Cutting Edge Law: http://cuttingedgelaw.com (last visited July 11, 2010).

Renaissance Lawyer Organization: www.renaissancelawyer.com (last visited July 11, 2010).

Humanizing Legal Education: http://www.law.fsu.edu/academic_programs/humanizing_lawschool/humanizing_lawschool.html (last visited July 11, 2010).

Law student listserv: thrive-subscribe@mail.fsu.edu.

Ethical Wills: www.ethicalwill.com (last visited July 11, 2010).

Coordination: All of Wright, King, and Macfarlane.

Chapter 4

Foundational Comprehensive Law Skills

This Chapter is excerpted and adapted from the author's 2006 law review article in Pepperdine Dispute Resolution Journal.[1]

There are certain basic, foundational skills that attorneys and law students require in order to successfully practice comprehensive law....

Law professor Leonard Riskin provides a terrific football analogy to understand the relevance of these skills to the comprehensive law movement. He reminds us that a football coach teaches his players the overall philosophy of football as well as how to throw, block, and tackle. The players learn the game and then practice the moves on the field. However, if the players do not actually go to the gym and become stronger through weight lifting, they do not become strong, effective football players. Just as strength training prepares football players to play football, the comprehensive law skills, outlined below, prepare comprehensive lawyers [to practice law by making them stronger human relations specialists]....[2]

These skills include: excellent interpersonal, human relations skills; self-knowledge (or intrapersonal skills); and rudimentary psychological sophistication....[3] [Some commentators label the combination of excellent interpersonal skills and intrapersonal skills "emotional intelligence," leadership skills, or communication skills. Others might simply view these skills as "good common sense" or "street smarts."]

Interpersonal Skills

First, there are communications and relational skills that attorneys need in order to form and maintain working relationships with their clients, opponents, judges, and other legal personnel. These basic communications skills are useful in creating trusting relationships

---

1. Susan Daicoff, *Law as a Healing Profession: The "Comprehensive Law Movement,"* 6 Pepperdine Disp. Resol. L. J. 1 (2006). This Chapter also relies heavily on the author's training in clinical psychology in the master's program at the University of Central Florida.

2. Personal communication with University of Florida law professor Leonard L. Riskin, April 6, 2003, at Touro College, Jacob D. Fuchsberg Law Center, Huntington, New York, at the symposium titled: "Lawyering and Its Discontents: Reclaiming Meaning in the Practice of Law" [hereinafter "Discontents"].

3. Marjorie A. Silver, *Love, Hate, and Other Emotional Interference in the Lawyer/Client Relationship*, 6 Clinical L. Rev. 259 (1999) (providing an excellent and exhaustive review of the skills needed to practice law comprehensively).

with clients, witnesses, and other individuals, interviewing individuals, or negotiating with other parties or lawyers. These skills include active or reflective listening, basic and advanced empathy, and questioning skills. These skills are often taught as part of law school clinical courses or externships, but a comprehensive approach would suggest that all law students need training in these skills.

Active Listening

Active listening is the ability to listen to another's statement, indicate attentiveness and interest, and then, when the speaker is finished, recite back to the speaker the content of his or her statement, in a paraphrased, not verbatim fashion. It is often the focus of communications training exercises, where one person speaks or tells a story for one minute to another person, then the listener tells the story back to the speaker in his or her own words. It serves the function of letting the speaker know they have been "heard," which can be very powerful and satisfying to the speaker, can forge bonds of connection between the speaker and the listener, and can motivate the speaker to go on to divulge more information, as he or she often feels "safe," heard, and understood, simply as a result of active listening. It has been used in conflict resolution training and parent effectiveness training. It is misapplied and misused when it devolves into parroting back to the speaker what he or she has said, in a rote and mechanical fashion. This has sometimes been parodied as, "What I hear you saying is ___(fill in the blank with the precise words the speaker used)___" as sort of a pop psychology "move" used to make someone feel more comfortable or "heard." One can convey active listening without using this stilted formula for one's response.

Exercise 1: Active Listening:

Try this exercise: Split up into pairs. Have Partner A tell a story about something that happened to them recently, for one minute, while Partner B is attentive but entirely silent. Then have Partner B recite back to Partner A the content of his or her story, without repeating it word for word. Have Partner A tell Partner B how complete and accurate B's account of A's story was. Then switch and have B tell a story to A, etc.

Advanced Reflection:

In the above Exercise, after the listener recites the story back to the speaker, have the speaker describe how it felt to hear his or her story from another's mouth. For example, did the speaker gain any new perspective on the story or feel more connected to the listener, afterwards? What possible uses could this technique have, for a practicing lawyer? When might it be useful and for what purpose?

Empathy

Empathy is often defined as the ability to stand in another's shoes and express an understanding of the other's thoughts and feelings.

Thoughts vs. Feelings

Because it is often much easier (particularly for lawyers, who are often not attuned to interpersonal or emotional dynamics) to identify and paraphrase another's thoughts, we will focus here on identifying and conveying an understanding of another's feelings or emotions, not thoughts. For example, suppose a client says in an initial client interview, "I'm so angry that I have all these injuries and bills from this accident. I did nothing to cause it — it came out of the blue and the person who hit me needs to pay up for my injuries." It might be easy to say, "So I understand that you feel that the accident was not your fault and that the person who hit you should pay for your injuries, is that right?" This statement identifies no emotions explicitly but only the idea that the speaker was not to blame and some other person was. It may be received as accurate active listening, but it focuses on a thought, not an emotion, even though the words "you feel" were used. It is not really empathy. Be on the watch for thoughts disguised as emotions in this way. It may be more difficult to identify that the speaker expressed at least one emotion, explicitly, saying "so angry," and perhaps another emotion of surprise or dismay in the words "out of the blue." Thus, a more empathetic statement might be, "Wow, it sounds like you feel furious that this accident came out of nowhere, caused all this trouble for you, and it wasn't your fault." This statement accurately reflects the two emotions expressed by the speaker (anger and surprise), without repeating them verbatim, and then gives the reason why those emotions are felt (losses were incurred and it was not the speaker's fault). You may be able to formulate an even more accurate and wellcrafted response, just be sure to reflect the expressed, explicit emotions presented by the speaker.

Empathy vs. Sympathy

Empathy is not sympathy, as when someone says to a grieving person, "I'm sorry for your loss" or "I'm sorry you are in pain or upset." It is not a rote recital of pat statements such as "I know just how you feel" or "my sister went through the same thing as you." These kinds of statements, even when well-intentioned, often have an unwantedly negative impact on the hearer, who may experience them as patronizing, hollow, or even self-centered.

Conveying Empathy

Empathy is not simply the *feeling* of understanding another's thoughts and feelings, but it is the ability or skill to convey and effectively communicate that understanding to the other person. It has also been parodied as, "What I hear you saying is that you feel ___(fill in the blank with the emotion expressed by the speaker)___," which, although it might be accurate, may be received as mechanical or formulaic.

However, when one is first learning to convey empathy to another, it is often useful to use the formula "You feel X because Y," where X is the explicit emotion expressed by the speaker and Y are the facts of the story that cause that particular emotion. In our example above, it would be "You feel angry because you have been injured, it was a surprise, and it wasn't your fault."

Basic and Advanced

There are two forms of empathy: basic and advanced.

Basic Empathy: Basic empathy accurately reflects back to the speaker the explicit or overt emotions expressed by the speaker. Basic empathy builds trust and connection between the speaker and the listener and it usually encourages the speaker to open up and relate more details of the story and his or her feelings about what happened. It is very useful when interviewing clients or witnesses to gain more information. It is also useful when building a relationship with a new client. You have perhaps noticed very skillful salespeople using this technique with you, as a customer, to build trust, relationship, and a feeling of comfort and safety, so that you will buy a product from them. If you want to stop or stem the flow of information issuing from a client or witness, basic empathy should be avoided, therefore.

Exercise 2: Basic Empathy:

Now return to your groups of two and see if the listener in each case can accurately identify and convey an understanding of the explicit or overt feelings and emotions expressed by the speaker. Have the speaker provide feedback to the listener as to how accurate he or she was in doing so. For example, "In the story you just told me, you felt X" or "You feel X about what happened to you in the story you just told me" where X is the express emotion displayed.

Advanced Reflection:

For the speakers, reflect on (and report, if you so choose) what it felt like to have someone accurately (or inaccurately, as the case may be) reflect the emotions you expressed in your story. What does this tell you about the possible uses of basic empathy in your work as a lawyer, as you interact with clients and others? How and when might you use this skill?

Advanced Empathy: Advanced empathy is much more challenging; it accurately reflects back to the speaker the implicit or covert emotions expressed in the speaker's story. Reflect for a moment upon the difference between explicit conditions or express terms and implicit conditions or implied terms in a contract. This is similar to distinguishing explicit emotions from implicit emotions. Advanced empathy refers to the ability to express the implicit thoughts and feelings under the surface of the other's actions and words. For example, a person facing major surgery might express anger, frustration, and irritation with the doctors but underneath might feel afraid, worried, and mistrustful of the surgeons. Basic empathy would reflect the person's anger; advanced empathy would recognize and acknowledge the underlying fear. It is challenging because it always runs the risk of being inaccurate, as the hearer must guess at the implicit or submerged feelings of the other. Inaccurate advanced empathy tends to have a negative impact on the speaker or may be experienced as a confrontation or challenge.

For example, in our story above, the client says, in an initial client interview, "I'm so angry that I have all these injuries and bills from this accident. I did nothing to cause it— it came out of the blue and the person who hit me needs to pay up for my injuries." The speaker only explicitly mentioned anger, he or she did not really express other emotions directly, other than perhaps the words "out of the blue" which might hint at surprise or shock. We are probably well able, however, to begin to guess at emotions the speaker is feeling but not expressing, such as feeling overwhelmed, shocked, surprised, victimized, sure, confident, or determined. After initially responding to the speaker with a basic empathy response, e.g., "You feel X (angry) because Y (you were hurt in an unexpected accident you didn't cause)," we might follow that up with an advanced empathy statement, e.g., "And it sounds like you feel outraged at what has happened to you," or one a bit more risky: "And despite perhaps feeling really determined to get compensated for your losses, you are still feeling a bit shocked and overwhelmed by the whole experience, so far."

Advanced empathy, when accurate, is very powerful. It usually causes the speaker to feel that they were heard and understood at a very deep level, builds trust and connection, and can even assist a speaker in identifying emotions they did not know they had.

It is therefore very useful in psychotherapy; its utility in legal counseling and interviewing should thus be carefully evaluated before it is used. When it is not accurate, however, and the speaker is not feeling the emotions the listener guesses he or she is feeling, it can be very offputting to the speaker and create distance and distrust between the speaker and listener. For example, in the story above, if the listener does a little amateur psychoanalysis and says, "It sounds as if you really feel afraid, deep down, that you caused this accident" and this guess is way off target for the speaker, then the speaker is likely to feel quite negatively towards the listener or feel challenged or affronted by the statement. The moral of the story is: use advanced empathy judiciously and do your best to be sure you are accurate in your guesses about the emotions "under the story."

Where do we learn what emotions might lie "underneath" someone's story? We obtain them from our own experiences, our own biases, our understanding of psychology, human relations, and emotions, and our theories. As a result, we may not always be accurate in our guesses, as our experience may differ from that of the speaker.

Exercise 3: Advanced Empathy:

Return again to your groups of two. This time, have each listener identify and convey an understanding of the implicit or implied emotions they believe were expressed by the speaker in the stories told. Have the speaker report to the listener as to the accuracy of the listener's guesses about his or her emotions "under the surface."

Advanced Reflection:

For the speakers, reflect on (and report, if you so choose) what it felt like to have someone accurately (or inaccurately, as the case may be) reflect your implicit emotions "behind the story." What does this tell you about the possible uses of advanced empathy in your work as a lawyer, as you interact with clients and others? How and when might you use this skill?

Questioning

Questioning skills refer to the ability to distinguish between closed-ended questions and open-ended questions and the ability to know when to use each type. Closed-ended questions are those requiring only a yes or no answer, known in Evidence classes as those used in cross-examination. For example, "Did you run the red light?" or "Have you decided that you want a divorce?" Open-ended questions are those requiring an answer other than yes or no; for example, "What happened?" or "Why did you run the red light?" or "What do you see as your goal in bringing this lawsuit?"

Closed ended questions tend to focus and direct the speaker, often closing down the flow of information emanating from the speaker. They can serve to redirect the conversation along specific lines, get "back on track," or shut down an overly loquacious speaker. Open-ended questions, particularly when combined with basic empathy, tend to encourage the flow of information and elicit more from the speaker. The combination of open-ended questions and basic empathy is particularly effective when establishing a trusting relationship with another person, such as a client, witness, or even an opponent in negotiations.

Exercise 4: Open and Closed Questions:

Return again to your groups of two. This time, have Partner A tell a story for about 2–3 minutes. Have Partner B ask only closed-ended questions during the story, making no other responses other than closed-ended questions. Have both partners discuss what effect the closed-ended questions had on the speaker (Partner A). Then, have Partner A tell the story again, this time allowing Partner B to respond during the story only with open-ended questions. Then, reflect on and discuss the differences in the effects on the speaker. Switch partners and repeat the exercise with B as the speaker and A as the listener.

Advanced Reflection:

For the speakers, reflect on (and report, if you so choose) what it felt like to receive only closed questions or only open questions. What did this exercise tell you about the strategic uses of closed and open questions in your work as a lawyer, as you interact with clients and others?

Confrontation

One skill that mental health therapists use with clients to help them grow and change is sometimes called "confrontation." It can be gentle, as when a therapist points out a conflict or some dissonance between a client's values or thoughts and his or her behavior (for example, "You say that you are no good at math and have great math anxiety, and yet when you graduated from college, you made A's in all of your math classes."). Or, it can be very challenging, such as, "Face it, you are an alcoholic and you need help." Confrontation is useful to propel the listener to make changes in his or her behavior, thoughts, or attitudes, but if the change is unwanted, confrontation is often received as very challenging, affrontive, and harsh. It can tear down trust and safety, within an interpersonal relationship, in this situation.

This skill might be useful to lawyers working with clients or in negotiations, but should be used very judiciously, strategically, and sparingly. One thing that is useful to lawyers, however, is knowing about the concept of confrontation as a communications skill, as it is likely that we may utilize this skill unwittingly and then wonder why we have alienated our listener. It also might be useful in negotiations to point out discrepancies between a party's position and their stated goals or needs, to assist them in compromising.

Rudimentary Psychological Sophistication

To practice law comprehensively, attorneys need a minimal amount of psychological sophistication and an ability to contain and help clients manage their emotions.

Identifying Emotions

For example, lawyers need to be able to identify emotions their clients are likely experiencing and be able to develop strategies for dealing with them, should they arise. One skill that lawyers particularly need is the ability to recognize and deal with individuals going through the grief process.[4] Many clients coming to a lawyer for help have experi-

---

4. Clinical psychologist Sanford Portnoy claims that over 40% of attorney-client communications involve the clients' emotions and yet attorneys routinely dismiss the need to address clients' emotions. For example, he says there are more complaints against attorneys brought by divorce clients and per-

enced a loss of some sort, whether it is a personal injury (tort), the disappointment of a failed marriage (divorce) or business relationship (contract dispute), the death of a loved one (probate), or getting caught committing a crime. Thus, each litigant is likely to be experiencing one or more of Elizabeth Kübler-Ross' famous five stages of grief: denial, anger, bargaining, depression, and acceptance.[5] As they progress through the course of litigation, therefore, they are also likely either to progress through these stages of grief, at various times reflecting these emotions to their attorneys, or to get "stuck" in one stage and fail to move through the grief process. For example, at various times in a divorce action, a client may express to his or her attorney: "This can't be happening to me" (denial), "I want you to nail my spouse to the wall. Take him/her for all he's/she's got" (anger), "If only I were more attractive and youthful, my spouse would not have left me for another" (bargaining), "I don't feel like dealing with this, I just feel paralyzed most of the time" (depression), or "I understand why the divorce had to happen and I'm ready to move on in my life" (acceptance). Alternatively, a litigation client might easily get "stuck" in the anger phase and consequently insist on taking intractable, rigid negotiation positions with the opposing party.

Clients who are not experiencing loss may instead be facing a fearsome possibility, such as imprisonment (criminal action), loss of driving privileges (driving while under the influence of alcohol charges), personal liability or shame (defending a contract or tort action), bankruptcy, and the like. These clients are likely to be feeling great fear even if they present a calm and confident exterior image. This fear may be reflected in their behavior, just as loss stages can be.

Managing Emotions

How should you respond if your client becomes excessively angry or excessively upset during an office conference with you? What if it occurs during a mediation or settlement negotiation session with the other side and his or her attorney? Some lawyers discuss the possibility of this occurring with their clients early in the legal representation, notably with divorce clients, and prepare the clients for the lawyer's intervention in this case. For example, they point out that individuals going through divorces are often not at their best, instead they often display some of their worst behavior during this time. They explain that, should this occur, they may ask the client to take a break or a "time out" during a conference, or to work with a divorce coach to better manage their rampaging emotions.

Making Appropriate Mental Health Referrals

Lawyers also need to know when they are in over their heads, psychologically speaking, and the client needs to be referred to a mental health professional. For example, when the lawyer's simple management strategies are ineffective or the lawyer becomes weary or frustrated with the client, it may be appropriate to refer. When it is appropri-

---

sonal injury clients, probably because those clients' emotions generally run high and they may displace anger onto the attorneys. Talk given by Dr. Portnoy at Touro College Law Center, April 7, 2003, "Discontents," *supra* note 2. Dr. Portnoy published these ideas in his book, SANFORD M. PORTNOY, THE FAMILY LAWYER'S GUIDE TO BUILDING SUCCESSFUL RELATIONSHIPS (2000).

5. ELIZABETH KÜBLER-ROSS, ON DEATH AND DYING 34–99 (1969) (discussing the five stages of coping in terminally ill patients).

ate to refer a client for professional therapy or counseling, the lawyer can be prepared to make the referral and perhaps offer personally to make the call to a suitable professional (and let the client know that the professional is expecting his or her call). The lawyer also must assess whether the referral to therapy in some way prejudices the client's legal case, for example, by raising doubt as to the client's mental state.

Maintaining Boundaries

Perhaps family lawyers understand best the importance of observing and maintaining firm, consistent boundaries with their clients, meaning knowing what behavior is inside or outside the bounds of appropriate lawyer-client relations. Allowing your client to live with you rent-free while he or she is going through a divorce, for example, might be inappropriate. Allowing your client to call you 24 hours a day, 7 days a week, to "vent," anytime he or she is upset or emotional about the case, may be inappropriate. Telling your client what to do, in a legal matter, when that directive conflicts with what your client wants to do, may be inappropriate and may overstep the bounds of the lawyer's role. From a psychological standpoint, a lawyer who cannot maintain appropriate boundaries with his or her clients not only risks malpractice actions and disciplinary complaints, but may also create distrust and feelings of insecurity in the client. Clients need to be able to trust that their attorney knows the proper role of the attorney, will maintain behavior in line with that role, and will not allow the client to step over the boundaries of what is appropriate between attorney and client, in order to feel safe and secure in the lawyer-client interactions.

Optimizing the Therapeutic Potential of the Legal Representation

While the vector of therapeutic jurisprudence, discussed *infra*, explicitly assesses how to maximize the healing potential of each case or matter handled for a client, even non-TJ-oriented lawyers may benefit from rudimentary psychological knowledge about the likely effects of their actions on their clients. Litigation can facilitate or suspend the grief process—the process of dealing with and resolving the loss that resulted in the legal problem. For example, in wrongful death actions, litigation can interrupt the process of grieving if it focuses too long on the cause of or responsibility for the death. On the other hand, litigation facilitates the grief process when it helps the survivors sort out the events leading to the death or fulfills their sense of duty to the deceased person, and is begun and concluded quickly after the death.[6]

Lawyers working with traumatized clients can help reverse the effects of trauma, using excellent interpersonal skills. For example, if the client was raped and experienced degradation and humiliation, the lawyer can provide the client with an additional measure of respect, autonomy, and control. The attorney can ask the client when and for how long he or she wants to talk about the event, listen well, and treat him or her with respect.[7]

---

6. David B. Wexler & Bruce J. Winick, Eds., Law in a Therapeutic Key 452–53 (Carolina Academic Press, 1996).

7. Ideas paraphrased from comments by University of Miami law professor Bruce Winick, April 7, 2003, "Discontents," *supra* note 2.

Intrapersonal Skills

In addition to the above communications and human relations skills, lawyers also need excellent intrapersonal skills.

Countertransference

First, they need the ability to know themselves well enough to determine when they are over- or under-reacting to a particular client, cause, or party. This is sometimes referred to as "countertransference," meaning when the lawyer's own internal feelings, experiences, biases, fears, frustrations, likes, or dislikes unduly influence or interfere with his or her work and the lawyer loses his or her ability to react neutrally and objectively to the client, cause, or party. This can only be detected if the lawyer is adept at knowing himself or herself and his or her strengths and weaknesses and can effectively evaluate and monitor his or her emotions, thoughts, and actions. Marjorie Silver provides an excellent example of countertransference, both positive and negative (see Chapter Assignments) and a very useful checklist to assess whether a lawyer is experiencing countertransference with a particular client. She credits Bastress and Harbaugh, who in turn credit a 1954 text by Wolberg, for this countertransference checklist:[8]

1. How do I feel about the client?

2. Do I anticipate the client?

3. Do I over-identify with, or feel sorry for, the client?

4. Do I feel any resentment or jealousy toward the client?

5. Do I get extreme pleasure out of seeing the client?

6. Do I feel bored with the client?

7. Am I fearful of the client?

8. Do I want to protect, reject, or punish the client?

9. Am I impressed by the client?

Silver explains that, if the answer is "Yes" to any of these questions, we might then ask ourselves "Why?" However, even if we cannot ascertain the cause or source of the countertransference, simply identifying it and acknowledging it may be sufficient to allow us to control or defuse the feeling enough to be able to adequately represent the client.[9] One might add to this list a few more questions; for example, *Do I want to rehabilitate or change the client? Does the client remind me of anyone in my life? Do I think this client's case is going to "make my career" or "put me on the map?" Am I anticipating making a lot of money (or, no money) in legal fees from this client?* Having countertransference towards opposing counsel in a case can also affect the lawyer's effectiveness in representing a client.

---

8. Marjorie A. Silver, *Love, Hate & Other Emotional Interference in the Lawyer/Client Relationship*, 6 Clinical L. Rev. 259 (1999), reprinted in Dennis P. Stolle, David B. Wexler, & Bruce J. Winick, Eds., Practicing Therapeutic Jurisprudence: Law as a Helping Profession 400 (Carolina Academic Press, 2000) (as Chapter 13), citing Robert M. Bastress & Joseph D. Harbaugh, Interviewing, Counseling, and Negotiating 297 (1990), citing Lewis R. Wolberg, M.D., The Technique of Psychotherapy 491 (1954).

9. Silver, *supra* note 8, at 400–401 (in Stolle, et al., *supra* note 8).

A lawyer who wants to impress opposing counsel perhaps in order to bolster his or her professional reputation in the local bar may take unneeded actions on behalf of a client, or make or avoid certain adversarial moves, that he or she might not, were a different opponent present. This can run up the client's legal fees or affect the course of the case's resolution positively or negatively. These responses are likely to be unavoidable; what is important is to be *conscious* of them and attempt to minimize their effects.

Thus, lawyers need the ability to manage one's own behavior, reactions, and emotions, deal effectively with countertransference,[10] and maintain personal emotional boundaries. Lawyers, particularly those who feel compassion and empathy for their clients, can become enmeshed with clients and their emotions. They can "take on" the client's strong emotions so much that they actually become angry at the opposing side and/or counsel and lose their objectivity and ability to assess the situation clearly. Inappropriate attachment or involvement can cause the lawyer stress, derail the lawyer-client relationship, distort the legal representation, distract the client from seeking professional psychological help, and give rise to ethical dilemmas.[11]

For example, lawyers working with clients who were sexually assaulted or abused or clients fighting human rights violations, can be vicariously traumatized by this exposure.[12] Comprehensive lawyers may be particularly vulnerable to this secondary trauma, because they are likely to respond to these clients with understanding and empathy. They might overidentify with such a client and thus might insist on vigorously prosecuting a case even when it is unlikely to win and sure to be very costly in legal fees and costs. Coping strategies therefore need to go beyond simple stress management; lawyers need the ability to identify, manage, and contain their own distressing emotions.[13]

Empirical Research and Summary

Most, if not all, of the skills in this chapter have been identified by practicing lawyers as important to the practice of law. For example, four surveys of practicing lawyers in the United States asked what skills they believe are important to the practice of law. Many of the skills on the lists were traditional skills taught in law school, such as legal analysis and reasoning, written and oral communication, legal research, legal drafting, factual investigation, interviewing and questioning, recognizing and resolving ethical dilemmas, pretrial discovery and advocacy, and trial advocacy. However, a surprising number of nontraditional "soft" skills were also identified in these studies as important. These often mirror social skills and competence making up what corporate America calls "emotional

---

10. Marjorie A. Silver, *Love, Hate & Other Emotional Interference in the Lawyer/Client Relationship*, 6 Clinical L. Rev. 259, 261–66 (1999).

11. Ideas paraphrased from talk given by Yale University law professor Jean Koh Peters, April 7, 2003, at "Discontents," *supra* note 2; *see also* Marjorie A. Silver et al., *Stress, Burnout, Vicarious Trauma, and Other Emotional Realities in the Lawyer/Client Relationship*, 19 Touro L. Rev. 847 (2004) (detailing a panel discussion that broadly looked at the emotional competence and intelligence of lawyers and the possibilities for positive intervention in legal education).

12. *See* Peters, *supra* note 11, and Silver, *supra* note 11.

13. *See* Leonard L. Riskin, *The Contemplative Lawyer: On the Potential Contributions of Mindfulness Mediation to Law Students, Lawyers, and Their Clients*, 7 Harv. Negot. L. Rev. 1 (2002); Douglas A. Codiga, *Reflection on the Potential Growth of Mindfulness Mediation in the Law*, 7 Harv. Negot. L. Rev. 109 (2002); and Steven Keeva, Transforming Practices, Finding Joy and Satisfaction in the Legal Life (Contemporary Books, 1999).

intelligence."[14] The nontraditional skills identified by these four surveys as essential to the practice of law were, in order of importance:

1. Survey of Chicago[15] and Minnesota[16] lawyers:
   a. Instilling others' confidence in you
   b. Negotiation
   c. Counseling
   d. Ability to obtain and keep clients

2. Survey of Montana lawyers:[17]
   a. Honesty
   b. Integrity
   c. Reliability
   d. Judgment
   e. Maturity
   f. Dealing effectively with others
   g. Motivation
   h. Continued professional development
   i. Tolerance and patience
   j. Understanding human behavior
   k. Self-confidence

3. Survey of Arizona lawyers:[18]
   a. Listening
   b. Working cooperatively with others as part of a team
   c. Problem solving
   d. Counseling
   e. Negotiation
   f. Obtaining and keeping clients
   g. Networking within the profession
   h. Mediation
   i. Strategic planning

---

14. JAMES M. KOUZES & BARRY Z. POSNER, THE LEADERSHIP CHALLENGE, 3d ed. 264 (Jossey-Bass, 2002) *citing* DANIEL GOLEMAN, WORKING WITH EMOTIONAL INTELLIGENCE (Bantam Books, 1998) (they say "Emotional intelligence is no passing fad" and assert its relevance to executive success and leadership).

15. Bryant G. Garth & Joanne Martin, *Law Schools and the Construction of Competence*, 43 J. LEGAL EDUC. 469 (1993).

16. John Sonsteng & David Camarotto, *Minnesota Lawyers Evaluate Law Schools, Training and Job Satisfaction*, 26 WM. MITCHELL L. REV. 327 (2000).

17. John O. Mudd & John W. LaTrielle, *Professional Competence: A Study of New Lawyers*, 49 MONT. L. REV. 11 (1988).

18. Stephen Gerst & Gerald Hess, *Professional Skills and Values in Legal Education: The GPS Model*, 43 VAL. U. L. REV. 513, 520–22, 524–40 (2009) (discussing the Phoenix School of Law's survey of area lawyers and description of subsequent development of professional skills and values course).

A Canadian study found that lawyers scored better than the norm in many areas: independence, stress management, problemsolving in particular, intrapersonal skills (self-reflection), and adaptability.[19] They scored even with the norm on stress management and general mood, which is unexpected based on studies showing greater levels of psychic distress among lawyers as compared to the general population. However, when "top stars" among the lawyers were assessed separately, distinct differences emerged.

- Top litigators scored much higher than all lawyers in **stress management, independence,** and **problemsolving.**
- Top dealmakers scored higher in **intrapersonal skills, general mood,** and **stress management.**
- Top women lawyers scored higher than their male counterparts in **interpersonal competencies** and **general mood.**

Therefore, the Canadian studies suggest that **top** lawyers excel in these areas:[20]

a. Intrapersonal skills (the ability to know and manage oneself, self-reflection)

b. Independence

c. Stress management

d. General mood

e. Interpersonal skills

f. Problem solving

These empirical studies support the importance of these skills, not just for comprehensive lawyers, but for all lawyers. The skills are also essential for leadership, according to Kouzes and Posner.[21] They group them into four quadrants, based on the "four fundamental capabilities" of "emotional intelligence" as explained by Goleman: "self-awareness, self-management, social awareness, and social skill."[22] These four quadrants are a good way to remember and summarize the skills in this chapter:

	Self	Social
Awareness	• Self-reflection • Countertransference • Identifying one's own emotions	• Active listening • Identifying emotions • Empathy • Rudimentary psychological sophistication
Management	• Self-control • Managing one's own emotions • Maturity • Judgment • Stress management	• Communicating basic & advanced empathy • Open and closed ended questioning • Confrontation • Maintaining boundaries • Making appropriate referrals

---

19. Irene E. Taylor, *Canada's Top 25 Corporate Litigators,* Lexpert Magazine, July 2002.

20. *Id.*

21. James M. Kouzes & Barry Z. Posner, The Leadership Challenge, 3d ed. 264 (Jossey-Bass, 2002).

22. *Id.* at 264–65, citing Daniel Goleman, *Leadership That Gets Results,* Mar–Apr 2000 Harv. Bus. Rev. 80, and Daniel Goleman, Working With Emotional Intelligence (Bantam Books, 1998).

Lawyers, judges, mediators, and other legal personnel can monitor their proficiency in these four areas by periodic self-assessments, asking questions such as: In what areas am I working well? In what areas might I benefit from additional training? In what areas did I recently demonstrate excellence (or deficiency), in a particular situation? Most importantly, while these skills are often developed through life experiences (the so-called "school of hard knocks") or sometimes seem to be innate, these skills *can* be learned and improved upon throughout one's lifetime.

Resources

There are many excellent, well-loved resources for interviewing, counseling, and negotiating skills; including:

Robert M. Bastress & Joseph D. Harbaugh, Interviewing, Counseling, and Negotiating: Skills for Effective Representation (Aspen Law & Business, 1990).

Roger S. Haydock, Peter B. Knapp, & Ann Juergens, Lawyering Skills: Interviewing, Counseling and Negotiation (West Publishing Company, 1995).

David A. Binder & Susan C. Price, Legal Interviewing and Counseling: A Client-Centered Approach (1977).

Roger Fisher, Bruce M. Patton & William L. Ury, Getting to Yes: Negotiating Agreement Without Giving In (Houghton Mifflin, 1981).

Newer resources focused explicitly on the vectors of the comprehensive law movement include:

Marjorie A. Silver, The Affective Assistance of Counsel (Carolina Academic Press, 2007) (Chapters 1–6, 10, 14–18).

Susan L. Brooks & Robert G. Madden, Relationship-Centered Lawyering: Social Science Theory for Transforming Legal Practice (Carolina Academic Press, 2010) (Chapters 3, 5–6).

Dennis P. Stolle, David B. Wexler, & Bruce J. Winick, Eds., Practicing Therapeutic Jurisprudence: Law as a Helping Profession (Carolina Academic Press, 2000) (designed for practicing lawyers as a guide to practicing law therapeutically) (Chapters 11–15 and pages 283–305).

Majorie A. Silver, *Love, Hate, and Other Emotional Interference in the Lawyer/Client Relationship,* 6 Clinical L. Rev. 259 (1999), in Dennis P. Stolle, David B. Wexler, & Bruce J. Winick, Eds., Practicing Therapeutic Jurisprudence: Law as a Helping Profession (Carolina Academic Press, 2000) (as Chapter 13).

Kate Paradine, *The Importance of Understanding Love and Other Feelings in Survivors' Experience of Domestic Violence,* 37 Ct. Rev. 40, 44 (Spring 2000).

Linda G. Mills, *Affective Lawyering: The Emotional Dimensions of the Lawyer-Client Relation,* in Dennis P. Stolle, David B. Wexler, & Bruce J. Winick, Eds., Practicing Therapeutic Jurisprudence: Law as a Helping Profession (Carolina Academic Press, 2000) (as Chapter 14).

These resources are focused on intrapersonal and interpersonal skills relevant to lawyers:

Douglas Stone, Bruce Patton, & Sheila Heen, Difficult Conversations: How To Discuss What Matters Most, 2d ed. (Penguin Books, 1999, 2010).

DAVID HALL, THE SPIRITUAL REVITALIZATION OF THE LEGAL PROFESSION (Edwin Mellen Press, 2005) (examines how to have a spiritual base in the practice of law).

Leonard L. Riskin, *The Contemplative Lawyer: On the Potential Contributions of Mindfulness Meditation to Law Students, Lawyers, and their Clients*, 7 HARV. NEGOT. L. REV. 1–66 (2002) (the seminal work by this world leader in the field of mindfulness meditation and law).

PATRICK LENCIONI, THE FIVE DYSFUNCTIONS OF A TEAM: A LEADERSHIP FABLE (Jossey-Bass, 2002) (providing valuable insight into leadership skills, teambuilding, and collaborative capabilities, which can be applied to lawyers).

JIM COLLINS, GOOD TO GREAT: WHY SOME COMPANIES MAKE THE LEAP ... AND OTHERS DON'T (2001) (describing the modern shift in corporate management from hierarchical, command-and-control to team- and humility-based leadership, among Fortune 500 corporations that prosper).

Coordination: Also read Silver (Chapters 1–6, 10, and 15–18), Brooks & Madden (Chapters 3, and 5–6), Stolle, et al. (Chapters 13–4), all of Macfarlane, and Wright (Chapter 5).

Chapter Assignments

Pre-Interview Exercise 4-1

In each of the following three vignettes, have someone role play the client and simply read the story, with feeling. Then, have another person identify the basic and advanced empathy emotions present and formulate a one-sentence empathic response to the client (with the most basic formulation being "You feel X because Y").

Vignette Scripts: Tom, Judy, and Jan

> *Tom:* "My name is Tom. I was diagnosed with inoperable throat cancer about 6 months ago. I am now in my 6th month of alternative cancer therapy and I'm doing really quite well. I think, though, that even though I don't think I'll need it, I should update my will. I have a daughter. I also have a best friend, and her daughter has been like a stepdaughter to me. Both girls are grown. I have a money market account and a car and house and that's about it for assets. I want to leave almost everything to my daughter, who really needs it, but the funny thing is, I've been closer to my best friend and her daughter than I have to my real family. Of course, there is no real rush on this. I just want to have all my bases covered, just in case."

> *Judy:* "My name is Judy. I need some help in tracking down my ex-husband. The child support hasn't been paid in two years. I had a restraining order put on him back when we got divorced, because he was abusive to me and the kids, so I've been afraid to deal with this until now. But now, my hours have been cut at work and I need the money. I think I can handle it if he shows up again at the house."

> *Jan:* "My name is Jan. Well, I want a divorce. I caught my husband having an affair with a man — can you believe it? It's the worst thing I could possibly imagine. I want to be divorced as soon as possible. We have two kids, 10 and 14 years old. I want the kids, the house, all the money, everything. I can't believe he could

do this to me and I want you to *make him pay*. I want you to nail him to the wall. I mean, the courts are going to *crucify* him for what he's done, right?"

Countertransference Exercise 4-2

Analyze what occurred in each one of these vignettes, presented by Marjorie A. Silver and Linda Mills in pages 377–79, 400, 419, 424, 428, and 439 of the book, Dennis P. Stolle, David B. Wexler, & Bruce J. Winick, Eds., Practicing Therapeutic Jurisprudence: Law as a Helping Profession (Carolina Academic Press, 2000). You may want to read Chapters 13 & 14 of this book in their entirety, as well. (If you do not have this book, think of some client interviews you have seen.)

> Client 1 — **Belle p. 377** — This criminal lawyer becomes enamored with the client and thus experiences inappropriate feelings of love or positive countertransference. As a result, the lawyer urges the client to go to trial, perhaps wrongly believing her case was stronger than it was, and refuses to accept a plea bargain offer from the prosecution. The result is that she gets twice the sentence she would have gotten under the plea bargain. Why does this occur?

Perhaps the lawyer is bored or unhappy in his marriage and this woman is thus exciting and attractive to him. How can you prevent this from occurring in your own law practice?

> Client 2 — **Carl p. 378** — This lawyer is irritated by the client and thus experiences inappropriate frustration with and dislike of the client, or negative countertransference. As a result, the lawyer urges the client to take a plea bargain despite the client's claim of innocence. This lawyer actually does emotional violence to the client by yelling at him for crying and telling him to grow up and act like a man. Why?

Perhaps the client reminds the lawyer of his own son, who the lawyer perceives as weak. Perhaps the lawyer is frustrated that his own son cries easily and wishes he could force his son to be tougher. How can you prevent this from happening in your own law practice?

> Client 3 — **Versie Hawkins p. 424** — This lawyer unwittingly elicits a suicide history from the client, near the very end of their interview, that ends up being the fact that tips the scales in favor of winning her disability claim (which had previously been denied for many years) for her. The lawyer here pauses to ask, "Is there anything else you have not told me?" (Note how this is a nice open-ended question likely to elicit more information.) Then, when the client responds with an ambiguous, "I've tried to finish things, get it all over," the lawyer does not dismiss or ignore this response. Instead, she follows up with another open-ended probe or question, asking "What do you mean?" which propels the client to disclose an 8-year history of emotional impairment (suicidal thoughts). This history is the critical fact that allows the lawyer to finally win the case for the client. What went right?

What could have happened instead, and why would it have happened?

How can you use this vignette in your own law practice to be a better lawyer?

> Client 4 — **John p. 428** — This lawyer terrorizes the client by ruthless interrogation, e.g., "grilling the witness." As a result, the client decides not to hire the lawyer or even accept a referral to another lawyer, despite a potentially winning

claim. The lawyer admits that she did this because she was operating to satisfy her agenda. She had decided that she needed to put the client through as ruthless an interrogation as the judge or opposing counsel might in court, she needed to see how he would look and respond when she interrogated him at his hearing (to see if his claim would be successful), and she needed to meticulously and persistently gather information. She also later admits negative countertransference — she didn't like this client because he reminded her of someone in her family who she disliked. She was also worried about trying to appear competent to this bright man who was her age peer. She felt that her status as an attorney permitted her secretly to test him in the name of good lawyering, but it backfired and alienated the client to the point that he did not hire her as a lawyer. How can you prevent this from happening in your own law practice?

Client 5 — Michelle p. 439 — In this script, the lawyer takes the reader through an initial client interview in a domestic violence clinic, pausing to insert her inner thoughts and feelings and strategies as the interview progressed. What went right?

What lawyer skills were utilized to improve the overall outcome?

What went wrong? Why?

How often do you pause, when interviewing someone, and silently reflect on your next move, your reactions, and your options, before responding?

Initial Client Interview Observation Exercise 4-3

Here are the typical tasks or goals of an initial client interview, along with their intended functions:

1. Icebreaking at first — builds relationship

2. Empathy and active listening in early part of the interview — builds relationship

3. Judicious use of open and closed questions to direct interview where you want it to go at times, other times let client tell the story — gathers information

   (Be aware that when you use closed questions or directive questions, it may shut client's flow of information down [this may be desirable, or not].)

4. As the interview proceeds, at some point stop and summarize the facts and identify the legal issues and extralegal issues. Begin to move towards identification of the problems and begin to provide your tentative or interim solutions to those problems, or say "I will have to research that and get back to you" — builds client's confidence in you, builds relationship, solidifies information gathering, begins advice and counsel role

5. Provide information and options to the client. Make your assessment, alone or with the client — builds client's confidence in you, furthers advice and counsel role

6. Summarize the interview, discuss options for future, discuss fees, costs, and attorney client relationship (retainer agreement, confidentiality), make assignments for next meeting — business matters and agenda for next meeting[23]

---

23. Summarized from Robert M. Bastress & Joseph D. Harbaugh, Interviewing, Counseling, and Negotiating: Skills for Effective Representation (Aspen Law & Business, 1990) and Roger S. Haydock, Peter B. Knapp, & Ann Juergens, Lawyering Skills: Interviewing, Counseling and Negotiation (West Publishing Company, 1995).

First, watch a video or simulation of an initial client interview. While you are watching, place a checkmark on the sheet, below, every time you observe the attorney exhibiting one of these moves, strategies, or behaviors. Think about the purpose for which the attorney is using them. How well are they received by the client?

Feedback Sheet for Initial Client Interviews

Put a checkmark each time you see the skill exercised by the interviewer/attorney:

Active Listening (restate facts):

Basic Empathy (restate explicit feelings):

Advanced Empathy (restate implicit feelings):

Closed-Ended Questions (yes/no answer):

Open-Ended Questions (not a yes/no answer):

Educate Client:

Competence Building/Educating Client About Attorney's Expertise:

Problemsolving/Exercising Judgment About Options:

Developing Action Plan For Future:

Advise/Suggest/Direct:

Self-Disclosure Re: Topic:

Business Matters (Fees, Costs, Retainer Agreement, Confidentiality):

Describe what the interviewer did that worked or was particularly good:

_____

_____

Other comments or suggestions:

_____

_____

_____

_____

Initial Client Interview Role-Play Exercise 4-4

Split into groups of three. Assign one person to play the role of the client, one to play the role of an attorney, and the third person to play the role of an observer. The "client" will play one of the three roles (Tom, Jan, or Judy) in the Vignette Scripts provided earlier in this Chapter, in the Pre-Interview Exercise, in the context of a simulated initial client interview. The "lawyer" will interview the "client" for about 15–20 minutes using the self-knowledge and communications skills outlined in this chapter. During this interview, the observer will place a checkmark on the rating sheet, above, every time he or she observes a particular behavior, strategy, or move being displayed by the attorney. When the interview is over, the observer will debrief the attorney, by showing him or her the rating sheet and discussing his or her observations with the attorney as to the effectiveness and effect of the attorney's responses to the client. The client will also debrief the attorney by disclosing what effects the attorney's various moves had on the client's attitudes, emotions, and overall experience in this simulated interview. If there is time, you may switch roles so that another person in the group has a chance to play an attorney.

Specific Instructions: Feel free to stop the action (press "Pause") and discuss what is happening in the interview, off the record, and then restart the action (press "Play") and finish the interview, as many times as you like. Be prepared to perform your rehearsed interview in front of all the other groups, afterwards. Feel free to practice your interview as many times as you like in preparation for this performance, later. Ask any questions you like as you work through this exercise.

Observers: The observer's job is to keep track of what type of responses the attorney makes and how often and how effective his or her choices are. After each interview is over, the observer will "debrief," meaning provide feedback to, the attorney about what he or she observed, what worked and what didn't, and then check out his or her perceptions with the "client" for accuracy. You also should serve as timekeeper, to make sure the interview does not exceed 20 minutes. Debriefing should take no more than 15 minutes.

Clients: Simply read the Vignette Script given to you and act out this client for the interview. Assume that this is an initial meeting with the attorney and that all you've done on the phone with his or her receptionist is make an appointment to see the attorney. Monitor the way you feel during the interview (comfortable, uncomfortable, unsure, intimidated, encouraged, affirmed, etc.) so that you can tell the attorney in the debriefing what effect his or her interactions had on you.

Attorneys: Assume that this is an initial meeting with the client and that all the client has done so far is make an appointment to see you. Assume that you are competent to handle the case. Debriefing will follow each interview. Each interview should take no more than 20 minutes. If you get stuck, feel free to call a "time out," meaning suspend the interview and call on others or ask the observer for help with the law or strategy.

Chapter 5

Vector 1 — Therapeutic Jurisprudence[1]

Description

Therapeutic jurisprudence ("TJ") emerged around 1990 and now is represented by more than a thousand articles and eighteen books. Its co-founders, law professors David Wexler and Bruce Winick, often define it by quoting law professor Christopher Slobogin's definition of TJ: "the use of social science to study the extent to which a legal rule or practice promotes the psychological or physical well-being of the people it affects."[2] Therapeutic jurisprudence explicitly acknowledges, like it or not, that law, legal personnel, and legal procedures have psychological effects upon the individuals and groups involved in each legal matter. According to Professors Wexler and Winick, it asks, "whether the law's antitherapeutic consequences can be reduced, and its therapeutic consequences enhanced, without subordinating due process and other justice values."[3] It acknowledges that law is a social force with inevitable if unintended consequences for the mental health and psychological functioning of those it affects. It proposes to study law and legal processes using the tools of social science research to evaluate and critique law and legal processes and, based on these insights, it suggests law reforms to "minimize anti-therapeutic consequences and to facilitate achievement of therapeutic ones."[4]

Because it grew out of an interdisciplinary, law, and psychology viewpoint, they explain that TJ was first applied to traditional mental health law topics such as "the civil commitment of the mentally ill, the insanity defense, and incompetency in both civil and criminal contexts."[5] TJ has rapidly grown and spread into many other areas that include

---

1. This Chapter reprints portions of the author's 2006 article, Susan Daicoff, *Law as a Healing Profession: The "Comprehensive Law Movement,"* 6 Pepperdine Disp. Resol. J. 1 (2006). It also incorporates material from Susan Daicoff & David B. Wexler, *Chapter 26: Therapeutic Jurisprudence*, in Comprehensive Handbook of Psychology: Volume 11: Forensic Psychology (Alan M. Goldstein, ed., John Wiley & Sons, Inc., 2003) (adapted for use in Chapters 5–7) Copyright © 2003, John Wiley & Sons, Inc. Reprinted with permission of John Wiley & Sons, Inc.

2. David B. Wexler & Bruce J. Winick, Eds., Law in a Therapeutic Key xvii (Carolina Academic Press, 1996) [hereinafter Wexler & Winick, Key], in part quoting Christopher Slobogin, *Therapeutic Jurisprudence: Five Dilemmas to Ponder,* 1 Psych., Pub. Pol. & L. 193 (1995) (reprinted in Wexler & Winick, Key, *supra* this note, at 775).

3. Wexler & Winick, Key, *supra* note 2, at xvii.

4. Dennis P. Stolle, David B. Wexler, Bruce J. Winick & Edward A. Dauer, *Integrating Preventive Law and Therapeutic Jurisprudence: A Law and Psychology Based Approach to Lawyering,* 34 Cal. W. L. Rev. 15, 16 (1997), reprinted in Dennis P. Stolle, David B. Wexler, & Bruce J. Winick, Eds., Practicing Therapeutic Jurisprudence: Law as a Helping Profession 7 (Carolina Academic Press, 2000).

5. Wexler & Winick, Key, *supra* note 2, at xix.

the civil commitment of sexual offenders and outpatient drug abusers. TJ has also reached sentencing and probation agreements, workers' compensation law, sexual orientation law and disability law, fault-based tort compensation schemes, domestic violence, crime victims, mandatory child abuse reporting, contract law,[6] and family law.[7] TJ has even explored the therapeutic consequences of practicing law upon lawyers.[8]

Importantly, therapeutic jurisprudence seeks to optimize the therapeutic effects of substantive rules of law, legal personnel's actions, and legal processes without elevating therapeutic concerns over traditional legal concerns such as rights or due process. It simply says, given two different options for achieving a particular legal result, if one option is more therapeutic than the other, the lawyer should attempt to pursue the more therapeutic course of action.

TJ has been applied to employment law to argue that the Americans with Disabilities Act's provision requiring confidentiality of employee claims made pursuant to the Act is countertherapeutic.[9] Confidentiality deprives the claiming employee's coworkers of an opportunity to assist and cooperate in designing and implementing reasonable accommodations for the employee's disability. Coworker assistance and participation can reduce resentment towards the accommodated employee, increase social support for the accommodation and the accommodated employee, and maintain or increase overall workplace morale.

TJ has also been applied to the United States military's policy on homosexuality of "don't ask, don't tell and don't pursue"[10] to demonstrate the policy's countertherapeutic aspects. Under this policy, the armed services do not require applicants to disclose whether they are homosexual or bisexual. The military will not discharge homosexual members unless homosexual conduct is engaged in, but making a statement that one is homosexual or bisexual constitutes "homosexual conduct." Thus, a member of the armed forces who states that he or she is gay or bisexual can be discharged from military service. However, no investigations or inquiries will be conducted solely to determine a member's sexual orientation.[11] From a TJ perspective, Kay Kavanagh argues that this policy is countertherapeutic for homosexual service members because, while it allows them to be homosexual, it requires them to refrain from discussing their sexual orientation. It requires deception and prevents them from talking about activities that would raise a presumption that they are engaging in homosexual acts. For example, they cannot discuss with whom they spent the weekend, from whom they are receiving a phone call, etc. This sets them apart from their colleagues and forces them to be emotionally distant and isolated from their co-workers.[12] It reduces the social support available to gay service mem-

---

6. *Id.* at xvii, xix, and Table of Contents.

7. Barbara A. Babb, *An Interdisciplinary Approach to Family Law Jurisprudence: Application of an Ecological and Therapeutic Perspective*, 72 IND. L. J. 775 (1997) (proposing an interdisciplinary approach to resolving family law issues).

8. Amiram Elwork, Ph.D. & G. Andrew H. Benjamin, Ph.D., J.D., *Lawyers in Distress*, 23 J. PSYCHIATRY & L. 205 (1995).

9. Rose Daly-Rooney, *Designing Reasonable Accommodations Through Co-Worker Participation: Therapeutic Jurisprudence and the Confidentiality Provision of the Americans with Disabilities Act*, 8 J.L. & HEALTH 89 (1994).

10. Kay Kavanagh, *Don't Ask, Don't Tell: Deception Required, Disclosure Denied*, 1 PSYCHOL., PUB. POL'Y & L. 142 (1995) (reprinted in Wexler & Winick, KEY, *supra* note 2, at 343).

11. Kavanagh, *supra* note 10, in Wexler & Winick, KEY, *supra* note 2, at 346–50.

12. Wexler & Winick, KEY, *supra* note 2, at 352–356.

bers, causes constant strain and tension in maintaining secrecy, causes distressing isolation, and lowers self-esteem due to inauthenticity.[13]

TJ asks lawyers to beware of "psycho-legal soft spots," which are, according to Bruce Winick, areas "in which certain legal issues, procedures, or interventions may produce or reduce anxiety, distress, anger, depression, hard or hurt feelings, and other dimensions of [emotional] ... well-being."[14] They can be psychological pitfalls, fallout, or opportunity spots, positive or negative. They explicitly recognize factors in a client's affairs that may give rise to future legal or psychological trouble, e.g., social relationships or emotional issues that ought to be considered in order to avoid conflict or stress when contemplating the use of a particular legal move or document. They explicitly acknowledge that certain legal moves create emotional distress or rifts.

For example, elderly clients may present developmental, end-of-life, health, and family relationship concerns. Clients with terminal cancer or HIV/AIDS may present needs relating to the dying process, the emotional stages of grief, and family relationships. Personal injury clients may display anger, depression, and a desire for revenge. Their anger can be misdirected onto the lawyer. They may need the opportunity to "tell their story" and be "heard." They may need to hear an apology from the defendant or need help to avoid becoming emotionally "stuck" in the grief process. Domestic violence victims may need extra understanding and support, suffer from low self-esteem, and have ambivalent feelings towards the offender. A lawyer or judge who insists that a domestic violence victim be completely finished with the relationship, or, at the other extreme, one who buys into the victim's denial and justification, can be countertherapeutic. For example, Kate Paradine relates a case in which the lawyer told the victim that the perpetrator was behaving poorly because he "still loves you," at a time when she said she most needed to hear, "You don't have to put up with that behavior."[15] Alcohol or drug dependent clients are likely to display denial, rationalization, and resistance and they are prone to relapse. A TJ lawyer considers the effects of these potential issues, includes them in lawyer-client discussions, and considers them in developing, with the client, a course of action that is most likely to have the desired legal *and* therapeutic outcome.

TJ recognizes the often-devastating effects of protracted, costly, and adversarial litigation as a "psycho-legal soft spot" and sometimes, therefore, seeks nonlitigation alternatives for certain clients. For example, it is a known phenomenon that doctors are more likely to either commit malpractice or have another malpractice action filed against them in the six months following the filing of a malpractice suit against them.[16] For this reason, a TJ defense lawyer might use this social science insight to recommend a nonlitigated, immediate settlement of his or her client's *first* malpractice case to minimize the effect of this phenomenon on the doctor's medical practice.

In cases where ongoing relationships are key, a nonlitigated settlement may preserve the interpersonal relationships between the parties and lead to a better overall outcome.

---

13. *Id.*

14. Bruce J. Winick, *The Expanding Scope of Preventive Law*, 3 Fla. Coastal Sch. L.J. 189, 195 n.15 (2002).

15. Kate Paradine, *The Importance of Understanding Love and Other Feelings in Survivors' Experience of Domestic Violence*, 37 Ct. Rev. 40 (Spring 2000).

16. Edward A. Dauer et al., *Transformative Power: Medical Malpractice Mediations May Help Improve Patient Safety*, ABA Disp. Resol. 9 (Spring, 1999) (reviewing successful pilot malpractice mediation programs in Massachusetts and Toronto). One wonders if perhaps the doctors' confidence is shaken and they become more prone to either mistakes or lawsuits as a result of the initial filing.

For example, a tenured professor who sues his or her school for gender discrimination may desire to continue working there, post-lawsuit. A mediated resolution might preserve a better future working relationship for employee and employer and thus a better outcome for all involved, in the long run.

Litigation itself, however, can at times be therapeutic. In cases that present a significant power imbalance between the parties, such as a sexual harassment suit where the employer is intractable, arrogant, and self-righteous and where the employee has a long history of victimization, litigation may be the most therapeutic process for both parties. It could allow the plaintiff to assert himself or herself, perhaps for the first time. It would also give the employer a terrific "wake up call" which might force it to reassess its treatment of its employees and make some positive changes.

TJ is probably the most visible and prolific vector, at least in academic and judicial circles. It has rapidly spread to all areas of the law and has been enthusiastically adopted by American judges in the form of "problem solving courts" (see Chapter 15, *infra*). It is perhaps most vibrant, however, when it is used in conjunction with preventive law; more detailed information about the uses of TJ will be presented after Chapter 6, on preventive law.

Example

Suppose that a mental health patient is involuntarily civilly committed to a long-term treatment center for chemical dependency. Suppose also that this patient has the legal right to receive a certain standard of care[17] and is not receiving that care. The lawyer representing this patient as a client might well proceed to bring legal action against the treatment center in order to force the center to provide more appropriate care for the client. However, the lawyer could either: (1) do this with the collaboration of and input from the client's treatment team, consisting probably of a unit director, psychiatrist, psychiatric nurse, and social worker or mental health counselor and maybe even with the involvement of and input from the client's family; or (2) do this alone with the client, following the client's wishes. The legal result may be the same in both situations; the client gets his or her legal standard of treatment care.

However, suppose that this particular client has been hospitalized many times before and is quite belligerent and resistant to treatment. The client's treatment team views the client's efforts to secure an attorney as simply more evidence of the client's resistance to treatment and, from a psychological perspective, as simply a diversion to allow the client to avoid making any real positive changes in his or her life. In the first scenario, the lawyer is more likely to accomplish the client's legal goal in a way that allows the treatment team to assist the client in gaining some psychological insights about why he or she is pursuing legal action. The lawyer and the treatment team might actually be able to collaborate to achieve the legal goal while making the process therapeutically meaningful for the client and thus enhancing his or her treatment. The lawyer in the second scenario is more likely to work at cross purposes to the treatment, actually becoming a distracting influence on the client, and hampering any real psychological progress the client is making in treatment.

---

17. Based on *Wyatt v. Stickney,* 344 F. Supp. 373 (M.D. Ala. 1972).

Given that both options are likely to achieve the same legal result, the TJ-oriented lawyer might encourage the client to allow him or her to pursue the first approach.[18]

Definitions and Key Points

Therapeutic jurisprudence has been defined by Slobogin as: "the use of social science to study the extent to which a legal rule or practice promotes the psychological or physical well-being of the people it affects."[19]

TJ explicitly acknowledges, like it or not, that law, legal personnel, and legal procedures have psychological effects upon the individuals and groups involved in each legal matter. It asks whether the law's countertherapeutic consequences can be minimized and its therapeutic consequences maximized without subordinating due process and other legal rights.[20]

According to Winick, "psycho-legal soft spots" are areas "in which certain legal issues, procedures, or interventions may produce or reduce anxiety, distress, anger, depression, hard or hurt feelings, and other dimensions of [emotional] ... well-being."[21]

Litigation itself, however, can at times be therapeutic.

Resources

There are over 1500 sources listed in the bibliography of the website of the International Network on Therapeutic Jurisprudence, below. These are just a few:

Dennis P. Stolle, David B. Wexler, & Bruce J. Winick, Eds., Practicing Therapeutic Jurisprudence: Law as a Helping Profession (Carolina Academic Press, 2000) (Chapters 1–4, 8–12, 15).

Marjorie A. Silver, The Affective Assistance of Counsel (Carolina Academic Press, 2007) (Chapters 11–14).

Susan L. Brooks & Robert G. Madden, Relationship-Centered Lawyering: Social Science Theory for Transforming Legal Practice (Carolina Academic Press, 2010) (Chapter 1).

David B. Wexler, Therapeutic Jurisprudence: The Law as a Therapeutic Agent (Carolina Academic Press, 1990) (introducing the concept of TJ).

David B. Wexler & Bruce J. Winick, Essays in Therapeutic Jurisprudence (Carolina Academic Press, 1991) (a collection of essays applying TJ to various areas of the law).

---

18. This hypothetical is a composite of situations encountered by the author in her capacity as a former mental health therapist in a substance abuse treatment center and contained in the "Mr. A" case study in Robert D. Miller, Gary J. Maier, Frederick W. Blancke and Dennis Doren, *Litigiousness as a Resistance to Therapy,* in David Wexler, Therapeutic Jurisprudence: The Law as a Therapeutic Agent 332–35 (Carolina Academic Press, 1990).

19. Christopher Slobogin, *Therapeutic Jurisprudence: Five Dilemmas to Ponder,* 1 Psych., Pub. Pol. & L. 193 (1995) (reprinted in Wexler & Winick, Key, *supra* note 2, at 775).

20. Wexler & Winick, Key, *supra* note 2, at xvii.

21. Bruce J. Winick, *The Expanding Scope of Preventive Law,* 3 Fla. Coastal Sch. L.J. 189, 195 n.15 (2002).

DAVID B. WEXLER & BRUCE J. WINICK, LAW IN A THERAPEUTIC KEY: DEVELOPMENTS IN THERAPEUTIC JURISPRUDENCE (Carolina Academic Press, 1996) (adding to the 1991 collection and extending the application of TJ to new areas, such as employment law).

Bruce J. Winick, David B. Wexler & Edward A. Dauer, *Preface—A New Model for the Practice of Law*, 5 PSYCHOL. PUB. POL'Y & L. 795 (1999).

Christopher Slobogin, *Therapeutic Jurisprudence: Five Dilemmas to Ponder*, 1 PSYCHOL. PUB. POL'Y. & L. 193 (1995).

DAVID B. WEXLER & BRUCE J. WINICK, REHABILITATING LAWYERS: PRINCIPLES OF THERAPEUTIC JURISPRUDENCE FOR CRIMINAL LAW PRACTICE (Carolina Academic Press, 2008).

BRUCE J. WINICK & DAVID B. WEXLER, JUDGING IN A THERAPEUTIC KEY: THERAPEUTIC JURISPRUDENCE AND THE COURTS (Carolina Academic Press, 2003).

Websites

Website of the International Network on Therapeutic Jurisprudence: http://www.therapeutic jurisprudence.org (last visited July 11, 2010) and http://www.law.arizona.edu/depts/upr-intj (last visited July 11, 2010).

Coordination: Also read Brooks & Madden (Chapter 1), Stolle, et al. (Chapters 1–3 and 15), Wright (p. 43–46) and King (Chapter 2).

Chapter 6

Vector 2 — Preventive Law[1]

Description

Preventive law ("PL") is perhaps the oldest vector of the movement. Preventive law emerged in the 1950s, although its founder, attorney and law professor Louis Brown, conceived of it in the 1930s. Its 1978 casebook, *Planning by Lawyers*, was revised and republished as a preventive law textbook in 1997.[2] The *Preventive Law Reporter* has been published since 1982.[3]

Preventive law is "a branch of law that endeavors to minimize the risk of litigation or to secure more certainty as to legal rights and duties."[4] It seeks to minimize potential legal liability and enhance legal opportunities. It believes preventing lawsuits is less costly than litigation and attempts to avoid or prevent litigation before it arises. As a lens, preventive law asks what measures can be put in place to prevent future litigation or future legal problems. It takes a proactive approach and allows the attorney to intervene in clients' lives before problems arise. By anticipating disputes before they arise, planning ahead, and intervening to prevent legal problems whenever possible, the lawyer serves the client's interests in a proactive, albeit nontraditional, way. The client may be spared the traumatizing effects of a litigated confrontation with another person or legal entity. Preventive law also considers the fact that some interpersonal relationships, such as husband-wife or employer-employee, may endure long after the current difficulty has passed, and a solution that irreparably ruptures the bond may lead to future legal problems and thus be really no solution at all. The emphasis in preventive law is on a good, ongoing lawyer-client relationship, open communication, and the prevention of legal disputes. It is a client centered approach, involving the lawyer and client in a joint decisionmaking process. It focuses on long term legal health instead of matter by matter analysis and utilizes legal "check-ups" for updates and planning with the client.

Check Ups and Audits

The lawyer can suggest that the client come in for annual or regular "check-ups" or "audits" to determine if there are any "soft spots" in the client's affairs. These soft spots

---

1. This Chapter incorporates portions of (and expands on) the author's 2006 article, Susan Daicoff, *Law as a Healing Profession: The "Comprehensive Law Movement,"* 6 Pepperdine Disp. Resol. J. 1 (2006).

2. Robert M. Hardaway, Preventive Law: Materials on a Non Adversarial Legal Process (2d ed. 1997) (the "textbook" for preventive law).

3. The first volume of the Preventive Law Reporter was published in July 1982 (Butterworth Legal Publishers) by the National Center for Preventive Law (U.S.), University of Denver, College of Law.

4. *See* Edward D. Re, *The Lawyer as Counselor and the Prevention of Litigation* 31 Cath. U.L. Rev. 685, 692 (1995), *citing* Webster's 3d New Intl. Dictionary 1798 (1961).

are situations which might lead to litigation and where the lawyer may be able to intervene early to put measures in place to prevent litigation from occurring. An audit might be a one-time overall evaluation of the client's affairs; checkups might be regular reviews for the same purposes.

For example, a preventive employment law attorney might assess a corporate client's employee policies and procedures manual and practices in order to assess whether the corporation has any potential exposure to harassment or discrimination suits. Then, the PL lawyer would put into place policies and procedures, perhaps including some in-service training, if any "legal soft spots" emerged as a result of the lawyer's "audit." Periodic "check ups" would be performed with the client in the future to intervene proactively with any troubled employee/employer situations.

Rewind and Fast Forward Techniques

Preventive law also uses the "rewind technique" and the "fast forward technique" to identify legal soft spots—potential legal problems that might arise in the future. The rewind technique evaluates current legal disputes or even reported cases to glean wisdom about how to prevent lawsuits. It asks, "if this situation were rewound back in time, what could have been done in an attorney's office to have prevented this lawsuit from arising?" The "fast forward" technique fast forwards a situation in time to evaluate whether there is any litigation potential in the future that may be avoided by taking preventive measures, today.

Example: Rewind

For example, in the often-used first-year contract case *Shell Oil Co. v. Nanakuli*,[5] the lawsuit arose because Shell underwent a corporate reorganization during the oil crisis of the 1970s and made a resultant change in personnel handling its asphalt supply contracts with its customers in Hawaii. Nanakuli was an asphalt paving contractor in Hawaii (a small market) and was one of these customers. Shell had been "price protecting" Nanakuli, meaning protecting it from price increases occurring between the time of order of the asphalt and the time Shell delivered it to Nanakuli, but their written contract clearly stated otherwise. When Shell reorganized, the new corporate managers enforced the written contracts as written and refused to continue "price protecting" Nanakuli, even though there was an oral tradition or policy of price protection between Shell and Nanakuli and in the asphalt paving trade in Hawaii, with respect to orders used to fulfill fixed-price contracts with governmental entities. Nanakuli expected the old policy of price protection to continue; Shell expected to be able to rely on the express terms of its written contract with Nanakuli.[6] Shell sent a letter to all of its customers indicating that it would no longer

---

5. Nanakuli Paving and Rock Co. v. Shell Oil Co., Inc., 664 F.2d 772, 32 UCC Rep.Serv. 1025 (9th Cir. 1981).

6. *Id.* at 786 (due to a "big organizational change at Shell in 1973 ... the philosophy toward asphalt pricing changed, [and] apparently no one was left who was knowledgeable about the peculiarities of the Hawaiian market or about Shell's long-time relations with Nanakuli or its 1969 agreement, beyond the printed contract").

"price protect" them; however, Nanakuli's officers believed the letter did not apply to them, as they believed they had an "understanding" with Shell for a special arrangement.[7]

The rewind technique would rewind this situation back in time to assess whether preventive measures could have been put into place, before the corporate reorganization of Shell, to prevent this lawsuit. For example, perhaps the management of Shell might have more carefully evaluated its contractual obligations to price protect Nanakuli based on course of performance and trade usage. Perhaps, if Shell chose to discontinue price protection, Shell could have had a more personal conference with the Nanakuli officers to discuss an orderly transition to the new "deal." Shell could have communicated its intentions to Nanakuli more directly and effectively. Since Nanakuli did not think Shell's letter applied to them, perhaps Shell could have arranged a face to face conference or written an individualized letter to Nanakuli, followed by an in person or telephone confirmation to discuss their future contractual dealings.

PL has been applied to copyright and entertainment law[8] and to end-of-life issues.[9] In both of these applications, a preventive lawyer started with a reported case, litigation by the band, Guns N' Roses, over the copyright of a song, and the Terry Schiavo case, respectively, and rewound them to ask how a lawyer might have set up a different plan to avoid the resultant litigation. For example, in the song ownership litigation, the preventive lawyer identified a graduated list of steps the plaintiff could have taken to protect his ownership claim in the song, early on, at the time that the song was actually composed. One of these steps is the filing of a copyright claim with the United States Copyright Office, but less positional options are simply writing a letter to the band members, claiming his ownership interest in the song, or documenting conversations between the plaintiff and the band about the ownership rights to the song. A preventive entertainment lawyer could have proposed any or all of these steps to the song composer, at the time that the song was created, to perhaps better establish his position and avoid the later litigation.

Example: Fast Forward

Dean Emeritus Edward Dauer gives this example:[10] Suppose a mature gentleman comes to see a lawyer about issuing some new shares of stock in the family corporation to his son-in-law. It turns out that the amount of stock involved would allow the son-in-law to exercise some influence over the direction of the business. In discussing the client's intentions, the lawyer realizes there are numerous risks the client may not have considered. Any competent lawyer would investigate the statutory, regulatory, and tax liability implications of the transaction, as well as issues of voting control, percentage ownership, and buy-sell agreements. Preventive law would take the additional steps of anticipating and pre-empt-

---

7. *Id.* ("the letter was addressed to 'Gentlemen' with Nanakuli's name typed in at the top; it was apparently addressed to all Shell's Hawaiian customers. . . . Nanakuli officials testified that they did not believe the letter was applicable to its unusual situation of already having a long-term contract with Shell").

8. Chiara St. Pierre, unpublished senior thesis, Florida Coastal School of Law, April, 2008.

9. Bruce J. Winick, *Symposium: The Schiavo Case: Interdisciplinary Perspectives—A Legal Autopsy of the Lawyering in Schiavo: A Therapeutic Jurisprudence/Preventive Law Rewind Exercise,* 61 U. MIAMI L. REV. 595 (April, 2007).

10. DENNIS P. STOLLE, DAVID B. WEXLER, & BRUCE J. WINICK, EDS., PRACTICING THERAPEUTIC JURISPRUDENCE 34–35 (Carolina Academic Press, 2000).

ing opportunities for conflict, dashed hopes, unfulfilled assumptions, and damaged relationships. If, for example, the client and his son-in law fail to get along after the stock is issued, their disagreements, frustrated expectations, and conflicting interests may result in shareholder deadlock or even civil litigation, impacting the family as well as the business. A fast forward technique might ask what is likely to happen if, three years in the future, the son-in-law and the father disagree over an important corporate matter or the son-in-law and daughter divorce. Careful deadlock planning and corporate document drafting might then be employed to address these concerns.

Going further, Dauer suggests that the preventive lawyer would ask the all-important question, "Why do you want to issue stock to your son-in-law?" (Note that this is an open ended question, designed to elicit information; it does not presuppose that the lawyer knows the answer.) The gentlemen then explains that his son-in-law has taken a path of which he does not approve, perhaps living in Boulder and eating but tofu and bean sprouts, and the father hopes to steer the young man into a more responsible, traditional lifestyle via a stock position and perhaps an employment position with the family business. Dauer reports that the lawyer would then say, "Ah!", and proceed with perhaps brainstorming with the father as to other options to achieve his goals that do not jeopardize his voting control of the corporation. Perhaps some alternative incentive scheme might be employed, for example.

Had the lawyer not asked the open ended question, "Why?" at the critical moment, however, this information might not have been elicited and the stock might simply have been issued. The client's stated objective might simply have been executed by the lawyer. This illustrates how important a close lawyer-client relationship is, in preventive law.

Concluding Thoughts

Some lawyers may protest that these examples simply illustrate "what good lawyers" already do, with every client. That may be the case and, if so, all is well with those lawyers. Some lawyers might benefit from taking an explicitly preventive approach with certain clients. Further, it may be helpful that preventive law has a vocabulary and set of clearly defined and named concepts (such as legal soft spots, rewind and fast forward techniques, audits, and check ups) that assist the lawyer in *intentionally* and explicitly practicing preventively, rather than leaving it to chance. They may also assist law students and new lawyers in consciously acquiring these "good lawyer" skills.

Critics have suggested that clients will not pay for what they perceive to be "extra," unnecessary legal fees generated by audits and checkups, when there is no legal crisis looming. However, corporate clients have been utilizing preventive law for years; they understand that it may be cheaper to pay a preventive lawyer than to wait and hire litigation counsel after the crisis has erupted.

Preventive law is perhaps the most easily accepted vector of the comprehensive law movement. If none of the other vectors appeals to you as a lawyer, this one vector may be the one "arrow" you can comfortably add to your "quiver" of legal skills and approaches you may use with various clients and cases. It is very useful in business law, corporate law, employment law, estate planning, and almost all transactional work. It is the theoretical basis for good contract, trust, and will drafting. The next Chapter explores the utility of the integration of preventive law with therapeutic jurisprudence, for practicing lawyers.

Definitions and Key Points

An ounce of prevention is worth a pound of cure.

Preventive law:

- Focuses on predicting legal disputes and avoiding or minimizing them before they occur
- Is analogous to preventive medicine
- Is skills-oriented

PL lawyers:

- Are proactive
- Emphasize planning, anticipating, and intervening in "legal soft spots"
- Value a good attorney-client relationship with open communication
- Try to preserve ongoing relationships
- Use "audits" and periodic "check-ups"
- Use the "rewind technique" and the "fast forward technique" to identify potential future legal problems

Resources

THOMAS D. BARTON, PREVENTIVE LAW AND PROBLEM SOLVING: LAWYERING FOR THE FUTURE (Vandenplas Publishing, 2009) (most recent PL book by the director of the National Center for Preventive Law; integrating PL with creative problem solving) (Chapters 4–8, 26).

Edward A. Dauer, *Preventive Law Before and After Therapeutic Jurisprudence*, in SUSAN L. BROOKS & ROBERT G. MADDEN, RELATIONSHIP-CENTERED LAWYERING: SOCIAL SCIENCE THEORY FOR TRANSFORMING LEGAL PRACTICE 50–63 (Carolina Academic Press, 2010) (in Chapter 1).

Bruce J. Winick, *The Expanding Scope of Preventive Law*, 3(2) FLA. COASTAL L. J. 189 (2002), in SUSAN L. BROOKS & ROBERT G. MADDEN, RELATIONSHIP-CENTERED LAWYERING: SOCIAL SCIENCE THEORY FOR TRANSFORMING LEGAL PRACTICE 57 (Carolina Academic Press, 2010) (in Chapter 1).

DENNIS P. STOLLE, DAVID B. WEXLER, & BRUCE J. WINICK, EDS., PRACTICING THERAPEUTIC JURISPRUDENCE: LAW AS A HELPING PROFESSION (Carolina Academic Press, 2000) (designed for practicing lawyers as a guide to practicing law therapeutically) (Chapters 1–6, 8, 9, 2–15).

Preventive Law Casebooks:

ROBERT M. HARDAWAY, PREVENTIVE LAW: MATERIALS ON A NONADVERSARIAL LEGAL PROCESS (Anderson Publishing Co. 1997) (a revision and update of preventive law founder Louis Brown's classic textbook on preventive law).

LOUIS M. BROWN & EDWARD A. DAUER, PLANNING BY LAWYERS: MATERIALS ON A NONADVERSARIAL LEGAL PROCESS (1977).

PETER WAHLGREN, ED., A PROACTIVE APPROACH: LAW LIBRARIES (SCANDINAVIAN STUDIES IN LAW) 109–128 (Stockholm, Sweden: Stockholm Institute for Scandinavian Law) (2006) (one of the contributors, Helena Haapio, is a Finnish corporate attorney and lecturer who presents preventive law as "proactive law").

GEORGE SIEDEL & HELENA HAAPIO, PROACTIVE LAW FOR MANAGERS: A HIDDEN SOURCE OF COMPETITIVE ADVANTAGE (Gower Pub. Co. 2010) (book on preventive law for corporate managers).

Preventive Law Website and Center:

The (Louis Brown) National Center for Preventive Law at California Western School of Law: www.preventivelawyer.com (last visited July 11, 2010).

Coordination: Also read Brooks & Madden (Chapter 1), Stolle, et al. (Chapters 1–3 and 6), Wright (p. 73) and King (Chapter 4).

Chapter Assignments

Exercise 6-1

Find a reported, litigated case that interests you. "Rewind" the situation back to a point in time at which intervention by a preventive lawyer, in his or her office, with one of the litigants, might have succeeded in preventing the later lawsuit. Explain what steps that preventive lawyer would have had to take, with the litigant as a client, to do so. Discuss the savings, in terms of financial or emotional resources, that would have resulted from such preventive action, if any.

Chapter 7

Vector 3 — The Integration of Therapeutic Jurisprudence and Preventive Law

Description[1]

Preventive law has been integrated with therapeutic jurisprudence, melding its processes and concepts with TJ's therapeutic goals, in order to provide a richer approach to practicing law.[2] This was particularly helpful, as each gave something to the other. TJ alone lacked practical procedures for law office application. PL alone lacked an analytical framework for justifying emotional wellbeing as one priority in legal planning. Therapeutic jurisprudence afforded preventive law a theoretical framework within which to evaluate and use various preventive law strategies, while preventive law gave therapeutic jurisprudence a set of concrete processes and skills to use in lawyering and adjudicating, to further TJ's goals and purposes.

The integration of TJ and PL, collectively referred to as therapeutically-oriented preventive law ("TOPL" or "TJ/PL"), merges the well-developed lawyering skills of PL with the psychological sophistication of TJ. From this integration developed the concept of lawyers foreseeing not just legal soft spots, but also "psycho-legal soft spots," and acting to prevent situations from occurring that were troublesome both legally and psychologically. To effectively practice TJ/PL, a lawyer must employ excellent communications skills and interpersonal sensitivity, as well as a familiarity with psychology.[3]

An analogy can be made to medical treatment: whereas traditional lawyering often intervenes at the point where the client has a "broken arm" and fixes it, a TJ/PL lawyer intervenes at the point in time where a client has, perhaps, "high blood pressure" which may lead to a more serious condition or crisis.

---

1. This chapter is adapted from Susan Daicoff, *Law as a Healing Profession: The "Comprehensive Law Movement,"* 6 PEPPERDINE DISP. RESOL. J. 1 (2006) and is used by permission.
2. Dennis P. Stolle, David B. Wexler, Bruce J. Winick & Edward A. Dauer, *Integrating Preventive Law and Therapeutic Jurisprudence*, 34 CAL. W. L. REV. 15 (1997).
3. Paragraph from Daicoff, *supra* note 1.

Practice Information

TJ/PL has a number of concepts or skills to be mastered:

Psycholegal soft spots are areas where the legal and psychological issues in the matter intersect. They can take one of several forms and can have negative or positive effects. For example, they can be a place where the legal issues cause or lead to psychological problems (negative impact), such as where a bitter, protracted divorce harms the children involved. Or, the law can create or result in improved psychological functioning (positive impact), such as where a disempowered, discriminated-against employee stands up for his or her rights and is vindicated by the courts against an intractable and violative employer.

They can also, however, be places where the psychology of the situation leads to legal problems (negative), such as where an employer is too fearful and nonassertive to deal effectively with a nonperforming employee and the pattern of nonassertiveness leads the employee to sue for arbitrary, wrongful termination when the employee is let go.

They can be places where the psychology leads to an improved legal outcome (positive), such as where rehabilitative efforts by a criminal defendant are persuasive and lead to a lighter sentence at formal sentencing.

They can also be situations where the psychology suggests taking a legal action that is not perhaps required, legally, but would be best emotionally (for example, a standby guardianship begun before death may be helpful to a terminally ill client who is the sole guardian of a minor child and who wants to name someone outside his or her immediate family as the child's guardian, upon death—it may provide more peace of mind to the client and facilitate a smoother transition, post-death, thus perhaps improving the mental status of all involved).

Finally, psycholegal soft spots can refer to "opportunity moments" when a lawyer, judge, or other legal personnel can have a positive impact on the parties involved in a legal matter, even when that impact does not have a legal effect. For example, in former judge Peggy Hora's Will Contest example, the judge was able to assist the plaintiff in progressing through the grief process and resolving his feelings of resentment towards his sister and deceased mother, when she chose to make an "extralegal" statement along with her ruling. She said something like, "I see no reason to contest the will here, there seems to be no undue influence. Given the relative financial situations of you and your sister, I understand why your mother might have divided her estate unequally. However, I do not think that it means that she loved you any less." Reportedly, the litigant cried upon hearing this legally irrelevant statement from a person of such authority as the judge.

Fast forwards, rewinds, checkups, and audits have all been described above in Chapter 6. It is helpful to have a nomenclature or taxonomy of TJ/PL "moves," as one learns to practice law in this way.

Examples

Here are a number of examples of cases in which a TJ/PL analysis and approach may be useful. Wexler and Winick have proposed that collecting cases and examples of TJ/PL in the law may be one of the most helpful ways of learning how to practice law and adjudicate cases from a TJ/PL approach.[4]

Sexual Harassment Example

Therapeutic jurisprudence/preventive law is particularly useful in the sexual harassment and discrimination law arena, as the area involves not only relationships between people, but can also involve the tender and delicate area of emotions, sexuality, and romance. TJ/PL has been applied to employment law in the area of accommodating employees with disabilities, for example.[5]

Facts

Imagine the following hypothetical case, facts and law, which have been excerpted from the author's 1999 article:[6]

Castaway Corporation hired Paula as a receptionist after the president of the company, Jackson, specifically took an interest in one of the applicants and convinced the hiring committee that she was the best candidate. He personally called her to offer her the job, told her he "really went to bat for her," was the first to greet her on her first day of work, and invited her to lunch shortly thereafter. In a few weeks, Jackson and Paula spent a great deal of time together during and after work and eventually their close working relationship developed into a consensual romance. During this time, Jackson frequently told Paula that he "saw a great future ahead for her in the company," her work performance was excellent, "you have to start at the bottom and work your way to the top," and "knowing people at the top" was critical to success. Within a year, Paula was promoted to the Assistant to the President position over several other candidates. This was a considerable wage, status, and responsibility increase for her. All the other candidates had a college education; Paula had a high school education. The position required close work with Jackson as the President, including business travel. Within three months of her promotion, however, Paula desired to end her personal relationship with Jackson. Although initially he was unwilling to end the relationship and continued to pursue her, after a few weeks he accepted her feelings and no longer made advances towards her. Shortly thereafter, Jackson approached Paula and asked her to step down as his assistant and return to her former receptionist position, stating that she was not able to meet the demands of the position of Assistant to the President. Jackson's position is that Paula never has been able to perform the duties required of the position, that he has been "covering for her" during the past few months (to the detriment of his own duties), and that other employees have been pressuring Jackson to demote or fire Paula because of her inadequacies. Paula's position is that the reassignment is a reprisal for her ending their romantic relationship and she has filed a claim for sexual harassment with the Equal Employment Opportunity Commission (EEOC).

---

4. Dennis P. Stolle, David B. Wexler, & Bruce J. Winick, Eds., Practicing Therapeutic Jurisprudence: Law as a Helping Profession 73–79 & 493–98 (Carolina Academic Press, 2000).

5. Rose Daly-Rooney, *Designing Reasonable Accommodations Through Co-Worker Participation: Therapeutic Jurisprudence and the Confidentiality Provision of the Americans with Disabilities Act*, 8 J.L. & Health 89 (1994).

6. This hypothetical, facts and law, are excerpted from Susan Daicoff, *Making Law Therapeutic For Lawyers: Therapeutic Jurisprudence, Preventive Law, and the Psychology of Lawyers*, 5 Psych., Pub. Pol'y. & Law 811 (1999). Copyright © 1999 by the American Psychological Association. Adapted with permission. The use of this information does not imply endorsement by the publisher.

In addition, Paula has experienced sexual relationships with superiors on the job before. She has a history of troubled relationships with men. She tends to defer to powerful males that she perceives as superior to her. She is a recovering alcoholic and drug abuser and has been clean and sober from alcohol and drugs for five years. Paula is about 35 years old and is attractive. She is divorced and has one child, a fifteen-year-old daughter. As part of her recovery from alcohol and drugs, she has had intermittent psychological counseling and at one time was taking antidepressant medication but has discontinued both at this time. She is angry, outraged, but not unreasonable. She wants and needs money since she is facing a demotion with a pay cut. She has bought a house and obligated herself on a mortgage based on her Assistant to the President position and its salary and now is afraid she will lose the house. She receives child support from her ex-husband for her daughter but it does not cover all of the child's expenses. She has never litigated before (her divorce ended in mediation). She believes she has an excellent case for sexual harassment, based on all the stories in the press in the past about inappropriate sexual relationships between employers and female subordinates. The Assistant to the President position is the best job, status and salary wise, that she has ever held. She also likes the company and likes working there.

Law

As applied to Paula's situation, the law provides as follows:

Sexual harassment is covered under Title VII of the Civil Rights Act of 1964 when it is a "term or condition of employment." There are two forms of sexual harassment: hostile work environment and quid pro quo. A hostile work environment is created by "unwelcome sexual advances, requests for sexual favors, and other verbal or physical conduct of a sexual nature." 29 C.F.R. § 1604.11(a)(3) (1997); see also Meritor Savings Bank, FSB v. Vinson, 477 U.S. 57, 106 S. Ct. 2399 (1986). Quid pro quo sexual harassment occurs when submission to sexual demands is made a condition of tangible employment benefits, 29 C.F.R. § 1604.11(a) (1997); for example, when an employer "conditions the granting of economic or job benefits upon the receipt of sexual favors from a subordinate, or punishes that subordinate for refusing to comply." Chamberlin v. 101 Realty, Inc. 915 F.2d 777 (1st Cir. 1990). Although making a case for a hostile work environment may not be impossible, it is unlikely because the sexual advances of Jack had ceased by the time of the lawsuit and her work environment had not become abusive or hostile in nature, Harris v. Forklift Sys., Inc., 510 U.S. 17, 114 S. Ct. 367 (1993) (terms and conditions of employment must be negatively affected by the employer's sexual activities before a hostile work environment can be established). Paula would be more likely to prevail on a claim for quid pro quo harassment. To make a claim for quid pro quo sexual harassment, Paula must show that her employer conditioned a tangible job benefit on her acquiescence to sexual favors. She would focus on the fact that she was promoted shortly after the beginning of her romantic relationship with Jackson and that she was demoted shortly after the end of the relationship. Castaway will in turn raise Paula's lack of credentials and poor work performance as legitimate business reasons for its actions. However, the timing of the duration of the relationship and the promotion and demotion are suspicious and might lead to a successful sexual harassment case. This case, however, is not clear-cut. It could be seen as simply a consensual sexual relationship the ending of which was unrelated to Paula's termination, which is not actionable, or as quid pro quo sexual harassment, which is.[7]

---

7. *Id.*

An employment lawyer would assess that Paula's case fell in the "gray area." Paula would have to file a complaint with the Equal Employment Opportunity Commission who would investigate Paula's case and issue a "right to sue" letter or dismiss her complaint. The EEOC might dismiss her case, finding that the advances were "not unwelcome" or that "no tangible job benefits were conditioned on assent to the advances" or that the situation simply does not rise to the level of "sexual harassment."

However, simply filing the complaint and pursuing this as a litigable claim may be fruitful, for Paula. She may be able to position herself to negotiate a settlement figure with the company, in exchange for not filing or dropping the complaint. The law gives Paula an incentive to bring a lawsuit and, at the very least, settle for some amount. Regardless of the fact that there are some "bad facts" working against her that would emerge at trial, she may be incentivized to at least proceed and try to obtain some compensation. Even a small settlement after filing a lawsuit may function as a reward.

TJ/PL Analysis

A therapeutic jurisprudence analysis of this case reveals the following: Paula has a pattern of behavior at the workplace that is disturbing. She has had similar difficulties in the past and they have negatively affected her employment success. She appears to be caught in a pattern of sexualizing relationships with male superiors on the job that may be gratifying in the short-term, but disastrous in the long-term. While the current lawsuit/complaint is at issue, a greater question is whether Paula would like to address and change this pattern of behavior, at this point in her life. It has been said that, for some people, a lawyer is the only mental health professional they will see. The TJ/PL lawyer might be prepared to discuss this pattern and her future employment plans with Paula, as she decides how to proceed in this matter. This conversation could be an "opportunity spot" for the lawyer to have a positive impact in Paula's life, even if a change in her behavior has no impact on her legal case against Castaway.

An academic TJ/PL analysis would recognize that the law may function untherapeutically when it (unintentionally) actually rewards Paula for engaging in this destructive pattern of behavior at yet another company. One might thus lobby to change sexual harassment and discrimination law to take these concerns into account. The law might be amended to remove the reward-for-destructive-behavior that is unwittingly contained in its current formulation and application.

Defense counsel, representing Castaway Corporation, also may be motivated to raise these issues with the plaintiff and her counsel, with the EEOC or the court, or with the legislature, with the intention of avoiding the antitherapeutic consequences of the law and avoiding liability on the part of the corporation.

The law's emphasis on consent, welcomeness, and consensuality does not adequately take into account the actual psychology behind cases like Paula's. The law does not encourage the plaintiff to address her pattern—it simply tells her that either: (1) she was victimized (therefore, she wins); or (2) she welcomed the behavior (therefore, she loses); or (3) even if she did not welcome the behavior, it either was not severe enough (this denigrates her experience, as it probably was distressing) or there were no tangible job benefits predicated on her assent to the behavior (which communicates that nothing can be done for you in this situation).

So the potential messages the law delivers are three-fold. Either:

1. *You win; you are not at fault, you have been wronged, others are to blame, you deserve compensation, you are the victim here. This may perpetuate a passive, victim*

role in life and encourage the individual to bring more lawsuits, in the future, when things go wrong;

2. *You lose; you asked for it. You are to blame for what happened. This perpetuates guilt and shame and does not adequately reflect the inner experience of the plaintiff. This can also perpetuate a defeatist attitude towards life; or*

3. *You are making too much of something that really bothered you and affected your job, so you are simply overly sensitive, perhaps histrionic, or melodramatic. Your experience at this job does not count, is not important, and is not weighty. This could also lead to feelings of hopelessness and personal powerlessness and also does not adequately reflect the inner experience of the plaintiff, who is likely to be distressed by the situation.*

All three of these potential outcomes of this case contain messages from the law that may be very antitherapeutic. What would be more helpful, perhaps, is something that encourages the plaintiff to examine whether she has a pattern of engaging in consensual sexual relationships with superiors on the job, take responsibility for her part, and become willing to end this pattern.

One possible solution is to move away from these "on-off" switches of liability/no liability based on "welcome/unwelcome," "consensual/nonconsensual," "tangible job benefits conditioned or not" in the law — and towards some type of comparative fault or apportionment of fault. This system of comparative fault would certainly rely on expert testimony about the relational dynamics involved, so that Paula's pattern of behavior would be admissible and relevant to liability, fault, and award. Compensation could be structured so that the amount of monetary compensation paid to the plaintiff was capped, or limited, so that the change did not result in more monetary compensation being paid out to plaintiffs than is paid under current law. However, unlike current law, monetary awards to plaintiffs would be reduced by an amount relative to their comparative percentage of fault. Perhaps rehabilitative efforts might be admissible and relevant in court or with the EEOC, so that if Paula voluntarily examined her behavior and took measures to change it, her legal position would be strengthened by these efforts.

However, sweeping changes to the law are not likely to be available quickly or easily to the practicing lawyer, nor are they always retroactively applied. A preventive lawyer representing Paula might have to work within the existing legal framework and at the same time help her identify this destructive pattern in the workplace so that these events do not reoccur in the future, with her next employer. Reframing the results and outcome of the matter, for Paula, so that the above destructive or negative messages are not internalized by her, might be very useful. Bruce Winick has written at length about how useful it can be for counsel to "reframe" or put into perspective the outcome of a case, for clients.[8] This is one possible example:

Cognitive Reframing Example: For example, Paula's counsel might say, at the conclusion of the case, "I'm sure this has been a very difficult and distressing time in your life and I know you have suffered as a result of what happened at Castaway. I'm glad you received some compensation for this. But I want to congratulate you on how you have been willing to admit your part in causing the difficulties that

---

8. Bruce J. Winick, *Therapeutic Jurisprudence and the Role of Counsel in Litigation*, in Dennis P. Stolle, David B. Wexler, & Bruce J. Winick, Eds., Practicing Therapeutic Jurisprudence 309 (Carolina Academic Press, 2000) (as Chapter 11) (discussing cognitive reframing).

arose and to commit yourself to making changes in your life so that this situation will not happen again for you in the future. I'm also delighted that your coming forward has raised the awareness level at Castaway so that the company won't let this happen again, in the future, either. Great job! It's been a pleasure working through this with you." Notice the basic or advanced empathy in the beginning of the statement, focused on her distress, suffering, and happiness with receiving some money (perhaps not all she asked for). This is intended to soften the blow, perhaps, of the next portion. The reframing portion is found here: "I want to congratulate you on how you have been willing to admit your part in causing the difficulties that arose and to commit yourself to making changes in your life so that this situation will not happen again for you in the future" which turns this event in her life into a positive opportunity to acknowledge a weakness and commit to change. More reframing is found here: "I'm also delighted that your coming forward has raised the awareness level at Castaway." This highlights the overall positive impact her complaint has had upon others, namely, Castaway and its employees.

Other options are to avoid court altogether and pursue negotiation and settlement and/or mediation, in order to avoid having Paula's history made public in the litigation (which could damage her reputation and self-concept), preserve her self concept, and perhaps encourage both Paula and Castaway to accept equal responsibility for the events leading to her complaint. Where litigation tends to encourage polarized, ossified positions of blame/no blame, mediation and settlement might allow for more reasonable apportionments of blame. If the client is in denial about her pattern of behavior, she may not tell the lawyer the entire truth about it and the lawyer may have to be prepared for her to reject the idea that she could lose this lawsuit due to the consensuality of the relationship. Finally, the lawyer may need to be ready to deal with the fact that she may be angry with Jackson and Castaway and a desire for revenge may be fueling her desire to pursue them, legally.

For defense counsel, a preventive lawyer representing Castaway would want to assist the company in putting into place policies and procedures designed to identify, intervene in, or prohibit these situations in the future, to avoid future threats of litigation. It is easy to see how therapeutic jurisprudence and preventive law can almost seamlessly be merged and applied in this case, whether on the plaintiff's or defense counsel side.

Automobile Personal Injury Lawsuit

In another example, in a tort action arising from an automobile accident involving two teenagers in the same car, the plaintiff teenager's (passenger's) counsel deposed the teenaged defendant driver. The plaintiff was not present, but the plaintiff's counsel mentioned to the defendant driver that the teenaged plaintiff passenger missed their friendship and hated what the lawsuit had done to it. Weeks later, the defendant driver died in a second car accident. The defendant's family called to thank the plaintiff's attorney for the peace he gave the defendant prior to his untimely death, by this comment. This move was totally extralegal, had no legal effect, and was not necessary or relevant from a legal standpoint, but was an opportunity to do something positive in the legal matter. It was a psycholegal soft spot, of sorts.[9]

---

9. This case was given to the author by attorney Wade Bettis in a personal communication around 2000.

Employment Disability Law

Another case involves an employee of a corporation who is entitled to an accommodation under the Americans With Disabilities Act that is not visible or obvious to his or her coworkers. For example, it could be prescription drug dependency or a medical condition that is not obvious. The employee has been out of work for a month, while being treated for the disabling condition. Now rehabilitated, the employee will return to work. The accommodation involved will, when it is implemented, allow the employee to arrive late to work, have a longer lunch break than other employees, and occasionally leave early from work, making up the time missed on a periodic basis by working at home. The law provides that the accommodated individual clearly has the right to have his or her disability remain entirely confidential, in the workplace.

From the other employees' perspective, it appears as if this employee was inexplicably gone from work for a month and now, upon return, will receive special treatment from the employer. Because the other employees are unaware of the situation and cannot see the disabling condition, they are likely to resent the accommodated employee and their general morale is likely to drop.

Rose Daly-Rooney argues that, because of this, the confidentiality right may actually be countertherapeutic. The TJ/PL lawyer might counsel the accommodated employee to consider waiving confidentiality to allow other employees to know, so they can help and support the accommodated employee. She suggests that the lawyer or client could request that the employer schedule a conference with the employee, his or her coworkers, and a representative of the employer, to explain the situation and the reason for the accommodations, to prevent this resentment and drop in morale. Here, potential stress is caused by nonlegal factors and by legal rights, but can be relieved by legal (waiver) and nonlegal actions (conference). The real difference here from traditional lawyering is in the consideration of the effect of this legal right (confidentiality) on the coworkers, on the client's relationships with his or her coworkers, and, thus, on the client's overall functioning.[10]

This is an example of a case where the law creates a psycholegal soft spot through its potential for mental and relational harm; it also illustrates when the psychology involved suggests that an additional legal move should be taken (the waiver and request) to protect the employee's relationships on the job.

Stolle, Wexler, and Winick, in their excellent book, Practicing Therapeutic Jurisprudence,[11] set forth a number of concrete examples of the potential application of TJ/PL in law practice; these are summarized below and examined again in a Chapter Assignment.

Elder Law: Burkes' Stay in Shape Example

In this example, an elderly couple comes to see a lawyer wanting a simple will for both of them. The issues are their future health, planning for possible incapacity, and the fact

---

10. Rose Daly-Rooney, *Designing Reasonable Accommodations Through Co-Worker Participation: Therapeutic Jurisprudence and the Confidentiality Provision of the Americans with Disabilities Act*, 8 J. L. & HEALTH 89 (1994), discussed in DENNIS P. STOLLE, DAVID B. WEXLER, & BRUCE J. WINICK, EDS., PRACTICING THERAPEUTIC JURISPRUDENCE 55–56 (Carolina Academic Press, 2000).

11. DENNIS P. STOLLE, DAVID B. WEXLER, & BRUCE J. WINICK, EDS., PRACTICING THERAPEUTIC JURISPRUDENCE (Carolina Academic Press, 2000).

that the wife's mother has Alzheimer's and is in a nursing home and may require more intensive care in the future. The third of their three adult children, Tom, has a drug problem, and they would like to leave his share of their estate to him in trust, while the other two adult children would receive their shares outright. They may need some advance directives (living will documents) and insurance for health care. The preventive lawyer might establish a legal check up system with the Burkes for updates and changes in their medical or financial status; it might be useful to establish a flat fee for this to reduce any perception that this is simply a fee-generating strategy of the attorney. This example is at the outer edge of the lawyer's role because it requires the lawyer to step into considering some health concerns, yet these nonlegal factors may cause the Burkes a great deal of stress in the future and during the current estate planning process. The lawyer might make some tentative statements, caveats, cautions, innocuous statements, and referrals to appropriate professionals for these matters. The lawyer's conduct is designed to encourage the clients to get extralegal help for their medical and health concerns. Finally, the law can create some solutions to the Burkes' stress, in leaving Tom's share in trust but setting up an explanatory conference, meeting, video, or letter so that everyone in the family, or perhaps just Tom, understands why this was done, to head off any potential will contests brought by Tom, after their death.[12]

Incompetence Labeling

In this example, a client faces a competency assessment in an incompetent to stand trial hearing in criminal law. The law itself causes stress for the client, as the client is likely to feel stigmatized by the label of "incompetent." The label may even have a self-fulfilling prophecy effect, such that the client begins to act in ways even less competent than he or she did, before the hearing. The TJ/PL lawyer can take some nonlegal actions to reframe the label of incompetent to stand trial in order to facilitate therapeutic improvement of the client, otherwise, the label can be pejorative and self-fulfilling. For example, the lawyer can reframe this as simply affording the client an opportunity to secure needed treatment and delay of trial, for better functioning. Here, the lawyer is putting a therapeutic spin on a legal matter/event, without treading too closely to another, nonlegal discipline. Yet, the lawyer's statements, attitude, and approach to the client and this label might have a positive effect in a potentially negative situation.[13]

HIV/AIDS Client

In this situation, an HIV-infected client comes to the lawyer for estate planning in the final stages of AIDS. He or she has a child and a same sex life partner. He or she is estranged from his or her family of origin, however, who do not approve of his or her lifestyle and do not accept his or her life partner as "family." The nonlegal issues abound: the client, child, partner, and family are all likely experiencing the grief process (denial, anger, bargaining, depression, acceptance) in a very intense way. The client may feel as if his or her life is out of control and yet not really want to deal with end of life issues (denial). The best interests of the child are at stake. There are likely medical and financial issues involved, such as health care costs, employment, insurance, disability insurance, life in-

---

12. *Id.* at 10–11, 15–16, & 49–51.
13. *Id.* at 53–54.

surance, and availability of governmental aid (Medicaid and Social Security disability benefits). The legal issues also abound: estate planning (will, trust, advance directives), a guardianship for or custody of the child post-death, planning for possible mental incapacity near the end of life (including problems of competency resulting from shifting lucidity), possible will contests by the family of origin, health care surrogate and surrogate decisionmaker status perhaps for the life partner, and employment discrimination.

Winick proposes a number of techniques the lawyer can use to deal with denial and resistance on the part of the client, such as putting the client at ease, self disclosure and modeling that one or one's family members have engaged in estate planning even when not sick, directly noting the client's anxiety (if present) and asking if it is ok to continue, using active listening with basic empathy and/or passive listening with use of silence, and using the attorney's well-honed skills of persuasion, perhaps noting, "You want to plan ahead, don't you?" The attorney can be aware of, and perhaps even comment on, the fact that dealing with the legal matters involved can afford the client a sense of some control over the end of life and a great sense of comfort knowing that all is planned for, which can help in an otherwise seemingly uncontrollable and frightening process. Winick suggests that the lawyer can try an extralegal, empathic statement such as, "It is not an admission of getting sicker to prepare for the possibility that one day a person might need these measures; I have a good estate plan in place, as do many of my clients and friends." The lawyer can encourage the client to get all of his or her affairs in order. Not talking about the stress the client is likely feeling and just proceeding with the legal work may actually create more distress, which is entirely avoidable. One possible psycholegal soft spot may be an opportunity spot; this end-of-life planning may afford a chance for the client to reconcile with alienated family members. Finally, setting up a guardianship for the client's child before death and beginning that transition now may ease the transition for the child and family, at death. This "standby guardianship" appears to be a real difference between what a traditional lawyer and a TJ/PL lawyer might do, in this case.[14]

Corporate and Business Planning Case

In corporate and business planning cases, most lawyers would identify a need for shareholder buy-sell agreements to resolve deadlocks in small business corporations, but may not always ask about or take into account the emotional and social relationships between the shareholder/owners, which may affect the legal planning of how to resolve deadlocks.

In the Fast Forward Example in Chapter 6, *supra,* Dauer points out the value of not taking a business client's direction at face value, but asking further questions. Upon asking, "Why?" and then listening carefully, the lawyer discovered that the client's objectives might be better achieved through means other than the legal moves the client was asking for, explicitly. Like medical patients, legal clients may not be adept at self-diagnosis. Attorneys need the freedom to diagnose the problem and then craft a solution. In corporate law, many businesspeople are more concerned with relationship building and creating goodwill than with anticipating litigation or ensuring legal enforceability of legal documents such as contracts. While the lawyer is charged with being concerned about these matters (anticipating litigation and ensuring enforceability of instruments), they can also attend to the nonlegal concerns the clients also care about. For example, most corporate lawyers are aware of the tension between insisting on contractual language that would be

---

14. *Id.* at 18–21, 51–52, & 76.

helpful to ensuring enforceability of the contract in your client's favor, and on maintaining the tenuous trust and accord between contracting parties. The lawyer's insistence on certain language can, at times, be a "deal breaker" that erodes the trust between the contracting parties. Finally, there has been a recent move towards including contractual language dealing with less legally binding aspects of the parties' ongoing relationship, perhaps based on the model of Japanese contracts which sometimes provide for simply "further negotiation" in the case of contractual disputes. For example, a divorce agreement might provide that the ex-spouses intend to collaborate on decisions regarding their minor children, in the future.

Criminal Defense Cases

Some TJ themes present in criminal defense work include the importance of "voice" for the criminal defendant and his or her participation in the decisionmaking process. Research shows that client participation in the sentencing process can lead to greater compliance with the judgment, sentence, or order. Also, litigation, particularly criminal charges, is/are distressing and this is something the attorney can be sensitive and responsive about. David Wexler and Bruce Winick set forth excellent and exhaustive material for the criminal lawyer desiring to practice with a TJ/PL approach.[15]

Rehabilitation, remorse, repentance, and a willingness to change can be therapeutic and legally beneficial. Legally, the criminal defense attorney may be able to ask for and receive a downward departure from the federal sentencing guidelines in the event of post conviction rehabilitation of the criminal defendant. However, the *Koon*[16] case says the rehabilitative efforts must be "extraordinary." Therefore, simple rehabilitation does not automatically lead to a lighter sentence, but the attorney may be able to make an argument for a reduced sentence in some cases, using his or her excellent advocacy skills.

Clearly, for criminal defendants whose criminal history shows a repeated pattern of behavior related to a mental health issue, rehabilitation makes sense. They are often initially reluctant, however, so the attorney may carefully choose to use his or her persuasive skills to encourage the criminal client (when appropriate) to enter into rehabilitation efforts. Attorneys can educate themselves about the client's options, assist in getting the client into a rehabilitation facility, use the fact of rehabilitation to request deferred sentencing and/or a plea bargain, bring it to the attention of the prosecutor and the parole board (who may prepare a presentence report), and use it at sentencing hearings. Legally, *Flowers* and the federal sentencing guidelines[17] permit attorneys to request deferred sentencing to buy time for defendants to complete rehabilitation programs. In Flowers, the

---

15. *Id.* at 237–326 (Chapters 9–11).

16. United States v. Koon, 518 U.S. 81 (1996) cited by Bruce J. Winick, *Redefining the Role of the Criminal Defense Lawyer at Plea Bargaining and Sentencing: A Therapeutic Jurisprudence/Preventive Law Model,* in DENNIS P. STOLLE, DAVID B. WEXLER, & BRUCE J. WINICK, EDS., PRACTICING THERAPEUTIC JURISPRUDENCE: LAW AS A HELPING PROFESSION 248–49 & 254–62 (Carolina Academic Press, 2000) (as Chapter 10).

17. United States v. Flowers, 983 F. Supp. 159 (E.D.N.Y. 1997); U.S. SENTENCING COMM'N, FEDERAL SENTENCING GUIDELINES MANUAL Section 2E1.1 (Nov. 1991), cited by Bruce J. Winick, *Redefining the Role of the Criminal Defense Lawyer at Plea Bargaining and Sentencing: A Therapeutic Jurisprudence/Preventive Law Model,* in DENNIS P. STOLLE, DAVID B. WEXLER, & BRUCE J. WINICK, EDS., PRACTICING THERAPEUTIC JURISPRUDENCE: LAW AS A HELPING PROFESSION 248–29 (Carolina Academic Press, 2000) (as Chapter 10).

deferment period was one year. John McShane, a board certified criminal defense attorney in Dallas, Texas (referenced in Chapter 10), has described providing the court with a "binder," containing affidavits of family, friends, therapists, doctors, and program staff attesting to the genuineness of the defendant's rehabilitation efforts, his or her progress, and his or her commitment to recovery, the defendant's sincere apology to the victim(s), and other supportive documentation. Some may even include the report of an expert on malingering with psychological testing to show the genuineness of the client's desires and commitment to rehabilitation.

When representing corporate clients with criminal charges, there are special provisions of the sentencing guidelines that allow a reduction in sentence if there is an organizational compliance program in place, designed to prevent law violations. These programs need to be genuine and followed, not merely present in name only, to be relevant.

Other creative criminal sentences may include: probation, house arrest, electronic monitoring, community service orders, sentencing to a bootcamp, pretrial diversion, deferred prosecution, restitution, continued employment, attendance at drug and alcohol treatment programs, and community service.[18] While these options may sound like restorative justice, they are not. The process operates within traditional criminal court, although the outcome may be more restorative than traditional criminal law.

Notes of caution to criminal defense attorneys are due, regarding paternalism, coercion, lecturing clients, and countertransference. Attorneys must be careful not to pressure criminal defense clients into treatment programs they do not want or need or are not willing to complete. Attorneys who have recovered themselves from various mental health issues must be careful not to project their feelings onto their clients and fail to listen carefully to what their clients actually want to do, not what the attorney thinks is best, if those conflict.

Miscellaneous Cases

In family law cases, there is a wealth of social science research on what is most therapeutic for the divorcing spouses and their children, as they go through the process. Maxwell points out that three factors are most important to the post-divorce functioning of the children and family: (1) the absence of interparental conflict; (2) maximizing stability for the children (financial, domicile, etc.); and (3) the emotional and physical availability of the parents to the children. Legal moves that create interparental conflict, distract the parents from parenting their children effectively, or create instability for the children, are all countertherapeutic. Sometimes they cannot be avoided, but if they can, TJ/PL suggests that we attempt to do so.

Another example involves the U.S. military's policy of "don't ask, don't tell" regarding sexual orientation of its members. This has been assessed as countertherapeutic, as it may foster social isolation, secretiveness, and low morale among affected members.

In civil commitment hearings, the TJ/PL lawyer might move to close the client's file, to prevent the public disclosure of embarrassing material. In litigation generally, there

---

18. Dennis P. Stolle, David B. Wexler, & Bruce J. Winick, Eds., Practicing Therapeutic Jurisprudence: Law as a Helping Profession 268 (Carolina Academic Press, 2000).

are a number of things lawyers can do to reduce the client's stress, such as sitting with the client in a civil case while the jury is out deliberating, to lessen the client's anxiety. The lawyer can then debrief the jury's decision with the client afterwards, to put it into perspective. In bringing a simple civil lawsuit between people who know each other, such as partners, former employers, buyers and sellers of real estate, or even divorcing spouses, the TJ/PL lawyer might be very careful about the timing and manner of delivery of demand letters and service of process, in order to minimize emotional anguish and interpersonal conflict between the parties. Finally, TJ/PL lawyers working with bankruptcy clients may realize that the law creates solutions to the client's financial stress, but also may cause additional stress to the client through the potential stigma associated with the label, "bankrupt."

Comment

The following is an excerpt from the author's short essay on preventive law:[19]

The Role of Preventive Law in the Transformation of the Legal Profession[20]

. . . .

As I understand it, preventive law emerged during the first half of the twentieth century; however, the remaining vectors of ... [the comprehensive law] movement have emerged more recently, gaining recognition only in the final decade of the last century. Perhaps Louis Brown [founder of preventive law in the 1930s] was years or decades ahead of his time, as is often the case with visionary individuals. I imagine he would be delighted with the direction of preventive law today.

What is different and vibrant about preventive law today is that the techniques and skills of preventive law are being combined with a philosophical approach to lawyering that reaches beyond simply preventing lawsuits and preventing legal problems and encompasses actually benefiting or improving human wellbeing. This adds a valuable normative dimension to preventive law. When combined with this philosophy, preventive law moves from being value-neutral to being value-laden. In turn, preventive law provides lawyers who want to practice law as a helping or healing profession with a set of specific, concrete, tested, and well-thought-out skills or tools for their new trade. It also provides a model for a lawyer-client relationship that is closer, warmer, more collaborative, probably longer lasting, and more like a partnership. This kind of lawyer-client relationship

---

19. Copyright © Susan Daicoff, 2000. A portion of this unpublished essay was quoted in Thomas D. Barton & James M. Cooper, *Preventive Law and Creative Problem Solving: Multi-Dimensional Lawyering,* 14–19 (2000), available at http://www.preventivelawyer.org/content/pdfs/Multi_Dimensional_Lawyer.pdf (last visited April 12, 2011).

20. [Original acknowledgement] Associate Professor of Law, Florida Coastal School of Law. Deep thanks are due to Dean Emeritus Edward A. Dauer, John D. Lyons Professor of Law David B. Wexler, Professor Bruce J. Winick, board-certified Dallas trial lawyer John D. McShane, collaborative law co-founding lawyers Pauline Tesler and Stuart Webb, Executive Director of the McGill Center for Creative Problem Solving James Cooper, Director and Professor Thomas Barton of the Louis Brown Center for Preventive Law, Professor Roberta Mitchell, Professor Donald A. Hughes, Jr., holistic lawyer William Van Zyverden, Kalamazoo lawyer Richard Halpert, the Honorable Peggy Hora, and all the many others who tirelessly toil in the furtherance of the comprehensive law movement.

is entirely appropriate for lawyers who want to function as healers and problemsolvers rather than gladiators or neutral, technical experts.[21]

.... Because preventive law, and especially the combination of preventive law with therapeutic jurisprudence, fit well with ... decisionmaking styles [that are often atypical of lawyers], they may serve an important role in ameliorating lawyer distress and dissatisfaction.

More specifically, preventive law is perfectly well-suited to the values and beliefs of atypical lawyers who prefer Feeling or have an ethic of care. Its emphasis on preventing harm, avoiding litigation, conflict, or controversy, and maintaining harmonious relationships is likely to satisfy the lawyer who cannot divorce his or her own personal morals and standards from his or her work for the client, who seeks to avoid harm to people, who seeks to restore and maintain relationships and harmony, and who values mercy over justice. While the traditional practice of law is likely to be agonizing for such a lawyer, preventive law offers this person an outlet for his or her innermost, deeply held values and beliefs. Further, this kind of lawyer is likely to be highly motivated to practice preventive law well, because of the excellent fit between his or her personal ethics and the ethic of preventive law.

In the last twenty to thirty years, the number of women and minorities in the legal profession has dramatically increased.[22] Some of the atypical lawyer traits, such as Feeling and an ethic of care, are more prevalent among women, even among women lawyers.[23] ... One would therefore expect the legal profession to begin to change, given its increased diversity. Yet empirical evidence exists to suggest that law school tends to silence these voices, or modes. Law students who come to law school with an ethic of care tend to shift to a rights-oriented decisionmaking style by the end of their first year.[24] The ascension of preventive law and the entire comprehensive law movement promise two things: first, to preserve space in the legal profession for lawyers with these atypical decisionmaking preferences and, second, to allow the transformation of the legal profession—through diversification—to come to full flower.

.... The time is ripe for approaches to law and lawyering, like preventive law, that deemphasize pitting individual parties against one another and instead seek to find creative, collaborative, forward-looking solutions to human and legal disputes. The time is also ripe for approaches that concern themselves with maintaining and fostering the client's ongoing relationships with his or her family, friends, workplace, community, and society. Preventive law clearly allows the lawyer to focus on and explicitly work towards both these goals, consistent with our apparent growing awareness of the need to acknowledge our "connectedness."

A note of caution is required, however. Despite the author's obvious approval of the notion of law as a healing profession, it is only one of several options. Traditional law practice, adversarial process, and gladiatorial, win-lose, hard-ball litigation are impor-

---

21. See Chapter 1 for more on these various professional roles of the lawyer.

22. ABA Comm. on Women in the Profession, *Basic Facts from Women in the Law: A Look at the Numbers* (1995) (reporting that 80% of female lawyers entered the profession after 1970 and the percentage of women in the profession rose from 3% in 1960 and 1971 to 23% in 1995).

23. *See, e.g.,* Erica Weissman, Gender-Role Issues in Attorney Career Satisfaction, at 74–76 (1994) (unpublished Ph.D. dissertation, Yeshiva University) (on file with author) (finding the ethic of care more prevalent among female lawyers as compared to male lawyers).

24. Sandra Janoff, *The Influence of Legal Education on Moral Reasoning,* 76 MINN. L. REV. 193 (1991) and RAND JACK & DANA C. JACK, MORAL VISIONS AND PROFESSIONAL DECISIONS: THE CHANGING VALUES OF WOMEN AND MEN LAWYERS (1988).

tant. In many cases, they are necessary and appropriate.... [Yet, t]he profession needs alternatives to the monolithic standard for law practice.... clients and society are calling for alternatives to what they encounter when they involve lawyers in their problems. These alternatives are found in preventive law, in the integration of preventive law with therapeutic jurisprudence, and in the broader comprehensive law movement—of which preventive law is an elder statesman.

Definitions and Key Points

Top characteristics of TJ/PL:

- Achieves a legal result equivalent to that achieved by traditional law, via the most therapeutic means
- Avoids counter-therapeutic legal moves
- Prevents litigation before it occurs

Advantages:

- Better overall outcome for clients, greater client satisfaction
- Repeat customers
- Better lawyer-client relationships
- Avoids future litigation

Challenges:

- Paternalism
- Guessing wrong about the therapeutic issues involved
- Boundaries blurred with mental health experts
- Clients not seeing the value of preventive law check-ups and audits

TJ/PL Skills:

1. Psycholegal soft spots—places where the legal and psychological issues intersect
2. Rewind technique
3. Fast forward technique
4. Legal audits
5. Checkups

Psycholegal Soft Spot Types:

Positive Psycholegal Soft Spot	Negative Psycholegal Soft Spot
Law results in a psychological benefit	Law results in psychological harm
Psychological dynamics create a legal benefit	Psychological dynamics result in legal problem
Psychology suggests taking a legal action	
Opportunity to do something legal or extralegal with a positive effect	

Resources

Dennis P. Stolle, David B. Wexler, Bruce J. Winick & Edward A. Dauer, *Integrating Preventive Law and Therapeutic Jurisprudence: A Law and Psychology Based Approach to Lawyering*, 34 Cal. W. L. Rev. 15, 16 (1997) (first proposing the integration of TJ and PL) in Dennis Stolle, David Wexler, & Bruce Winick, Eds., Practicing Therapeutic Jurisprudence: Law as a Helping Profession (Carolina Academic Press, 2000) (as Chapter 1).

Dennis Stolle, David Wexler, & Bruce Winick, Eds., Practicing Therapeutic Jurisprudence: Law as a Helping Profession (Carolina Academic Press, 2000) (Chapters 1–6, 8–12).

Thomas D. Barton, Preventive Law and Problem Solving: Lawyering for the Future (Vandenplas Publishing, 2009) (Chapter 18).

Coordination: Also read Brooks & Madden (Chapter 1), Stolle, et al. (Chapters 1–6, 8, and 9–12), and Silver (Chapters 11–12 and 14).

Chapter Assignments

Exercise 7-1

Return to the three vignettes presented in Chapter 4, Tom, Judy, and Jan. Identify the psycholegal soft spots in each case, by first identifying (1) the legal issues, (2) the psychological issues, (3) the ways in which they intersect, and (4) possible moves or measures the TJ/PL lawyer might take to avoid problems resulting from the intersection, as follows:

VIGNETTE	LEGAL ISSUES	PSYCHOLOGICAL ISSUES	PSYCHOLEGAL SOFT SPOTS	TJ MEASURES
Tom	Will, advance directives (living will), health care surrogate designation	Denial Desire not to admit physical condition and desire not to deal with end of life concerns due to denial Pain medication for cancer can ultimately impair cognitive abilities Rivalry or conflict between heirs	May procrastinate estate planning May cancel or no-show for appointments May resist naming health care surrogate May become incompetent due to pain medication	Normalize will w/self-disclosure (I have a will; it's good business practice to have a will) Establish time frame to finish legal work Explanatory letter or video to heirs
Jan	Divorce	Anger Shame Embarrassment Sense of rejection Outrage, shock Need to coparent kids with ex-husband Need for counseling to process emotions so client doesn't use lawyer for that purpose Client going through normal stages of grief	Anger can blind client to "reality check" of what she can expect to get in divorce Anger can obstruct client's decision-making re: kids and re: coparenting concerns Anger can subside Passage of time can change client's emotional state (normal grief process) Client may ultimately want something other than initially stated	Sensitive timing issues re: when to ask client to make decisions Appropriateness of mediation? Delicate balance for lawyer re: role in assessing client's deepest goals below the surface anger, if any
Judy	Enforce child support order	Domestic violence survivor in past Fear Need for new courage and confidence	Filing of petition can escalate threat potential for client and kids Filing petition can encourage new strength for client and be a positive step	Delicate timing issues re: filing, service of process Need to assess safety plans of client and kids Suggest coterminous mental health counseling?

Exercise 7-2

Read the following hypothetical cases summarized on pages 100–05 hereof and drawn from the book, Dennis P. Stolle, David B. Wexler, & Bruce J. Winick, Eds., Practicing Therapeutic Jurisprudence: Law as a Helping Profession (Carolina Academic Press, 2000): Burkes' Stay In Shape, p. 10 & 49; Tom's Drug Problem, p. 50; HIV/Aids Client p. 18 & 51–52, 76; Bob & Jane, Jack & Sally Corporation, p. 23 & 25; Hora's Will Contest p. 64 & 74; Adoption p. 76; ADA Client p. 78. (If you do not have this book, you can use reported cases or legal cases described in the media, see last row of the Grid, below.)

Evaluate the legal issues, psychological issues, psycholegal soft spots (areas of inter-section), skills needed, and then what moves were taken by the legal personnel involved, in each case, as a TJ/PL strategy, and complete the following "TJ/PL Grid":

Matter	Legal Issues	TJ/PL Issues	Intersection of Law & TJ/PL	Lawyering Skills Used	TJ Measures
Burkes' Stay In Shape p. 10 & 49; Tom's Drug Problem p. 50 (p. 100 hereof)	Will Trust Advance directives (living wills)	Sibling rivalry Children's attitudes and relationships Health in future Alzheimer's potential Need for money for medical care	Sibling rivalry may lead to will contest, after death, if there are unequal shares Sibling rivalry may lead to challenge to trustee selection Tom will resent receiving his share in trust and may bring will contest Tom/trustee relationship may suffer Medical care needs may deplete estate	Questioning Exploring children's relationships Listening Education re: elders' concerns Inheritability of Alzheimer's Raise issue of sibling rivalry if using a trust	Suggesting a family conference or video or letter to children to reduce sting of trust Careful selection of trustee Health care insurance
HIV/AIDS Client p. 18 & 51, 52, 76 (p. 101–02 hereof)					
Bob, Jane, Jack & Sally Corp. p. 23, 25 (p. 102–03 hereof)					
Hora's Will Contest p. 64 & 74 (p. 94 hereof)					
Research your own case and analyze it:					

Exercise 7-3

Assess the following cases using a TJ/PL approach:

Therapeutic Jurisprudence/Preventive Law Family Law Problems

These are problems a law school class compiled, from their own experiences or from events reported in the media, that they believed would benefit from a TJ/PL perspective:

1. Wanting to initiate a divorce as the victim in a domestic violence situation. No financial resources; few emotional resources.

Appropriate legal actions:

Psycholegal soft spots:

Possible TJ/PL actions:

2. Fighting an action by an abusive ex-spouse seeking child support payments.

Appropriate legal actions:

Psycholegal soft spots:

Possible TJ/PL actions:

3. Child custody arrangement resulting in true, 50/50 joint custody. Does this meet the "best interests of the children" test in the law?

Appropriate legal actions:

Psycholegal soft spots:

Possible TJ/PL actions:

4. Dealing with an ex-spouse with primary residential custody, who denies visitation to noncustodial parent in violation of their divorce decree.

Appropriate legal actions:

Psycholegal soft spots:

Possible TJ/PL actions:

5. Eleven-year-old child who wants to "divorce" his crack cocaine-addicted mother, against the recommendation of the state.

Appropriate legal actions:

Psycholegal soft spots:

Possible TJ/PL actions:

6. Private adoption where the biological mother changes her mind and does not want to proceed with the adoption.

Appropriate legal actions:

Psycholegal soft spots:

Possible TJ/PL actions:

Exercise 7-4

TJ in Employment Law: Review the facts of the Employment Disability Law case summarized on p. 100 of this chapter. Read the Americans with Disabilities Act/employment law case on pages 55 and 78 of DENNIS P. STOLLE, DAVID B. WEXLER, & BRUCE J. WINICK, EDS., PRACTICING THERAPEUTIC JURISPRUDENCE: LAW AS A HELPING PROFESSION (Carolina Academic Press, 2000) (same case). Draft two letters on behalf of the plaintiff to the employer corporation: first, one from a traditional approach simply requesting the accommodation and, second, one from a TJ/PL approach, requesting the accommodation and this conference.

Chapter 8

Vector 4 — Procedural Justice

Description

This excerpt from the author's 2006 article introduces procedural justice:[1]

In 1990, social scientist Tom Tyler published an empirical study with a very surprising finding: that litigants' evaluation of the "fairness" of judicial processes depended more on three psychological factors than on the actual win-lose outcome of the process.[2] In other words, whether these factors were present dictated how fair one thought a legal process was, regardless of whether one won or lost. These three factors were:

1. *being given an opportunity to speak and be heard;*

2. *being treated with dignity and respect by the judge and the other legal personnel; and*

3. *how trustworthy those in authority appeared and behaved.*

Being allowed to participate in the decisionmaking process and having the judge explain his or her reasons for making his or her decision were also relevant to these factors and thus to litigants' satisfaction. Tyler concluded:

> People's evaluations of the fairness of judicial hearings are affected by the opportunities which those procedures provide for people to participate, by the degree to which people judge that they are treated with dignity and respect, and by judgments about the trustworthiness of authorities. Each of these three factors has more influence on judgments of procedural justice than do either evaluations of neutrality or evaluations of the favorableness of the outcome of the hearing.[3]

Procedural justice ("PJ") suggests that litigation in itself may not necessarily be what people want from the law; they want a voice, an opportunity to tell their story, to be treated with respect by the authority figures, and to have the decision (if made by a third party) explained to them.[4]

---

1. This Chapter incorporates portions of (and expands on) the author's 2006 article, Susan Daicoff, *Law as a Healing Profession: The "Comprehensive Law Movement,"* 6 Pepperdine Disp. Resol. J. 1 (2006) [hereinafter Daicoff, 2006].

2. Tom R. Tyler, *The Psychological Consequences of Judicial Procedures: Implications for Civil Commitment Hearings,* in David B. Wexler & Bruce J. Winick, eds., Law in a Therapeutic Key 3, 6–7 (Carolina Academic Press, 1996) [hereinafter Wexler & Winick, Key].

3. *Id.* at 12.

4. Daicoff, 2006, *supra* note 1.

What happens if litigants do not feel that "procedural justice" was present? Tyler reported that they are likely to have lowered satisfaction with the process, even if they "won" in terms of monetary compensation or the judge's decision as to culpability. They are also likely to be reluctant to accept the decision and comply with it or with legal rules. They are likely to have diminished respect for the judge, mediator, or third-party decision-maker, if present, and for the court and legal system generally. Finally, they may experience lowered self-esteem and morale.

These consequences reach beyond mere subjective satisfaction to actual compliance with legal orders and rules and one's overall respect for the legal system and rule of law. Therefore, procedural justice is something lawyers, judges, mediators, legislators, and other legal personnel should consider implementing in all legal procedures. Procedural justice alone is not a way of practicing law or administering justice, but its insights have weighty consequences for lawyers, clients, and judges. It applies to and can inform all approaches, traditional or comprehensive, to legal practice and the administration of laws.

For example, every lawyer dealing with a litigation client can be aware of these psychological needs and, if the lawyer wants to maximize the client's satisfaction with the process of the legal matter and legal representation, the lawyer can intentionally build into the representation opportunities for the client to have a voice, to have an opportunity to tell his or her story, to be treated with respect by the authority figures, and to have the decision (if made by a third party) explained to him or her. For example, in mediation negotiations, the lawyer should be very aware that the client may have these needs and may negotiate to allow the client to be heard in the mediation process or include an opportunity for the client to be heard in the final settlement agreement. For example, in one medical malpractice wrongful death case, even though the lawyers settled the case, the grieving family insisted on meeting the doctor defendant face to face, to ask questions and to be heard, as part of the settlement. In another case, when the lawyer litigated the plaintiff's case successfully (so he or she thought) and "won," the client later exploded in fury to the attorney, "That was not justice! I never got to tell my story to the judge!" Even if the client never gets to tell his or her story to the judge or to the opposing party or counsel, the lawyer can allow the client a chance to "vent" to the lawyer in his or her law office.

Lawyer personality research suggests that many lawyers may not be attuned to these kinds of emotional and psychological needs and motivations, in their clients. Lawyers as a group may be more insensitive to emotional, psychological, and relational dynamics than are, perhaps, social workers.[5] Law school also does not tend to emphasize these concerns, so lawyers may have to be very intentional to be aware of and integrate these needs into their work with clients.

Procedural justice may also be useful in traditional legal settings, as well. Bruce Winick was successful in using procedural justice to argue for the appointment of separate counsel for juveniles facing civil commitment in Florida. While the juveniles were afforded court-appointed guardians ad litem, these lawyers often functioned as "best interests" lawyers and may not have represented the actual wishes of the juveniles involved. Winick argued that the juveniles, needing a "voice" in the process, needed their own representational attorney. An excerpt from his amicus brief to the Florida Supreme Court is set forth in the Examples in this Chapter, *infra*.

---

5. Susan Daicoff, Lawyer Know Thyself: A Psychological Analysis of Personality Strengths and Weaknesses (American Psychological Association Books, 2004).

Health Care Compliance Research: A Related Concept

A related effort is David Wexler and Bruce Winick's use of Meichenbaum and Turk's health care compliance research findings, in the law.[6] Wexler reports that Meichenbaum and Turk found that certain factors were associated with whether or not patients would follow or not follow, respectively, doctors' orders.[7] Patients were less likely to comply with health care providers' orders if the health care professional failed to instruct the person as to the treatment regimen, was distant, looked and acted busy, read case notes during the interview, asked patients closed ended questions, cut off the patient, did not permit them to tell the story in their own words, failed to state the exact treatment regimen or stated it in unclear or technical terms, used jargon, adopted a moralizing, high-powered stance, or terminated the interview abruptly. They were also less likely to comply if they were not actively involved in negotiating and designing the treatment program.

They were more likely to comply if the actual written order provided incentives for the patient's achievement of treatment objectives, was individually tailored to the needs and desires of the patient, defined target behavior with specificity, spelled out the positive and negative consequences of compliance or noncompliance, and included specific dates for contract initiation, termination, and renewal.[8] Public commitment to the plan led to greater compliance, when patients were given the chance to announce to one or more people, including a prestigious professional, their intentions to comply with the plan.

The parallels with procedural justice are clear, as the concepts of voice and decision-making participation are again present; however, there are a number of other concepts present in this research that may be useful for legal personnel. Wexler argues that legal personnel can implement these findings, if they want to enhance the likelihood that clients or litigation parties will comply with legal orders. For example, he asserts that lawyers and judges should avoid directive language, have high prestige, present themselves as competent, attentive, practical, and motivated by the best interests of the client or party, raise mild counterarguments about the client's prospective compliance and allow the client to refute them, bring up obstacles and drawbacks to compliance, involve significant others, such as family members, in the decisional process, and allow for public commitment to the order, by giving the client an opportunity to announce to a prestigious professional his or her intention to comply or to inform one or more people of his or her decision to follow the plan. The written document memorializing the agreement, decision, or order should also follow the wisdom of this research; it should contain incentives for the party's achievement of various objectives and be individually tailored to the needs and desires of the party. It should define target behavior with specificity, spell out the positive and negative consequences of compliance or noncompliance, and include specific dates for contract initiation, termination, and renewal, for maximal compliance.[9]

---

6. David B. Wexler, *Therapeutic Jurisprudence and the Criminal Courts, in* Wexler & Winick, Key, *supra* note 2, at 167 (Carolina Academic Press, 1996). Bruce Winick also discusses this research in the context of TJ criminal lawyering in Chapter 10 of Dennis P. Stolle, David B. Wexler, & Bruce J. Winick, Eds., Practicing Therapeutic Jurisprudence: Law as a Helping Profession 280–81 (Carolina Academic Press, 2000).

7. Donald Meichenbaum & Dennis C. Turk, Facilitating Treatment Adherence: A Practitioner's Guidebook (1987), cited in Wexler, *supra* note 6.

8. Wexler, *supra* note 6.

9. *Id.*

Examples

The following three examples are from the author's 2006 article:[10]

Sexual Harassment

If a sexual harassment plaintiff brings a lawsuit against her former employer and ultimately receives back pay and a fair damage award but is poorly treated by the judge, the attorneys, and the employer's representatives throughout the proceeding, the glow of the "win" is likely to fade substantially. If she feels as if she was not given an opportunity to tell her story because of the restrictions placed on witness' testimony, or if her credibility and character are impugned during cross-examination in a way that leaves her feeling decimated afterward, and if she gets the impression that the judge does not want her to speak freely, then she may feel violated by the process rather than vindicated. Tyler's work would suggest that she would feel less satisfied, or even be unhappy, with the outcome under these circumstances.[11]

Drug-Related Criminal Offenses

Another example can be seen in the treatment of a chronic substance-dependent man who is facing sentencing for a minor, drug-related criminal offense. The sentence is likely to consist of a multitude of measures, including mandatory inpatient and outpatient substance abuse treatment, jail time, house arrest, community service, and community restitutionary measures. It will likely take 18 months to complete. Wexler has applied Meichenbaum and Turk's empirical research on factors enhancing patients' compliance with health care professionals' directions (i.e., "doctor's orders") to situations like this and concluded that this man will be more likely to comply with the terms of his sentence if he is given a chance to participate with the judge in the formulation of its terms, among other things.[12] If he is given a voice in the decisional process, is treated with dignity and respect by the judge and the other legal personnel, and is given an explanation by the judge as to how he came to his decision, he is more likely to "buy in" to the program and follow it. In the long run, this approach will be more likely to facilitate this man's successful recovery from substance abuse.

Employment Law

Another example can be found in corporate hierarchical decisionmaking. Suppose that a medium-sized corporation (without unionized employees) has just revised its employment contracts with its employees, because it just concluded an expensive and painful lawsuit with an ex-employee over the terms of her contract. In an effort to prevent future lawsuits, the corporation unilaterally amends its annual employment contracts and policies and procedures manual in order to minimize future disputes over its employment-related decisions, acting on the advice of its lawyer (who may even be practicing preventive

---

10. Daicoff, 2006, *supra* note 1.
11. DAICOFF, KNOW THYSELF, *supra* note 5, at 179–80.
12. David Wexler, *Inducing Therapeutic Compliance Through the Criminal Law*, 14 L. & PSYCHOL. REV. 43 (1990).

law). The employees receive the new contracts in the mail, with no explanation as to the changes. They are furious, feel betrayed by the corporation, and perceive the new contracts as undercutting their legal rights, to their detriment and to the corporation's unilateral benefit. Now the corporation has to engage in "damage control" to preserve the morale of its employees. Procedural justice would have dictated that the corporation should have included its employees or a representative group thereof in the process of revising the standard employment contracts. If they had been involved in the process, understood the reasons for the changes, were given a voice and an opportunity to be heard and to participate in revising the contracts, they would have been more likely to accept the new contracts without question. Morale and favorable employer-employee relations would have been preserved. Future employee lawsuits might have been prevented.

Synthesis: Juvenile Civil Commitment

Here is an excerpt from Professor Bruce Winick and Judge Ginger Lerner-Wren's amicus brief to the Supreme Court of Florida in the case *Amendment to the Rules of Juvenile Procedure, Fla. R. Juv. P. 8.350*,[13] arguing for procedural justice and "voice" to be afforded to juveniles being civilly committed to residential treatment facilities against their wishes, after adjudication of dependency.[14] In this brief, they argue that juveniles will not have an adequate opportunity to be heard, and thus will be denied procedural justice, unless they are represented by appointed counsel, not simply guardians ad litem, at their commitment hearings. This position was ultimately successful and the Florida Supreme Court agreed with requiring appointed counsel for juveniles facing civil commitment.[15]

> The central difference between the majority and minority relates to whether a juvenile facing civil commitment should be represented at the commitment hearing by an attorney, who is ethically bound to represent the juvenile's articulated wishes, in addition to a guardian ad litem, who is statutorily bound to articulate the guardian's views of the juvenile's best interest. A variety of constitutional, legal, and policy considerations are relevant to deciding whether the majority or minority proposal should be adopted by this Court. This brief will limit its consideration to the therapeutic impact of representation by guardians ad litem or by attorneys on juveniles subjected to such hearings. This brief argues that considerations of therapeutic jurisprudence strongly support the minority proposal that attorneys in addition to guardians ad litem be used.

> Empirical studies of how litigants experience judicial and administrative hearings have led to the development of a literature on the psychology of procedural justice. Research on the psychology of procedural justice suggests that people are more satisfied with and comply more with the outcome of legal proceedings when they perceive those proceedings to be fair and have an opportunity to participate in them. The process or dignitary value of a hearing is important to lit-

---

13. Case No. SC00-2044, 842 So. 2d 763, 28 Fla. L. Weekly S221 (March 6, 2003) (opinion by Justice Pariente). Winick is a co-founder of therapeutic jurisprudence and Lerner-Wren is a Florida judge who is the nation's first mental health court judge.

14. Amicus brief reproduced in Bruce J. Winick & Ginger Lerner-Wren, *Do Juveniles Facing Civil Commitment Have a Right to Counsel?: A Therapeutic Jurisprudence Brief*, 71 U. CIN. L. REV. 115 (2002).

15. *In Re* Amendment to the Rules of Juvenile Procedure, FLA. R. JUV. P. 8.350, 804 So.2d 1296 (Fla. 2001).

igants. People who feel they have been treated fairly at a hearing—dealt with in good faith and with respect and dignity—experience greater litigant satisfaction than those who feel treated unfairly, with disrespect, and in bad faith. People highly value "voice," the ability to tell their story, and "validation," the feeling that what they have had to say was taken seriously by the judge or other decision-maker. Even when the result of a hearing is adverse, people treated fairly, in good faith, and with respect are more satisfied with the result and comply more readily with the outcome of the hearing. Moreover, they perceive the result as less coercive than when these conditions are violated, and even feel that they have voluntarily chosen the course that is judicially imposed. Such feelings of voluntariness rather than coercion tend to produce more effective behavior on their part. For many litigants, these process values are more important than winning.

Social psychologist Tom Tyler, applying these principles to the civil commitment hearing, has argued that increasing the individual's sense of participation, dignity, and trust during the commitment proceedings is likely to increase his or her acceptance of the outcome of the hearing, lead to a greater willingness to accept hospitalization and treatment, and enhance treatment efficacy. Civil commitment hearings that appear to juveniles who are subjected to them to be a sham violate their need to be treated with "respect, politeness, and dignity" and to feel that "their rights as citizens are acknowledged." When legal authorities treat juveniles with dignity in this sense, their status as competent, equal citizens and human beings is confirmed. When legal proceedings do not treat people with dignity, they feel devalued as members of society. If juveniles who are sought to be committed attribute this denial of dignity to the legal and political authorities who run the hearing, the judge, the attorney and social worker for the Florida Department of Children and Families, the guardian ad litem and his or her attorney, and the clinicians who testify—this perception will threaten their feelings of self-esteem, self-worth, and sense of personal responsibility. Because juveniles with mental illness or behavioral problems who are sought to be committed on the basis of these difficulties already have been marginalized and stigmatized by a variety of social mechanisms, self-respect and their sense of their value as members of society are of special importance to them. Perhaps nothing can threaten a person's belief that he or she is an equal member of society as much as being subjected to a civil commitment hearing. Juveniles involved in civil commitment hearings are likely to be particularly sensitive to issues of participation, dignity, and trust, and the psychological effects posited by the literature on the psychology of procedural justice are especially applicable in this context. In addition, this Court also recognized the applicability of therapeutic jurisprudence to juvenile commitment proceedings when it said, "Indeed, the issue presented by this case extends beyond the legal question of what process is due; rather, this case also presents the question of whether the child believes that he or she is being listened to and that his or her opinion is respected and counts."

Civil commitment hearings that are perceived by juveniles as phony rituals violate their sense of participation, dignity, and equal citizenship. Civil commitment hearings for juveniles that deny them the ability to articulate their wishes through counsel, but which solely use guardians ad litem to present the guardian's views of the juvenile's best interests, will not fulfill the juvenile's participatory or dignitary interests. Instead, such hearings may actually produce feelings of worthlessness and loss of dignity, exacerbating the juvenile's mental illness or behavioral problems, and perhaps even fostering a form of learned helplessness that can further diminish performance, motivation, and mood in ways that can be antitherapeutic.

The proposed civil commitment hearings are very likely to be perceived by the juveniles subjected to them to be phony rituals. The proposed rule promises the juvenile the chance to present evidence. However, a juvenile is not able to prepare his own case or cross-examine adverse witnesses effectively on his own. A guardian ad litem along with the attorney for the guardian ad litem is not responsible for assisting the juvenile in preparing his case. If in fact, the guardian ad litem disagrees with the juvenile about his best interests, then the guardian ad litem and the attorney for the guardian ad litem are statutorily bound to prepare a case against the juvenile's articulated position. Without someone to assist the juvenile to articulate his position, he will not be able to fully participate in the hearing. This lack of participation undermines the juvenile's participatory interests, making the hearing appear to be a phony proceeding conducted by adults.

III. The Psychological Effects of Coercion and Voluntary Choice

The recent research by the MacArthur Network on Mental Health and the Law on patient perceptions of coercion also supports the conclusion that the minority report should be adopted. This research examined the correlates and determinants of individuals' perceptions of what makes them feel coerced. Patient perceptions of coercion in the mental hospital admission process were found to be strongly associated with the degree to which that process was seen to be characterized by procedural justice. The MacArthur research found that people feel noncoerced even in coercive situations such as civil commitment when they perceive the intentions of state actors to be benevolent and when they are treated with dignity and respect, given voice and validation, and not treated in bad faith. Patients who are provided procedural justice in this sense, even if involuntarily committed or pressured by family members and clinicians to be hospitalized, reported experiencing considerably less coercion than patients who were not afforded procedural justice.

The MacArthur work on coercion is significant when considered in connection with a body of theoretical work on the psychology of choice that suggests that people perform more effectively and with greater motivation when they choose voluntarily to do something, and perform less well, with poor motivation and sometimes with psychological reactance, when they are coerced into doing it. Principles of cognitive and social psychology including the goal setting effect, expectancy theory, intrinsic motivation, the psychology of commitment, and cognitive dissonance in general support the positive value of choice and the negative effects of coercion. In the treatment context, this research suggests that people who feel less coerced into accepting treatment and who believe that entering treatment reflects their own choice are more invested in treatment and benefit more from it than patients who feel coerced and disrespected by the treatment process.

The attorney is the primary vehicle for effectuating the juvenile's participatory interests. Both the American Psychological Association and the American Psychiatric Association have recognized the therapeutic importance of having a juvenile represented by an attorney in their Model Act and Guidelines. Without representation by an individual (such as an attorney) who is professionally bound to articulate the juvenile's wishes and preferences, juveniles will not experience the sense of voice and participation in the proceedings that are essential to their having a positive response to the outcome of the hearing.

The attorney also is in an excellent position to diminish the potential for coercion and its perception by the juvenile in the admission process. By effectuating, rather than compromising, the juvenile's participatory interests in the commitment process, the attorney can contribute to the juvenile's sense that he or she was treated fairly and to his or her ability to accept the outcome of the proceeding, even if adverse, and to comply with the court's decision in ways that can better achieve the goals of hospitalization. Without this, the juvenile is more likely to experience the hospital admission that may be ordered as coercive, with potentially devastating consequences for his or her ability to gain the benefits that such hospitalization may offer.

IV. Conclusion

The purpose of committing juveniles to mental health facilities is the treatment of their mental health and behavioral problems. The procedures we use in the commitment process can have an enormous impact on whether juveniles so committed respond favorably or unfavorably to such treatment. A process that allows guardians ad litem to "represent" these juveniles but which frustrates the juveniles' ability to experience voice and participation in their own hearings will be antitherapeutic, frustrating the treatment purpose of their commitment. It will reinforce feelings of worthlessness and lack of self-efficacy, and will exacerbate the feeling that their dignity and personhood are disrespected by the legal system. It will make them feel coerced by the legal process in ways that are likely to diminish their motivation to accept treatment and their ability to respond favorably to it.

By contrast, juveniles who are treated with dignity and respect at the hearing and given the right to participate through counsel are less likely to experience the process as coercive, and will predictably respond better to any treatment that is ordered. An attorney representing a juvenile who articulates the juvenile's own wishes will fulfill the sense of voice and validation that the literature on the psychology of procedural justice stress as essential to litigant satisfaction and compliance with the outcome of the proceeding.

Representation only by a guardian ad litem who does not advocate the juvenile's wishes and instead presents arguments based on the guardian's perception of the juvenile's best interests will frustrate the sense of voice and validation that are so important. Proceedings using such guardians, without providing the juveniles with attorneys, will be perceived by juveniles as phony rituals conducted by adults that only pretend to allow the juvenile the opportunity to participate. The feelings such hearings will produce will reinforce the disaffection and alienation that such juveniles already experience. Allowing them to participate through counsel, by contrast, will increase their sense of self-worth and self-efficacy, and in turn, increase the likelihood that they will benefit from the treatment they are thought to need. [Citations omitted.][16]

---

16. Winick & Lerner-Wren, *supra* note 14.

Practice Information

The following practical suggestions are based on the conclusions drawn by Tyler's research and may be valuable for lawyers and/or judges who want parties to feel that the legal process was "fair":

- **Voice**

  Give clients and parties "voice": a chance to present evidence, present their own views, and be heard.

- **Participation**

  Give clients and parties a chance to participate and share in the decisionmaking *process*, even if their participation does not affect the ultimate decision.

- **Respect**

  Have legal authorities treat parties with respect, politeness, and dignity, acknowledge their rights as citizens, and acknowledge their status as competent, equal human beings.

- **Explanation**

  Have legal authorities express concern for parties' welfare, appear to want to treat them fairly, allow parties to present evidence, and explain or account for their decisions.

These suggestions are based on Meichenbaum and Turk's research and are useful for legal personnel (lawyers, judges, or other officers) who want a client to comply with an order, decision, decree, contract, or agreement, such as a court order, settlement agreement, criminal sentence, plea bargain, probation conditions, conditions of release, or other contract (collectively, called the "Contract," below):

- **Avoid directive language.**

- Appear to have **high prestige** and be **competent, attentive, practical, and motivated by the best interests of the client.**

- **Raise mild counterarguments** about the client's prospective compliance and **allow the client to refute** them. Bring up obstacles and drawbacks to compliance.

- **Involve significant others,** such as family members, in the decisional process leading to the Contract (if possible).

- Give the client a chance to make a **public commitment** to the Contract, by giving the client an opportunity to announce to a prestigious professional his or her intention to comply or to inform one or more people of his or her decision to follow it.

- In the Contract, provide **graduated incentives** for achievement of various objectives. **Individually tailor** the Contract to the needs and desires of the client, **define target behavior** with specificity, spell out the **positive and negative consequences** of compliance or noncompliance, and include **specific dates** for Contract initiation, termination, and renewal.

Definitions and Key Points

Litigants want:

- Voice: a voice, an opportunity to tell their story,
- Participation: a chance to participate in making the decision,
- Respect: to be treated with respect by the authority figures, and
- Explanation: to have the decision (if made by a third party) explained to them.

Participation: A chance to present evidence, one's own views, and voice and have shared decisionmaking. Need not actually affect decision.

Dignity: Legal authorities treat participants with respect, politeness, and dignity; rights as citizens are acknowledged; and their status is affirmed as competent, equal citizens and human beings.

Trust: Legal authorities are concerned about participants' welfare; want to treat them fairly; and allow them to present evidence. If so, they are perceived as more trustworthy. Trustworthiness increases also if legal authorities treat participants with respect and dignity, try to explain or account for their decisions, and appear motivated to treat them fairly.

Resources

Tom R. Tyler, *The Psychological Consequences of Judicial Procedures: Implications for Civil Commitment Hearings,* in David B. Wexler & Bruce J. Winick, Law in a Therapeutic Key: Developments in Therapeutic Jurisprudence 3–16 (Carolina Academic Press, 1996).

Susan L. Brooks & Robert G. Madden, Relationship-Centered Lawyering: Social Science Theory for Transforming Legal Practice (Carolina Academic Press, 2010) (Chapter 4, collecting four articles on procedural justice).

Dennis P. Stolle, David B. Wexler, & Bruce J. Winick, Eds., Practicing Therapeutic Jurisprudence: Law as a Helping Profession 320–23, 280–83, and 288–93 (Carolina Academic Press, 2000) (applying Tyler's and Meichenbaum and Turk's research to lawyering).

Coordination: Also read Brooks & Madden (Chapter 4) and Stolle, et al. (Chapter 11, particularly p. 320–24).

Chapter Assignments

Exercise 8-1 — TJ, PL, PJ Discussion Questions

Background Reading: If the answers to the below questions are not readily apparent, read Chapters 10–11 of the book, Dennis P. Stolle, David B. Wexler, & Bruce J. Winick, Eds., Practicing Therapeutic Jurisprudence: Law as a Helping Profession (Carolina Academic Press, 2000) and apply the concepts in the reading to the following questions:

1. Briefly discuss how these alternative sentencing options for the TJ/PL criminal defense lawyer would be employed, in a particular criminal case:

   a. Probation

   b. House arrest

   c. Electronic monitoring

   d. Community service

   e. Shock sentencing to a boot camp

   f. Restitution

   g. Employment

   h. Attendance at drug and alcohol treatment programs

   i. Pretrial diversion

   j. Deferred prosecution

2. Clients' participation in sentencing leads to lower compliance with the judgment or sentence imposed: T   F

3. Rehabilitative efforts of a criminal defendant, to be given weight by the court, must be:

   a. Extraordinary

   b. Voluntary

   c. Approved by the court

4. Clients need _____ in decisionmaking:

   a. Voice

   b. Participation

   c. To be treated with respect and dignity

   d. All of the above

Exercise 8-2 —
Integration Case: TJ, PL, & PJ in Criminal Law

Background Reading: Read Chapters 9–11, 13 & 14 of the book, DENNIS P. STOLLE, DAVID B. WEXLER, & BRUCE J. WINICK, EDS., PRACTICING THERAPEUTIC JURISPRUDENCE: LAW AS A HELPING PROFESSION (Carolina Academic Press, 2000).

Apply a TJ/PL and PJ analysis to the following case:

"10-20-Life": A 37-year-old father who is raising two children, ages 4 and 9, on his own, feels overwhelmed by financial pressures and frustrated with his situation and challenges in general. He is a reformed alcoholic and drug addict; 8 years ago, he had a series of criminal charges that led to him finally "getting sober" at age 29. At that time, he underwent some treatment and recovery, but in the last 4 years, since he has been a single parent, he has not attended any continuing treatment or recovery meetings, stating that he has "no time." His children's mothers (two separate women) are both active alcoholics and drug addicts and do not have unsupervised visitation with the children. He makes a poor choice and robs a convenience store using a gun. A struggle ensues with the store clerk and, while fighting, the gun fires, injuring the clerk. Applying the 10-20-life law, since he used a gun in the commission of a crime, he will receive at least 10 years if convicted; if he fired the gun, he receives 20 years, if he shot someone, he receives a life sentence if convicted. If this father is convicted, he could receive a life sentence, leaving his children are parentless. Suppose that the convenience store clerk is a 45-year-old divorced mother of two grown children and that she has one grandchild, age 3.

Gather in groups of three and have two assume the role of criminal defense attorney for one person playing this client. Assess: the issues you see presented, how you apply the concepts in the background reading and in Chapters 4–8 (listed below) to this case, your strategy for his defense, and your hopes for the outcome. Conduct an attorney-client meeting in which you cover or grapple with some of these ideas:

1. *Deferred sentencing*

2. *Creative sentencing options*

3. *Countertransference*

4. *Paternalism/coercion*

5. *Lecturing vs. listening*

6. *Sincerity of the client*

7. *Client voice and participation in decisionmaking*

8. *Client compliance with the judgment/sentence*

9. *Distressing nature of litigation*

10. *Dealing with denial and resistance*

Debriefing: Have the person playing the client give feedback to the two "attorneys" as to their efficacy in these ten areas, during the interview, balancing praise with suggestions for future interviews. Also, have that person relate his or her reactions to the attorneys' interview.

Chapter 9

Vector 5 — Creative Problem Solving

Description

Creative problem solving[1] ("CPS") refers to a broad approach to lawyering and legal problems that takes into account a wide variety of non-legal issues and concerns and then seeks creative, win-win solutions to otherwise win-lose scenarios. Creative problem solving is the discipline of conceptualizing and framing problems so as to permit the broadest possible array of solutions. A creative problem solver systemically seeks many points of view, engaging in multi-cause investigation and analysis. Problems are examined for their relational implications at all levels: individual, institutional, and societal. Creative problem solving avoids simplistic, "silver bullet" solutions. Instead it seeks to develop solution systems based upon what is learned about a problem, rather than on what is habitually done. It is a caring approach that seeks transformative solutions to redefine problems, expand resources, and facilitate enhanced relationships among the parties.

The website of the Center for Creative Problem Solving at California Western School of Law explains that, "clients and society are increasingly asking lawyers to approach problems [not always as fighters, but] more creatively. The Center develops curriculum, research, and projects to educate students and lawyers in methods for preventing problems where possible, and creatively solving those problems that do exist. The Center focuses both on using the traditional analytical process more creatively and on using nontraditional problem solving processes, drawn from business, psychology, economics, neuroscience, and sociology among others."[2]

CPS points out that the traditional model of lawyering relies on the following:

- An adversary system with rights and liabilities
- Decisionmaking that is rule based, not relational
- A single decisionmaker, the judge
- The binary lens of the judge (win/lose)
- Reliance on precedent (theory is more important than cases)

---

1. This Description is adapted from, and reprints portions of, Susan Daicoff, *Law as a Healing Profession: The "Comprehensive Law Movement,"* 6 Pepperdine Disp. Resol. J. 1 (2006).

2. CPS is associated with the Center for Creative Problem Solving at California Western School of Law (whose website is http://www.cwsl.edu/main/default.asp?nav=creative_problem_solving.asp& body=creative_problem_solving/home.asp) (last visited July 11, 2010), which sponsors a number of law school courses on CPS, national and international projects, and periodic conferences.

- Lawyers as advocates and neutral partisans
- Lawyers focused only on legal rights
- A focus on the past and assigning blame, as opposed to being forward-looking or planning-oriented

In contrast, CPS focuses on:

- Nonadversarial collaboration rather than adversarial advocacy
- Relational decisionmaking
- Group decisionmaking
- Win/win outcomes, not win/lose
- Case by case decisionmaking
- Lawyers as part of a collaborative team
- Lawyers who are focused on rights, goals, needs, etc.
- Being forward-looking and planning-oriented

In 1998, in the course of providing a brilliant explanation of the theoretical underpinnings and assumptions of CPS, Thomas Barton provided very useful concepts for understanding problem solving. First, he asserted that problems are a "mismatch" of needs with the environment. Second, he argued that there may be no inherent, empirical "truth" of the problem. Third, he explained that, in any problem, there are only three possible solutions: one can attempt to change the situation or other people involved (a "change you" solution), one can attempt to change oneself or one's attitudes toward the situation or other people involved (a "change me" solution), or one can exit the situation and attempt to find a substitute (an "exit and substitute" solution).[3]

One can easily apply this clear, three-step analysis to almost any conflict, for example, one at the workplace. Most people have found themselves in conflict with someone or some policy, at work. Barton's options are: ask the employer for a change (e.g., "may I work flex hours?"); change one's attitude (e.g., accept that this is a good job and in order to keep this good job, one must compromise and accept the working conditions present there); or exit and substitute (resign and find an alternate job). Importantly, Barton points out that exiting and substituting is a solution that depends entirely on the market and one's ability to control those resources (e.g., can another job be obtained?). Changing the others involved or changing oneself are technical solutions depending on insight, understanding, and the ability to redesign either the situation, other people, or one's attitudes. The law often steps in to resolve problems when none of these three options works, by employing social norms (such as the "best interests of the child" test in family law) and exercising power over the disputants. This provides an excellent framework for understanding problem solving and the law's role in that process.[4]

Janeen Kerper and Linda Morton explain how to apply creative problem solving to legal problems.[5] Kerper asserted that CPS assumes, first, that not all problems require

---

3. Thomas D. Barton, *Conceiving the Lawyer as Creative Problem Solver,* 34 Cal. W. L. Rev. 267 (1998).

4. *Id.*

5. Janeen Kerper, *Creative Problem Solving vs. The Case Method: A Marvelous Adventure in Which Winnie-the-Pooh Meets Mrs. Palsgraf,* 34 Cal. W. L. Rev. 351 (1998) (introducing the emergence of creative problem solving as a legal discipline in response to the need for change in legal education); Linda Morton, *Teaching Creative Problem Solving: A Paradigmatic Approach,* 34 Cal. W. L. Rev. 375, 376–78 (1998) (applying CPS in law school courses).

legal solutions and not all legal problems require a lawsuit. Second, CPS views problems as multidimensional with nonlegal, multidisciplinary solutions. It views "win/win" solutions as optimal. Finally, it defines the lawyer's role as assisting the client in solving problems. Part of this role includes helping the client build, maintain, and strengthen positive relationships with others to prevent future conflicts.[6]

Law professor Linda Morton gives an example of how the principles of CPS can be applied to and reinforced in other areas of the law school curriculum.[7] She starts with the example often given in Property class of the client who has been sued by a neighbor who is claiming adverse possession:

> The students' initial reaction might be to examine legal doctrine learned through the study of appellate cases (e.g., Was there sufficient use of the premises? Was the use permissive?). In teaching substantive law, this process must be undertaken in order to learn both content and legal analysis. However, analysis of the issue should not end there. A creative problem solving paradigm can teach other methods that lawyers might use to resolve the issue. In doing so, students would inevitably incorporate more humanistic and creative concepts in their thinking. In using the model offered, students would first have to identify the problem, taking into account interests and needs of those involved (e.g., Is this a case of neighborhood hostility? Land acquisition? What does the client want to happen? What can she afford? How do her values and interests compete with others involved?). Understanding the problem is the next step (e.g., What further research would have to be undertaken? What other disciplines should be consulted? How could the problem have been prevented?). Once the problem is thoroughly understood, solutions, in addition to that of litigation, are posed (e.g., Can this be resolved through a negotiation, mediation, or neighborhood coffee? Or should the client simply sell the property? What are the possible results of each?). After a full range of solutions is offered, the next step is to choose among them, keeping in mind the effects of implementing each one (e.g., Who decides? And, according to whose values? Who might be harmed?). Ultimately, an analysis is required as to whether the "best" solution has been chosen (e.g., Will such choice prevent future problems?). By framing class discussion in a creative problem solving context, the student is exposed to a much richer variety of approaches to the issue than legal analysis alone can offer.[8]

Law professor Janeen Kerper in her 1997 article on CPS gives a most vivid example of CPS, when she applies it to the famous *Palsgraf* explosion-on-the-railroad-platform case.[9] She asserts that in most first-year torts classes across the country, Cardozo's opinion in this case is analyzed as a "brilliant piece of legal reasoning,"[10] deciding just how far liability extends. In contrast, Kerper points out that the ultimate result of this famous torts case for Helen Palsgraf was dismal, if not entirely devastating. A single mother, struggling to provide for her children by working two menial jobs, and suffering from a speech impediment as an after effect of the incident that impaired her ability to work and communicate with her children, Mrs. Palsgraf was ultimately held liable for costs roughly equivalent to a year's earnings. Not only did Mrs. Palsgraf lose the case on appeal, but she

---

6. Kerper, *supra* note 5.
7. Example and questions from Morton, *supra* note 5, at 386–87.
8. *Id.*
9. Kerper, *supra* note 5.
10. *Id.* at 365.

also had to pay her own and the railroad's attorneys' fees. Financially, she ended up poorer as a result of the lawsuit and she achieved none of her nonlegal goals. Anecdotal evidence suggests that she even became mute as a result of the lawsuit's eventual outcome.[11] From a CPS perspective, it is "an example of particularly bad lawyering."[12]

Kerper re-evaluates Mrs. Palsgraf's case from a creative problem solving standpoint and contrasts what the CPS lawyer might do, with what her lawyer, Matthew Wood, did. For example, solutions that would have addressed Mrs. Palsgraf's physical problems, medical expenses, limited employment opportunities, and childcare obligations might well have been fashioned with the railroad's concurrence. By "brainstorming" to identify mutually acceptable alternatives to litigation, Mrs. Palsgraf's attorney may have better served her needs. Indeed, Kerper suggests, had Mrs. Palsgraf been afforded the opportunity to thoroughly explore her options and acknowledge her needs, she might have avoided the risks of a lengthy lawsuit that ultimately left her worse, physically and financially, than when she started.[13] Kerper's entire article is recommended reading, in connection with this vector (*see* Janeen Kerper, *Creative Problem Solving vs. The Case Method: A Marvelous Adventure in Which Winnie-the-Pooh Meets Mrs. Palsgraf,* 34 CAL. W. L. REV. 351 (1998)).

Practice Information

Lawyering Skills

Kerper, Barton, and other writers on creative problem solving include the following as lawyering skills required in CPS:[14]

- Listening, asking "dumb" (open) questions
- "Aporia"—adopting an attitude of not knowing, bafflement, curiosity, perplexity, ignorance, state of surrender, emptiness, readiness to learn
- Being TPWRQs—"The Person With the Right Questions" versus TPWA—"The Person With the Answers"
- Fact investigation
- Interest clarification
- Collaboration
- Negotiation
- Planning
- Using the adversarial process as a last resort
- Seeing emotions as integral to the problem solving process
- Self reflection on values and personal choice
- A problem solving model such as "SOLVE"

---

11. *Id.*
12. *Id.*
13. *Id.* at 368–70.
14. Barton, *supra* note 3, Kerper, *supra* note 5, and Morton, *supra* note 5.

Application of SOLVE to the Palsgraf Case

The "SOLVE" analysis explicated by Kerper in her article, above, is particularly useful for practicing attorneys.

SOLVE Five-Step Method of Problem Solving

- **State** the Problem Broadly
- **Observe and Organize** Problem
  - Identify initial conditions, goals, resources, constraints
- **Learn by Questioning** All Parts of the Problem
- **Visualize Possible Solutions**, Pick One, & Refine It
- **Employ Solution** & Monitor Results

Kerper applies the SOLVE analysis to the Palsgraf case as follows:[15]

- **Statement of the Problem**

What is the problem, state it as broadly as possible, are there emotional concerns involved or political concerns, is it simple and single or complex and multiple?

Palsgraf: The problem is that she was poor (earned $536.00 a year), had developed a speech impediment which seriously impacted her employment status, and was having trouble communicating with and caring for her children. There are multiple emotional associations and concerns, including her mental health and her relationship with her daughters.

There are political issues relating to wage and class structures. The problem was multiple and complex, meaning it was multicausal, as are minority juvenile delinquency or drug use, today.

- **Observe and Organize Problem**

State problem alternatively and from others' viewpoints, define current status, resources and conditions, define goals and resources, identify constraints.

Palsgraf: Her daughters were probably more concerned with her emotional health than her poverty. The railway saw it as no problem at all, but instead a freak accident that is unlikely to reoccur. Society would see it as a minor problem and of no consequence. It is not a major social problem that would require or be likely to receive vindication by a court of law.

Her goals were probably to: cover her medical expenses, stop stammering, and get a better paying job.

The constraints were: her lack of education, her low wages, her lack of time due to working two jobs and raising three children, no support from her husband, and the unemployment rate.

Available resources were: her husband, other family members, churches, charities, herself, her family, her employer, and her landlord.

- **Learn by Questioning All Parts of the Problem**

Why solve it, when and why does it happen, how often ... (ask who? what? why? where? how?). Have you ever had a similar problem? If so, how was that problem solved?

---

15. Kerper, *supra* note 5.

What does intuition tell us about solving this problem? Can we make the problem smaller or bigger?

Palsgraf: This analytical process would have had to have been done in a dialogue between the lawyer and the client and would have involved excellent listening, active listening, and empathy skills in order to elicit information from her. It would naturally have led into the next phase:

- **Visualize Possible Solutions, Pick One, and Refine It**

  Free associate and brainstorm. Effective brainstorming requires the suspension of judgment. Do not evaluate or criticize ideas during a brainstorming session. Accept all ideas. The leader of the session adopts a "no criticism, no judgment, no evaluation" rule in order to make the process work well.

  Palsgraf: Perhaps Matthew Wood and Helen Palsgraf would have decided to pursue other options instead of or alongside litigation, which would have helped build and strengthen her position so that the ultimate outcome would not have been so devastating.

- **Employ Solution and Monitor Results**

  a. *Select a solution or set of solutions, create an action plan, and monitor criteria that will indicate success. In choosing a solution, the lawyer should be judgmental and list pros and cons, evaluate, and critique, etc.*

  b. *Refine and improve the selected solution.*

  c. *Employ the solution by designing an action plan. List all things that need to be accomplished to get from Point A to Point B, with sequence and timing and responsibilities noted (i.e., a "to do" list).*

  NOTE: Here is where all the lawyer's typical lawyer-like personality characteristics are likely to be most useful (e.g., critiquing, judgmentalness, discrimination, critical thinking, objectivity, rational decisionmaking, logic, analysis).

  d. *Test on a small scale, if possible, and see how it works.*

As lawyers and hopeful people-with-the-answers, we are often likely to jump to the E of the SOLVE acronym without adequately exploring the SOLV processes. We also may tend to resolve the S part of the process all alone, without much input or collaboration from our clients and colleagues and others. As people who are likely to be Introverts on the Myers-Briggs Type Indicator (see Chapter 1), we are more likely to engage in the SOLVE processes alone, in our offices, not in a team atmosphere with other people. As people who are likely to prefer Judging on the Myers-Briggs Type Indicator and being a competent, socially ascendant leader (see Chapter 1), we are also likely to shun "aporia" and proceed directly to the E stage.

There are other, alternative models for problems solving, such as "ADDIE: Analyze, Design, Develop, Implement, and Evaluate." Related concepts are the approach to negotiation in Fisher, Patton, and Ury's 1981 book, *Getting to Yes*,[16] Goleman's concept of emotional intelligence,[17] and modern concepts of corporate management.[18]

---

16. ROGER FISHER, BRUCE M. PATTON & WILLIAM L. URY, GETTING TO YES: NEGOTIATING AGREEMENT WITHOUT GIVING IN (Houghton Mifflin, 1981).

17. DANIEL GOLEMAN, EMOTIONAL INTELLIGENCE: WHY IT CAN MATTER MORE THAN IQ (2005). *Cf.* John D. Mayer, Peter Salovey, & David R. Caruso, *Emotional Intelligence: New Ability or Eclectic Traits?*, 63 AM. PSYCHOL. 503, 504–05 (2008) (questioning the modern meaning of EQ).

18. *See, e.g.,* JIM COLLINS, FROM GOOD TO GREAT: WHY SOME COMPANIES MAKE THE LEAP ... AND OTHERS DON'T (2001); JAMES M. KOUZES & BARRY Z. POSNER, THE LEADERSHIP CHALLENGE

Kerper concludes that Palsgraf is an example of particularly bad lawyering, i.e., using the "hammer" excessively. She also argues that legal reasoning is circular in that, once one frames the issue, one decides the holding. She proposes that the issues could be re-framed this way:

- Cardozo intentionally omits the stammer to prevent future cases' distinguishing it;
- Cardozo was scandalously partial due to the American Law Institute lecture; and
- Wood did not make bad decisions for a trial lawyer (he won twice).[19]

Core Skills of Creative Problem Solving Being Taught in Law Schools

In early 1999, the McGill Center for Creative Problem Solving and California Western School of Law unveiled a pilot legal course in Creative Problem Solving. This course offered students hands-on experience in the art of asking questions and listening to people in contexts similar to those encountered in the actual practice of law, direct and cross-examination, client interviewing, jury selection, and negotiation. Other creative problem solving courses were later added to the curriculum; topics covered included: problem diagnosis, fact investigation, problem solving models and analysis, professional judgment and decisionmaking, professionalism, creativity, leadership, cross-cultural communications, group processes, collaboration with other professionals, brainstorming, identification of interests and stakeholders, strategic planning, risk analysis, and obstacles to sound decisionmaking. Many of these topics are taught in other law schools as leadership skills (see Chapter 4, *supra*); for example, at Santa Clara University School of Law, in courses on "leadership for lawyers."[20]

Definitions and Key Points

Creative Problem Solving:

- seeks solutions to problems that are genuine improvements for all persons.
- defines problems as: a mismatch of the physical, relational, cultural, organizational, or political **environment** with the **human purposes of people**.
- believes that problems can be solved by manipulating the environment rather than by a pronouncement of legal rights, vindication of power, or validation of identity.
- focuses on a concern for connections, relationships, and the common good.

Problems are a mismatch of people's needs with their environments.

In any problem, there may be no inherent, empirical "truth."

Three options to solve a problem:

1. Change you,

(2002); and Patrick Lencioni, The Five Dysfunctions of a Team: A Leadership Fable (2002) (all describing the modern forms of corporate management noted in Chapter 2 of this book).

19. Kerper, *supra* note 5.

20. *See, e.g.,* http://law.scu.edu/academics/courses/leadership-for-lawyers-521.cfm (last visited April 6, 2011).

2. Change me, or

3. Exit the situation and substitute.

SOLVE Model of Problem Solving:

- State the Problem

- Observe and Organize Problem (initial conditions, goals, resources, constraints)

- Learn By Questioning All Parts of the Problem

- Visualize Possible Solutions, Pick One, & Refine It

- Employ Solution & Monitor Results

Resources

Thomas D. Barton, Preventive Law and Problem Solving: Lawyering for the Future (Vandenplas Publishing, 2009) (most recent PL book by the director of the National Center for Preventive Law; integrating PL with problem solving) (Chapters 1–3, 10–25).

California Western Law Review, volume 34, issue 2, 1998 (entire issue devoted to creative problem solving).

Janeen Kerper, *Creative Problem Solving vs. The Case Method: A Marvelous Adventure in Which Winnie-the-Pooh Meets Mrs. Palsgraf,* 34 Cal. W. L. Rev. 351 (1998).

Linda Morton, *Teaching Creative Problem Solving: A Paradigmatic Approach,* 34 Cal. West L. Rev. 375 (1998).

Thomas D. Barton, *Conceiving the Lawyer as Creative Problem Solver,* 34 Cal. W. L. Rev. 267 (1998).

Website

Creative Problem Solving: Center for Creative Problem Solving at California Western School of Law, San Diego, California: www.cwsl.edu/main/default.asp?nav=creative_problem_solving.asp&body=creative_problem_solving/home.asp (last visited July 11, 2010).

Coordination: Also read King (Chapter 5) and Wright (p. 74).

Chapter Assignments

Exercise 9-1—Applying CPS in Practice

Return to the Paula/Castaway example in Chapter 7 and apply a CPS analysis to your representation of Paula, as follows:

(a) First, apply Barton's three options to the problem: 1. change you, 2. change me, or 3. exit the situation and substitute, and identify how these would apply, in this situation.

(b) Next, apply Morton's series of questions: Examine and apply legal doctrine learned through the study of appellate cases, to the facts of this case. Then, identify the problem, taking into account interests and needs of those involved (e.g., What does the client want to happen? What can she afford? How do her values and interests compete with others involved?). Understanding the problem is the next step (e.g., What further research would have to be undertaken? What other disciplines should be consulted? How could the problem have been prevented?). Once the problem is thoroughly understood, solutions, in addition to that of litigation, are posed (e.g., Can this be resolved through a negotiation, mediation, or conference? What are the possible results of each?). After a full range of solutions is offered, the next step is to choose among them, keeping in mind the effects of implementing each one (e.g., Who decides? And, according to whose values? Who might be harmed?). Ultimately, an analysis is required as to whether the "best" solution has been chosen (e.g., Will such choice prevent future problems?).

(c) Finally, specifically apply the steps of the SOLVE analysis, based on Kerper's work, summarized below (note: there is overlap between the steps):

SOLVE method of problemsolving

State the Problem: What is the problem? State the problem as clearly as you can; does the problem have emotional associations? Does the problem have political ramifications? Is the problem single and simple, or complex and multiple?

Observe, Organize, and Redefine the Problem: What are some alternative ways of stating the problem? Use perspectives of different actors. What is the starting place for the problem—any initial conditions, resources, current status? Define the goal; what is the desired end result upon successful completion? Are there constraints (any limiting factors or obstacles)?

Question the Problem: Why solve it? Why is it a problem? What specifically is the problem? Where does the problem occur? Why does it occur there? When does the problem occur? Why does it occur then? Who is involved? Why are they involved? How does it happen? Why does it happen that way?

Visualize Possible Solutions, Select One, and Refine It: Brainstorm possible solutions. Have you ever had a similar problem? If so, how was that problem solved? (Note that experience and precedent are only one aspect of brainstorming.) What are the numbers involved? Can the problem or possible solutions be graphed? Is there a logical solution (i.e., one which can be arrived at through logic, deduction, or inference)? What are the applicable analogies? What are the similar items, processes, or ideas? What does intuition tell us about how to resolve this problem? Does anyone have any hunches or gut feelings? Is there any way we can make the problem bigger? Is there any way we can make it smaller? Can we add something? Can we take something away? Can we exchange two parts? Can we replace something with something else? Can we combine two elements? Does anything else come to mind? (Use the process of free association here.)

The leader of a brainstorming session is trained to enforce a "no criticism, no judgment, no evaluation" rule.

Employ the Solution and Monitor Results: Select a solution or set of solutions, be judgmental, list pros and cons for each, and feel free to combine or modify. Refine and improve—review the selected idea carefully and improve or tweak it. Employ the solution and monitor results by designing an action plan. Create a path from here to there—list all the things that need to be accomplished or gathered in sequence with timing and responsibilities noted. Test on a small scale—if applicable, put the solution in place, and monitor criteria that will indicate success.

Chapter 10

Vector 6 — Holistic Law

Description

Holistic lawyering[1] encompasses many forms of practice that would easily fit within some of the other vectors, such as TJ or CPS; many of the other vectors would also easily fit within a "holistic" approach to law and justice. Holistic law or holistic justice ("HJ") is hard to define because it refers to approaches taken by a loose coalition of practicing lawyers in the United States and world, rather than an academic discipline. These lawyers also embody a rather diverse set of approaches. Most see themselves as healers and peacemakers; some focus more expressly on spiritual principles. The former website of the International Alliance of Holistic Lawyers stated that holistic justice "envisions a world where lawyers are valued as healers, helpers, counselors, problem-solvers, and peacemakers. Conflicts are seen as opportunities for growth. Lawyers model balanced lives and are respected for their contributions to the greater good." It sought "to transform the practice of law, through education and support of holistic practice" and "create peace within ourselves [and] between people."[2]

Holistic law, like preventive law, may parallel recent developments in the medical field. As preventive law analogizes to preventive medicine, so may holistic law analogize to holistic medicine, as compared to traditional medicine. Similarly, perhaps, preventive law has been a bit more readily accepted in the law, compared to holistic law; however, the move towards an integrative form of practice, both in law and in medicine, appears to be growing. Ruth Rickard explained HJ beautifully, in her June, 2008 article in the Michigan Bar Journal, *Practicing Wellness*, available at http://www.michbar.org/journal/pdf/pdf4article1374.pdf (last visited July 21, 2010).

Holistic lawyers often view the client's situation as an opportunity for growth for both the client and the lawyer, although they might be inclined to define growth along spiritual lines rather than along psychological lines. Some explicitly hold that "everything happens for a reason" and seek to find a greater purpose for or meaning in the legal problem or the interaction of the lawyer and client. Some explicitly follow their own personal values in their professional work and refuse to take actions that conflict with those personal values, always of course discussing those actions and values with the client. Some try to elicit from their clients their deepest desires, use the client's heartfelt goal as the goal of

---

1. This Description and other parts of this Chapter are adapted from, and reprint portions of, Susan Daicoff, *Law as a Healing Profession: The "Comprehensive Law Movement,"* 6 Pepperdine Disp. Resol. J. 1 (2006).

2. Website: http://www.iahl.org (last visited July 11, 2010). The organization dissolved in 2011, perhaps because its transformative goal had been accomplished. Its work continues in www.cuttingedgelaw.com (last visited July 6, 2011).

the lawyer-client relationship, and view their role as helping the client achieve that deeper goal.

Examples

The following[3] references three attorneys who, although they would not label their work "holistic," embody a truly "comprehensive" approach to lawyering, utilizing all of the vectors of the comprehensive law movement, even if implicitly.

Arnie Herz

Wall Street attorney Arnie Herz, who was profiled in the American Bar Association Journal in 2001,[4] describes holistic practice well when he gives this example of his lawyering work:[5]

> Attorney Arnie Herz. . . . represented an imposing ex-football player we shall call John Smalls, in a dispute with the new owners of the company Smalls had just sold, after ten years of successful solo ownership. Smalls was furious with the new owners' treatment of him as employee post-sale and with their mismanagement of the company. Unfortunately, he had signed a noncompete agreement as part of the sale and felt bound by it, despite his frustration. Determined to sue the new owners for mistreatment and mismanagement, he approached Herz, who opined that a lawsuit might succeed but would cost well over $100,000 in fees and costs to litigate. Smalls was ready to move, but Herz decided to slow him down a bit and asked, "If you could have anything you wanted in your life, what would you want your life to look like six months from now?" Smalls said, more than anything, he wanted to be free of the new owners and wanted to make more money. He thought he could make a lot more money without them but didn't want to "let them off the hook." Frustrated that Herz was trying to talk him out of suing, Smalls commented, "You're too nice — I need a tough litigator," packed up, and started to walk out the office. Taking a big risk, Herz responded with something like, "I know you think I'm not tough, but in all my years of experience, I think you may be the weakest person I've worked with. You set out a vision that was to be free of these people — you didn't mention that you wanted to punish them, teach them a lesson, or spend $100,000 of your own money and five years of your life doing so. What I see is that you don't have the strength to hold on to your own vision and deal effectively with your own anger. And I'll bet you've been doing this all your life." At first Smalls

---

3. This Section reprints portions (including the Sidebar, featuring Arnie Herz) of the author's article, Susan Daicoff, *Resolution without Litigation: Are Courtrooms Battlegrounds for Losers?* GPSOLO 44–50 (October/November 2003) (republished as a book chapter, Susan Daicoff, *The Comprehensive Law Movement: An Emerging Approach to Legal Problems*, in PETER WAHLGREN, ED., A PROACTIVE APPROACH, 49 SCANDINAVIAN STUDIES IN LAW 109–129 (2006)).

4. Steven Keeva, *What Clients Want: People Who Come to Arnie Herz Seeking Legal Help Leave with Some Unexpected Solutions*, 87 A.B.A.J. 48 (June 2001).

5. Sidebar from Susan Daicoff, *Resolution without Litigation: Are Courtrooms Battlegrounds for Losers?* GPSOLO 44–50 (October/November 2003).

flushed with anger. But something in what Herz said rang true. He slowly sat down and began listening and discussing; together, they agreed on a plan of action that involved a more collaborative, nonlitigious approach to resolving the matter. Smalls was freed from his noncompete clause three months later. The new owners teetered on the edge of bankruptcy for years—as Herz had predicted, even had Smalls sued, he would not have been able to collect a dime. Freed of the new owners, Smalls was in fact able to make a lot more money. Financially, the plan was a huge success. Personally, Smalls later said, the process of resolving this legal matter had allowed him to learn how his anger had been controlling his life, affecting his relationship with his wife and children, and blocking him from his full potential.

Herz's approach to representing Smalls is one illustration of how a comprehensive lawyer might conduct such a law practice. Herz went beyond the law to ask about the client's deepest needs, goals, and desires and then used that information to create, with the client, the best strategy. Admittedly, he took a major risk early in the lawyer-client relationship, and not all comprehensive lawyers would be comfortable doing so. Using excellent interpersonal skills, though, Herz assessed that Smalls was a no-nonsense person who would respond only to straight talk—which he did. Litigation in this case only would have wasted time and money and fueled the client's excessive anger. The final process and outcome were not only financially successful but also personally and emotionally beneficial for Smalls.[6]

Richard Halpert

Conduct an internet search on Richard Halpert. Read the May, 1999 American Bar Association Journal article by Steven Keeva featuring attorney Rick Halpert, *The Nicest Tough Firm Around,* available at http://www.tgpgraphics.com/customers/iahl %20test/articles/05_The_nicest_tough_firm.htm (last visited July 21, 2010).

John McShane

Conduct an internet search on John McShane. Read the June, 2000 American Bar Association Journal article by Steven Keeva featuring attorney John McShane, *Passionate Practitioner,* available at http://johnvmcshane.com/passion.html (last visited July 21, 2010).

Practice Information

Holistic law was advanced in the active practice of law by the International Alliance of Holistic Lawyers, founded by attorney William Van Zyverden.[7] It has been hard to define. As Jennifer Foster points out in Ruth Rickard's 2008 article, cited above, holistic law

---

6. Susan Daicoff, *Resolution without Litigation: Are Courtrooms Battleground for Losers?,* GP Solo, Oct./Nov. 2003 at 45–46.

7. www.iahl.org (last visited July 11, 2010).

often is most visible in how attorneys approach and interact with their clients, both attitudinally and in their communications. It denotes both an interior, attitudinal or values difference and an exterior, behavioral shift difference from traditional lawyering. Holistic law explicitly allows attorneys to incorporate and follow their own morals and values in their representation of clients, rather than setting them aside, as they engage in legal work.

Resources

J. Kim Wright, Lawyers as Peacemakers: Practicing Holistic, Problem-Solving Law (American Bar Association, 2010) (a most complete and extensive work by an American lawyer, dispute resolver, collaborative lawyer, author, and journalist exploring in detail how to practice law holistically).

Websites

www.cuttingedgelaw.com (last visited July 11, 2010).

www.renaissancelawyer.com (last visited July 11, 2010).

John McShane: www.johnvmcshane.com (last visited July 11, 2010).

Arnie Herz: http://www.legalsanity.com (last visited July 11, 2010).

Rick Halpert: http://www.leadersinlaw.com/attorneys/halpert (last visited July 11, 2010).

International Alliance of Holistic Lawyers: www.iahl.org (last visited July 11, 2010).

Coordination: Also read King (Chapter 6) and Wright (p. 23–26).

Chapter Assignments

Exercise 10-1—Employing Holistic Law in Practice

Assume your client is a part owner of a company that is being sued for product liability. Your client has been personally named as a defendant in this lawsuit. The lawsuit alleges that the company manufactured and sold a defective product that caused serious personal injury to children. Your client says it is possible that the allegations in the complaint are true, but he is not completely sure, since he is not a "hands-on" owner of the business. Your client is terribly distressed by the lawsuit and afraid of what will happen as a result of it. He has never been sued before or had any experience with litigation. He tells you very quickly in your initial interview that he has deeply held spiritual beliefs that people draw experiences to themselves in order to learn important life lessons, that any harm he does to any other person will have negative consequences, ultimately, for him, that all people are connected to one another, and that any harm one person inflicts on another creates a deep wound in the spiritual health of society/the world in general. He also has a deeply held moral belief that, when attacked, one should "turn the other cheek." He wants to hire you as his defense counsel and he needs somehow to respond to the plaintiffs' complaint, which he has not yet done. How do you propose to represent this client or handle his case?

How would this differ from a traditional approach to his case?

NOTE: This was based on a real case in which the defendant's heartfelt apology motivated the plaintiffs to drop that defendant out of the lawsuit entirely, while proceeding forward with suing the remaining defendants.

.

Chapter 11

Comprehensive Dispute Resolution

While many of the vectors of the comprehensive law movement are nonlitigative, avoiding litigation is not a universal goal of the comprehensive law movement approaches. Litigation is, in some cases, restorative, sanative, therapeutic, empowering, and appropriate, for example, when dealing with an intractable opponent. However, when nonlitigative alternative dispute resolution can be successfully used, many of the vectors of the comprehensive law movement advocate for its use. This chapter will introduce how comprehensive dispute resolution might differ from "traditional alternative dispute resolution," such as negotiation and settlement and mediation and then explore some basic conflict resolution processes and principles, including the utility and elements of apologies.

Conflict Resolution Processes

Modern dispute resolution takes many forms, ranging from more traditional forms, such as litigation and negotiated settlements, to alternative dispute resolution methods such as mediation, arbitration, private trials, and the like. Alternative dispute resolution ("ADR") emerged in the 1960s and 1970s for efficiency (as a way to avoid the cost and time involved in litigation) and empowerment (as a way to give power back to the people, rather than to the government). However, according to law professor Roberta Mitchell, when lawyers and psychologists vied for control of ADR in the 1970s, the lawyers won. As a result, traditional ADR has more of a legal flavor, today, than a psychological/social science flavor. In other words, while it resembles neither of these extremes precisely, it looks more like a trial than group therapy. Many forms of ADR reflect concerns about the fairness or equity of the outcome and the denigration of legal rights in the process, and tend to continue to have a third-party decisionmaker or facilitator involved.

In contrast, cooperative or comprehensive dispute resolution downplays or eliminates the presence of a third-party decisionmaker and of attorneys. Parties are encouraged to consider the emotions, motives, needs, and goals of the others involved in the process, even those traditionally thought of as "opponents." It emphasizes active listening, empathy, and decisionmaking by consensus among those present and participating in the process.

Comprehensive conflict resolution tends to emphasize cooperation, collaboration, honesty, full disclosure, transparency, and humility. It often reflects fundamental assumptions that collaboration is preferable (or equal) to adversarialism;[1] collectivity, in-

---

1. *See, e.g.,* J. Kim Wright, Lawyers as Peacemakers: Practicing Holistic, Problem-Solving Law (American Bar Association, 2010); Michael King, Arie Frieberg, Becky Batagol, & Ross

terdependence, and interrelationships should be valued;[2] needs are important along with legal rights;[3] and healing and reconciliation are important goals.[4] It also often recognizes three concepts: first, many legal disputes result simply from failure to manage interpersonal relationships well.[5] Better communication or conflict skills might have prevented the lawsuit altogether. Second, "truth," which the traditional legal system prizes, can be relative, in conflict resolution. Each party can see the situation from a different perspective and hold firm to the position that their view is the "truth," teaching us that there can be more than one "truth." For example, divorcing spouses may see an alimony dispute differently. The husband may say that the truth is that his wife is lazy and does not want to work full-time outside the home; his wife may say that the truth is that she is a devoted parent and that there is not enough money in her budget to cover all of the expenses she now has, post-separation. Third, global environmental interdependence has taught us that we cannot harm another without harming ourselves. For example, one country can dump toxic waste thinking it cannot harm itself, only to find later that its pollution affected another country halfway around the globe, which is its only source of a needed resource. Aggressive or hostile action by one party, which is intended to harm another party, may backfire. Therefore, it is discouraged in comprehensive conflict resolution.

Attorneys' Function

Attorneys continue to function as advocates and advisors for their clients, but do not usually argue points of law or fact with the other participants. They do not typically engage in oral argument or positional or argumentative opening statements. They may function more as coaches or full participants in the dispute resolution processes. They may assist their clients in crafting well-drafted apologies. They are expected to have an excellent understanding of their own reactions to conflict, the stages of grief (denial, anger, bargaining, depression, and acceptance), the process of conflict resolution — including apology, forgiveness, and reconciliation (if appropriate), and the possible pitfalls and blocks to resolution that can occur.

Clients' Function

Unlike traditional mediation, for example, clients are more likely to function as full participants with equal rights to speak as any other participant. They may be expected to

---

HYAMS, NON-ADVERSARIAL JUSTICE (The Federation Press, 2009); JULIE MACFARLANE, THE NEW LAWYER: HOW SETTLEMENT IS TRANSFORMING THE PRACTICE OF LAW (UBC Press, 2008) (Law & Society Series).

2. *See, e.g.,* Thomas D. Barton, *Troublesome Connections: The Law and Post-Enlightenment Culture,* 47 EMORY L.J. 163 (1998) (arguing that a sea change has occurred in society's philosophies).

3. *See, e.g.,* PAULINE H. TESLER, COLLABORATIVE LAW (2001) (indicating the importance of focusing on needs as well as legal rights in resolving family law disputes "collaboratively" rather than adversarily).

4. *See, e.g.,* works documenting the rise of a healing, peacemaking approach to practicing and adjudicating law such as MARJORIE A. SILVER, THE AFFECTIVE ASSISTANCE OF COUNSEL (Carolina Academic Press, 2007); DENNIS P. STOLLE, DAVID B. WEXLER, & BRUCE J. WINICK, EDS., PRACTICING THERAPEUTIC JURISPRUDENCE: LAW AS A HELPING PROFESSION (Carolina Academic Press, 2000); WRIGHT, *supra* note 1, KING, *supra* note 1, and MACFARLANE, *supra* note 1.

5. See, e.g., the example of the possible interpersonal communication errors that led to the litigation in Nanakuli Paving and Rock Co. v. Shell Oil Co., Inc., 664 F.2d 772, 32 UCC Rep.Serv. 1025 (9th Cir. 1981) (discussed in Chapter 6, text accompanying nn. 5–7).

participate and voice their thoughts more often than in traditional ADR processes. They are also expected to be able to manage their own strong emotions and learn how to "fight fair," express their needs and concerns, and refrain from needlessly incendiary words and actions.

Third Parties' Function

If third parties are present, they are more likely to fulfill the role of a facilitator of the process rather than act as a decisionmaker regarding substantive issues in the matter. They are expected to be very knowledgeable about, and skilled at managing, the process of dispute resolution, particularly needs- or interest-based processes. They need to be able to identify what the parties and attorneys need, at any particular moment, in order to continue moving forward in a productive manner. They also need to be able to halt or redirect the process when it has become nonproductive. Rarely will the parties and attorneys ask the facilitator to render a decision on an unresolved issue in the case.

Size and Personnel

Processes may be two- (two parties alone), three- (two parties plus a mediator or facilitator but no attorneys), four- (two parties and their attorneys but no third party), five- (two parties, their attorneys, and a third party mediator or facilitator), or multiple-party (e.g., circle sentencing, family group conferences, reparative boards, with and without facilitators) in size.

Conflict can be resolved in various processes; for example, conflict resolution may be:

- Two-party (two disputing parties)
- Three-party (two disputing parties and a third party process facilitator or decisionmaker)
- Four-party (two disputing parties and two lawyers advocating for each side)
- Five-party (four party, with the addition of a third party process facilitator or decisionmaker)
- Community decisionmaker (more than five parties present, an entire community comes together to make a decision and resolve a conflict, see Chapter 14, *infra*, on restorative justice circles, for example)

Conflict Resolution Basics

Recall Barton's three options for problem solving in Chapter 9 on creative problem solving. These are applicable to conflict resolution as well:

Type A. **Attempt to Change You (the other's behavior or the environment)**

Type B. **Attempt to Change Me (change one's own attitudes or behavior)**

Type C. **Exit the Situation and Get a Substitute (e.g., job, friend, etc.)**

Recall that Type A depends on the malleability of other people and situations; Type B depends on one's own self awareness and ability to self manage; and Type C depends upon one's ability to obtain substitutes on the "open market." None will work in all situations to resolve the problem; thus, each has limitations and constraints.

There are many models of conflict resolution; one proposes five types of conflict resolution, as follows:

Type 1. Denial or withdrawal

Type 2. Suppression or smoothing over

Type 3. Power or dominance

Type 4. Compromise or negotiation

Type 5. Collaboration

This table sets forth when to use each of these five types:[6]

Methods	What happens when used	Appropriate to use when	Inappropriate to use when
Denial or withdrawal	Person tries to solve problem by denying its existence. Results in win/lose.	Issue is relatively unimportant; timing is wrong; cooling off period is needed; short-term use.	Issue is important; when issue will not disappear, but build.
Suppression or smoothing over	Differences are played down; surface harmony exists. Results in win/lose and forms of resentment.	Same as above; also when preservation of relationship is more important at the moment.	Reluctance to deal with conflict leads to evasion of an important issue.
Power or dominance	One's authority, position, majority rule, or a persuasive minority settles the conflict. Results in win/lose.	Power comes with position of authority; when this method has been agreed upon.	Losers have no way to express needs, could result in future disruptions.
Compromise or negotiation	Each party gives up something in order to meet midway. Results in win/lose if "middle of the road" position ignores the real diversity of the issue.	Both parties have enough leeway to give; resources are limited; when win/lose stance is undesirable.	Original inflated position is unrealistic; commitment is doubted by parties involved.
Collaboration	Abilities, values, and expertise of all are recognized; results in win/win for all.	Time is available to complete the process; parties are committed.	The conditions of time, abilities, and commitment are not present.

---

6. This table was given to the author circa 2002–03 by Professor Michael Z. Green, formerly of Florida Coastal School of Law. However, its origin is unknown and apologies are due to its creator for missing attribution.

Example

For example, imagine that you are in a hurry to get to school or work and you realize, on your drive in, that you are almost out of gas. Spotting one of your favorite gas stations ahead, with the cheapest gas in town, you quickly wheel into the station and begin to pull into a bay. The gas station is full of customers and this is the only open bay; as you pull forward into the bay, another car is simultaneously pulling into the bay from the opposite direction. Pause for a moment and reflect on your immediate reaction; what would you do? It can suggest your preferred or default mode of conflict resolution, which is useful information to have when entering into negotiations. Every mode of conflict resolution has its advantages, disadvantages, and appropriate uses. Some of these will be explored below:

You might resolve the problem via the **raw exercise of power**. Either you quickly try to drive into the bay before the other car does, you inch forward slowly, forcing the other car to reverse and back out of the space, or you ram the other car with your car forcefully.

> Pros—The advantage of this is that it solves the problem; it's efficient.

> Cons—The disadvantages are that it could cause an accident that could be your fault, you may not be in the right under the law so you subject yourself to further sanctions, the other side may retaliate, it tends to keep those in power in power, and those with no power stay disempowered (might makes right).

You might resolve the problem via an **appeal to a higher authority**, arbiter, or judge—some sort of third party decisionmaker, like the store clerk at the station—who will decide who gets the bay.

> Pros—The situation gets resolved; it is somewhat efficient.

> Cons—There is a loss of control over the outcome or the process, you don't know if you'll be heard in the process, the other side may not comply with the decree, and the outcome can be unfair.

This is what R. Baruch Bush[7] calls "imposed judgment." He says that when people resort to this process for dispute resolution, it is because one or both are functioning at the lower level of human nature, relationally speaking, and thus the institution dealing with the conflict must be protective in character (i.e., have constitutional protections and evidence laws, not be like mediation), because the individuals involved need the protection.

You could resolve the problem via **subordination**—like a subordinate animal showing its soft underbelly to the dominant, "alpha" male, you might simply allow the other party to go first.

> Pros—This resolves the problem and is efficient.

> Cons—You don't get anything you want or need, you lose entirely, this is the flip side of might makes right, overuse of this strategy can lead to long term oppression and passive-aggressive reactive behavior on your part, and it could be stress producing for you.

You could resolve the problem by **arguing over rights and entitlements determined by rules and regulations** of the environment.

---

7. Robert A. Baruch Bush & Joseph P. Folger, The Promise of Mediation: The Transformative Approach to Conflict (1st ed. 1994; 2d ed. 2005).

Pros—Where there are black and white answers, this is efficient and should yield an answer.

Cons—There may not be black and white answers or rules and regulations that apply, people may see the answer differently (legal realism), there is too much "grey," people may not agree about the rules and may not abide by the decision made, parties may not respect the person/body promulgating the rule, and the rules may be unenforceable in practice, due to the high cost of litigation.

You could resolve the problem via **communication re: needs, wants, and fears**, leading to mutual **compromise** and understanding between the parties.

Pros—This affords the parties maximum control over the process and may create a working relationship between the parties that can be relied on in future conflicts.

Cons—This usually takes longer than the previous modes; it takes time and requires a certain level of honesty and self-knowledge.

You could resolve the problem by **simple economics/game theory**, exchanging bargaining pieces (one party could offer to pay for the other's spot) or making competing offers (this is often used in real estate sales and car buying).

Pros—This makes the process simply a matter of money and can be efficient.

Cons—This may not create a working relationship between the parties; it does not enhance empowerment or understanding by one party of the other side; there may be nonmonetary issues involved; and it relies on the availability of money to resolve the problem.

It is useful to begin to identify your own default conflict resolution strategies and the modes you prefer, in various situations, as you begin to hone your conflict resolution competency.

Basic Conflict Resolution Skills

The following skills are useful in comprehensive dispute resolution processes:

(1) **Be Real and Nondefensive; Communicate Well**—The parties need to be in touch with their own feelings, motives, needs, goals, vulnerabilities, and fears and be able to "own" or disclose them to the other parties. Optimally, they should be able to do this by using "I statements," not "You statements" (e.g., "I am afraid I'll lose money on this deal" instead of "You aren't a trustworthy business partner."). This can be viewed as humility, being real and non-defensive, and communicating well. This is also similar to needs-based bargaining instead of position-based bargaining.

(2) **Recognize the Other**—Each party needs to be able to put aside his or her own position/ego/self just long enough to stand in the shoes of the other parties. Empathy and active listening are tools one can use if one isn't "feeling it" at all, a way to act "as if" until one's understanding kicks in.

(3) **Ask for Solutions**—An additional tool is openness to solutions, brainstorming, and asking the other parties what kinds of solutions they see, as opposed to being a Person With The Answers/a "know it all." This also falls in the category of humility.

(4) **Tolerate Ambiguity and Silence**—Another skill is being able to accept and be comfortable with ambiguity, impasse, absence of solutions, silence, and silent conflict. We

are so quick to jump into the chasm with a solution or words when letting it sit, "sleeping on it," or getting more time will help.

(5) **Refocus on the Goal**—This tool is reminding everyone what the ultimate goal is and/or reaffirming the parties' commitment to or motivation for resolving this.

(6) **Fair Fighting**—If there is a basic commitment to a process or relationship, then constant threats to end that process or relationship are not fair game and create undue stress and fear in the participants.

Apology, Forgiveness, and Reconciliation

The following (at pages 147–157 hereof) has been adapted from an unpublished law review article by the author.[8]

Everyone has committed a wrong, made a mistake, broken a rule, or done something that violated their own morals and values, at some point in their life. We would hardly be human if we had not done so. It may even be natural and healthy to go through a process of personal wrongdoing that leads to greater maturation and growth.

A. A Natural Wrongdoing Process

When we committed our transgression, we may have been fully conscious that we were committing a wrong. Or, we may have been oblivious to the harm being done until later, perhaps when we reflected on it or were "caught" by another person. If we knew we were doing wrong at the time, we might have justified our actions by pointing out the misdeeds of others or some perceived injustice that fueled our behavior. Or, we chalked up our acts to "really poor judgment" or a "mistake." Sometimes we complained that we could not help ourselves; we were helpless to change or stop our own behavior. Our natural feelings of guilt over our actions existed alongside the undeniable reality that we were doing "wrong," but they did not stop us in our descent into transgression.

If we were of innocent mind, originally, and later realized we were wrong, we felt ashamed when we realized what we had done. We may at that point have engaged in justification and rationalization of our behavior or we may instead have dissolved into self-flagellation and despair.

We may have harmed only ourselves with our transgression or we may have harmed others. Either way, we suffered. We suffered the consequences upon ourselves of our wrongs and we suffered, watching the harm to others that we knew our behavior caused. Again, the pain of this suffering often caused us to attempt to reject or cast off responsibility for it. We turned instead to justifying, rationalizing, defending, arguing, and explaining away our behavior in a vain attempt to feel better about it.

However, this is only part of the natural process of committing, reflecting on, and learning from our wrongs. Eventually, we stop justifying. We can then look squarely at our behavior and the consequences it has wreaked upon us and those around us. We pri-

---

8. Article based on speech by the author, entitled *Therapeutic Jurisprudence: From Adversarialism to Mutuality in the Practice of Law* (April 10, 2009) (delivered at a symposium held by the Center for the Interdisciplinary Study of Conflict and Dispute Resolution on "Forgiveness, Reconciliation, and the Law," Case Western Reserve University School of Law, Cleveland, Ohio). Article manuscript submitted to symposium for publication; publication expected in 2012.

vately and publicly accept responsibility for what we have done and the harm it has caused others. We use the events and emotions strategically to aid us in, first, reflecting on our condition and, then, changing our minds, thoughts, reactions, and even personalities to become better people. Wrongs, properly utilized, help us become committed to aligning our future actions with our true values and morals. Finally, we learn humility and accountability, which foster greater self-esteem, when we make restitution to those we have harmed, including ourselves, by our actions. This may result in reconciliation of relationships with other people (what some call "horizontal harmony"); it will always result in reconciliation of us to ourselves (or, if it is to God, what some call "vertical harmony").[9] The entire process might be expressed as: acceptance; accountability; healthy shame; expressions of remorse; restitution; positive change; and reconciliation.

B. How The Law Deals With Wrongs

The traditional legal system aids our denial of personal responsibility and thus arrests this natural process. It encourages us to deny responsibility, cast off shame and guilt, point the finger at others' behavior or unjust rules, paint ourselves "lily white," tell only one side of the story, never admit fault or blame, and live in a polarized, binary system of thought: right/wrong, guilty/innocent, win/lose. This is true for both civil and criminal cases. It discourages horizontal harmony by fostering distance and "no communication" rules between people involved in lawsuits. It provides scarce avenues for restitution of wrongs by offenders directly to those they have harmed, preferring instead the impersonal measures of monetary damages, incarceration, and fines.

Surprisingly, those we have harmed find little solace in the legal process' treatment of our wrongs. Victims of crime and civil plaintiffs alike often express dissatisfaction with legal process, either feeling revictimized by the discovery and trial processes or disenfranchised by the lack of opportunity to "be heard" in court.[10]

These failings have spurred the development of vectors of the comprehensive law movement such as restorative justice and transformative mediation, which directly or indirectly can foster the natural process of "acceptance — accountability — healthy shame — expressions of remorse — restitution — positive change — reconciliation" described above. Also, not only is the natural process of wrongdoing therapeutic for the wrongdoer, in it the victim's needs can also be addressed and some form of restitution can be made.

---

9. Definition attributed to Dean Emeritus David T. Link, former dean of Notre Dame Law School and former president of the International Centre for Healing and the Law (personal communication with the author, circa 2003), *see* http://people.forbes.com/profile/david-t-link/72392 (last visited May 8, 2011). *See also* comments by Hon. Ray Austin, Supreme Court, Navajo Nation, and Chief Justice of the Navajo Nation, Hon. Robert Yazzie, describing Navajo peacemaking process, in the 2000 film by James M. Cooper, Jurist Voices (McGill Center for Creative Problem Solving, California Western School of Law, 2000), *citing* Judge Robert Yazzie, *Hozho Nahasdlii — We are Now in Good Relations: Navajo Restorative Justice*, 9 St. Thomas L. Rev. 117, 124 (1996) (which means "may the good way be restored").

10. Tom R. Tyler, *The Psychological Consequences of Judicial Procedures: Implications for Civil Commitment Hearings*, in David B. Wexler & Bruce J. Winick, Eds., Law in a Therapeutic Key 9–12 (Carolina Academic Press, 1996). Tom Tyler presents stunning empirical evidence that litigants' satisfaction with legal process and perceptions of fairness are related more to three intangible factors than they are to the actual win/lose outcome of the case; these are discussed in more detail in Chapter 8.

C. An Alternative Process to Resolve Wrongdoing: The "Core Sequence"

What are the steps of such a process? Sociology professor Thomas Scheff describes a "core sequence" of apology-forgiveness-reconciliation, in successful victim/offender mediations in criminal law.[11] This core sequence involves an exchange between the victim and the offender (in civil cases, it would involve the plaintiff and defendant, instead). Usually, this exchange consists of a sincere apology by the offender to the victim directly, containing the following elements: an expression of regret, remorse, or "I'm sorry;" a plan or intention not to do it again; and an acknowledgement of the harm done to the victim and the impact of the wrong on the victim's life. The offender (or defendant) takes personal responsibility for the act and the victim (or plaintiff) receives some acknowledgement from the offender.

This can be followed by acceptance of that apology by the victim or plaintiff. Forgiveness means more than simply hearing; it involves acceptance, believing in the offender's sincerity, and feeling that the defendant or offender is truly remorseful and either wishes that he or she did not do the acts that caused harm or is taking steps never to do them again. The effect of forgiveness is to restore humanity and status to the offender.

The apology-forgiveness exchange is often memorable, usually poignant, and sometimes even magical. When sincere, there is almost always deep emotion visible at this point in one or both parties. There is almost a tangible, perceptible shift in the room when, as a mediator, one sees this exchange occur. Before it happens, there is usually anxiety, tension, anger, and resistance in the room. Afterwards, there is often calm, relaxation, and peace. The parties sometimes collaborate and there is often smooth progress towards resolution. Ideally, after this exchange, the resolution of the dispute or offense is relatively simple, with both sides quickly agreeing to material reparations to be made by the offender to the victim. Something is actually given to the victim by the offender in this process, perhaps symbolically partially replacing what was taken from the victim by the offender in the offense.

Reconciliation may or may not happen after this "core sequence." It involves re-establishing a relationship of trust between the victim and offender afterwards. This is not a necessary sequel to apology and forgiveness, but it may occur. The parties' relationship may be restored and they may now be on "good terms" with each other. At the least, closure may occur for the victim or offender, or both.

However, this is only likely to occur if there has been a sincere apology which was made directly to and accepted by the victim or plaintiff. There is a classic example of a failed apology in an interview of the mother of a victim tortured and killed due to apartheid in a 1999 documentary titled *Facing the Truth with Bill Moyers*. In this film about the South African Truth and Reconciliation Commission's post-apartheid efforts to bring victims and offenders together for reconciliative purposes, she says justice was not done. When asked why not, she emphatically expressed that the apology was not directed to her: "[T]hey should have apologized to me, *to me*, ... first to me, and then to God."[12]

---

11. Thomas J. Scheff, *Community Conferences: Shame and Anger in Therapeutic Jurisprudence*, 67 Rev. Jur. U.P.R. 97, 104–06 (1998).

12. DVD: *Facing the Truth with Bill Moyers*, Gail Pellet, Films for the Humanities & Sciences (1999) (on file with author).

While much of the apology-forgiveness-reconciliation literature focuses on criminal actions, in civil disputes, there is a similar exchange that occurs and, indeed, arguably must occur for lasting resolution to be present.[13] However, in civil actions (particularly contract disputes or domestic relations matters), sometimes both parties feel as if they were wronged, so both may be looking for an apology and for a dual "core sequence" to occur.[14]

D. Benefits of Apologies

Apologies are useful for several reasons. First, they have been demonstrated to reduce the threat of civil litigation. In 1987, 2001, and 2002, respectively, when hospitals in Kentucky,[15] Maryland,[16] and Michigan[17] adopted apology policies, reportedly their malpractice claims dropped significantly (30% in one case and 50% in another). Apology by a physician can be particularly important; Colorado surgeon Michael Woods has been quoted as attributing litigation more to a "doctor's attitude" than to the actual act of malpractice.[18]

Second, apologies facilitate guilt, which can be therapeutic for the apologizer. Scheff distinguishes between unhealthy shame, which says, in effect, "I am wrong; there is something wrong or defective about me," and reintegrative shame (or guilt), which says, "I have done something wrong."[19] Reintegrative shame, or guilt, is linked to acceptance of personal accountability and responsibility and a willingness to change. This is particularly true if the apology is done publicly. Unhealthy shame, on the other hand, is linked to recidivism, low self-esteem, and alienation from society.[20] Therefore, reintegrative shame or guilt can lead to changed behavior, ultimately.

Third, apologies can facilitate movement through the grief process in litigants or parties. Recall psychologist Elizabeth Kübler-Ross' familiar five stages of grief—denial, anger, bargaining, depression, and acceptance.[21] Due to most litigation's emphasis on blame and fault, it is possible for parties to remain "stuck" in anger, which may be countertherapeutic. For example, Scheff asserts that anger in litigants is often disguised as moral indignation and lecturing of the wrongdoer.[22] Allowing plaintiffs and crime victims to express anger and be heard, and allowing offenders and defendants to express remorse and ask for forgiveness, may reduce anger and thus facilitate the parties' movement towards acceptance, resolution, and closure.

A more specific application is in divorce actions; there is empirical evidence that interparental conflict is one of the top three factors in poor post-divorce functioning of

---

13. Based on the author's personal experiences informally mediating various disputes, circa 2003.

14. Somewhat similarly, transformative mediation (explored in Chapter 13) uses the concept of "recognition" to encourage both parties to express to each other an understanding of each other, *see* Robert A. Baruch Bush & Joseph P. Folger, The Promise of Mediation: The Transformative Approach to Conflict 77 (1st ed. 1994).

15. The Hardest Word, Folio Weekly (Nov. 16, 2004) (Author unknown) (referring to a veterans hospital).

16. Martin Lasden, *Esq.: Saying You're Sorry,* California Lawyer (June, 2005) available at http://www.callawyer.com/story.cfm?pubdt=NaN&eid=718449&evid=1 (last visited July 8, 2010).

17. The Hardest Word, *supra* note 15 (referring to the Johns Hopkins children's hospital).

18. *Id.,* referring to Dr. Woods' book, Michael S. Woods, Healing Words: The Power of Apology in Medicine (2007).

19. Thomas J. Scheff, *Community Conferences: Shame and Anger in Therapeutic Jurisprudence,* 67 Rev. Jur. U.P.R. 97, 104–06 (1998).

20. *Id.*

21. Elisabeth Kübler-Ross, On Death and Dying (1969) (discussed in Chapter 4).

22. Scheff, *supra* note 19, at 111–14.

children.[23] Focusing on opportunities for apology and forgiveness in divorce actions may reduce the parties' anger and thus their conflict, which, in turn, may result in better post-divorce functioning of their children.[24]

E. Practice Tips for Legal Personnel

Legal personnel can use apologies in several ways. First, lawyers can consider incorporating opportunities for apology, forgiveness, and reconciliation in their criminal and civil cases. Partisan lawyers representing criminal or civil defendants may specifically consider whether their clients would benefit from (and are ready for) making an apology. They can refer clients to mental health professionals to assess their readiness to apologize. They can study the components of an effective apology and then coach their clients in how to craft an effective apology. They may prepare their clients for the possibility that forgiveness might not be received. They can help their clients thread through the legal ramifications of making an apology; in many jurisdictions, expressions of remorse are not admissible in court, later. For example, there may be state statutes preventing expressions of sympathy from being admitted as evidence.[25] Federal evidence law may provide that apologies made in the course of settlement negotiations are not admissible as evidence of liability.[26] Lawyers representing plaintiffs or counseling crime victims can coach them in accepting or asking for apologies. Finally, lawyers serving as mediators can foster opportunities for the core sequence of apology, forgiveness, and reconciliation to occur. For example, Scheff explains that a mediator can use gentle questions to stop moral indignation and lecturing and refocus the parties and the process, if bickering develops.[27]

Apologies are most effective when they are done publicly, as opposed to privately. They are also best when they are made by the apologizer directly to the intended audience (victim or plaintiff, affected community, etc.). Philosophy professor Nick Smith proposes these strategies: using written letters or videos when face-to-face encounters are unavailable, using performed apologies in addition to written ones, and apologizing in postings on social networks such as Facebook and Twitter.[28] The efficacy of apologizing by phone, by email, or interactively over the internet, if face-to-face encounters are impossible, should be evaluated.

Apologies are most effective when they state all acts done and are sincere, complete (as opposed to incomplete or missing some components), made voluntarily, and made directly to the victim. There must be no factual disputes; the apologizer must be ready to apologize and must believe he or she did something wrong. The apologizer must not defend, excuse, justify, or rationalize his or her acts. The apologizer should take personal responsibility and not blur the actor ("I am sorry for what I did," not, "The company is

---

23. Kathryn E. Maxwell, *Preventive Lawyering Strategies to Mitigate the Detrimental Effects of Client's Divorces on Their Children*, 67 Rev. Jur. U.P.R. 137 (1998).

24. Speech by Solangel Maldonado, Professor of Law, Seton Hall University Law School, titled *Forgiveness in the Context of Family Law: "Healing Divorce"* (April 10, 2009) (delivered at a symposium held by the Center for the Interdisciplinary Study of Conflict and Dispute Resolution on "Forgiveness, Reconciliation, and the Law," Case Western Reserve University School of Law, Cleveland, Ohio).

25. Lasden, *supra* note 16.

26. *Id.*

27. Scheff, *supra* note 19, at 111–14.

28. Speech by Nick Smith, Associate Professor of Philosophy, University of New Hampshire, titled *Forgiveness: What, When, Why?*, with Charles Griswold, Professor of Philosophy, Boston University (April 10, 2009) (delivered at a symposium held by the Center for the Interdisciplinary Study of Conflict and Dispute Resolution on "Forgiveness, Reconciliation, and the Law," Case Western Reserve University School of Law, Cleveland, Ohio) (discussing the elements of an effective apology).

sorry for your loss."). Finally, there should be no recidivating; an apology loses meaning when the apologizer repeats the behavior, afterwards.[29]

Empirical studies have shown that lawyers do not view apologies to be as important as nonlawyers do, so they should be aware of this tendency in themselves to downplay the effect of an apology.[30] There is also evidence that lawyers, particularly prosecutors, may view apologies as a display of weakness by a criminal defendant.[31]

A law school class on comprehensive law practice developed the following recommended components of a successful apology-forgiveness-reconciliation exchange, in this table, below (excerpted from the author's unpublished article):[32]

---

29. Smith, *supra* note 28.

30. There is actually empirical research comparing how lawyers and nonlawyers rated the desirability of various settlement offers in hypothetical civil actions; the nonlawyers rated the offers that were accompanied by apologies higher than those that were not, while lawyers saw no difference between the two offers (which were equal in dollar amount). Russell Korobkin & Chris Guthrie, *Psychology, Economics, and Settlement: A New Look at the Role of the Lawyer*, 76 TEX. L. REV. 77 (Nov. 1997). *See also* SUSAN DAICOFF, LAWYER, KNOW THYSELF 25–42 (2004) (lawyers are also generally less sensitive to interpersonal concerns and emotions, compared to nonlawyers).

31. Margareth Etienne & Jennifer K. Robbenolt, *Apologies and Plea Bargaining*, 91 MARQ. L. REV. 295, 309–10 (2007).

32. *See* note 8, *supra.* This was developed in the author's Comprehensive Law Practice class at Florida Coastal School of Law, Jacksonville, Florida, 2008–09. The class drafted written apology letters from the perspective of a hypothetical offender, then drafted written acceptance letters from the perspective of the victim. The author observed these common themes in their collective written work.

Concept	Victim's Need	Offender's Apology
Consequences	To express the impact the O's actions had on the V's life, including expressing the painful emotions caused in V by the event	To understand and acknowledge the impact the O's actions had on the V's life
Apology/Remorse	To believe, have faith that the O really is sorry for what he or she did, is remorseful, regrets what happened not solely for selfish reasons	To apologize, say I'm sorry, express remorse, regret that the event happened to the V, in a sincere, non-selfish, non-self-focused manner, with O being visibly ashamed of what he or she did and not being angry, which allows V to see O as human—forges bond between V & O
Responsibility	To have all blame shifted entirely off the V and entirely onto the O for the event	To accept responsibility for what happened, to express awareness that the event was "wrong" and that O did wrong
Forgiveness	To forgive the O, stop being angry with O, stop lecturing O from hilltop, see the O as a fellow human being—forges bond between V & O NOTE: relentless anger at O may be moral indignation, which may be unacknowledged (projected) shame	To receive V's forgiveness
Understanding	To ask why, to understand more about why this happened to the V May also include understanding the O as a fellow human being	Explains why the offense was done May also include understanding the V as a fellow human being
Positive Outcome/ Rehabilitation	To have faith that something good can come out of this event, that the O will improve as a result	To admit that O has a problem and express O's willingness to change
Restitution to the Victim	To receive material restitution from the O to "make whole" the loss that arose from the event	To express willingness to make material restitution to V, outline a plan for it
Plan for the Future	To know that this will not happen again	To describe his or her plan for changing and not recidivating

Example

These concepts can be applied to any real or hypothetical apology. For example, in 2010, professional golfer Tiger Woods publicly apologized for his marital unfaithfulness.[33] Most of the above concepts are present in the Woods apology, as analyzed in this table, below (excerpted from the author's unpublished article):[34]

---

33. Tiger Woods' public apology, entire text available at http://www.huffingtonpost.com/2010/02/19/tiger-woods-transcript-ap_n_469208.html (last visited May 9, 2011) and http://www.ajc.com/sports/text-of-tiger-woods-314300.html (last visited May 9, 2011).

34. *See* note 8, *supra.*

Concept	Offender's Apology	Mr. Woods' Statement
Consequences	To understand and acknowledge the impact the O's actions had on the V's life	*I am also aware of the pain my behavior has caused to those of you in this room. I have let you down. I have let down my fans. For many of you, especially my friends, my behavior has been a personal disappointment. To those of you who work for me, I have let you down, personally and professionally. My behavior has caused considerable worry to my business partners.* To everyone involved in my foundation, including my staff, board of directors, sponsors, and most importantly, the young students we reach, … *I know I have severely disappointed all of you. I have made you question who I am and how I have done the things I did.…* *I hurt my wife, my kids, my mother, my wife's family, my friends, my foundation, and kids all around the world who admired me.*
Apology/Remorse	To apologize, say I'm sorry, express remorse, regret that the event happened to the V, in a sincere, non-selfish, non-self-focused manner, with O being visibly ashamed of what he or she did and not being angry, which allows V to see O as human—forges bond between V & O	*I want to say to each of you, simply, and directly, I am deeply sorry for my irresponsible and selfish behavior I engaged in.…* I am embarrassed that I have put you in this position. For all that I have done, *I am so sorry.* I have a lot to atone for. … Parents used to point to me as a role model for their kids. I owe all of those families a special apology. *I want to say to them that I am truly sorry.*
Responsibility	To accept responsibility for what happened, to express awareness that the event was "wrong" and that O did wrong	Many of you have cheered for me, or worked with me, or supported me, and now, *every one of you has good reason to be critical of me.…* *The issue involved here was my repeated irresponsible behavior. I was unfaithful. I had affairs. I cheated. What I did is not acceptable. And I am the only person to blame.… … I knew my actions were wrong.…* *I was wrong. I was foolish.* I don't get to play by different rules. The same boundaries that apply to everyone apply to me. *I brought this shame on myself…*
Forgiveness	To receive V's forgiveness	Finally, there are many people in this room and there are many people at home who believed in me. Today, I want to ask for your help. *I ask you to find room in your hearts to one day believe in me again.*
Understanding	Explains why the offense was done May also include understanding the V as a fellow human being	I know people want to find out how I could be so selfish and so foolish. People want to know how I could have done these things to my wife, Elin, and to my children.… I knew my actions were wrong. But *I convinced myself that normal rules didn't apply. I never thought about who I was hurting. Instead, I thought only about myself. I ran straight through the*

		boundaries that a married couple should live by. I thought I could get away with whatever I wanted to. I felt that I had worked hard my entire life and deserved to enjoy all the temptations around me. I felt I was entitled. Thanks to money and fame, I didn't have far—didn't have to go far to find them.... I stopped living by the core values that I was taught to believe in.... As I proceed, I understand people have questions. I understand the press wants me to—to ask me for the details of the times I was unfaithful. I understand people want to know whether Elin and I will remain together. Please know that as far as I'm concerned, every one of these questions and answers is a matter between Elin and me. These are issues between a husband and a wife.
Positive Outcome/ Rehabilitation	To admit that O has a problem and express O's willingness to change	It is hard to admit that I need help. But I do. For 45 days, from the end of December to early February, I was in inpatient therapy, receiving guidance for the issues I'm facing. I have a long way to go. But I've taken my first steps in the right direction. ... I've had a lot of time to think about what I have done. My failures have made me look at myself in a way I never wanted to before.
Restitution to the Victim	To express willingness to make material restitution to V, outline a plan for it	Elin and I have started the process of discussing the damage caused by my behavior. As she pointed out to me, *my real apology to her will not come in the form of words. It will come from my behavior over time....* It is now up to me to make amends. And that starts by never repeating the mistakes I have made. It is up to me to start living a life of integrity.... I do plan to return to golf one day. I just don't know when that day will be. I don't rule out that it will be this year. *When I do return, I need to make my behavior more respectful of the game.*
Plan for the Future	To describe his or her plan for changing and not recidivating	I recognize I have brought this on myself. And I know above all I am the one who needs to change. I owe it to my family to become a better person. I owe it to those closest to me to become a better man. That is where my focus will be. *I have a lot of work to do. And I intend to dedicate myself to doing it....* *Part of following this path for me is Buddhism,* which my mother taught me at a young age. People probably don't realize it, but I was raised a Buddhist, and I actively practiced my faith from childhood until I drifted away from it in recent years. Buddhism teaches that a craving for things outside ourselves causes an unhappy and pointless search for security. It teaches me to stop following every impulse and to learn restraint. Obviously, I lost track of what I was taught.

		As I move forward, I will continue to receive help because I have learned that is how people really do change. Starting tomorrow, I will leave for more treatment and more therapy. ... In therapy, I have learned that looking at— the importance of looking at my spiritual life and keeping in balance with my professional life. *I need to regain my balance and be centered so I can save the things that are most important to me: my marriage and my children.* *That also means relying on others for help.* I have learned *to seek support from my peers in therapy, and I hope someday to return that support to others who are seeking help....* (italics added)[35]

However, his apology could have been criticized or ill-received as a result of three additional features. First, he might have seemed defensive when he included the italicized comments, in his apology, as follows:

> But there is one issue I really want to discuss. Some people have speculated that Elin somehow hurt or attacked me on Thanksgiving night. *It angers me that people would fabricate a story like that.* She never hit me that night or any other night. There has never been an episode of domestic violence in our marriage. Ever....
>
> *Some people have made up things that never happened. They said I used performance-enhancing drugs. This is completely and utterly false....*
>
> Some have written things about my family.... *However, my behavior doesn't make it right for the media to follow my 2½-year-old daughter to school and report the school's location. They staked out my wife and pursued my mom.* Whatever my wrong-doings, for the sake of my family, please leave my wife and kids alone (italics added).[36]

Second, he refused to answer questions posed by the audience. Finally, the apology occurred several months after his unfaithfulness was discovered and became public, as opposed to immediately.

Nevertheless, examples such as Mr. Woods' apology are encouraging evidence of a growing recognition of the utility of apologies. In addition, study of these public apologies can be useful to legal professionals seeking to assist parties in crafting or requesting an effective apology. The field of apology-forgiveness-reconciliation research and literature is vast[37] and this brief treatment in this chapter does not do it justice. However, as

---

35. Tiger Woods' public apology, entire text available at http://www.huffingtonpost.com/2010/02/19/tiger-woods-transcript-ap_n_469208.html (last visited May 9, 2011) and http://www.ajc.com/sports/text-of-tiger-woods-314300.html (last visited May 9, 2011).

36. Tiger Woods' public apology, entire text available at http://www.huffingtonpost.com/2010/02/19/tiger-woods-transcript-ap_n_469208.html (last visited May 9, 2011) and http://www.ajc.com/sports/text-of-tiger-woods-314300.html (last visited May 9, 2011).

37. For example, Jonathan R. Cohen has written extensively about apologies in the law, *see, e.g.,* Jonathan R. Cohen, *The Immorality of Denial,* 79 Tul. L. Rev. 903 (2005); Jonathan R. Cohen, *The Culture of Legal Denial,* 84 Neb. L. Rev. 247 (2005); Jonathan R. Cohen, *Apology and Organizations: Exploring an Example from Medical Practice,* 27 Fordham Urb. L. J. 1447 (June 2000); Jonathan R. Cohen, *Legislating Apology: The Pros and Cons,* 70 U. Cin. L. Rev. 819 (Spring 2002); Jonathan R. Cohen, *Encouraging Apology Improves Lawyering and Dispute Resolution,* 18 Alternatives to High Cost Litig. 171 (October 2000); Jonathan R. Cohen, *Apologizing for Errors,* 6 No. 4 Disp. Resol. Mag. 16 (Summer 2000); Jonathan R. Cohen, *Advising Clients to Apologize,* 72 S. Cal. L. Rev. 1009

the field may continue to grow, legal personnel may want to consider adding these concepts to their conflict resolution skills.

Resources

There are many well-loved resources on conflict resolution/dispute resolution; however, these are a few that specifically focus on dispute resolution within the comprehensive law movement:

SUSAN L. BROOKS & ROBERT G. MADDEN, RELATIONSHIP-CENTERED LAWYERING: SOCIAL SCIENCE THEORY FOR TRANSFORMING LEGAL PRACTICE (Carolina Academic Press, 2010) (Chapter 2).

MARJORIE A. SILVER, THE AFFECTIVE ASSISTANCE OF COUNSEL (Carolina Academic Press, 2007) (Chapters 7, 9–11).

DANIEL BOWLING & DAVID HOFFMAN EDS., BRINGING PEACE INTO THE ROOM (John Wiley & Sons, Inc., 2003) (this book, by two experienced mediators, one of whom is also a collaborative lawyer, challenges mediators to learn to be peacebuilders in the mediation process).

BARBARA ASHLEY PHILLIPS, THE MEDIATION FIELD GUIDE: TRANSCENDING LITIGATION AND RESOLVING CONFLICTS IN YOUR BUSINESS OR ORGANIZATION (Jossey-Bass 2001) (covering changes in the area of mediation toward a more holistic practice).

Jonathan R. Cohen, *The Immorality of Denial*, 79 TUL. L. REV. 903 (2005).

Jonathan R. Cohen, *The Culture of Legal Denial*, 84 NEB. L. REV. 247 (2005).

Jonathan R. Cohen, *Advising Clients to Apologize*, 70 S. CALIF. L. REV. 1009 (May, 1999).

Jonathan R. Cohen, *Encouraging Apology Improves Lawyering and Dispute Resolution*, 18 ALTERNATIVES HIGH COST LITIG. 171 (2000).

Edward A. Dauer, et al., *Transformative Power: Medical Malpractice Mediations May Help Improve Patient Safety*, DISP. RESOL. MAG. 9 (1999) (this article is authored by a preventive law expert).

Coordination: Also read Silver (Chapter 7 and 9), King (Chapter 7), and Wright (p. 55–60 and Chapter 5).

Chapter Assignments

Exercise 11-1 — Your Conflict Resolution Style

Answer these questions:

(1) How do you normally resolve conflict?

(May 1999); Jonathan R. Cohen, *Nagging Problem: Advising the Client Who Wants to Apologize*, 5 No. 3 DISP. RESOL. MAG. 19 (Spring 1999).

(2) Notice how many times during the day do you encounter a potential argument—did it get resolved and in what manner; of the various styles of conflict resolution, how was it resolved? Begin to notice dispute resolution and dispute conflagration.

(3) What is your concept of optimal dispute resolution/conflict resolution? Describe.

Exercise 11-2 — Practicing Identifying Conflict Resolution Skills

For each response, below, characterize it by one or more of the five methods of dealing with conflict listed below. Write: (a) the method(s) being portrayed and (b) the likely result of each response (interpersonally, legally, and emotionally), on the blank line below the response. These results can come from this Chapter or from your personal experiences.

Type 1. Denial or withdrawal

Type 2. Suppression or smoothing over

Type 3. Power or dominance

Type 4. Compromise or negotiation

Type 5. Collaboration

For example: (a) Type = subordination; (b) Result = conflict is solved but one party still feels frustrated and dissatisfied.

Case 11-A

Student: Professor, there is just no way that I could possibly have gotten a C- in this class. I mean, I nailed that exam! We have gone over my exam and the way I see it, I got every issue that you were looking for. How did you come up with a C-, did you have your dog grade the exams? (*attack*) I followed your instructions to a T; I did everything you asked me to (*this is your fault*). You explain to me how this grade is justified! (*angry "you statement"*) I demand that you regrade my exam and change my grade in the course (*furious demand, "you statement"*) (*tone of voice is angry, bewildered, and demanding*).

Professor Aggressive: You think you could do a better job than me at my job? (*attack*) Do you think you have what it takes to get to where I am? (*attack on other's ability*) Do you see all those degrees on my wall? (*puffing*) What's the matter with you that you come in here making demands of me? (*direct personal attack*) You must have some kind of deep seated mental problem to come in here with an attitude like you have (*direct personal attack*). What is your major malfunction? (*the problem is all you, not me*)

Type/Result? _____ (1)

Professor Defensive: Look, Mr./Ms. X, I have gone over the exam with you. I've pointed out to you what you missed on the exam, what you left out, and the grade is the grade. I've made my decision and it's final (*the answer is no*). I simply can't take any more time to discuss this with whiney students like you (*patronizing subtle attack*). Someday you are just going to have to grow up and face reality (*attack*). You earned this grade, fair and square (*it's all you*). The issue is closed (*closed mind*).

Type/Result? _____ (2)

Professor Perfect: Well! I know what I am doing. I think you would find, if you had been teaching law school for 25 years like I have, that this grade is perfectly justified. I haven't made a mistake in 25 years; the grade is correct (*puffing up self, subtle patronizing of other by reference to one's competence; I couldn't possibly be wrong or have done wrong*).

Type/Result? _____ (3)

Professor Rule Book: The rule in the students' handbook is that a grade can only be changed for a math error. The rule does not allow professors to regrade an exam and change someone's grade as a result, unless the error was simply a matter of misadding the scores. The matter is out of my hands (*denying all personal involvement by relying on the rules and regulations*).

Type/Result? _____ (4)

Professor Empathy: Wow, I'm so sorry that this grade has upset you like this (*empathy*). Let's see if we can go over the exam again—perhaps I made a mistake (*collaboration; team building; joint effort; information gathering; opening possibility of wrongdoing*). I'd like to understand why your view of your work and mine are so different (*empathy*). [They engage in another round of comparing the student's exam to the exam grading key—the professor makes the key completely available to the student and explains the grading procedure—no mistake is found (*collaboration; information gathering*).] I know you worked really hard in the course and I could always count on you to be prepared and to be on top of the material in class (*empathy, stating facts positive to opponent's side*). It is really frustrating that your grade does not reflect your abilities or effort in this class (*empathetic reality check; reframing of the problem*). I can't change the grade unless there is a math error, so that option isn't available to us (*providing info, referring to us as a team; team building*). Is there something else I can do (like write an explanatory letter to your file) to explain that this grade does not really adequately reflect your performance in this class? (*brainstorming options; offering a conciliatory alternative*) Are the problems that I identified on your exam ones that you have encountered in other classes? (*offering academic help as an alternative to changing the grade*) Is this grade way out of line with your grades in your other classes? (*reality check; information gathering*)

Type/Result? _____ (5)

NOTE: Outcome is ultimately the same with all the professors: no grade change. But in the last example there are some alternative solutions proffered.

Case 11-B

Clients have met to discuss resolving a dispute over performance of software sold by seller to buyer:

Buyer: Look, we both know we have a problem. We believe the software you sold us is defective and we believe you can't fix it, despite months of trying. We are being deluged with complaints from our customers and at this point we just want to return the software and receive a refund on the purchase price. Your position is that you are not required to issue us a refund, that you provided us software that does what we asked it to, and we are stuck with it. We are at a point of needing a third party to decide who is right and who is wrong, but before we go down that costly road, can we work on a solution?

Alternative 1:

Seller 1: Absolutely not.

Buyer 1: Then we are out of here.

Type/Result? _____ (6)

Alternative 2:

Seller 2: Absolutely not.

Buyer 2: OK, then what do you have in mind?

Seller 2: You just give us a settlement figure in writing and we'll get back to you. I can't promise you anything, but we can have Legal review your proposal.

Buyer leaves and later has its attorney mail a written demand letter with a dollar figure in it, to Seller. Negotiations proceed by mail.

Type/Result? _____ (7)

Alternative 3:

Seller 3: Why would we want to settle this with you? It's your problem. We have no responsibility here.

Type/Result? _____ (8)

Alternative 4:

Seller 4: Sure. First, though, give me a little more information about what's happening on your end, as a result of the software (probing for more information about the effects of the problem on the Buyer). Then, let me tell you a little bit about our goals and the effects of this dispute on our company.

Type/Result? _____ (9)

Case 11-C

Ms. Gideon, a 55-year-old female corporate executive, to her boss (company management): I have worked for this company for 12 years. You know, I have poured my heart and soul into this company and I was promoted and promoted and promoted, because everybody knows that I worked harder and produced more than any other person at the company. For you to demote me now, when I am this close to retirement, and replace me with some young guy just out of MBA school, is intolerable. It's demeaning! It's discrimination! That's what it is. You are looking right down the barrel of a lawsuit and you can bet that I am going to win. If you don't get rid of him and reinstate me immediately to my old position with full benefits and a salary increase, I will sue you for age discrimination, sex discrimination, and disability discrimination.

Manager 1: Our decision is final. This conversation is over. If you have anything more to say, talk to our attorneys.

Type/Result? _____ (10)

Manager 2: Now, now, Ms. Gideon. You're just upset. You haven't been demoted at all. All we did was restructure the management of the company and reorganize the job responsibilities. You are still just as valuable to the company as ever.

Ms. Gideon: Don't blow smoke up my dress. You are lying—you have stuck me out in the middle of nowhere in a job that has half the potential for year-end bonuses that my old job did and half the responsibility. You're not fooling anyone.

Type/Result? _____ (11)

Manager 3: You don't have a claim. You were never qualified for the position you held at the company. The only reason you were promoted is because you were best friends with the former president of the company. You were wrongly promoted; now we are simply moving you to a position that fits better with your abilities. You can't do the job this fellow can do; you are simply not qualified and not capable.

Type/Result? _____ (12)

Manager 4 (**position based bargaining**): We are not in a position to do that. We can offer you the job you have now or an attractive severance package, which would you like?

Type/Result? _____ (13)

Manager 5 (**recognition bargaining**) Would use empathy to defuse the anger inherent in her statement and presenting position. Might use active listening to buy a little time, defuse the emotional valence, and be correct about her position.

Type/Result? _____ (14)

Now, write a script of a model response to the Buyer in Case 11-B and a model response to Ms. Gideon in Case 11-C. These model responses should be your idea of the best, ideal, or optimal response in these situations that embodies or exemplifies Styles 4 (compromise), 5 (collaboration), or a combination thereof. (If you feel strongly that Style 4, 5, or 4+5 is not appropriate for this situation, then it is fine to craft a differently styled response, but please explain.) These responses should be relatively short; no more than a paragraph.

(15) **Optimal Response to Buyer:**

(16) **Optimal Response to Ms. Gideon:**

Exercise 11-3 — Practicing Conflict Resolution

Split into groups of three, two disputing parties and one observer. Have the two disputing parties identify and role-play a conflict and attempt to resolve it in about 20 minutes. Have the observer write the initial of the party in the margin of the "feedback sheet," below, during the process, each time he or she observes that party demonstrating a particular behavior. Have the observer share his or her observations with the two disputants, afterwards.

Observer Feedback Sheet

Persons Being Observed and Their Initials: _____

Put the person's initial in the left margin of this page EACH time you see that person display one of the following behaviors:

(1) **Be Real and Nondefensive; Communicate Well** — are they in touch with their own feelings, motives, needs, goals, vulnerabilities, and fears and able to disclose them to the others in "I statements," not "you statements," and "own" them? This is similar to needs-based bargaining instead of position-based bargaining and is sometimes known as "transparency."

(2) **Recognize the Other**—are they able to put aside their own position/ego/self just long enough to stand in the shoes of the other? (Empathy and active listening are tools one can use if one isn't feeling it at all, a way to act "as if" until the understanding kicks in.) This is sometimes called empathy.

(3) **Ask for Solutions**—are they open to solutions and do they brainstorm or ask the others what kinds of solutions they see, as opposed to being a PWTA ("know it all")? This is also called humility.

(4) **Tolerate Ambiguity and Silence**—are they able to accept and be comfortable with ambiguity, nonsolution, impasse, silence, and silent conflict? We are so quick to jump into the chasm with a solution or words when letting it sit, sleeping on it, or getting more time to think, will help.

(5) **Refocus on the Goal**—do they remind everyone what the ultimate goal is, reaffirming parties' commitment to or motivation for resolving this?

(6) **Unfair Fighting**—if there is a basic commitment to a process or relationship, then constant threats to end that process or relationship are not fair game and create undue stress and fear in the participants. See this?

<u>Types of conflict resolution: Put a checkmark (or initial) EACH time you see one of these used:</u>

_____ Type 1. Denial or withdrawal

_____ Type 2. Suppression or smoothing over

_____ Type 3. Power or dominance

_____ Type 4. Compromise or negotiation

_____ Type 5. Collaboration

_____ Type A. Attempt to Change Me (change one's own attitudes or behavior)

_____ Type B. Attempt to Change You (the other's behavior or the environment)

_____ Type C. Exit the Situation and Get a Substitute (job, friend, etc.)

<u>Results:</u> What were the results of each person's approach to conflict resolution? Describe.

Exercise 11-4 — Apologies

1. Find the transcript of a public apology and analyze its completeness and deficiencies as the Chapter text did with Tiger Woods' apology (for example, consider the 2010 public apology by the officers of Toyota, the car manufacturer, for its cars' braking defects[38] or one of the apologies made by officers of BP Oil for the Gulf oil spill in 2010–11[39]). What was present and where, and what was missing?

_____

38. http://www.themoneytimes.com/featured/20100202/toyota-issues-public-apology-restart-production-8-models-id-1099124.html (last visited May 9, 2011).

39. http://www.msnbc.msn.com/id/37739658/ns/disaster_in_the_gulf/t/bp-boss-sorry-about-small-people-remark (last visited May 9, 2011).

2. (a) Write an apology to the plaintiff on behalf of a personal injury defendant in a fictional automobile accident case. You may make up facts as necessary for this exercise. Assume the apology will not be admissible in court.

    (b) Describe how you would change this written apology if you knew it was admissible in court.

Chapter 12

Vector 7 — Collaborative Law

Description

The author's 2006 article[1] introduces collaborative law as follows:

Collaborative law is a non-litigative method for resolving divorce and custody actions that allows the clients and their attorneys control over the resolution, without a third-party decision-maker.[2] It originated among practicing family lawyers who were seeking a better, less emotionally damaging, more economical way for divorcing spouses to resolve their differences. The theory is that the traditional methods of resolving family law disputes often create more animosity between the divorcing spouses and harm family relationships. This is in part because the traditional approach takes people whose behavior and emotional state are at their worst and then engages them in an adversarial process. If the clients' attitudes indicate that they are appropriate for a collaborative process, collaborative law allows the ex- or divorcing spouses and their attorneys to meet in a series of four-way conferences outside of court to resolve the issues in divorce and custody cases. The attorneys and clients work together in a collaborative atmosphere with a foundation of mutual, contractual agreement to the process and a commitment to participate in good faith.

There are two forms of collaborative practice: In collaborative law, the attorneys and spouses resolve the conflict, perhaps employing neutral financial and psychological experts in the process. In another form of collaborative law known as "collaborative divorce," the divorce is resolved by meetings between and among interdisciplinary teams for each side consisting of legal, psychological, and financial experts for each spouse. There may also be neutral experts in this latter form, as well, such as child specialists and the like. In this Chapter, "collaborative law" will be used to refer to both forms of practice.

---

1. Excerpt from Susan Daicoff, *Law as a Healing Profession: The "Comprehensive Law Movement,"* 6 Pepperdine Disp. Resol. L. J. 1 (2006) [hereinafter Daicoff, 2006].
2. This description is adapted from the author's article, Daicoff, 2006, *supra* note 1. *See* Pauline H. Tesler & Peter B. Sandmann, *Ten Questions For Clients Weighing Litigation v. Collaborative Law*, 21 Alternatives High Cost Litig. 11 (2003); Pauline H. Tesler, *Collaborative Law: Achieving Effective Resolution in Divorce Without Litigation*, 40 Fam. Ct. Rev. 403 (2002); Pauline H. Tesler, *The Basic Elements of Collaborative Law*, 21 Alternatives High Cost Litig. 9 (2003); Pauline H. Tesler, *Collaborative Law: A New Paradigm for Divorce Lawyers*, 5 Psych. Pub. Pol'y & Law 967 (1999); Pauline H. Tesler, *Collaborative Law: What It Is and Why Family Law Attorneys Need to Know About It*, 13 Am. J. Fam. L. 215 (1999); Pauline H. Tesler, *Collaborative Law: A New Approach to Family Law ADR*, 2 Conflict Mgmt. 12 (1996); Pauline H. Tesler, *Collaborative Law Neutrals Produce Better Resolutions*, 21 Alternatives High Cost Litig. 1 (2003); Pauline H. Tesler, *Client Relations: Tips From a Collaborative Practitioner*, 21 Alternatives High Cost Litig. 13 (2003).

Collaborative law offers the opportunity for divorcing spouses to dissolve their marriages with less anger, hostility, cost, time, and negative emotion than result from most litigation processes. Through the collaborative law process, they can also begin to develop a workable, cooperative post-divorce relationship that may be useful if they must continue to co-parent children in the future.

The main features distinguishing collaborative law from simple mediation or negotiation are the six-way communication (among and between the two spouses and two lawyers), the parties' commitment to the collaborative law process, and the binding agreement of the attorneys to withdraw if the parties go to court. No formal litigation is usually instituted until settlement is reached. There is a strong psychological component to the lawyer-client relationship in that emotions, needs, transference, etc. are openly acknowledged and dealt with in order to maximize the results of the four-way conferences. According to one of the trailblazers in the field, attorney Pauline Tesler, one of the most important features of collaborative law is the fact that the attorneys are contractually forbidden from representing their clients in court should the collaborative process break down. This feature aligns the attorneys' financial interests with that of their clients' and greatly incentivizes the attorneys to work towards creative solutions to the outstanding issues. Without this, the attorneys can easily lapse into, "Why worry if my client is misbehaving or the clients aren't agreeing? I get paid either way." Tesler maintains that this feature produces unprecedented creativity and resolutionary energy in both attorneys and clients.[3] This contrasts with the usual process, where the lawyers simply litigate if negotiations break down, thus they collect a fee and thereby "win," whether or not the clients settle.

In a collaborative law process, the lawyer first assesses, with the client, the appropriateness of the client for a collaborative process. The client must be able to deal effectively with his or her negative emotions (what Tesler calls the client's "shadow self") and must be able to negotiate with honesty and in good faith with his or her spouse. Second, the lawyers create in the four-way conferences what psychologists might recognize as a container, or safe space, within which conflicts and issues between the spouses can be aired and resolved. Establishing ground rules, guidelines, boundaries, and consequences of inappropriate behavior by a participant creates this "container."[4]

Collaborative law has spread rapidly to many metropolitan areas in the United States.[5] Groups of specially trained lawyers in these areas offer collaborative law processes to divorcing spouses, as long as the opposing side's attorney is also trained in the collaborative law process. In 1997, Pauline Tesler conducted a training session at the annual meeting of the American Bar Association and, in 2001, the American Bar Association published her practice-oriented book, Collaborative Law.[6] At least three states have collaborative law statutes (Texas, North Carolina, and California) and there is currently a Uniform Collaborative Law statute being drafted. Collaborative law is being experimented with in other areas of law, such as employment law disputes.[7]

---

3. Pauline H. Tesler, *Collaborative Law: A New Paradigm for Divorce Lawyers,* 5 Psych. Pub. Pol'y & Law 967 (1999) [hereinafter Tesler, 1999].

4. *Id.*

5. *See, e.g.,* http://www.collaborativefamilylawfl.com/index.html (regional websites for South Florida group; last visited July 11, 2010).

6. Tesler, 1999, *supra* note 3. Tesler was the first recipient of the "Lawyers as Problem-Solvers" Award given by the Dispute Resolution Section of the American Bar Association.

7. Daicoff, 2006, *supra* note 1.

The following reprint of the author's essay on collaborative law (at pages 167–188 hereof) explores the field in more detail:

Collaborative Law:
A New Tool for the Lawyer's Toolkit[8]

Introduction

What we are doing in civil family law litigation in America has not been satisfactory for many years. Massive reforms have been attempted, from the inception of "no-fault" divorce in the 1970s[9] to recent reforms such as nonlawyer "parenting coordinators" to assist divorced parents in resolving conflicts, post-divorce.[10] Early reforms initially appeared to result in a sharp increase on the divorce rate; it doubled from 1965 to 1975,[11] peaking around 1980,[12] most likely due to the widespread institution of no-fault divorce. Recently, however, it has dropped to its lowest rate since 1970[13] — some commentators believe it is due to fewer people marrying, more couples cohabitating, and people waiting longer to get married, suggesting a general lack of confidence in American family law.[14]

In addition, the current system of no-fault divorce has not necessarily improved the post-divorce lot of ex-spouses, particularly divorced women, and children. For example, economist Allen Parkman[15] argues that, even though most cases are settled rather than litigated, settling a case under a no-fault divorce system tends to produce an outcome that provides "divorced women with smaller financial settlements" than they would receive if settling a case under a fault system.[16]

---

8. This is a reprint of the author's article titled, *Collaborative Law: A New Tool for the Lawyer's Toolkit*, 20 U. Fl. J. L. & Pub. Pol'y. 135 (2009), used with permission from the *University of Florida Journal of Law and Public Policy* © 2009.

9. Allen M. Parkman, No-Fault Divorce: What Went Wrong 1, 8–9 n.1 (1992) (reporting that, after California passed the first "pure" no-fault divorce statute in 1969, other states rapidly followed suit; all of the states but three had no-fault divorce by 1977 and all states permitted some form of no-fault divorce by 1985).

10. Parenting coordinators have developed in recent years; for example, the Association of Family and Conciliation Courts reported the development of Parenting Coordinator standards (and a 94% increase in its membership) during 2002–07; http://www.afccnet.org/pdfs/AFCC%20Five-Year%20Report%20Web.pdf (last visited July 11, 2010).

11. Parkman, *supra* note 9, at 72.

12. Parkman, *supra* note 9, at 72–73 (noting that the divorce rate for married women peaked at 22.8 per 1000 people in 1979); David Crary reported that the overall divorce rate peaked at 1981 at 5.3 per 1000 people, David Crary, *U.S. Divorce Rate Lowest Since 1970, The Associated Press (April 10, 2007), available at* http://www.breitbart.com/article.php?id=d8p1mg601&show_article=1 (last visited July 11, 2010) [hereinafter Crary].

13. Crary, *supra* note 12, asserting "[s]ome experts say relationships are as unstable as ever — and divorces are down primarily because more couples live together without marrying. Other researchers have documented what they call 'the divorce divide,' contending that divorce rates are indeed falling substantively among college-educated couples but not among less-affluent, less-educated couples."

14. Crary, *supra* note 12, asserting "[t]he number of couples who live together without marrying has increased tenfold since 1960; the marriage rate has dropped by nearly 30 percent in past 25 years; and Americans are waiting about five years longer to marry than they did in 1970."

15. Parkman, *supra* note 9, at 112.

16. *Id.* Parkman explains that there was a veto power that afforded some leverage to spouses in negotiations in a fault divorce scheme; this veto power is absent in no-fault divorce. The result is that

Family law attorneys have described the litigation process for divorce as "grueling, expensive, dragged out, unpredictable, stressful, and many other unflattering terms."[17] While mediation can avoid some of these results, the mini-trial-like nature of some mediation processes, the use of a third-party mediator, and the involvement of attorneys who are operating in a traditional advocacy mode limits mediation's ability to reach its full potential, in many instances. These failings have spurred experimentation in the family law area with alternative ways to resolve divorce and child custody cases other than traditional negotiation, settlement, mediation, and trial.

Finally, some perceive a recent shift in the way people approach relationships. For example, North Carolina divorce lawyer Lee Rosen was reported in 2007 as noticing "a trend toward increased realism and civility among couples with marital strains. Many seek mediation as they split, and arrange for joint legal custody of their children."[18] He added, "People are coexisting more peacefully, whether they stay together or come apart" and "are more contemplative and serious about their relationships ...."[19]

All of these developments, conditions, and attitudes appear to have coalesced to herald the emergence of a quite innovative reform in family law: the movement for "collaborative law."[20] Collaborative law is a nonlitigative, nonadversarial mode of dispute resolution that emerged in 1990 as an alternative to existing modes of dispute resolution in family

---

negotiations in a no-fault scheme tend to track closely the outcome that the spouses would have obtained from a trial and tend to emphasize property settlement over alimony and child support awards, which can provide less wealth to certain divorcing spouses when there is little property to be divided but large income earning potential. *Id.* at 112–13.

17. Gary L. Voegele, Linda K. Wray, & Ronald D. Ousky, *Family Law: Collaborative Law: A Useful Tool for the Family Law Practitioner to Promote Better Outcomes*, 33 Wm. Mitchell L. Rev. 971, 1012 (2007) (note that Mr. Ousky is the co-author, with Stuart G. Webb, of The Collaborative Way to Divorce, The Revolutionary Method That Results in Less Stress, Lower Costs, and Happier Kids—Without Going to Court (2006) (a book primarily designed for clients)).

18. Crary, *supra* note 10, *quoting* Lee Rosen (who also reported that family law business at his large firm was "booming").

19. *Id.*

20. Pauline H. Tesler & Peggy Thompson, Collaborative Divorce: The Revolutionary New Way to Restructure Your Family, Resolve Legal Issues, and Move on with Your Life (2006) [hereinafter Tesler & Thompson]; Stuart G. Webb & Ronald D. Ousky, How the Collaborative Divorce Method Offers Less Stress, Lower Cost, and Happier Kids Without Going to Court: The Smart Divorce (Hudson Street Press, 2006) [hereinafter Webb & Ousky]; Pauline H. Tesler, Collaborative Law: Achieving Effective Resolution in Divorce Without Litigation (American Bar Association, 2001) [hereinafter Tesler, 2001]; Nancy J. Cameron, Collaborative Practice: Deepening the Dialogue (Continuing Legal Education Society of British Columbia, 2004); *see also* Pauline H. Tesler & Peter B. Sandmann, *Ten Questions For Clients Weighing Litigation v. Collaborative Law*, 21 Alternatives High Cost Litig. 11 (2003); Pauline H. Tesler, *Collaborative Law: Achieving Effective Resolution in Divorce Without Litigation*, 40 Fam. Ct. Rev. 403 (2002); Pauline H. Tesler, *The Basic Elements of Collaborative Law*, 21 Alternatives High Cost Litig. 9 (2003); Pauline H. Tesler, *Collaborative Law: A New Paradigm for Divorce Lawyers*, 5 Psych. Pub. Pol'y & Law 967 (1999); Pauline H. Tesler, *Collaborative Law: What It Is and Why Family Law Attorneys Need to Know About It*, 13 Am. J. Fam. L. 215 (1999); Pauline H. Tesler, *Collaborative Law: A New Approach to Family Law ADR*, 2 Conflict Mgmt. 12 (1996); Pauline H. Tesler, *Collaborative Law Neutrals Produce Better Resolutions*, 21 Alternatives High Cost Litig. 1 (2003); Pauline H. Tesler, *Client Relations: Tips From a Collaborative Practitioner*, 21 Alternatives High Cost Litig. 13 (2003). Collaborative law websites exist in many metropolitan areas; *see, e.g.,* http://www.collaborativefamilylawfl.com/index.html (regional CL website for South Florida; last visited July 11, 2010).

law.[21] It has had a "meteoric rise"[22] throughout the United States and Canada;[23] it is most often utilized in family law cases,[24] but has expanded and been experimented with in civil and employment suits as well.[25]

This Essay will describe collaborative law and then place it within a larger movement in American jurisprudence towards making law "sustainable" for human wellbeing—the "comprehensive law movement." It will argue that the development of collaborative law, along with the other disciplines that make up the comprehensive law movement, bodes well for the future of the legal profession and indeed of society itself.

The Emergence of Collaborative Law

A Brief History

Collaborative law was founded in 1990 by Minnesota lawyer Stuart Webb.[26] He describes himself as a disgruntled family lawyer who, in 1990, was so dissatisfied with the current practice of law that he was on the verge of quitting, if he could not conceive of a satisfactory way to be a lawyer.[27] He writes:

> As a divorce litigator, I'd felt for a long time that I was living in a siege mentality merely waiting for the next battle to start and, finally, I got to the point where I was ready to quit the practice of law. I enrolled in college and was ready to start educating myself for a new career, when I had one last thought about practicing law: *"If I'm actually willing to quit being a lawyer, why don't I at least see whether there's some out-of-the-box way I can look at things. Maybe there's a better way of handling divorce."*[28]

With this backdrop, he created the concept of collaborative law and devoted himself to its full-time practice.[29] San Francisco Bay Area family lawyer Pauline Tesler quickly discovered, and began practicing and training others in, collaborative law.[30] Its original model relies on two attorneys and two clients. Family psychologists Peggy Thompson and Rodney Nurse were developing a model for working with divorcing couples; when Tesler introduced them to collaborative law, they quickly incorporated it into their developing model and thus expanded the concept to include interdisciplinary teams of professionals working with and for the divorcing spouses to accomplish the dissolution of marriage.

---

21. Tesler, 2001, *supra* note 20.

22. Christopher M. Fairman, *Growing Pains: Changes in Collaborative Law and the Challenge of Legal Ethics*, 30 Campbell L. Rev. 237, 240 (2008) (symposium issue) (calling its meteoric rise "well known").

23. *Id.* at 239, claiming that, between 1990 and 2007, "tens of thousands of cases have been resolved with it in the United States and Canada" … "Collaborative law practice groups exist in virtually every state in the nation" and "major law firms are … hiring partners to head up … collaborative law sections." *Id.*

24. *Id.* at 239–43 (arguing also for its expansion outside family law).

25. *Id.* at 243–46 (arguing for the use of collaborative law in employment and labor law cases, wills and probate, landlord/tenant disputes, royalty, construction project cases, and medical malpractice cases).

26. Webb & Ousky, *supra* note 20.

27. *Id.*

28. *Id.*

29. *Id.*

30. Tesler, 2001, *supra* note 20.

These teams consisted of mental health experts (serving as divorce "coaches"), financial experts, child specialists, and sometimes other experts, in addition to the lawyers and clients. Tesler and Thompson began training individuals in "collaborative divorce," described below as a similar and related form of practice.[31] Tesler and Webb also conducted trainings in collaborative law (in its original form, utilizing two attorneys and two clients) around the country.[32]

In 1997 the International Academy of Collaborative Professionals was founded,[33] encompassing both collaborative law and collaborative divorce; it currently boasts over 3,000 members, provides trainers, and holds an annual meeting.[34] The American Bar Association published Tesler's book on collaborative law in 2001. Also in 2001, the Canadian Department of Justice commissioned a three-year study of the effectiveness of this rapidly growing phenomenon in Canada by Professor Julie Macfarlane, a "leading scholar in family law conflict resolution;"[35] it was completed in 2005.[36] Collaborative law pioneers Webb and Tesler were awarded the first "Lawyer as Problem Solver" Award by the American Bar Association ("ABA") in 2002. In 2006, Webb and practicing attorney Ronald Ousky published a book on collaborative law and Tesler and Thompson co-authored a book on collaborative divorce. Collaborative law is now found in most metropolitan areas in "virtually every state and province in"[37] the United States and Canada.[38]

While a flurry of critiques and concerns about collaborative law have been vetted in the academic literature[39] and in various state bar ethics opinions since its incep-

---

31. TESLER & THOMPSON, *supra* note 20.

32. The author attended one of these early trainings by Webb and Tesler, in Dallas, Texas, in January, 2000.

33. http://www.collaborativepractice.com/ is the national website for the International Academy of Collaborative Professionals (last visited July 11, 2010).

34. *Id.*

35. Voegele, et al., *supra* note 17, at 975. These authors' history of the development of collaborative law is summarized in this Article and is quite extensive and detailed, *id.* at 974–77.

36. *Id.* at 975 n.18, citing Professor Macfarlane's study published as Department of Justice Canada, *The Emerging Phenomenon of Collaborative Family Law (CFL): A Qualitative Study of CFL Cases (2005)* at http://www.justice.gc.ca/en/ps/pad/reports/2005-FCY-1/2005-FCY-1.pdf (no longer available) and Julie Macfarlane, *Experiences of Collaborative Law: Preliminary Results from the Collaborative Lawyering Research Project*, 2004 J. DISP. RESOL. 179.

37. Voegele, et al., *supra* note 17, at 975.

38. Fairman, *supra* note 22, at 239–40; *see also* Susan Daicoff, *Law as a Healing Profession: The "Comprehensive Law Movement*," 6 PEPP. DISP. RESOL. L.J. 1, 27 (2006). Besides the website of the International Academy of Collaborative Professionals ("IACP"), found at http://www.collaborativedivorce.com (last visited July 11, 2010), there are many other collaborative law websites in the United States, United Kingdom, and Canada, such as: http://www.collaborativefamilylawfl.com/collaborative.html (last visited July 11, 2010); http://www.collaborativelaw.com (last visited July 11, 2010); http://www.collaborativelaw.org (last visited July 11, 2010); http://nycollaborativelaw.com (last visited July 11, 2010); http://www.collablawtexas.com (last visited July 11, 2010); http://www.collaborativelaw.us (last visited July 11, 2010); http://www.collablaw.com (last visited July 11, 2010); http://www.collablaw.org (last visited July 11, 2010); http://www.collablawil.org (last visited July 11, 2010); http://www.collabdivorce.com (last visited July 11, 2010); http://www.collaborativelaw-swfla.org (last visited July 11, 2010); http://www.collaborativepractice.com (last visited July 11, 2010); http://www.qldcollablaw.com.au (last visited July 11, 2010); http://www.collaborativelaw.ca (last visited July 11, 2010); and http://www.collaborative-law.ca (last visited July 11, 2010).

39. Critical articles include Penelope Eileen Bryan, *"Collaborative Divorce": Meaningful Reform or Another Quick Fix?*, 5 PSYCH., PUB. POL'Y & L. 1001 (1999) (criticizing collaborative law as failing to address the post-divorce economic and financial plight of women and children, power disparities between husbands and wives, and gender bias and incompetence of lawyers and judges, overemphasizing relational and nonlegal concerns, and thereby possibly contributing to inequitable post-divorce results for disempowered parties). Tesler replied to Bryan in Pauline H. Tesler, *The Believing Game,*

tion,[40] those concerns have been stalled recently by a formal ABA ethics opinion that, in 2008, opined that collaborative law practice was ethical.[41] Several states have enacted laws permitting and encouraging collaborative law,[42] others are considering it,[43] an ABA Committee for collaborative law has been formed, the National Conference of Commissioners on Uniform State Laws appointed a drafting committee for a Uniform Collaborative Law Act, which is currently generating a working draft.[44] It appears that collaborative law, as Professor Christopher Fairman argues, is no longer in its infancy but has reached at least adolescence, complete with the "growing pains"[45] of controversy about its features.

A Brief Description

Collaborative law refers to at least two forms of dispute resolution, first and most frequently used in dissolution of marriage and other domestic relations matters. It includes "collaborative law"[46] and "collaborative divorce law,"[47] as well as disciplines sometimes

---

The Doubting Game, and Collaborative Law: A Reply to Penelope Bryan, 5 Psych., Pub. Pol'y & L. 1018, 1021–22 (1999) (noting that collaborative law is not intended as an overall remedy for "problems inherent in the American culture within which all U.S. divorces take place, and indeed, inherent in the human condition itself" and noting the absence of anecdotal or empirical evidence of the abuses Bryan warns of). Other commentators often focus on concerns that the practice of collaborative law might run afoul of the ethics rules for lawyers, *see, e.g.,* John Lande, *Principles for Policymaking About Collaborative Law and Other ADR Processes,* 22 Ohio St. J. Disp. Resol. 619 (2007) (critiquing proposals by Professor Christopher Fairman and Professor Scott Peppet for new ethical rules for collaborative law) and Larry R. Spain, *Collaborative Law: A Critical Reflection on Whether a Collaborative Orientation Can Be Ethically Incorporated Into the Practice of Law,* 56 Baylor L. Rev. 141 (2004) (outlining a number of ethical concerns with collaborative law and concluding that "careful attention," redefinitions of ethical rules, and "consensus" may be required); and Joshua Isaacs, *A New Way to Avoid the Courtroom: The Ethical Implications Surrounding Collaborative Law,* 18 Geo. J. Legal Ethics 833 (2005). Others focus on how well attorneys will execute the principles and practices of collaborative law, *see, e.g.,* John Lande, *Possibilities for Collaborative Law: Ethics and Practice of Lawyer Disqualification and Process Control in a New Model of Lawyering,* 64 Ohio St. L. J. 1315, 1379–82 (2003) (analyzing collaborative law, raising many issues regarding the effectiveness of its practice, and concluding that "it is too early to declare it a success").

40. *See, e.g.,* Colo. Bar Ethics Comm., Formal Op. 115 (Feb. 24, 2007) (finding collaborative law ethical, in contrast) available at http://www.cobar.org/index.cfm/ID/386/subID/10159/Ethics-Opinion-115:-Ethical-Considerations-in-the-Collaborative-and-Cooperative-Law-Contexts,-02/24// (last visited July 11, 2010).

41. ABA Commn. on Ethics and Prof'l Responsibility, Informal Op. 07-447 (2007).

42. For example, Texas, North Carolina, and California; *see* Tex. Fam. Code Ann. §6.603 (2006); N. C. Gen. Stat. §50-77 (2007); and Cal. Fam. Code §2013 (2008).

43. For example, a state bar committee on family law in Florida has been drafting a proposed collaborative law statute for consideration by the Florida Legislature, titled the "Collaborative Process Act," Sections 61.601–604, 12.745.

44. Fairman, *supra* note 20, at 238 (reporting that a model act is already in working draft form "with its core feature being provisions to answer ethical concerns about confidentiality and privilege"); Jennifer M. Kuhn, *Working Around the Withdrawal Agreement: Statutory Evidentiary Safeguards Negate the Need for a Withdrawal Agreement in Collaborative Law Agreements,* 30 Campbell L. Rev. 363 n.21 (2008) (citing the Uniform Collaborative Law Act and indicating that its tentative draft is dated August, 2007, available at http://www.law.upenn.edu/bll/archives/ulc/ucla/oct2007draft.htm) (last visited July 11, 2010).

45. Fairman, *supra* note 22, at 237–40 (claiming that collaborative law is undergoing the "growing pains of an ADR process").

46. Tesler, 2001, *supra* note 20, describes this form of collaborative law.

47. Tesler & Thompson, *supra* note 20, describe this form of collaborative law.

referred to as "collaborative practice."[48] While there may be differences in the sub-variations of collaborative law, all share certain common features, described below.

Structure and Process

Collaborative law seeks to resolve legal disputes, most often family law matters such as dissolutions of marriage and custody disputes, through an alternative dispute resolution process that occurs outside of litigation, without the use of a third-party decision-maker.[49] Collaborative law engages the two clients and their two respective partisan attorneys, who each represent their own client, in a series of four-party conferences at which the attorneys and clients working together ultimately resolve the issues in the case and reach agreement.[50] All four contractually agree at the outset: (1) that the attorneys will withdraw from the representation of the clients if the process fails to reach agreement and the matter proceeds to litigation (this is a "linchpin" feature, meaning it is a necessary component of collaborative practice); and (2) to a variety of other mutual agreements, such as negotiating in good faith, voluntary disclosure of information to the other spouse in the collaborative process, maintaining confidentiality of the collaborative meetings, and refraining from litigative motions (such as unilaterally filing a dissolution action without all parties' assent).[51]

Collaborative divorce law engages in a similar process for the same goal, but relies on an interdisciplinary team comprised of the two clients, their two respective attorneys, and financial, vocational, and psychological experts to resolve the issues, in the conferences.[52] In this model, the two collaborative attorneys and two clients may be joined by two "divorce coaches" (one for each party), a financial neutral and, if applicable, a child specialist,"[53] who work together to resolve issues and reach agreement. Some variations engage one mental health professional, either as a neutral coach or as a neutral expert.[54] In the two mental health professional model, the professionals can serve more as divorce "coaches" than as detached, neutral opiners.[55] There is also a hybrid or "referral model," in which the parties "start the case with Collaborative attorneys and bring in other professionals ... when needed."[56]

While there was initially some intradisciplinary controversy due to the differences in these various models, all forms of collaborative practice now coexist relatively peacefully under the umbrella organization of the International Academy of Collaborative Professionals.[57] Collaborative professionals can choose which model in which to practice, as they wish. Collaborative law was described in Tesler's 2001 book, Collaborative Law,[58] published by the American Bar Association, while collaborative divorce law was described in a 2006 book co-authored by Tesler and Peggy Thompson, titled "Collaborative Di-

---

48. Voegele, et al., *supra* note 17, at 977.
49. Daicoff, *supra* note 38, at 24.
50. *Id.* at 25.
51. Voegele, et al., *supra* note 17 at 1017–21 (discussing ethical implications of these contractual agreements).
52. *Id.* at 976 n. 25.
53. Voegele, et al., *supra* note 17, at 976.
54. Daicoff, *supra* note 38, at 27.
55. Voegele, et al., *supra* note 17, at 976, n. 25.
56. Voegele, et al., *supra* note 17, at 976–77, n. 28.
57. IACP website, *supra* note 38.
58. TESLER, 2001, *supra* note 20.

vorce."[59] This Essay will use the term "collaborative law" to refer to all models of collaborative practice, including collaborative divorce.

Another option, often termed "cooperative" law or divorce, resembles collaborative law in that it seeks to resolve legal disputes using the same team or process, *without* collaborative law's identifying feature of mandatory disqualification of the attorneys if the process breaks down and the matter proceeds to litigation.[60] Some collaborative lawyers are firm in their view that this form of practice may be useful to resolve legal disputes, but it does not fall within collaborative law, and thus this form of practice is not included in this Essay.

Philosophy and Goals

Collaborative law is founded on the principle that avoiding conflictual, adversarial litigation, particularly in family law matters, is optimal for the post-divorce functioning of the parties, who are often required to work together as co-parents of their children for many years to come.[61] It acknowledges that litigation often escalates parties' level of conflict and hostility and that attorneys' traditional approaches to litigation can be part of the reason for this escalation.[62] The effects of divorce on children are well-documented; Kathryn Maxwell reported in 2000 that there are three factors that have been empirically shown to account for the majority of poor functioning, post-divorce.[63] These are: the amount of conflict between the divorcing spouses; the instability in the child's life, and the absence of effective parenting during and after the divorce process.[64] Collaborative law is designed to promote positive interactions between divorcing spouses, or at least not create more hostility, animosity, and conflict between them, in order to promote their post-divorce individual functioning and their ability to collaborate in the future, particularly if they are co-parenting minor children.[65]

"Linchpin Feature": Withdrawal of Counsel before Litigation

Possibly the most controversial aspect of collaborative law is its "disqualification agreement," "withdrawal provision," or "collaborative commitment feature," which is the requirement that the attorneys mandatorily withdraw from representation of their respective clients in the event that the collaborative process fails to reach agreement and the case

---

59. TESLER & THOMPSON, *supra* note 20.

60. John Lande & Gregg Herman, *Fitting the Forum to the Family Fuss: Choosing Mediation, Collaborative Law, or Cooperative Law for Negotiating Divorce Cases*, 42 FAM. CT. REV. 280 (2004). A controversial Colorado ethics opinion discussed cooperative law at length and concluded that its practice was ethical, while the practice of collaborative law, with the "linchpin" feature, was *per se* unethical; Colo. Bar Ethics Comm., Formal Op. 115 (Feb. 24, 2007) (finding collaborative law ethical, in contrast) available at ⟨http://www.cobar.org/index.cfm/ID/386/subID/10159/Ethics-Opinion-115: -Ethical-Considerations-in-the-Collaborative-and-Cooperative-Law-Contexts,-02/24//⟩ (last visited July 11, 2010)

61. Daicoff, *supra* note 38, at 25.

62. Fairman, *supra* note 22, at 243 (discussing the limitations of traditional family law litigation).

63. Kathryn H. Maxwell, *Preventive Lawyering Strategies to Mitigate the Detrimental Effects of Clients' Divorces on their Children*, in DENNIS P. STOLLE, DAVID B. WEXLER, & BRUCE J. WINICK, EDS., PRACTICING THERAPEUTIC JURISPRUDENCE: LAW AS A HELPING PROFESSION 161 (Carolina Academic Press, 2000) [hereinafter "PTJ"].

64. *Id.*

65. Ted Schneyer, *The Organized Bar and the Collaborative Law Movement: A Study in Professional Change*, 50 ARIZ. L. REV. 289, 298–99 (2008).

proceeds forward in a litigation mode.[66] In both collaborative law and collaborative divorce, the clients and the attorneys contractually agree, at the outset and with full informed consent, to enter into a dispute resolution process that is designed to resolve their conflict, divorce, or dispute before proceeding forward with litigation.[67] If the process breaks down and the parties and their attorneys are not able to reach agreement during the collaborative law process, then the attorneys are contractually bound to withdraw from representation and transfer their respective clients to new counsel for the purpose of proceeding forward with the litigation.[68] This is sometimes referred to as the "linchpin"[69] feature of collaborative law, as collaborative law experts have said that, without this contractual undertaking, the process simply "isn't collaborative law."[70]

For example, Pauline Tesler writes: "There is really only one irreducible minimum condition for calling what you do 'collaborative law': **you and the counsel for the other party must sign papers disqualifying you from ever appearing in court on behalf of either of these clients against the other.** Beyond that requirement, all else is artistry, and you are free to accept, reject, and adapt what is presented here to suit your personal style."[71]

One purpose of this dramatic feature is to align the attorneys' financial interests in legal fees with the clients' interests in settling their dispute.[72] Without this, collaborative lawyers argue, attorneys have no incentive to settle the matter, since they "make money either way,"[73] reaping legal fees whether their clients settle before trial or go to trial to resolve the case. With the attorneys' interests now aligned with the clients', they argue, the attorneys' great creativity and intelligence often is fully engaged in service of finding resolutions to the parties' disagreements, unlike traditional settlement negotiations.[74]

Voegele, Wray, and Ousky give three formal justifications for this feature: "(1) the ability to enhance the commitment of all participants to the Collaborative process, (2) creation of a safe environment outside of the courtroom, and (3) resolving the 'prisoner's dilemma' to increase cooperation."[75] They explain that an early commitment to settlement and to a nonadversarial process that does not allow the attorneys to "drift to court" appears to reduce "the posturing and gamesmanship of traditional lawyer-to-lawyer negotiation."[76] It creates a "safe" environment by reducing emotional pressures and tendencies to withhold "best proposals" and "critical facts," because it rewards candor, openness, and cooperation.[77] Finally, in family law cases, the "prisoner's dilemma" occurs when spouses prefer to utilize cooperative attorneys, but feel pressure to choose an aggressive

---

66. Voegele, et al., *supra* note 17, at 978 (noting these different names given to the feature).

67. *Id.* at 1012.

68. *Id.*

69. Jennifer M. Kuhn, *Working Around the Withdrawal Agreement: Statutory Evidentiary Safeguards Negate the Need for a Withdrawal Agreement in Collaborative Law Agreements*, 30 CAMPBELL L. REV. 363, 364 (2008).

70. *Id.* at 367. *See also* Voegele, et al., *supra* note 17, at 983.

71. TESLER, 2001, *supra* note 20, at 6.

72. Daicoff, *supra* note 38, at 25.

73. Based on anecdotal evidence collected by the author from her practice experience, circa 1985–1994.

74. Daicoff, *supra* note 38, at 26. *See also* TESLER, 2001, *supra* note 18, and Webb & Ousky, *supra* note 18, on this point.

75. Voegele, et al., *supra* note 17, at 979–983.

76. *Id.* at 979–80, citing the results of Professor Macfarlane's three-year study, *supra* note 36.

77. Voegele, et al., *supra* note 17, at 979–980.

attorney out of fear that their spouse will choose an aggressive attorney; collaborative law removes this pressure and gives spouses the freedom to choose an attorney who fits with their "wishes and long-term interests."[78]

The linchpin feature has generated substantial controversy; when lawyers first learn about the practice of collaborative law, they often question the value of this feature and ask, "why can't you have collaborative law without the withdrawal undertaking?"[79] They see it as an unnecessary burden on the attorneys and clients and argue that, in cases of failure, the clients will spend more on legal fees than they would have without collaborative law.[80] However, proponents of collaborative law point out that cases of failure are relatively rare and the value of this feature is worth the risk of failure and the need for and expense of new counsel.[81] For example, recent statistics conclude that about 86% of collaborative cases reach agreement, in 4% of the cases the parties reconcile and stay married, and in only about 10% does the process fail, according to the International Academy of Collaborative Professionals.[82]

It has been so controversial that states have felt it necessary to opine as to whether or not this feature is ethical, meaning in compliance with the state ethics codes of behavior for attorneys.[83] The Colorado Bar Association, for example, issued an opinion in March, 2007[84] declaring the linchpin feature of collaborative law *per se* unethical, while finding the remainder of collaborative law to be permissible.[85] However, the American Bar Association responded in November, 2007 with an ethics opinion of its Standing Committee on Ethics and Professional Responsibility explicitly finding this feature "ethical," as long as clients give informed consent, thus apparently ending the controversy over the ethical nature of this contractual undertaking.[86]

Nuts and Bolts

In collaborative law, the parties agree to operate in good faith.[87] They agree to full voluntary disclosure of all information and documents to each other in the collaborative process.[88] They agree to maintain confidentiality of what is disclosed in the collaborative process.[89] There is "six-way" communication, meaning that the attorneys speak to each other between meetings, the clients may speak to each other between meetings, and each

---

78. *Id.* at 979–83.

79. *Id.* at 1013.

80. *Id.*

81. *Id.* at 1013–14 (comparing and contrasting the advantages and disadvantages of a traditional litigation process and of the collaborative law process).

82. IACP Collaborative Practice Survey Cumulative Data Results, Oct. 15, 2006–Dec. 31, 2007 (reporting the results of one survey of 403 cases and another survey of 30 cases in Georgia; in Georgia, 97% of the cases were completed and only 3% terminated the collaborative process).

83. Kuhn, *supra* note 69, at 372.

84. This Colorado Bar Association Ethics Opinion was decided in February, 2006 but not released until 13 months later and found the linchpin feature *per se* unethical; *see* Colo. Bar Ethics Comm., Formal Op. 115 (Feb. 24, 2007) available at http://www.cobar.org/index.cfm/ID/386/subID/10159/Ethics-Opinion-115:-Ethical-Considerations-in-the-Collaborative-and-Cooperative-Law-Contexts,-02/24// (last visited July 11, 2010).

85. *Id.*

86. Debra Cassens Weiss, *ABA Ethics Opinion Approves Collaborative Law*, ABA Journal website (Posted Nov 7, 2007, 01:12 pm CDT) (reporting that the ABA Formal Opinion had been issued).

87. Daicoff, *supra* note 38 at 25.

88. Kuhn, *supra* note 69 at 371.

89. *Id.*

attorney and client will speak to each other between meetings.[90] In the collaborative meetings themselves, all participants speak freely to each other, so even opposing counsel may speak to a client.[91] As long as the client's own attorney is present, no ethical violations are presented.[92] See Figure 1, below:

Figure 1. Six-Way Communication with Everyone at the Table

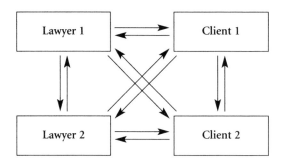

Depending on the local practice, the parties may agree to file a suit for dissolution of marriage before or during the collaborative process, agreeing not to proceed forward with that litigation until the collaborative process ends in resolution or breaks down.[93] If it ends in resolution, a written agreement is drawn up and becomes the parties' settlement agreement, attached to their uncontested petition for dissolution of marriage.[94] Typically, this petition is filed after the collaborative process is complete, unless the filing is done before or during the process; if done before or during the collaborative process, the parties do not prosecute the action during the process' pendency.[95] If the collaborative process breaks down, then the parties engage new counsel and proceed to litigation in the traditional mode.[96] All parties are contractually bound to keep confidential any information revealed during the collaborative process, in later litigation (if it occurs).[97]

Collaborative law is not appropriate for all cases; commentators reiterate that it is likely not appropriate in cases involving domestic violence, serious mental health issues, chemical dependency, or other abuse issues.[98] It is not appropriate when a party is not willing to make voluntary disclosure to the other of facts, is using the collaborative process strategically to obtain "free discovery," or cannot or will not negotiate in good faith. It may be inappropriate in cases of severe power imbalance between the parties.[99]

---

90. Daicoff, *supra* note 38, at 27.

91. Schneyer, *supra* note 65, at 297–98.

92. *See, e.g.,* American Bar Association Model Rule 4.2, reprinted in SUSAN R. MARTYN, LAWRENCE J. FOX, & W. BRADLEY WENDEL, THE LAW GOVERNING LAWYERS: NATIONAL RULES, STANDARDS, STATUTES, AND STATE LAWYER CODES (Aspen Publishers, 2009) at 73 (making clear that an attorney cannot communicate with a represented person without that person's attorney's consent).

93. Tesler & Thompson, *supra* note 20, at 256 (showing example of filing after the process has begun); *see also* TESLER, 2001, *supra* note 20, at 146–151 (showing example of collaborative law filing at the beginning of the process).

94. Daicoff, *supra* note 38 at 27.

95. Voegele, et al., *supra* note 17, at 987.

96. Daicoff, *supra* note 38, at 27.

97. Voegele, et al., *supra* note 17, at 1022.

98. *Id.* at 1012.

99. *Id.*

A Case Example

One example that founders and attorneys Pauline Tesler and Stewart Webb have used in their trainings is the hypothetical "Henry/Ruth" divorce. I have elsewhere[100] described this case as follows:

> ... In this case, Henry has a Type "A" personality and is very organized and conscientious, but a bit controlling. Ruth has been a homemaker for years but is now living on her own and making her way, financially. Henry and Ruth have been married for 20 years and have one 17-year-old son, Justin, who is currently being treated in-patient for drug and alcohol abuse. Ruth has moved out of the house into her own apartment and begun working part-time. Henry is providing her with spousal support that is inadequate, as it is below the statutory guidelines in amount.
>
> Because they have seen so many of their friends go through agonizing, lengthy, and costly divorces, they elect to use collaborative law attorneys for theirs. Henry and Ruth, despite their differences, some distrust, and a bit of hostility, both agree that for Justin's sake, this process needs to be as amicable and cooperative as possible. They agree that they need to resolve their differences and come to agreement on property division, child and spousal support, and custody in an amicable fashion, in order to maximize their son's chances of success in his treatment program and in the future. However, they are not in agreement on all of the financial issues.
>
> Despite their disputes over money, they are ultimately able to resolve the issues, divide their property, develop a plan for Justin, and agree on spousal and child support, in a series of four-way conferences involving Henry, Ruth, and their respective attorneys. The process takes four months and costs about a fourth of what a traditional uncontested divorce would cost in legal fees and costs. At the end of the process, the parties attach their signed agreement to their petition for dissolution, file it, and are promptly divorced. The attorneys and the spouses agree at the outset to honor the specific guidelines of the collaborative law process, which includes a contractual undertaking by the attorneys to withdraw from representation if the process breaks down and the parties end up litigating the issues. Neutral third-party evaluators are agreed to, engaged, and used to explore and help resolve the psychological and financial issues involved in Henry and Ruth's lives. Full and honest disclosure of assets and financial matters is required. In the four-ways, communication flows in six directions, between all members of the four-party conference. Between the four-ways, the attorneys and their clients talk, the two clients may talk, and the two attorneys talk.[101]

Statutory Support

Several states have enacted laws specifically approving the practice of collaborative law;[102] Texas was a leader in this area,[103] under the guidance of Dallas collaborative attorney

---

100. Daicoff, *supra* note 38, at 26–27.
101. *Id., citing* Tesler, 1999, *supra* note 3, at 967, 998–1000.
102. Tex. Fam. Code Ann. §6.603 (2006), N.C. Gen. Stat. §50-77 (2007), Cal. Fam. Code §2013 (2008).
103. Tex. Fam. Code Ann. §6.603.

John McShane, who pioneered collaborative law in Texas.[104] More states are likely to follow, including Florida, where a bar committee is currently drafting a proposed statute.[105] The National Conference of Commissioners on Uniform State Laws is also drafting model statutory language for state statutes approving the practice of collaborative law.[106]

Education and Training in Collaborative Law

There are a few law schools who have taught collaborative law courses, reportedly at Florida Coastal School of Law, Santa Clara University, and in Texas and Virginia;[107] currently, Professor Nancy Dowd of the University of Florida is proposing one.[108] The author has taught collaborative law as part of a survey course on the comprehensive law movement at Florida Coastal School of Law since 2001.

Individuals in the United States are typically trained in local training conferences held in each city or town, which train local family law attorneys and experts on collaborative law; after these training sessions and perhaps after observing some collaborative cases, the participants are often deemed ready to practice collaborative law.[109] For example, John McShane introduced collaborative law in his home state by holding a training in 2000 led by founder Stuart Webb and early advocate Pauline Tesler and inviting top family law practitioners to the event.[110] A similar process occurred in Tampa, Florida. Collaborative law has spread, and is likely to continue spreading, via these locally-held trainings and possibly law school courses, after which participants are often eager to begin practicing collaboratively.

Analysis of Collaborative Law

Advantages

Most of the advantages of collaborative law are relatively obvious: proponents claim that successful collaborative cases require much less time and money,[111] engender less anger and hostility between the parties,[112] preserve family relationships, are self-paced

---

104. Steven Keeva, *The Passionate Practitioner,* A.B.A. J. (June, 2000) (profiling attorney John McShane).

105. Personal communication with attorney Nicole K. Habl, Jacksonville, Florida, September 12, 2008 (indicating that attorney Matthew B. Capstraw of Longwood, Florida was then chairing the bar subcommittee responsible for drafting the Florida proposal).

106. Jill Schachner Chanen, *A Warning To Collaborators: Colorado Bar Ethics Panel Takes Aim at a Growing ADR Practice,* A.B.A. J. (May, 2007) at http://www.abajournal.com/magazine/a_warning_to_collaborators/ (last visited July 11, 2010).

107. Personal email communication with collaborative lawyer and former professor Jeanne Fahey, October 7, 2008.

108. Telephone communication with Professor Nancy Dowd, Chesterfield Smith Professor of Law and Co-Director of the Center on Children & the Law, University of Florida Levin College of Law, Gainesville, Florida (Fall, 2008).

109. First Coast Collaborative Law Group's criteria for readiness to practice collaborative law includes attendance at a training plus observation of collaborative law cases, see http://www.firstcoastcollaborativelaw.com (last visited July 11, 2010).

110. The author was in attendance at this training; approximately 50 attorneys were trained in collaborative law at this time, some of whom then went on to practice collaborative law in Texas thereafter. Texas has thus been one of the leaders in the collaborative law movement.

111. Voegele, et al., *supra* note 17, at 1012.

112. Daicoff, *supra* note 38, at 24.

and self-directed, and provide a better overall outcome for families, post-divorce, than do litigated (or even mediated) family law cases.[113]

Less Time and Money

Litigated cases can take up to two years or more to conclude, even with mandatory pre-suit mediation;[114] collaborative cases often take only four to six conferences over a few months' time.[115] The International Academy of Collaborative Professionals reported in 2007 that, of 403 cases, the average number of meetings with one or more professionals was 8 for an average time of 15.2 hours; in a Georgia survey, the vast majority of cases (73%) were completed within 3–8 months.[116] The International Academy of Collaborative Professionals reported that, of 710 American reported collaborative cases between 2006 and 2009, 61% completed within eight months and 80% completed within a year.[117] The average total costs of a collaborative process in 2007 ranged from $20,519 for a lawyers-only form to $28,188 for a team form; the average legal costs were approximately $18,000.[118] In 2009, the average cost of a full-team collaborative divorce was about $23,000, with legal fees constituting about $20,000 of that amount.[119] The majority (approximately 40 to 50%) of the 433 cases surveyed in 2007 had marital estates worth between $500,000 and $2 million; the rest were split above and below this bracket.[120] … Eighty-one to 84 percent of the couples had children and the largest percentage (45%) of cases had a marital estate worth between $200,000 and less than $1 million, suggesting that CL may be greatly useful for the "justice gap," referring to those middle income families who have assets but cannot afford high legal fees. Lower- and higher-value marital estate couples used CL less frequently.[121]

Proponents also claim that there are very few unsuccessful collaborative processes, where the clients must engage new counsel and proceed to trial;[122] in recent surveys, only 10% and 3%, respectively, of collaborative cases terminated (in one survey, 4% of the couples reconciled).[123] The International Academy of Collaborative Professionals reported that, of 710 American reported collaborative cases between 2006 and 2009, 87% completed the CL process, 10% terminated the collaborative process, and 3% of the couples reconciled.[124]

---

113. Voegele, et al., *supra* note 17, at 1012.

114. Anecdotal evidence reported to the author by various family law attorneys in Ohio and Florida, between 2000 and 2008.

115. TESLER & THOMPSON, *supra* note 20, at 250–56 (giving an example of a collaborative divorce that took about six months).

116. IACP Collaborative Practice Survey Cumulative Data Results, Oct. 15, 2006–Dec. 31, 2007 (the number of meetings and number of hours spent with professionals in Georgia was higher than the national survey, but the costs in Georgia were a bit lower, so there were some variations; the national survey included 403 cases while the Georgia survey only looked at 30 cases).

117. Data provided by Attorney Nicole Habl, of Jacksonville, Florida, in a collaborative law training in Jacksonville in 2009.

118. IACP Collaborative Practice Survey Cumulative Data Results, Oct. 15, 2006–Dec. 31 (average costs were $26,235 for a team form, in Georgia).

119. Habl, *supra* note 117.

120. IACP Collaborative Practice Survey Cumulative Data Results, Oct. 15, 2006–Dec. 31 (in Georgia, more clients with higher income marital estates were surveyed than in the national survey reported by the IACP).

121. Habl, *supra* note 117.

122. TESLER, 2001, *supra* note 20.

123. IACP Collaborative Practice Survey Cumulative Data Results, Oct. 15, 2006–Dec. 31, 2007.

124. Habl, *supra* note 117.

Reduced cost and time is likely to benefit the families and children of divorcing spouses, as more money will be available for their needs.[125] Spending less time and energy on the legal process means the divorcing parents may be more available to spend time and energy on their children.[126] Empirical research shows that the absence of ineffective parenting, even temporarily, is one of the three most important reasons children and families experience poor family functioning post-divorce,[127] thus this benefit of collaborative law may have a direct, positive effect on the post-divorce condition of the family and children involved.[128]

Greater Privacy

Proponents point out that collaborative law affords the parties greater privacy than traditional litigation, since the process can occur entirely outside litigation, with a short formal court process at the end, once the parties have come to agreement. This feature is precisely why collaborative law has been expanded into civil cases, particularly cases involving probate, employment disputes, and the breakup of business entities, such as partnerships and joint ventures.

Greater Satisfaction: "Procedural Justice"

Parties to the collaborative case, typically divorcing spouses, have more control over and input into the process and the outcome of their legal matter, which is likely to lead to greater satisfaction with the process and outcome[129] and greater compliance with the settlement agreement provisions.[130] Social scientist Tom Tyler has reported that greater satisfaction with the litigation process and perceptions of its fairness have been empirically reported among litigants when three factors are present: they have more "voice" in the process, they have greater input into the decisionmaking process, and they are treated with respect and dignity by the authorities.[131] This is known as "procedural justice."[132]

Collaborative law is likely to satisfy several of these elements, if not all, in that it allows the parties to have more input and participation in the ultimate outcome, thus affording them both "voice" and participation.[133] The egalitarian nature of the "team" approach to resolving the case, in the collaborative sessions, is also likely to make clients feel as if they are being treated with respect and dignity by the lawyers and experts on the

---

125. TESLER & THOMPSON, *supra* note 20, at 233.

126. *Id.* at 129 (chart comparing what children need during a divorce and how collaborative divorce provides those needs)

127. Maxwell, *supra* note 63.

128. Schneyer, *supra* note 65.

129. Tom Tyler, *Procedural Justice*, in DAVID B. WEXLER & BRUCE J. WINICK, LAW IN A THERAPEUTIC KEY: DEVELOPMENTS IN THERAPEUTIC JURISPRUDENCE 3–15 (1996) [Wexler & Winick hereinafter referred to as KEY] notes that greater satisfaction and perceptions of fairness have been empirically reported among litigants when they have more "voice" in the process, greater input into the decisionmaking process, and are treated with respect and dignity by the authorities.

130. David B. Wexler, *Health Care Compliance Principles and the Insanity Acquittee Conditional Release Process*, 27 CRIM. L. BULL. 18 (1991) (utilizing the health care compliance concepts found in DONALD MEICHENBAUM & DENNIS C. TURK, FACILITATING TREATMENT ADHERENCE: A PRACTITIONER'S GUIDEBOOK (1st ed. 1987) to suggest ways to enhance compliance by those in the legal system).

131. Tyler, *supra* note 129.

132. *Id.* at 6 n.23, 6–12.

133. Voegele, et al., *supra* note 17 at 1006–10 (discussing the four practices of collaborative law: listening, respecting, suspension, and voicing).

team, who, as professionals, may arguably be "authorities" in the eyes of the clients.[134] The more these three factors are fulfilled, Tyler says, the more likely the parties are to feel satisfied with the process and perceive it as "fair."[135]

Compared to typical mediation processes, collaborative law may encourage more participation by the parties in the process.[136] This is due to its "team" approach to dispute resolution and its emphasis on egalitarianism among the members of the collaborative team.[137] In collaborative law, the *parties* craft their resolution with the assistance of their counselors, not solely the attorneys.[138] The attorneys serve more as advisors, equal partners with their clients, and managers of the process to ensure that it progresses smoothly.[139]

Greater Compliance

Other empirical research exists to suggest that the more involved the parties are in crafting the ultimate outcome of their case, the more likely they are to comply with its provisions.[140] In other words, the more participation one has in a decisionmaking process, the more likely one is to comply, behaviorally, with the decision.[141] Greater compliance with settlement agreements, particularly with the terms of visitation and child support payments, can reduce friction and future litigation between ex-spouses, thus saving additional time and money.[142] It can also ensure that children receive more financial support and attention from their parents,[143] which is a desirable outcome.

"Therapeutic Jurisprudence"

... Collaborative law is arguably much more therapeutic for the individuals and families involved in the legal matter, compared to the hostility, adversarialism, posturing, and polarization involved in traditional litigation, because of the above two benefits and because it is designed to minimize destructive conflict between the parties.[144]

Less Conflict

Collaborative law affords divorcing spouses the opportunity to resolve the dissolution of their marriage in an atmosphere of collaboration and cooperation, with a foun-

---

134. Tyler, *supra* note 129, at 10.

135. *Id.* at 6–7.

136. Voegele, et al., *supra* note 17, at 986–88 (discussing differences between ADR processes such as mediation compared to collaborative law, stating that the collaborative process' primary goal is to allow clients to make as many decisions as possible on their own).

137. *Id.* at 988.

138. *Id.*

139. *Id.* at 987.

140. Bruce J. Winick, *Redefining the Role of the Criminal Defense Lawyer at Plea Bargaining and Sentencing: A Therapeutic Jurisprudence/Preventive Law Model*, in PTJ, *supra* note 63, at 279–80; *see also* Maxwell, in PTJ, *supra* note 63 (finding that noncustodial parents in mediated divorces were more likely to comply with child support awards than were noncustodial parents in litigated divorces).

141. David B. Wexler, *Therapeutic Jurisprudence and the Criminal Courts*, in KEY, *supra* note 129, at 157; *see also* Maxwell, *supra* note 63, at 171.

142. Maxwell, *supra* note 63, at 171–72.

143. *Id.*

144. Schneyer, *supra* note 65, at 300–02 (exploring Tesler's paradigm shift required for collaborative law practice).

dation of mutual contractual agreements to abide by the collaborative process and a commitment to participate in good faith.[145] It was founded in part in order to avoid the animosity and hostility traditionally associated with litigation and thus may allow divorcing spouses to reach resolution with less anger, hostility, and negative emotions than result from traditional processes.[146] Not only is this possibly psychologically beneficial for the divorcing spouses, but it also benefits their children, as the amount of conflict between divorced parents has been empirically shown to negatively impact the post-divorce adjustment of the children involved.[147] This reduction in conflict may also assist in fostering a workable, cooperative post-divorce co-parenting relationship between the parties that will serve them well in the future, as they attempt to parent their children.[148]

Interdisciplinary Decisionmaking

Parties in collaborative law, particularly in its interdisciplinary forms, may also have greater access to the input and wisdom of nonlawyer experts, such as financial advisors, vocational experts, psychologists, family counselors, and other mental health experts, in crafting a resolution to their case.[149] With both parties having access to this information, having the input of these experts in the process, and sharing evenly this information and advice, arguably the most optimal outcome, financially and psychologically, can be crafted.[150] Further, if the experts engaged are "neutral," then the courtroom "battle of the experts," each of whom testifies vigorously for and suspiciously in favor of their "side," is eliminated.[151] Instead of receiving two divergent, partisan reports, the parties can operate with information given by a truly neutral expert, which may present a more balanced and useful view of their concerns.[152] The parties can also ask those experts to opine on matters and concerns that arise during the course of the collaborative law process, for example, "if we grant custody to this parent, what effect will that have on the family as a whole?" or "how much money can this spouse actually earn; what is realistic?" or "what's the optimal way to cut up the financial pie, in this family, post-divorce?"[153]

Disadvantages

Collaborative law does, however, have some potential disadvantages. These mostly relate to either a break down in the collaborative process[154] or participants misbehaving, either by operating in bad faith[155] or without sufficient training.[156]

---

145. Fairman, *supra* note 22.
146. Daicoff, *supra* note 38 at 25.
147. Maxwell, *supra* note 63 at 162–63.
148. Schneyer, *supra* note 65, at 298–99.
149. Pauline H. Tesler, *Collaborative Law: Practicing Without Armor, Practicing With Heart*, at 271–73 *in* Marjorie A. Silver, The Affective Assistance of Counsel (2007).
150. *Id.*
151. Tesler, 2001, *supra* note 20, at xv.
152. *See generally* William H. Schwab, *Collaborative Lawyering: A Closer Look at Emerging Practice*, 4 Pepp. Disp. Resol. L. J. 351, 359–60 (2004).
153. *See generally id.*
154. Voegele, et al., *supra* note 17, at 995.
155. *Id.* at 1018–21.
156. Fairman, *supra* note 22, at 246–48.

Ethical Concerns

Collaborative attorneys report "less stress, renewed career satisfaction, easier scheduling and time management, renewed enthusiasm developing and applying new skill sets, increased client appreciation, and improved professional relationships";[157] however, these advantages can cause attorneys to develop positive countertransference or a bias towards collaborative law. This can cause attorneys to "oversell or spin advice" in favor of it,[158] in cases where it is either inappropriate or the client does not really want to engage in the collaborative process, thus impairing the client's autonomy and true, informed consent.[159]

Ethical concerns cited by commentators often include concerns about (1) clients' informed consent to the limited scope of representation in collaborative law,[160] (2) conflicts of interest,[161] (3) candor, (4) termination and the linchpin feature (mandatory disqualification);[162] (5) use of neutral experts; (6) maintaining confidentiality of material information, proposals, and discussions revealed in the collaborative process;[163] and (7) interest-based negotiations and negotiating in good faith.[164] These concerns have been explored at length by commentators, who generally conclude that these concerns are surmountable, but that careful lawyering and attention to ethical concerns is critical, if collaborative law is to succeed.[165]

As these ethical difficulties of practice are explored more carefully, it becomes evident that the collaborative concept is strong, yet some of the intricacies of the process must be modified.[166] For example, a widespread ethical concern involves collaborative attorney/ client relationship termination and primarily points to the disqualification agreement all participants are required to sign. If the collaborative process breaks down and a settlement is not reached, the lawyer is disqualified and a third party lawyer must step in for traditional litigation.[167] This may encourage the collaborative lawyer to unreasonably pressure the client to settle,[168] or end up putting the client at unnecessary risk of extra time, expense and emotional distress if they do not settle.[169] Although solutions to the disquali-

---

157. Voegele, et al., *supra* note 17, at 1012.

158. Voegele, et al., *supra* note 17, at 1012. Note that, under ABA Model Rule 7.4, reprinted in Martyn, et al., *supra* note 92, at 95, attorneys can communicate that they practice collaborative law but cannot state or imply certification as a specialist in it; there is no formal certifying organization, yet.

159. This could be a conflict of interest with the lawyer's own desires, under ABA Model Rule 1.7(a)(2), reprinted in Martyn, et al., *supra* note 92, at 25–31.

160. ABA Model Rules 1.2, 1.1, 1.3, and 1.4, reprinted in Martyn, et al., *supra* note 92, at 13–18, allow for clients and lawyers to agree upon a limited scope of representation at the outset, but the client must render full informed consent to this limitation, after disclosure by the attorney of the risks involved.

161. See, e.g., ABA Model Rule 1.7(a)(2), reprinted in Martyn, et al., *supra* note 92, at 25–31.

162. Fairman, *supra* note 22, at 246.

163. Confidentiality is generally covered by ABA Model Rule 1.6, reprinted in Martyn, et al., *supra* note 92, at 21; however, disclosure in four-way conferences may affect confidentiality of the information and the applicability of attorney-client privilege to the information.

164. Voegele, et al., *supra* note 17, at 1013–23. Note that, under ABA Model Rule 2.1, reprinted in Martyn, et al., *supra* note 92, at 57, the lawyer has the ability to consider and discuss nonlegal factors in his or her representation of the client, in his or her capacity as counselor and advisor.

165. Fairman, *supra* note 22, at 247.

166. *Id.* at 251–52.

167. Schneyer, *supra* note 65, at 317.

168. Voegele, et al., *supra* note 17, at 1017.

169. Schneyer, *supra* note 65, at 317.

fication agreement include stringent lawyer disclosure and informed client consent; these solutions have their own challenges. There is an inherent need in the collaborative law process for candor and confidentiality.[170] The client must be candid with their attorney in order for the attorney to fully analyze all relevant, even sensitive, information; in turn allowing the attorney to act as an effective counselor.[171] Clients, even though fully informed and consenting to participate with these requirements, may underestimate the difficulty in following through with them.[172] This suggests that perhaps clients are not truly able to give full and adequate informed consent.[173] Furthermore, a breakdown of either candor or confidentiality is fatal to the process as the attorney is no longer able to effectively represent the client on several levels.[174] A lack of cooperation by clients may manifest itself in various ways. For example, a client may display a lack of candor in their use of neutral experts. Clients in the collaborative law process have the ability to disqualify neutral experts from their case.[175] If they use this capability in bad faith for strategic or timing reasons, it could put the collaborative relationship at risk.[176] However, this ethical concern may be put to rest during the informed consent and contractual phase of the process if done carefully.[177]

Another emerging concern with the collaborative law process is potential conflicts of interest. Model Rule of Professional Conduct 1.7(a)(2) prohibits lawyers from representing clients when there is a significant risk that the representation may be limited by, among other things, the lawyer's personal interest.[178] The Ethics Committee of the Colorado Bar Association also found a conflict in the requirement that both lawyers sign a four way agreement.[179] This Committee opined that in this act the lawyer essentially agrees to impair their ability to represent the client.[180] As stated previously, many of these ethical dilemmas are avoided by the lawyer carefully constructing guidelines and standards for their own practice of collaborative law. It has also been suggested that precise and appropriate selection of clients tailored to the collaborative process reduces the possibility that ethical issues will materialize.[181]

Bad Faith

Collaborative law relies on a mutual, cooperative agreement to engage in the collaborative process in good faith, with honesty, and a spirit of openness.[182] It relies on voluntary disclosure of financial and other information,[183] for example. Therefore, if one participant (attorney or client) engages in the process without good faith, seeking to conceal or misrepresent facts, or for an ulterior motive, such as simply seeking "free" discovery to be used in later litigation, then the process will not work properly and may

170. Voegele, et al., *supra* note 17, at 1016.
171. *Id.*
172. Fairman, *supra* note 22, at 248.
173. Voegele, et al., *supra* note 17, at 1017.
174. *Id.* at 1016–17.
175. *Id.* at 1015.
176. *Id.*
177. *Id.*
178. ABA Model Rule 1.7(a)(2), reprinted in MARTYN, ET AL., *supra* note 92, at 25.
179. Fairman, *supra* note 22, at 250–51.
180. *Id.*
181. *Id.* at 248.
182. Daicoff, *supra* note 38, at 25.
183. Voegele, et al., *supra* note 17 at 985 (discussing voluntary disclosure and transparency in the collaborative law process).

harm other participants who are operating in good faith.[184] However, it is the responsibility of all of the participants (particularly the attorneys) to query whether any of these dynamics are present and, if so, to terminate the process promptly.[185]

Failed Collaborative Processes

Critics argue that a failed collaborative process can take more time and money (in legal fees) than a traditional, litigated (or mediated) divorce.[186] This is mainly due to the "linchpin" feature that the attorneys must withdraw from representation if the process breaks down and the parties proceed to court.[187] They argue that there will be some duplication of effort and legal fees, as the new counsel learns the facts of the case and prepares to represent their clients. Advocates argue that failed collaborative cases are rare,[188] and that even if the process fails, important resolutionary energy may have been generated during the process, and some agreements may have been reached, before the process terminates.[189] For example, statistics indicate that only about 10% of collaborative cases fail.[190]

Inexperienced Attorneys and Attorney Personality Traits

One significant danger of collaborative law is that it may be practiced by attorneys without sufficient training or expertise to guide and direct the process appropriately.[191] Inexperienced attorneys may behave in an extreme manner, either acting overly adversarially or overly conciliatorily, failing to continue to advocate for and advise their clients in the collaborative process. Attorneys in the collaborative process are required to assist their clients in maintaining composure and remaining cooperative, but they still are required to put forth their clients' best interests and position; they do not simply agree to whatever is proposed.[192] On the other hand, they are not acting as gladiators, as they might in a litigation posture.[193]

Second, because there is no neutral third-party mediator present, the attorneys are also responsible for maintaining the "process," meaning they must monitor the progress of the collaboration, terminate it if it becomes destructive, call caucuses when clients become unable to continue productively in the process (for example, if they become overly angry, hostile, or distrustful), and enforce the ground rules that were agreed upon at the outset of the process.[194] Inexperienced attorneys might fail to perform these functions adequately and the process might derail or fail, as a result.[195]

Third, the "attorney personality" itself may be an obstacle to effective collaborative practice. Tesler has mentioned the need for significant retooling of experienced attorneys

---

184. TESLER, 2001, *supra* note 20, at 184–85.

185. *Id.*

186. NANCY J. CAMERON, COLLABORATIVE PRACTICE: DEEPENING THE DIALOGUE 18–19 (2004).

187. Kuhn, *supra* note 69.

188. Cameron, *supra* note 186.

189. Daicoff, *supra* note 38, at 25–26.

190. *See* IACP statistics from 2006–2009, presented by Attorney Nicole Habl, of Jacksonville, Florida, in a collaborative law training in Jacksonville in 2009, discussed at notes 116–24, *supra.*

191. Fairman, *supra* note 22, at 247.

192. Voegele, et al., *supra* note 17, at 1002–10 (discussing the importance of the four basic practices in maintaining a working collaborative process, while still advocating for the client's needs).

193. Pauline H. Tesler, *Collaborative Law: What It Is and Why Lawyers Need to Know About It*, in PTJ, *supra* note 63, at 189–90.

194. Voegele, et al., *supra* note 17.

195. *Cf.* TESLER, 2001, *supra* note 20, at 192–93 (explaining that it is not impossible to collaborate with an untrained attorney, though it may be difficult).

and the need for a "paradigm shift," before they can practice collaborative law.... [The] traits that distinguish lawyers from nonlawyers based on empirical studies ... are: an insensitivity to or decreased emphasis on interpersonal relationships and emotions, a focus on extrinsic rewards and the economic bottom line, competitiveness, a need for achievement, a focus on rights, duties, justice, clearly defined role obligations, logical analysis, and rationality, and a tendency to become more ambitious and aggressive when placed under stress.[196] These traits, while not descriptive of all attorneys, may tend to be present among lawyers more often than in nonlawyer groups and may tend to predominate in those in the legal profession. They also may work against the values of cooperation, collaboration, a sensitivity to and an ability to manage emotions of oneself and of others, the preservation of human relationships and wellbeing, and a focus on other nonlegal concerns, which may be useful in collaborative practice.

For example, the collaborative lawyer may need a keen sensitivity to knowing when to press for an advantage and when to allow the process to develop in the four-way conference without the attorney's input. The collaborative attorney may need to be able to consider and value relationships, psychological wellbeing, mental health, finances, values, morals, needs, and beliefs involved in the matter as well as legal rights. He or she may need to be able to assist the client in participating effectively in the process instead of collapsing into a negative, hostile, "shadow state" (Tesler's phrase),[197] as is common in divorce cases. To the extent that these capabilities are unfamiliar to lawyers, some retooling, retraining, coaching, and perhaps supervision by more experienced collaborative lawyers may be appropriate.

....

Commentary

Despite its potential risks and shortcomings, collaborative law is almost a necessary next step for the American legal system, because of ... an increased emphasis in society and in the law on relational matters, interpersonal harmony, cooperation, collaboration, team-building, and community, instead of a more traditional emphasis on individual rights, freedom, rugged individualism, and self-determinism.[198]

.... the traditional, adversarial manner of resolving civil cases, particularly family law cases, appears to have been brought into question, psychologically, economically, and philosophically. Since at least 1990, innovators in the law have been experimenting with a panoply of alternatives to traditional negotiation, settlement, mediation, and trial; collaborative law is one of these developments.[199] It fits with these shifts in emphasis in society in its explicit use of collaboration, cooperation, openness, and honesty in bringing adversaries together towards a common goal: the optimal resolution of their marital dissolution. It may allow clients to resolve their cases in ways that may more accurately reflect their own values and beliefs, particularly if their values and beliefs are changing to reflect the above developments. It reflects an egalitarian approach rather than a top-down,

---

196. Based on 40 years of empirical research summarized in SUSAN DAICOFF, LAWYER KNOW THYSELF: A PSYCHOLOGICAL ANALYSIS OF PERSONALITY STRENGTHS AND WEAKNESSES 2–98 (2004), summarized concisely at 40–42 thereof.

197. TESLER, 2001, *supra* note 20, at 30–32.

198. Thomas D. Barton, *Troublesome Connections: The Law and Post-Enlightenment Culture*, 47 EMORY L. J. 163, 163–64 (1998).

199. *See generally* Daicoff, *supra* note 38.

hierarchical approach to decisionmaking, by allowing clients to have a chance to have more control over and participation in the process by which their case will be resolved. Finally, in light of very recent economic downturns, it may become even more attractive as it can minimize the amount of client wealth spent on legal fees (making that money available for other purposes which, in divorce cases, means more money can be available for family purposes).[200]

In 2001, several students in one of my early comprehensive law practice courses were initially very skeptical of collaborative law, along with other comprehensive law approaches. At one point in the semester, one asked, "Professor Daicoff, is this a *paradigm shift*?" indicating his understanding that an overall fundamental change in approach to legal matters and dispute resolution was being proposed. This is precisely what collaborative law asks of attorneys, clients, experts, and society. A second student raised a number of concerns with collaborative law, until at one point he finally concluded something like, "What you are teaching me is just one more tool for my toolkit. When I graduate, I will have to compete with many other attorneys in the local legal community. The more tools I have for my toolkit, the more marketable and valuable I am, so I can see its value." These two insights have stayed with me ever since and proved to be persuasive for later students.

Professor Fairman also argues that collaborative law is one more tool for the lawyer's toolkit, along with litigation, mediation, and other dispute resolution mechanisms.[201] He describes this toolkit as now including a "rich spectrum" of alternative dispute resolution options, including collaborative law, and argues for its extension outside the family law realm into general civil cases.[202] Refining the tool of collaborative law and retooling lawyers to be able to appropriately triage cases, so that the right tool is used for the right case and client, are our next tasks. We also must continue to analyze, critique, study, and evaluate the efficacy and effectiveness of each tool in our toolkit, ever improving our implements.

The fact that collaborative law has grown as quickly as it has and the fact that experimentation with collaborative law in other substantive areas of the law, such as employment law, is occurring suggest that it was needed and that it does, indeed, work, at least in appropriate cases. It also suggests a receptiveness within society and the legal profession to this innovative way of resolving disputes.

Conclusion

Our current, traditional system of family law litigation is often disastrous emotionally and financially for families and divorcing couples. Attorneys may feel pressure to zealously advocate for their clients, demonstrate their competence and value to their clients, defend against draconian moves by their opposing counsel, and bill and collect legal fees; these pressures can create hostility, antagonism, excessive amounts of legal moves and posturing, and expensive discovery and trial. The end result for some families is that they can spend their life savings on accomplishing a divorce and feel dissatisfied if not emotionally and financially bankrupt by the end. The added emotions of a divorce multiply the emotional angst of litigation.

---

200. For example, the recent Wall Street downturns and the foreclosure/housing crisis may make collaborative law more attractive, *see* the statistics on costs at text accompanying notes 114–25, *supra.*

201. Fairman, *supra* note 22, at 270 (noting that "there may be few clear lines of demarcation" between the various dispute resolution forms).

202. *Id.*

While these concerns and pressures might be manageable or tenable in typical civil cases, in family law cases the financial and emotional pressures have direct consequences for families and children, which in turn are likely to affect the psychological functioning of tomorrow's adults.... [T]oday's litigation process might create tomorrow's mental health or criminal justice concerns, in the adult children of divorce.[203] With divorce rates as high as they are, these concerns affect a huge proportion of the population. Collaborative law ... is one step towards conceiving of a "better way" to resolve interpersonal disputes, thereby working towards greater wellbeing for many individuals affected by divorce. However, as with all of the disciplines making up the comprehensive law movement, careful implementation, evaluation, and further refinement of collaborative law are necessary and expected to continue.

Resources

Stuart G. Webb & Ronald D. Ousky, The Collaborative Way to Divorce: The Revolutionary Method That Results in Less Stress, Lower Costs, and Happier Kids Without Going to Court (Hudson Street Press, 2006). (This book is authored by the founder of collaborative law and is a good resource also for clients to read.)

Pauline H. Tesler & Peggy Thompson, Collaborative Divorce: The Revolutionary New Way to Restructure Your Family, Resolve Legal Issues, and Move On With Your Life (Harper Collins, 2006). (This book is authored by two pioneers and trainers in the collaborative law field, dealing primarily with the interdisciplinary, team-oriented collaborative divorce model of collaborative law.)

Pauline H. Tesler, Collaborative Law: Achieving Effective Resolution in Divorce Without Litigation (American Bar Association, 2001) (This book is authored by a pioneer and trainer in the collaborative law field, speaking primarily to lawyers who wish to become collaborative lawyers).

Forrest S. Mosten, Collaborative Divorce [Handbook]: Helping Families Without Going to Court (Jossey-Bass, 2009).

Nancy J. Cameron, Collaborative Practice: Deepening the Dialogue (Continuing Legal Education Society of British Columbia, 2004).

Dennis P. Stolle, David B. Wexler, & Bruce J. Winick, Eds., Practicing Therapeutic Jurisprudence: Law as a Helping Profession (Carolina Academic Press, 2000) (Chapters 6–8).

Susan L. Brooks & Robert G. Madden, Relationship-Centered Lawyering: Social Science Theory for Transforming Legal Practice (Carolina Academic Press, 2010) (Chapters 3 & 7).

Marjorie A. Silver, The Affective Assistance of Counsel (Carolina Academic Press, 2007) (Chapter 8).

---

203. Thanks are due to Circuit Judge John M. Alexander in St. Johns County, Florida, for these insights and for connecting adversarial family law litigation with the psychological and financial wellbeing of the children involved in the cases (personal communication with Judge Alexander, September 30, 2008). Judge Alexander formerly served in the criminal, civil, probate, juvenile, and domestic relations areas and currently presides in the unified family court at the Richard O. Watson Judicial Center in St. Augustine, Florida.

Websites

International Academy of Collaborative Professionals ("IACP"): http://www.collaborative divorce.com (last visited July 11, 2010).

Association of Collaborative Lawyers of Alberta: www.collaborativelaw.ca (last visited July 11, 2010).

Cincinnati Academy of Collaborative Professionals: www.collaborativelaw.com (last visited July 11, 2010).

Collaborative Law Association of the Rochester Area, Inc.: http://nycollaborativelaw.com (last visited July 11, 2010).

The Collaborative Family Law Council of Wisconsin, Inc.: www.collabdivorce.com (last visited July 11, 2010).

Collaborative Family Lawyers of South Florida: www.collaborativefamilylawfl.com/ collaborative.html (last visited July 11, 2010).

Collaborative Law Institute of Illinois: www.collablawil.org (last visited July 11, 2010).

Collaborative Law Institute of Minnesota: www.collaborativelaw.org (last visited July 11, 2010).

Collaborative Law Institute of Texas: www.collablawtexas.com (last visited July 11, 2010).

Collaborative Law: International Academy of Collaborative Professionals: www.collab orativepractice.com (last visited July 11, 2010).

Collaborative Practice Center: www.collablaw.com (last visited July 11, 2010).

Global Collaborative Law Council, Inc.: www.collaborativelaw.us (last visited July 11, 2010).

Queensland Collaborative Law: www.qldcollablaw.com.au (last visited July 11, 2010).

Coordination: Also read Brooks & Madden (Chapters 3 and 7), Silver (Chapter 8), Stolle, et al. (Chapters 7 and then 6 and 8), King (Chapter 8), and Wright (p. 47–54).

Chapter Assignments

Exercise 12-1—Collaborative Law Case Analysis: Antwhistles

Your client is Ricardo Antwhistle, a 58-year-old man who wants to be divorced from his 58-year-old wife, Avery Antwhistle. They have one grown daughter, Triley (25 years old), who is married and has children of her own. The husband has a son from a previous marriage, Leif (30 years old), and the wife has a daughter from a previous marriage, Carley (31 years old). The child and two stepchildren are all adult, married, and have their own children. Your client and his wife have been married for 26 years. Both spouses had very unpleasant, acrimonious divorces in the past and wish to "do this one differently." Your client was also dissatisfied with his attorney in the previous divorce because of the animosity and unpleasantness of the divorce and remarks that "once we got the lawyers involved, it was all about money and everything got a whole lot worse. I hope you can do a better job." Your client is a real estate developer whose work has been declining in recent years; he is contemplating retirement or a career change. They have a large house that is now not worth the amount they have invested in it. He says because of the close-knit relationship between the three children and their children (the grandchildren), the spouses want to remodel the house to divide it up into two homes and continue to live together after the divorce. His wife takes care of some of the grandchildren after school and he and she do not want to disrupt the grandchildren's relationships with their grandparents. Further, they live in a gated community with a golf and tennis club and neither wants to move out of that exclusive community. Each parent would have his or her own wing of the house. Your client also wants his wife to have half of his retirement, half the house, and half of their assets, because she has been a good mother and grandmother. She has not been employed outside the home during their marriage. He is willing to pay her some short term alimony but fears that she is going to want more alimony than he wants to pay. The divorce is his idea and she is less excited about it than he is, but she is not going to fight him in an attempt to stay married. How do you propose to handle his case?

Case Analysis: Antwhistles

This is a divorce, so the most appropriate vector for family law is collaborative law, which is almost exclusively used for family law matters (although it is proposed to be extended into other civil disputes). If they had no issues, then it would be a straight mediated, uncontested divorce, but these two are going to have ongoing relations and we do need to resolve the alimony issue, so CL is most appropriate.

(a) Legal issues:	(b) Psycholegal issues:	(c) Intersections:
Divorce Property settlement Alimony—long term marriage, W not working = W likely entitled to some alimony. Agreement re: division of time and financial responsibility for house. NOTES: Only alimony and property division; no minor children. No domestic violence is alleged. They are in agreement about the property division, but most likely there are issues of finances and use relating to the house that they will not agree on, once those issues are identified (things they have not considered or contemplated, yet). Also, it appears that alimony will be a point of contention. With the length of the marriage and the age of the parties, it is possible that the wife would be entitled to alimony, but the husband may be completely unwilling to pay it.	Neither wants an acrimonious divorce, based on past experience. H disliked previous attorney due to animosity. Grandchildren, close relationships between children and spouses. W provides child care for minor grandchildren in home. Spouses in different places re: readiness for divorce. May have different expectations re: alimony; property settlement should be easily agreed to, in contrast. Want to continue living together in divided house; don't want to move. Will have close working relationship post-divorce. H needs financial planning for his future career change or retirement. Marital home is an unrealized loss asset.	Legal actions of divorce may strain relationships within family with adult children and spouses and minor grandchildren. Need divorce process to minimize this strain (thus, use CL). Divided house idea may not work according to plan. Need to plan in settlement agreement for eventual sale of house and move out of both spouses. Educate both spouses re: typical alimony awarded in court in these type of cases to converge their expectations about this. W may resist legal actions due to psychological unreadiness for the divorce; may delay. Coaching for her might be helpful to expedite emotional process. Acrimonious, hotly contested divorce, alimony, or property settlement may run up legal fees and costs and thus deplete financial resources needed for H's future career or retirement.

Comprehensive law skills used would include: a psychological understanding of the stages of grief or divorce, the ability to identify which stage each spouse is in, an understanding of relationships in the family, the ability to conduct a CL 4-way, the ability to work with financial and psychological experts in a team format, and the ability to identify and defer "hot-button issues" to later 4-ways.

Processes: Here you would identify hot-button issues that would be agenda-ed for later 4-ways, not the initial ones (alimony, for example). Consider how and when to serve the W with the petition for dissolution (this is a psycholegal soft spot, as she does not really want the divorce and can be upset by it). You might want to include her in the filing process so it's a true collaboration. You would want to consider whether to use collaborative law (with neutral third-party financial and psychological experts) or collaborative divorce (with interdisciplinary teams). Since there are no minor children, collaborative law might be appropriate and less costly.

Collaborative law is clearly the choice, since the spouses appear to be in agreement, appear to have the ability to be honest and fair, and want to continue living together. They are going to need a positive divorce experience that improves or at least does not damage their relationship because they are going to have a close relationship post-divorce.

They clearly should avoid litigation because it is indeed likely to make their relationship worse. If they are truly as cooperative as the husband presents, then CL is a good choice and will resolve the case with the least time and money and the most good will between the spouses. There are probably some issues with alimony; we have no facts about whether or not the wife works but it does not sound like she does. Be aware that their idea of living together is likely unrealistic and plan for its eventual breakdown in the future (as each one begins dating and having serious romantic relationships).

Exercise 12-2 — Collaborative Law Marital Settlement Agreements

Locate the form marital settlement agreement commonly used in your jurisdiction. First, identify all of the provisions in this form that might work at odds with a collaborative law approach (i.e., that seem adversarial or "non-collaborative"). Then, redraft those provisions to harmonize more seamlessly with a collaborative law approach to dissolution cases, where children are involved.[204]

Exercise 12-3 — Collaborative Law Case Simulations

Split up into groups of eight, consisting of: two spouses, two attorneys, one mental health neutral expert; one financial neutral expert; one child specialist; and one vocational rehabilitation expert. The neutral experts will also serve as observers of the process who will debrief with the "spouses" and "attorneys" their impressions of the process, what worked, and what did not. Choose one of the following three cases to simulate. Identify the nonlegal issues. Identify which issues the collaborative attorneys would want to table for later four-ways as "hot button issues" and which would be issues appropriate to discuss in the first four-way.

Prepare for and conduct the first four-way conference in this case, including a five-minute pre-conference attorney-attorney phone call in which the attorneys set the agenda for the first four-way meeting (clients leave the room during this call). In the first four-way simulation, you can skip over some of the lengthy reading of the collaborative agreement that usually occurs during the first four-way, but not all of it. You may not have time to conduct an entire four-way, so be prepared to condense it. You may use the neutral experts for consultation and participation at any appropriate point in the process. When it is over, debrief the exercise with the neutral experts. (What worked? What could have been done differently?) *Optional: You may choose to write up any agreements you reached, using the revised form agreement you created in Exercise 2.*

Case 12-A: Nicholas/Sally

* Nicholas: age 45

* Sally: age 42

---

204. *See, e.g.*, Dax J. Miller, *Applying Therapeutic Jurisprudence and Preventive Law to the Divorce Process: Enhancing the Attorney-Client Relationship and the Florida Practice and Procedure Form "Marital Settlement Agreement for Dissolution of Marriage with Dependent or Minor Child(ren)," 10 Fla. Coastal L. Rev. 263 (2009) (providing an excellent and thorough deconstruction of the Florida form marital settlement agreement, from a collaborative and preventive approach).

- Nicholas and Sally have been married for 22 years.
- They have two children:
  - Nick, Jr.: age 14
  - Tyler: age 10
- Nicholas has a master's degree in engineering. Nicholas is the vice president of an engineering firm, making $120,000 annually. Nicholas' job requires him to travel about two days a week.
- He has a 401K retirement account. The parties own their own home and have a money market account, a stock portfolio, and individual retirement accounts (IRAs). They each have a late model car which is paid for and no significant debt. Nick is willing to help with college, but does not want to be legally obligated to do so.
- Nick, Jr. has become a challenge to Sally. He has a close relationship with Nick through mutual sports interests and would like to live with Nick. Tyler adores Nick, Jr. and would be devastated if Nick, Jr. went to live with Nick. Nick really wants to have Nick, Jr. live with him and he is somewhat oblivious to any negative implications.
- Sally has been a stay-at-home parent and care giver, thus making valuable contributions to the family. Nick appreciates some of these contributions, but this does not translate into him giving them a dollar value. Sally has not worked throughout the marriage and recently started a part time job in at an after school program at a recreation center. Sally quit college to marry Nick and has no marketable skills. Sally assumes that Nick will take care of her the rest of her life in the same manner that he has so far. Sally is afraid that if Nicholas remarries, he will forget about his promise to pay for college.

Legal Issues:

- Children's Issues
- Primary Residential Parent vs. Secondary Residential (Noncustodial) Parent
- Shared Parental Responsibility
- Time Sharing
- Financial Support/Alimony
- Child Support
- College Expenses
- Life Insurance (to fund child support and alimony)
- Asset/Debt Division

Assets:

- The parties purchased their home 10 years ago. The value is $220,000. The mortgage is $200,000 resulting in $20,000 net equity.
- 401K account $90,000
- IRAs: Nicholas $20,000, Sally $10,000
- Money market $25,000
- Stock portfolio $50,000
- Two cars (paid for; worth $5,000 each)

- Income after taxes $6,500/month

Debts:

- Mortgage, monthly payment $2,000 includes taxes and insurance

- One credit card with an outstanding balance of $5,000

Case 12-B: John/Kathy

Common Facts: John and Kathy are the clients. They are a professional couple; she is 35 and he is 40 years old. Kathy is an environmental law attorney and John has been the primary caregiver for their only son, Jake. John has a degree as an architect and worked before their son was born, but did not work for the six years prior to the time of their separation. John and Kathy have been married for eight years. They have been separated for one year. Kathy is living in their former marital home (in town) and John is living in a condo that they own at the beach (their former second home). Jake is now six years old and in school part of the day, but has been with John during every afternoon. The parties have been attempting to split Jake's time equally between them and so far this arrangement has been successful. The parties both desire to have joint custody of their son and to split visitation equally (50/50). John is currently employed as a freelance draftsman and architect part time while Jake is in school; however he desires to go back to full-time work but has not been able to find a job that he likes and is worried about the quality and cost of Jake's after school child care. Furthermore, John does not want to work as an architect, but would rather start up his own business or go back to school for retraining. He is also worried about being able to get a job and about what his earning capacity is. Kathy is sure that he can get a job and earn at least half of what she earns as a young, junior partner in her law firm. Kathy is very hardworking, conscientious, and career oriented, while John appears more "laid-back." Kathy is more conservative in her approach to life while John's lifestyle is a bit more alternative. Their conflicts (while married) centered around money, different values, and John's unemployment. Both, however, feel that the other is a good and devoted parent and they agree that the best interests of their child, Jake, are very important.

Kathy makes $100,000 per year. John has the ability, she feels, to make $60,000 per year but is currently earning $35,000 per year in his part time, free-lance work. John does not agree; he thinks he cannot make more than $35,000 per year and continue to care for Jake after school. The marital home where Kathy lives is worth $200,000 and has a mortgage on it of $180,000. The condo where John lives is worth $135,000 and has a mortgage on it of $120,000. Their cars are of approximately equal value and require equal car payments. Kathy has a retirement account worth $100,000 ($60,000 after tax value). Kathy currently carries all three of them on her health insurance. Kathy has life insurance; John does not. They have savings of $20,000 in a money market account held jointly.

Instructions for Kathy only:

You want this divorce to do as little harm to your son, Jake, as possible. You are committed to maintaining a good relationship with John and co-parenting Jake with him, in a 50/50, shared or joint custody arrangement. You want Jake to spend half his time with you and half his time with his dad, because you know how important fathers are to children, particularly sons. You are a devoted and involved parent, as much as you can be.

Also, you realize that your marriage has had a role reversal; you have been the breadwinner and John has been the stay home, primary child caregiver. You are worried about what effect this will have on you in a divorce setting; for example, your fear is that John will threaten to ask for custody of Jake and you are afraid that if you are the noncustodial parent you will only see your son every Wednesday night and every other weekend, which is not enough visitation for you. You believe John is a good parent but firmly believe that Jake needs both his parents equally in order to thrive. For now, you have worked out a visitation schedule that approximates a 50/50 split of time.

You are not willing to pay alimony. You do not want to pay child support because you are afraid that John will fritter the money away, use it as an excuse not to work full-time, and not spend the money on Jake. You also feel that you have worked very hard to get where you are and do not want your assets depleted by this divorce or by John. You want to make sure that your assets are used for Jake's education and his future needs. You are disappointed and a bit angry with John because you feel that he is lazy when it comes to working and you think he could be working harder (like you do) and making more money. However, you do realize that John's taking over Jake's after-school care is valuable both in terms of savings on child care expenses and emotionally, since you believe parental care is always better than babysitting care. However, you are also worried that John and Jake are spending their afternoons watching insipid television shows.

You were not the one to move out. You don't really want the divorce but you are resigned that it is going to happen. You are aware that John moved out in order to start dating other people. You are not dating. The marriage fell apart because you felt John was being lazy and you began to fight about money and work. You buried yourself in your work and neglected the relationship and eventually he wanted to see someone else. You recognize this but are still (now) stuck in anger at John for being lazy ("if he hadn't been so lazy to begin with, we wouldn't have had these conflicts and we would still be together. This marriage would work if he would just….").

Remember that you are committed to the collaborative process and that you have made a commitment to resolve all the issues and points of disagreement in the collaborative model, without resort to a third-party decision maker.

Based on this bare bones information, feel free to embellish and make up any facts or emotions consistent with the character and the situation.

Instructions for Kathy's attorneys only:

You have a few problems with this client's legal position. First, recent cases in the state indicate that, despite the traditional presumption that wives get primary residential custody of the children, courts are now willing to grant primary residential custody to husbands who have been stay home, primary caregivers for children. In the state where this couple lives, there is no such thing as "joint or shared custody"; there is only primary residential custody and secondary custody. One party is going to have to have the label of primary custodial parent, which makes the other parent sound a bit subordinate. Neither of these spouses wants to be subordinate to the other in terms of their responsibility for, control over, or time with their son. Indeed, they truly want a joint, shared, 50/50 situation but the labels used by state family law are not conducive to this arrangement. You have to create some facsimile of this arrangement, using the existing law.

Further, the nonresidential parent usually owes child support to the primary residential or custodial parent, so whoever is nonresidential would (if you went to court) end up having to pay child support based on the statutory guidelines (there is a fixed amount calculable in the statute). The client needs to be prepared for this issue, also.

The best way to resolve this is to give Kathy primary residential custody and give John very liberal visitation rights (e.g., up to 50% of the son's time spent with John), because this will relieve her of any obligation to pay child support to John. A court however, would probably make John pay her child support in this situation, which he isn't going to want to do. Basically, you have to be a bit creative in order to accomplish a joint custody arrangement that works for this couple, in this state.

However, if John fights for custody, there is a good chance he will win. If so, then Kathy as the nonresidential parent faces the risk that her visitation with Jake could be as little as every Wednesday night and every other weekend, far less than the 50% she wants (unless John agrees otherwise). And, she will owe child support to John calculated under the statutory guidelines.

She may be at risk for paying alimony to him, however, although the short term of the marriage and his education level and his ability to work all militate against her liability for alimony. He still may ask for it or demand it and she needs to be prepared that in court, there could be a risk that she would pay at least some short term rehabilitative alimony.

Regarding the property settlement, the presumption here is that all their assets and debts are marital assets and debts and thus they will all be split 50/50. You have to find a way to do this that equalizes their relative positions.

Instructions for John only:

You are the one who moved out. You love Kathy but can't live with her anymore. She is no longer the free spirit she was when you met her and fell in love with her. Now all she seems to want to do is work and fight with you about you working and making money. She is holding you back, being a negative and destructive force in your life, and you have determined that you have to divorce her to keep your sanity. You are sad about the end of this marriage but rather philosophical about it. You are not angry or vindictive. You are resigned to the situation. You understand that people grow apart and their priorities change. You felt, however, very lonely and unappreciated in the marriage, you enjoy companionship, and so you eventually moved out in order to start dating. Kathy is not dating.

You are a devoted and involved parent who is proud of the fact that you have been a stay home dad. You even formed a network of stay home dads in the area. Your plan was to move out, get a part time job, take care of Jake, and continue doing what you are doing. You think that it's crazy to put Jake in afterschool child care and you want to continue taking care of him while he is not in school. You want this divorce to do as little harm to your son, Jake, as possible. You are committed to maintaining a good relationship with Kathy and co-parenting Jake with her, in a 50/50, shared or joint custody arrangement. You want Jake to spend half his time with you and half his time with Kathy. You believe that no job is more important than your son and you plan to fit your work schedule around his school schedule. You are afraid that Kathy will ask for custody of Jake and you are afraid that if you are the noncustodial parent you will only see your son every Wednesday night and every other weekend, which is not enough visitation for you. You believe Kathy is a good parent but you can't imagine her becoming Jake's primary caregiver and displacing you, when you have been his primary caregiver for the first six years of his life. For now, you have worked out a visitation schedule that approximates a 50/50 split of time.

You also believe that you have worked hard as the primary caregiver for those six years and that you should be rewarded financially for fulfilling that role. Your position is that Kathy is where she is today in her career because of your unfailing support and care. You would like to have some kind of permanent child support from Kathy to help equalize your incomes, since you will be equal parents of Jake. You would like alimony as well, but aren't sure whether it's obtainable and are willing to forego it as long as you can cover your expenses. You are worried about not being able to make enough money in your part time job but you are not willing to work full-time. You have never been a high wage earner or enormously ambitious. You are more of a free spirit yourself.

Remember that you are committed to the collaborative process and that you have made a commitment to resolve all the issues and points of disagreement in the collaborative model, without resort to a third-party decision maker.

Based on this bare bones information, feel free to embellish and make up any facts or emotions consistent with the character and the situation.

Instructions for John's attorneys only:

John has a good chance of getting custody of Jake, if he wants it, based on some recent cases giving custody of children to stay home dads, in spite of the usual presumption that wives get custody of children. In a role reversal situation like this one, John may have a case for custody, some short term rehabilitative alimony, and certainly child support calculated under the statutory guidelines, since Kathy makes so much more money than he does. However, his education level, his earning capacity, and the short term of the marriage all militate against his getting alimony. On the other hand, her earning capacity and his role as stay home dad work in favor of his getting alimony.

In the state where this couple lives, there is no such thing as "joint or shared custody"; there is only primary residential custody and secondary custody. One party is going to have to have the label of primary custodial parent, which makes the other parent sound a bit subordinate. Neither of these spouses wants to be subordinate to the other in terms of their responsibility for, control over, or time with their son. Indeed, they truly want a joint, shared, 50/50 situation but the labels used by state family law are not conducive to this arrangement. You have to create some facsimile of this arrangement, using the existing law.

Further, the nonresidential parent usually owes child support to the primary residential or custodial parent, so whoever is nonresidential would (if you went to court) end up having to pay child support based on the statutory guidelines (there is a fixed amount calculable in the statute). John needs to be prepared for this issue, also. He is definitely not going to want to pay Kathy child support when she makes so much more money than he does. Probably, it would be best for him to be the primary residential/custodial parent and ask for child support from her.

Also, if he is the nonresidential parent, he faces the risk in court that his visitation with Jake could be as little as every Wednesday night and every other weekend, far less than the 50% he wants (unless Kathy agrees otherwise). And, as the nonresidential parent, he will owe child support to Kathy calculated under the statutory guidelines, unless she agrees otherwise. Basically, you have to be a bit creative in order to accomplish a joint custody arrangement that works for this couple, in this state.

Regarding the property settlement, the presumption here is that all their assets and debts are marital assets and debts and thus they will all be split 50/50. You have to figure out a way to do this that equalizes their relative positions.

Case 12-C: Jessica/Carter

Common Facts: Jessica and Carter are the clients. They are a professional couple; she is 35 and he is 40 years old. Carter is an environmental law attorney and Jessica has been the primary caregiver for their only son, Jake. Jessica has a degree as an architect and worked before their son was born, but did not work for the six years prior to the time of their separation. Jessica and Carter have been married for eight years. They have been separated for one year. Carter is living in their former marital home (in town) and Jessica is living in a condo that they own at the beach (their former second home). Jake is now six years old and in school part of the day, but has been with Jessica during every afternoon. The parties have been attempting to split Jake's time equally between them and so far this arrangement has been successful. The parties both desire to have joint custody of their son and to split visitation equally (50/50). Jessica is currently employed as a freelance draftsman and architect part time while Jake is in school; however she desires to go back to full-time work but has not been able to find a job that she likes and is worried about the quality and cost of Jake's after school child care. Furthermore, Jessica does not want to work as an architect, but would rather start up her own business or go back to school for retraining. She is also worried about being able to get a job and about what her earning capacity is. Carter is sure that she can get a job and earn at least half of what he earns as a young, junior partner in his law firm. Carter is very hardworking, conscientious, and career oriented, while Jessica appears more "laid-back." Carter is more conservative in his approach to life while Jessica's lifestyle is a bit more alternative. Their conflicts while married centered around money, different values, and Jessica's unemployment. Both, however, feel that the other is a good and devoted parent and they agree that the best interests of their child, Jake, are very important.

Carter makes $100,000 per year. Jessica has the ability, he feels, to make $60,000 per year but is currently earning $35,000 per year in her part time, free lance work. Jessica does not agree; she thinks she cannot make more than $35,000 per year and continue to care for Jake after school. The marital home where Carter lives is worth $200,000 and has a mortgage on it of $180,000. The condo where Jessica lives is worth $135,000 and has a mortgage on it of $120,000. Their cars are of approximately equal value and require equal car payments. Carter has a retirement account worth $100,000 ($60,000 after tax value). Carter currently carries all three of them on his health insurance. Carter has life insurance; Jessica does not. They have savings of $20,000 in a money market account held jointly.

Instructions for Carter only:

You want this divorce to do as little harm to your son, Jake, as possible. You are committed to maintaining a good relationship with Jessica and co-parenting Jake with her, in a 50/50, shared or joint custody arrangement. You want Jake to spend half his time with you and half his time with his mom, because you know how important mothers are to children, particularly sons. You are a devoted and involved parent, as much as you can be.

Also, your fear is that Jessica will threaten to ask for custody of Jake and you are afraid that if you are the noncustodial parent you will only see your son every Wednesday night and every other weekend, which is not enough visitation for you. You believe Jessica is a good parent but firmly believe that Jake needs both his parents equally in order to thrive. For now, you have worked out a visitation schedule that approximates a 50/50 split of time.

You are not willing to pay alimony. You do not want to pay child support because you are afraid that Jessica will fritter the money away, use it as an excuse not to work full-time, and not spend the money on Jake. You also feel that you have worked very hard to get where you are and do not want your assets depleted by this divorce or by Jessica.

You want to make sure that your assets are used for Jake's education and his future needs. You are disappointed and a bit angry with Jessica because you feel that she is lazy when it comes to working and you think she could be working harder (like you do) and making more money. However, you do realize that Jessica's taking over Jake's afterschool care is valuable both in terms of savings on child care expenses and emotionally, since you believe parental care is always better than babysitting care. However, you are also worried that Jessica and Jake are spending their afternoons watching insipid television shows.

You were not the one to move out. You don't really want the divorce but you are resigned that it is going to happen. You are aware that Jessica moved out in order to start dating other people. You are not dating. The marriage fell apart because you felt Jessica was being lazy and you began to fight about money and work. You buried yourself in your work and neglected the relationship and eventually she wanted to see someone else. You recognize this but are still (now) stuck in anger and bargaining at Jessica for being lazy ("if she hadn't been so lazy to begin with, we wouldn't have had these conflicts and we would still be together. This marriage would work if she would just….").

Remember that you are committed to the collaborative process and that you have made a commitment to resolve all the issues and points of disagreement in the collaborative model, without resort to a third-party decision maker.

Based on this bare bones information, feel free to embellish and make up any facts or emotions consistent with the character and the situation.

Instructions for Carter's attorneys only:

You have a few problems with this client's legal position. First, there is a traditional presumption that wives get primary residential custody of the children, particularly if they have been stay home, primary caregivers. In the state where this couple lives, there is no such thing as "joint or shared custody"; there is only primary residential custody and secondary custody. One party is going to have to have the label of primary custodial parent, which makes the other parent sound a bit subordinate. Neither of these spouses wants to be subordinate to the other in terms of their responsibility for, control over, or time with their son. Indeed, they truly want a joint, shared, 50/50 situation but the labels used by state family law are not conducive to this arrangement. You have to create some facsimile of this arrangement, using the existing law.

Further, the nonresidential parent usually owes child support to the primary residential or custodial parent, so whoever is nonresidential would (if you went to court) end up having to pay child support based on the statutory guidelines (there is a fixed amount calculable in the statute). The client needs to be prepared for this issue, also.

If Jessica fights for custody, there is a good chance she will win. If so, then Carter as the nonresidential parent faces the risk that his visitation with Jake could be as little as every Wednesday night and every other weekend, far less than the 50% he wants (unless Jessica agrees otherwise). And, he will owe child support to Jessica calculated under the statutory guidelines.

He may be at risk for paying alimony to her, however, although the short term of the marriage and her education level and her ability to work all militate against his liability for alimony. She still may ask for it or demand it and he needs to be prepared that in court, there could be a risk that he would pay at least some short term rehabilitative alimony.

Regarding the property settlement, the presumption here is that all their assets and debts are marital assets and debts and thus they will all be split 50/50. You have to figure out a way to do this that equalizes their relative positions.

Instructions for Jessica only:

You are the one who moved out. You love Carter but can't live with him anymore. He is no longer the free spirit he was when you met him and fell in love with him. Now all he seems to want to do is work and fight with you about you working and making money. He is holding you back, being a negative and destructive force in your life, and you have determined that you have to divorce him to keep your sanity. You are sad about the end of this marriage but rather philosophical about it. You are not angry or vindictive. You are resigned to the situation. You understand that people grow apart and their priorities change. You felt, however, very lonely and unappreciated in the marriage, you enjoy companionship, and so you eventually moved out in order to start dating. Carter is not dating.

You are a devoted and involved parent who is proud of the fact that you have been a stay home mom. You even formed a network of stay home moms in the area. Your plan was to move out, get a part time job, take care of Jake, and continue doing what you are doing. You think that it's crazy to put Jake in afterschool child care and you want to continue taking care of him while he is not in school. You want this divorce to do as little harm to your son, Jake, as possible. You are committed to maintaining a good relationship with Carter and co-parenting Jake with him, in a 50/50, shared or joint custody arrangement. You want Jake to spend half his time with you and half his time with Carter. You believe that no job is more important than your son and you plan to fit your work schedule around his school schedule. You are afraid that Carter will ask for custody of Jake and you are afraid that if you are the noncustodial parent you will only see your son every Wednesday night and every other weekend, which is not enough visitation for you. You believe Carter is a good parent but you can't imagine him becoming Jake's primary caregiver and displacing you, when you have been his primary caregiver for the first six years of his life. For now, you have worked out a visitation schedule that approximates a 50/50 split of time.

You also believe that you have worked hard as the primary caregiver for those six years and that you should be rewarded financially for fulfilling that role. Your position is that Carter is where he is today in his career because of your unfailing support and care. You would like to have some kind of permanent child support from Carter to help equalize your incomes, since you will be equal parents of Jake. You would like alimony as well, but aren't sure whether it's obtainable and are willing to forego it as long as you can cover your expenses. You are worried about not being able to make enough money in your part time job but you are not willing to work full-time. You have never been a high wage earner or enormously ambitious. You are more of a free spirit yourself.

Remember that you are committed to the collaborative process and that you have made a commitment to resolve all the issues and points of disagreement in the collaborative model, without resort to a third-party decision maker.

Based on this bare bones information, feel free to embellish and make up any facts or emotions consistent with the character and the situation.

Instructions for Jessica's attorneys only:

Jessica has a good chance of getting custody of Jake, if she wants it, because of the usual presumption that wives and primary caregivers get custody of children. Jessica may have a case for custody, some short term rehabilitative alimony, and certainly child support calculated under the statutory guidelines, since Carter makes so much more money than she does. However, her education level, her earning capacity, and the short term of the marriage all militate against her getting alimony. On the other hand, his earning capacity and her role as stay home mom work in favor of her getting alimony.

In the state where this couple lives, there is no such thing as "joint or shared custody"; there is only primary residential custody and secondary custody. One party is going to have to have the label of primary custodial parent, which makes the other parent sound a bit subordinate. Neither of these spouses wants to be subordinate to the other in terms of their responsibility for, control over, or time with their son. Indeed, they truly want a joint, shared, 50/50 situation but the labels used by the state's family law may not be conducive to this arrangement. You have to create some facsimile of this arrangement, using the existing law.

Further, the nonresidential parent usually owes child support to the primary residential or custodial parent, so whoever is nonresidential would (if you went to court) end up having to pay child support based on the statutory guidelines (there is a fixed amount calculable in the statute). Jessica needs to be prepared for this issue, also. She is definitely not going to want to pay Carter child support when he makes so much more money than she does. Probably, it would be best for her to be the primary residential/custodial parent and ask for child support from him.

Also, if she is the nonresidential parent, she faces the risk in court that her visitation with Jake could be as little as every Wednesday night and every other weekend, far less than the 50% she wants (unless Carter agrees otherwise). And, as the nonresidential parent, she will owe child support to Carter calculated under the statutory guidelines, unless he agrees otherwise. Basically, you have to be a bit creative in order to accomplish a joint custody arrangement that works for this couple, in this state.

Regarding the property settlement, the presumption here is that all their assets and debts are marital assets and debts and thus they will all be split 50/50. You have to figure out a way to do this that equalizes their relative positions.

Chapter 13

Vector 8 — Transformative Mediation

Description

Transformative mediation ("TM") is a form of mediation that emerged in the 1990s.[1] Its founder, law professor R. Baruch Bush, co-authored a book in 1994[2] with communications professor Joseph Folger, the second edition of which was published in 2005, introducing TM. In this book, Bush and Folger explain that transformative mediation differs substantially from traditional mediation (both the facilitative and evaluative forms) in both its goals and process.[3] Unlike traditional mediation, which focuses on dispute resolution, transformative mediation focuses less on the outcome of the mediation or the solution to which the parties agree, and more on how the process of mediation might change the individuals involved. Specifically, transformative mediation seeks to foster a sense of "empowerment" and the experience of "recognition" in each of the parties. TM views conflict as a destabilizing "crisis in human interaction"[4] rather than a violation of rights or conflict of individual interests. Its three-person mediations seek to restore balance between self and other, transform conflict into a positive, constructive process, and encourage parties to do two things: (1) regain their sense of strength and self-confidence (the "empowerment" shift); and (2) expand their responsiveness to each other (the "recognition" shift). By focusing on these goals, the parties are moved towards increased personal development, enhanced personal and interpersonal skills, and moral growth.[5]

Empowerment

Empowerment, as defined by Bush and Folger, means the parties grew in maturity by developing and owning their own solution. It does not refer to the experience of having a third party enforce one's rights; instead, it refers to an internal condition in which the person feels more capable of solving his or her problems.[6] A party is empowered when

---

1. This Chapter is adapted from the author's article, Susan Daicoff, *Law as a Healing Profession: The "Comprehensive Law Movement*," 6 Pepperdine Disp. Resol. J. 1 (2006).
2. Robert Baruch Bush & Joseph Folger, The Promise of Mediation: Responding to Conflict Through Empowerment and Recognition (1994) (now in its second edition, 2005) [hereinafter Bush & Folger, 1994].
3. *Id.* at 1–12, 82–101, and 261–271.
4. Robert A. Baruch Bush & Sally Ganong Pope, *Changing the Quality of Conflict Interaction: The Principles and Practice of Transformative Mediation*, 3 Pepp. Disp. Resol. L.J. 67, 72 (2002).
5. *Id.* at 82–83.
6. *Id.* at 89–94.

he or she is able to see more than a limited set of solutions to his or her problem and realizes that he or she has the capacity to freely choose between those options.

Recognition

Recognition, as defined by Bush and Folger, means that it resembles a feeling of empathy for another person, in which one person is able to "stand in the shoes" of the other
and see the matter from another's perspective.[7] It often results in feelings of compassion
for the other and in its finest form, culminates in forgiveness. Once a party can experience recognition, the next goal is for that party to communicate those insights or feelings
to the other party. This is called "giving recognition."[8] Bush and Folger explain that the
ability to see a matter from the other person's standpoint is a mark of personal growth,
just as rigid egocentrism is a measure of emotional immaturity.[9]

Moral Growth

Transformative mediation thus explicitly seeks to foster personal and moral growth in
the parties as its goal, rather than the resolution of the dispute, which is secondary in
importance to growth.[10] It does so by focusing on fostering empowerment and recognition in the parties.

Critiques and Challenges

Bush and Folger answer some common critiques of TM in their books, as follows. In
response to the charge that TM takes more time and costs more, and settlement rates are
lower, than traditional mediation, they state that there is no evidence that this is true.
They assert that TM settlements are of better quality, as traditional mediated settlements
may be illusory due to the potential for a forced, directed nature. They assert that there
is nothing lost by losing a settlement that would have required a directive approach to
get. This is consistent with other research showing that parties' compliance with orders
is higher when they are more involved in the decisionmaking process (e.g., there is greater
"buy-in"), see Chapter 8 on procedural justice, above. In response to the charge that TM
results in more unfair settlements because the mediator is not evaluating the fairness of
the outcome, they assert that TM is actually more likely to produce fairer outcomes. They
believe that directive, evaluative mediation is more likely to force a solution on a weaker
party, whereas in TM that weaker party would be empowered to reject the forced settlement and perhaps go to court instead.[11]

TM has been a bit controversial in its explicit goals and methods. It is part of the comprehensive law movement because it seeks to improve the relational, moral, and personal
functioning of the parties involved, in the resolution of legal disputes. It focuses explicitly on processes that can foster growth in the parties' ability to communicate, under-

---

7. *Id.*
8. *Id.* at 96.
9. *Id.* at 92.
10. *Id.* at 81–84, 87.
11. Bush & Folger, 1994, *supra* note 2.

stand each other, solve their own problems, resolve conflicts, and interact with other people.

Example

Bush and Folger use the example of the "Sensitive Bully" to illustrate TM, in their 1994 book.[12] In this case, Charles, an adult, is charged with assault and battery of an adolescent, Jerome. Jerome's father, Regis, an imposing, stern African-American man, who enters mediation visibly angry, accompanies Jerome to the mediation. Charles, in contrast, appears undefensive, quiet, and even cowed. Charles is contrite and ashamed of what he has done. However, Regis begins with a very aggressive and unforgiving attitude towards what Charles has done to his son.

The mediator asks Regis and Charles to take turns describing what happened. Charles is a young, slight, African American man who walks with a limp. Charles routinely cut through Jerome's neighborhood on his way from the bus stop to see his girlfriend, and Jerome and his friends routinely "razzed" Charles as he passed. The two had had verbal altercations before the incident. On this occasion, Jerome was with a group of his friends when the dispute arose. On this day, Jerome took it a bit far with his verbal insults and Charles physically assaulted Jerome. Charles finally snapped and retaliated, albeit inappropriately.

Through this mediation, Regis realizes that his son, Jerome, and his friends had been making fun of Charles' physical disability and that, finally, Charles couldn't take it anymore. Once Regis realizes this, something shifts. He scolds his son for making fun of Charles. He gives "recognition" by telling Charles he understands "how cruel kids can be." Charles explains that all he wants to do is see his girlfriend and he is happy to walk a different route through the neighborhood.

By subtly focusing on Charles' physical condition, the content of the verbal interactions between Charles and Jerome pre-assault, and how each party's comments in the mediation had affected the other, the mediator was able to elicit what TM calls "recognition," a sort of empathy or standing in the other's shoes, from both Charles and Regis. Each was able to appreciate the other's feelings and motivations. Then, by having the parties jointly develop the solution to the problem, the mediator facilitated what TM calls "empowerment." The parties worked together to develop a way that Charles can walk through Jerome's neighborhood without encountering Jerome and his friends. The mediator did not offer or impose a solution for the future, but encouraged the parties to work it out themselves.

Practice Information

There is a marked difference in the focus and input of the mediator, in TM. The TM mediator focuses on opportunities to ask questions and make comments that might result in an empowerment or recognition opportunity, rather than asking about positions,

---

12. *Id.* at 5–11.

needs, or goals, evaluating various options, or proposing possible solutions. Even compared to nondirective, facilitative mediation, the TM mediator's "moves" and contributions differ in their focus and goals.

The following summarizes various skills and processes used by a transformative mediator that may, in some cases, vary from those used by more traditional mediators:[13]

To Empower

- Do not redistribute power within the process in order to protect weaker parties.
- Practice empowerment with both parties regardless of power imbalances.
- Do not control or influence the mediation process to produce outcomes that redistribute resources or power outside the process from stronger to weaker parties.
- Do not function as an advocate, advisor, or counselor.
- Do not take sides, express judgments, or be directive.
- Encourage parties to make choices without leading them to a preferred direction.

To Enhance Recognition

- Do not worry about the parties' reconciliation or restoration of their relationship, or seek to have them fully accept each other.
- Ask questions that reveal how each party wants to be seen by the other.

Three Hallmarks of a TM Mediator

1. Microfocusing on Parties' Contributions

- Focus on the details of how the case unfolds.
- Scrutinize parties' individual statements, challenges, questions, and narratives for transformative opportunities.
- Look for points where choices arise that the parties can be empowered to make.
- Search for openings that afford parties the chance to acknowledge each other's perspectives.
- Identify "signpost events" that mark opportunities for empowerment and recognition.

2. Encouraging Parties' Deliberations and Choice Making

- Clarify parties' available choices at all key junctures.
- Encourage parties to reflect and deliberate with full awareness of their options, goals, and resources.
- Avoid shaping issues, proposals, or terms for settlement.
- Encourage parties to define problems and find solutions for themselves.
- Endorse and support the parties' own efforts to do so.

3. Encouraging Perspective Taking

- Explore each party's statements for openings that allow one party to consider the other's situation or self.

---

13. This Section is summarized by the author from Bush & Folger's two editions of THE PROMISE OF MEDIATION (1994 & 2005), *see* BUSH & FOLGER, 1994, *supra* note 2. It may not adequately or accurately reflect their vision of transformative mediation, thus, the reader is directed to their excellent books in any case in which the author's summary raises questions. This Section is designed simply to introduce TM, rather than provide an exhaustive training guide.

- Look for places within each party's statements that would allow each party to consider the other's point of view.

- Reinterpret, translate, and reframe parties' statements (not to shape issues or solutions) but to help make each party more intelligible to the other.

- Ask parties to consider the significance of such reformulations, pointing out opportunities for recognition without forcing them.

- Focus on and pull apart relational issues for recognition opportunities.

- Include in final settlement terms broader language, such as statements of misunderstandings that were removed or more positive views of the other party that were developed.

In The TM Process

Opening Statements

Emphasize that all decisionmaking power is left in the parties' hands. Note that the process offers a chance for people to achieve greater understanding of their own options and each other. Mention that if the parties agree to take steps to deal with their situation, those steps can be written into a final agreement. However, even if a specific solution to the problem cannot be found, other accomplishments of the session can also be written up. These might include: understandings reached, new information that was exchanged during the session, and descriptions in the parties' own words of new ways of communicating that were followed in the session (that might help in their interactions after this session).

Ground Rules

- Not interrupting: Part of our ground rules here today include not interrupting while the other party gives his or her account of what the dispute is about.

- Taking notes: If the listener disagrees with or objects to what is being said, you are asked to write down your concerns so that you do not forget them. You will have a chance to raise your points after the other party is finished speaking.

- Listening for news: In addition to simply listening while the other party gives their account, you are also asked to take notes of "news" you hear as they speak, meaning writing down points of information you did not know, things you did not realize about the other party that are now evident from hearing the other party's opening statement. (After each party finishes speaking, turn to the other and ask what he or she heard in the other party's statement.)

  NOTE: It may be necessary to allow each side to vent, speak openly, and register the depth of their feelings about the dispute, first, before getting into this active listening.

Q & A Time

- After both parties' opening statements, encourage them to ask questions that arise from their genuine curiosity as to the other party, past events, or future possibilities. Possible goals are to break down barriers stemming from misunderstandings, false assumptions, and stereotypical thinking. Even if this Q & A time goes poorly, the mere fact that the mediator has set aside time to do it sets up a procedural expectation that will reorient the parties towards more transformative processes.

- Identify a point in the process in which each party indicates what they think the other still does not understand about them (after opening statements and discussion). This fosters discussion about differences and misunderstandings, curiosity, and recognition.

Summaries and Restatements

- Offer summaries of parties' views and positions without reshaping them. *(We can learn to do this by listening to a party's statement, summarizing it, and receiving feedback from others as to our skewness or biases apparent in our summary. Then, we offer an alternative summary, consciously avoiding our biases this time.)*

- Translate one party's statement so the other is more likely to hear him or her accurately or consider him or her sympathetically.

- Reinterpret parties' actions or motives without trying to sell one interpretation or the other. *(We can learn to do this by role-playing segments of a session in which one party asserts a negative interpretation of the other party's behavior or past actions. Then, we brainstorm 4 or 5 other possible explanations for the behavior that are less negative. Then, we practice tentatively offering these alternative interpretations to the accusing party in ways that encourage him or her to become openminded or consider if he or she is making unnecessary assumptions. We phrase them provisionally.)*

Caucuses

Use caucuses in ways that help parties understand their own choices and consider the other's perspective. These are best used in TM when the parties are unclear about how they view the situation and what their options are, to enhance their sense of personal control. It helps parties clarify their positions and what they want. Caucuses also help the mediator learn what recognition each party wants from the other. Caucuses can be helpful early on, if the parties are unclear; they may be less helpful later on and are not useful if there is transformative momentum already going (e.g., where recognition is already being given and received).

Written Agreements

Write up agreements that reflect the transformative accomplishments of the session, even if agreement on resolving the conflict is not fully reached. Expand what can be included in the written agreements resulting from the session. This document can be a "memorandum of understanding" that provides a summary, even in each party's own words, of what occurred. It can include points of agreement and commitments the parties have made about what to do about the situation. It can also include a record of:

(a) new understandings each party has gained about his or her own choices and options;

(b) misunderstandings that were cleared up;

(c) summaries of new ways they found to communicate with each other;

(d) summaries of the points on which they could not agree ("clarity on impasse," which may facilitate ultimate settlement after the session in an ongoing stream of conflict interaction between the parties).

Key Points

- Moral Growth
- Empowerment
- Recognition

Resources

Robert A. Baruch Bush & Joseph P. Folger, The Promise of Mediation) (Jossey-Bass Publishers 1994) (2d ed. 2005) (This book is the primary resource for understanding transformative mediation, written for mediators. The editions are different; I recommend reading both.)

Susan L. Brooks & Robert G. Madden, Relationship-Centered Lawyering: Social Science Theory for Transforming Legal Practice (Carolina Academic Press, 2010) (Chapter 2, which includes *Clarifying The Theoretical Underpinnings of Mediation: Implications for Practice And Policy*, by Dorothy J. Della Noce, Robert A. Baruch Bush, & Joseph P. Folger).

Websites

Institute for the Study of Conflict Transformation (ISCT): www.transformativemediation.org (last visited July 11, 2010).

Mediate.com—Everything Mediation: www.mediate.com/transformative (last visited July 11, 2010).

http://grebel.uwaterloo.ca/certificate/courses/tm.shtml (last visited July 11, 2010).

Coordination: Also read Brooks & Madden (Chapter 2, p. 95–105), King (p. 105 in Chapter 7), and Wright (p. 55–57).

Chapter Assignments

Exercise 13-1—TM Discussion Questions

1. A party can be empowered in mediation as to (check all that apply):

   a. Options

   b. Skills

   c. Decisionmaking

   d. Legal rights

   e. Resources

   f. A more favorable settlement for her or him

2. Empowerment is independent of any particular outcome of the mediation; a fair or optimal outcome or settlement is not required in order for empowerment of a party to have occurred. A less-than-optimal settlement in the eyes of the mediator might occur, even when empowerment occurs.

   T / F

3. The mediator's job is to steer the party to a better or fairer outcome because that creates greater satisfaction, which is one of the goals of transformative mediation.

   T / F

4. Recognition is not just a party having the capacity to consider and acknowledge another's situation, it is also when a party wants to do so.

   T / F

5. Recognition can be given in (check all that apply):

    a. Thought

    b. Words

    c. Deed

    d. Actions

    e. Internal insight

    f. Monetary form

    g. Material reparations

6. One party making a concrete accommodation to the other party, in mediation, is a form of compromise or negotiation; however, it can also constitute the giving of recognition, in TM.

    T / F

7. Transformative mediation can have positive effects in the parties' lives, in the future, once mediation has concluded.

    T / F

8. Empowerment includes advising, advocating for, and counseling a party to add to their strength.

    T / F

9. Recognition can include when a party realizes that he or she can get more of what he or she needs or wants by giving the other party some of what he or she needs or wants.

    T / F

10. The mediator's job in TM is to (check all that apply):

    a. microfocus on the parties' interactions

    b. ask each party to listen for news in what the other party is saying

    c. use caucuses when the emotions run high, in the mediation, and conflict appears imminent

    d. reinterpret actions and motives of each party, to the other

    e. offer alternative explanations of one party's behavior to the other party, tentatively

    f. persuade and pressure a party to change their views on why the other party behaves as they do

    g. break into caucus immediately following the opening statement in cases such as the Sensitive Bully

11. Describe why disputing parties might want mediators to take a transformative mediation approach, instead of a strong hand to guide them out of their conflicts:

12. Describe, in a few words, situations or cases in which transformative mediation might not be appropriate:

13. Transformative mediation's most important explicit goals are (check all that apply):

   Benefits to both parties

   Consensual agreements

   Efficiency

   Empowerment

   Moral growth

   Recognition

   Satisfactory resolutions of disputes

14. To achieve these goals, transformative mediation explicitly focuses on: (check all that apply)

   Engendering the parties' moral growth

   Improving the parties' interaction

   Improving the parties' mental health
   Improving the parties' situation

   Increasing the parties' capacity to relate to others

   Increasing the parties' strength of self

   Problem solving

   Reconciling the parties

   The settlement or outcome

15. TM is a   2   3   4   5   -party process (circle one). The participants are (list):

16. Name and define (in two sentences or so, each) the main goals of TM:

17. True (T) or False (F) or Unclear (U) (according to the Chapter):

   _____ (a) TM costs more and takes more time than traditional mediation.

   _____ (b) TM's solutions can be fairer for the weaker party.

   _____ (c) In TM, the weaker party might well reject a directed settlement and go to court instead.

   _____ (d) TM is not appropriate for civil cases.

   _____ (e) Like collaborative law, TM aims to ensure that the parties do not litigate in court.

Exercise 13-2 — TM "Fish-Bowl" Practice

Simulate portions of a modified transformative mediation process with six people: two parties, two attorneys, and two mediators in a "fish-bowl" format, meaning the six players are in the center of the room with the rest observing from a circle around them. Role-play a few segments of one or more of the practice hypotheticals in Exercise 13-3 as follows:

First, have the mediators practice opening statements and ground rules based on the material in this Chapter. Second, have the parties or attorneys give their opening statements. If the parties are unclear or vague about their positions, then caucus with each party to clarify his or her position and issues, always keeping in mind not to lead or direct the party. (Here we focus on <u>empowerment</u> of the parties.) After opening statements, go around the room and allow the observers to practice restating what they heard. Have others provide feedback as to biases heard, things emphasized and things ignored, and work on creating as neutral a restatement of the parties' opening statements as possible. (Here we work on not being directive, biased, or taking sides. This helps our mediators begin to help the parties focus on <u>recognition</u>.) Then, resume the mediation with the six players.

Have the parties flare up and accuse each other of bad past behavior. Then, have the observers work on brainstorming several possible alternative explanations for the person's behavior and then practice offering this explanation to the accusing party in a provisional, tentative fashion.

Here is a summary of TM skills and processes, to use in Exercises 13-2 and 13-3:

TM Mediator Skills

1. "Microfocus," meaning look for opportunities for empowerment and recognition at all times; microfocus on the parties' interaction.

2. Focus on choices and options.

3. Focus on relational issues; be more focused on the past than problemsolving approaches are (which are often future-oriented).

4. Summarize/restate parties' views and positions without reframing or casting them.

5. Restate one party's statements so the other can "hear" them better.

6. Offer possible reinterpretations or restatements of parties' actions or motives that are objective/ambiguous.

7. Use caucuses with parties to increase options, choices, and thus empower (but don't lead).

TM Processes

1. Opening statement should emphasize that all decisionmaking power is in the parties' hands.

2. Ask parties not only not to interrupt each other, but to take notes of "news" they hear in the other's narrative (this is like active listening, which promotes empathy).

3. Give parties a time to ask questions out of curiosity, to learn more about the other—this sets up an expectation that recognition is important in the process (even if unsuccessful).

4. Set aside a time when each says what the other still does not understand about them (to encourage recognition).

5. A written settlement agreement might include a description in parties' words of what occurred, memorialize points of agreement as well as points of new clarity about their options or choices, list misunderstandings that were cleared up, state new ways they found to communicate, and describe issues they reached impasse on (acknowledging that mediation is only part of an ongoing stream of conflict interaction).

Exercise 13-3—TM Mediation

Then, split up into groups of six to actually try out some TM mediations. Decide which of the following scenarios (below) you would like to simulate as a modified transformative mediation process. Assign roles within your group to the relevant players in the process—two mediators, two parties, and two attorneys. Run your simulation and debrief afterwards with all players.

Practice Hypotheticals for TM Mediation Exercises

1. Band Practice

Donald Dalton is the sole owner of a magazine publishing company specializing in current legal-trend works. His neighbor, William Westoni, owns a graphics company that is world renowned for its legal artwork. William is also a talented jazz musician who performs in a local band. Donald and William have known each other ever since they met at the president's inaugural ball and have remained best friends ever since. Donald has used William's graphics continuously for about 10 years and has a contract to exclusively use William's services. Recently, William became upset when Donald called to complain about William's late-night jazz sessions. William tried to explain that he had to practice for an upcoming gig but Donald was not sympathetic. Donald explained that he was lacking the sleep required to publish his magazine and his work was suffering as a result. William refused to stop playing, saying that the time of day of his band practice was reasonable, so Donald called the police who fined William for noise-ordinance violations. The publication is set to go out in four days and William now refuses to provide any illustrations to Donald. Donald knows the magazine is nothing without the pictures and thus demands that William conform to his contractual agreement. William refuses and says he won't comply unless Donald agrees to pay the $900 noise ordinance fine. Donald says he will not pay the fine.

2. Locals

Bob Hatfield was driving his '95 Ford pick-up truck along the outskirts of the small town of Rosford, when he was negligently hit by a tractor owned by Bufford "Cooter" McCoy. Bob's truck was totaled and his leg was severely injured, resulting in a permanent limp. Cooter's insurance company is willing to settle out of court for a sizable amount of money, but Bob wants his day in court. During the accident, Bob's favorite hunting dog, Reckless, was thrown from the bed of the truck and fatally wounded. Bob demanded an apology from Cooter as well as the civil litigation monetary settlement. Cooter did say he was sorry for the loss of the animal, but Bob did not believe that Cooter was sincere and refused the apology and the settlement offer.

3. Home Improvement

Arch Archway is a home owner that purchased hardwood flooring for the downstairs of his home. Natural Nails is a privately owned and operated construction company dealing with home improvements. Arch and Nathan, the owner of Natural Nails, entered into a Home Improvement Contract for the amount of $20,000. The Home Improvement Contract stated that defendant is properly licensed, would install the flooring, and would do the work within one month in a workman-like manner. Nathan, d/b/a Natural Nails, did not have a proper construction license and drilled holes in the frame of the house to install the flooring. The drilling of the frame caused massive structural damage to the house and created an uneven floor. Arch has brought suit against Nathan and Natural Nails for fraud in the inducement, breach of contract, and breach of warranty. The case has been mediated twice, both times ending when Nathan became verbally insulting to Arch.

4. Lemon Car

Mr. and Mrs. Genovia bought a car from ABC Car Sales on February 1. The car was bought from salesman Ralph Tucker. The car was bought with a check at 5:30 p.m. for the amount of $5,500. Prior to giving Mr. Tucker the check, a number of documents were signed by Mr. Genovia, with Mrs. Genovia witnessing his signature. One of these documents contained an "as is" clause which stated that the car would not be repaired or returned for any reason unless there was a warranty between the parties. The wording of the clause was in the same color, font, and size as wording in other documents such as the bill of sale. At no time did Mr. Tucker explain the clause. The car bought was a five-year-old Lexus. Prior to the sale, Mr. Tucker told Mr. Genovia that the car had not been wrecked and needed no repairs. Mr. Genovia looked under the hood and noticed a significant amount of oil. Genovia questioned the presence of the oil and Tucker stated that it was due to a recently installed air compressor on the car. Other than that, the car appeared fine and ran well. On the night of the sale, Mrs. Genovia drove the car to the local market. Upon returning home, the engine started smoking and making loud noises and then came to a sudden stop just as Mrs. Genovia was entering the parking lot. It would make no attempt to start after this. Mr. Genovia called Tucker the next morning (February 2) and stated that he wanted his money back. Tucker explained that the only way this could happen was if the car was returned to him just as it was sold (i.e., in running condition). Genovia stated that was impossible since the engine was now blown. Genovia placed a stop payment order with his bank on his check immediately following his conversation with Tucker. After Tucker heard of this, he called Genovia and threatened to prosecute him for writing a worthless check. Genovia wants his money back and nothing to do with the car. Tucker wants Genovia's money and nothing else to do with him. As of now, the car sits in Genovia's parking area in its current state of disrepair.

5. Caveat Employee

Nancy Beanhouse responded to an employment advertisement for a sales position. The terms of employment were a base salary of $26,000 annually plus a 5% commission on all sales. The employee was also obligated to document all potential customers that she had contact with, regarding sales. There was a mandatory requirement that the employee solicit business from 100 individual businesses and 500 residential customers on a weekly basis. The employee did her best at sales and documented all customer contacts as requested; however, her sales figures were not satisfactory to the management of the company. The general manager of the company, Graciela Green, then approached Nancy about switching from a base salary plus commission compensation structure to a straight commission (at 20%) on all sales. The employee, as a single mother of two who had a family to support, was unwilling to change to a straight commission structure. She needed to have a definite dollar amount of salary so that she might be able to budget her expenditures accordingly. The general manager then brought the employee into her office and explained to the employee that she was being placed on a two-week probationary period where she would be compensated at the salary plus commission (5%) structure during the probationary period. The employee closed three deals during the probationary period, for a total of $10,000 in revenues. Green called Beanhouse into her office at the end of the probationary period and informed the employee that she would not be receiving any compensation whatsoever (neither base salary nor straight commission). Although this seemed unfair, when the employee complained and stated that the only way she could receive any justice was to litigate the matter, Green responded that the company would just countersue for an amount greater than $15,000, thus kicking the claim out of small claims court. Because the employee has limited financial resources that have to be directed towards living expenses, she is reluctant to pay for a trial. Nancy is full of questions: What can the employee do to recover the monies that are rightfully due her? What can the employee do to prevent other employees from being victimized in this way? How can the employee shake a feeling of being victimized merely because someone else has the financial resources to keep them oppressed?

Exercise 13-4—Drafting the TM Mediation Settlement Agreement

Now, revise and complete the following sample mediation agreement form to reflect a comprehensive law/TM approach with respect to the simulated dispute you negotiated.

MEDIATION SETTLEMENT AGREEMENT

This Settlement Agreement and Mutual Release (this "Agreement") is entered into this _____ day of _____, 20____ by and between _____ and _____ (hereinafter individually and collectively referred to as "Plaintiff") and ____ and ____ (hereinafter individually and collectively referred to as "Defendant").

RECITALS

WHEREAS, Plaintiff and Defendant are parties to the above styled litigation ("Dispute"); and

WHEREAS, the Plaintiff and Defendant have resolved the Dispute with each other and execute this Agreement to fully and finally resolve all issues with respect to the Dispute and any and all claims that have been raised or could have been raised in connection with the Dispute.

NOW, THEREFORE, in consideration of the undertakings, promises and conditions contained in this Agreement, and other valuable consideration, the receipt and sufficiency of which are hereby acknowledged and warranted, Plaintiff and Defendant agree as follows:

AGREEMENT

1. Recitals. The above referenced Recitals are true and correct and incorporated herein by reference into this Agreement.

2. Plaintiff's Settlement Obligations: _____

3. Defendant's Settlement Obligations: _____

4. Release By Plaintiff. Upon completing the obligations set forth in paragraphs 2 and 3 above, Plaintiff, for themselves, their heirs, affiliates, attorneys, agents, successors and assigns, hereby fully releases and discharges Defendant and their heirs, affiliates, attorneys, agents, successors and assigns, from any and all claims, known and unknown, which Plaintiff has or may have, in any way directly or indirectly arising out of the Dispute between Plaintiff and Defendant.

5. Release by Defendant. Upon completing the obligations set forth in paragraphs 2 and 3 above, Defendant, for themselves, their heirs, affiliates, attorneys, agents, successors

and assigns, hereby fully releases and discharges Plaintiff and their heirs, affiliates, attorneys, agents, successors and assigns, from any and all claims, known and unknown, which Defendant has or may have, in any way directly or indirectly arising out of the Dispute between Plaintiff and Defendant.

6. <u>Dismissal of Dispute.</u> Within ten (10) days of completing the obligations set forth in paragraphs 2 and 3 above, Plaintiff and Defendant shall dismiss with prejudice all claim(s) and counterclaim(s) filed in the Dispute.

7. <u>Non-Waiver.</u> No delay or failure by any Party to exercise any right under this Agreement, and no partial or single exercise of that right, shall constitute a waiver of that or any right, unless otherwise expressly provided herein.

8. <u>Attorney Fees and Costs.</u> Each party is responsible for its own attorney's fees and costs with respect to the negotiation, settlement, execution of this Agreement, and Dispute referenced herein. In the event any legal proceeding is brought to enforce, interpret or contest this Agreement, in whole or in part, the prevailing party in such action shall be entitled to costs, expenses and reasonable attorney's fees from the non-prevailing party.

9. <u>Laws and Venue.</u> This Agreement shall be governed by and interpreted in accordance with the laws of the State of _____ and venue for any action shall exclusively be in the County of _____, State of _____.

10. <u>Survival.</u> Any and all warranties, provisions, rights and obligations of the parties herein described and agreed to be performed subsequent to the termination of this Agreement shall survive the termination of this Agreement.

11. <u>Whole Agreement.</u> This Agreement contains the entire understanding of the parties, and there are no contemporaneous or prior oral or written agreements between the parties which would supplement, add to or modify this Agreement in any way.

12. <u>Confidentiality.</u> The parties agree to keep this Agreement and all facts and the situation from which any and all claims arose or may have arisen, confidential, except to the extent necessary for disclosure for accounting purposes or pursuant to any legal process.

13. <u>Enforceability.</u> The parties reserve the right to enforce this Agreement.

Dated:_____

Plaintiff:

_____

_____

Plaintiff's Attorney

Defendant:

_____

_____

Defendant's Attorney

Mediator:

_____

Exercise 13-5—Integrative Cases

These cases, below, ask you to consider how to integrate and use the vectors of the comprehensive law movement (particularly CL and TM), in various situations:

Case 13-A

Your client is a 32-year-old white male who was, until two weeks ago, employed as a salesperson for a large company. He was employed on the understanding that he would be paid a base salary and would also receive commissions on each of his sales on a quarterly basis. He worked for the company for just under 12 months before his employment with the company was terminated by the company. He tells you that he is owed about $50,000 in commissions by the company, for the last quarter's sales. The company has refused to pay him these commissions, saying that he was a probationary employee only, he was on probation, he had no guarantee of a permanent job, and as a probationary employee he was not entitled to receive any commissions. The fact that he had received commissions for the previous three quarters was, according to the company, simply optional or voluntary by the company. Further, the company says that his performance on the job during the last quarter was unacceptable and substandard and this entitles them to decide not to pay him any commissions on the final quarter's sales. Your client is completely frustrated and feels helpless. He believes he has a good case against the company for his $50,000 in commissions due him, but he has nothing in writing about his compensation scheme and no witnesses or other corroborating evidence. No other employees of the company are compensated in the same fashion as he was, with the same "deal." The company has no written policies about compensation, probationary employees, or permanent employee status. You estimate that it will cost your client approximately $15,000 to $20,000 to have you litigate this case for him. How do you propose to handle this case?

Case 13-B

Your client is a 26-year-old woman who was hired by a truck driving company to drive trucks cross-country. She has the appropriate professional licenses and is duly qualified to drive the trucks. She tells you that she was fired by the company because she is a "woman in a man's job" and she wants to sue the company for sex discrimination. When she initially comes to see you, she is belligerent, angry, and hostile towards the company. She insists that she was a model employee and that the company's behavior towards her was unfair and oppressive at all times. You file a lawsuit on her behalf against the company for sex discrimination. In the course of discovery, the company's attorneys depose your client. In this deposition, with you present, the company's attorneys confront your client with internal, company personnel memoranda indicating that your client had been caught drunk on the job twice, had been confronted, and had agreed to submit to whatever measures the company required of her in order to ensure that it didn't happen again. Your client had not told you of these two incidents and had, up til now, told you continually that her behavior on the job was exemplary, perfect. After the deposition is over, you talk with your client and she continues to admit that she did drink on the job and that she was still struggling with this problem. Her attitude is less belligerent, less accusatory, and less blaming than it was when you first met her. She also tells you, after the deposition, that last week she had a run-in with the local police. She got into a fight in a local bar and hit another patron. The police were called, they arrived, but did not charge your client with anything. Assume you clearly have the right to withdraw from representing her, because she has lied to you and misrepresented facts. How do you propose to handle her case against the company?

Case 13-C

Your client is a 33-year-old lesbian woman whose long-term relationship with her partner is breaking up. They have been in a committed relationship for seven years and her partner has an eight-year-old son that they have both been raising for the last seven years. Your client wants help in splitting up their shared assets (a home, savings accounts, checking accounts, retirement accounts, two cars, a small collection of original paintings, and three dogs) and in drafting a dissolution-type agreement. Your client wants some rights to visitation of her partner's son, since she has been involved in his life since he was a year old and feels very close to him, yet she realizes that she has no legal rights to visit him since she is unrelated to him. His father does not exercise his visitation rights nor does he fulfill his obligations to pay child support to his mother. There is no written agreement between the two women. All of their assets are jointly titled and jointly owned, except the cars which are both in your client's name. The break-up is your client's idea; her partner does not want the relationship to end. How do you propose to handle this case?

The following are initial analyses of these cases; see if you can expand upon and refine these analyses and plans.

Case 13-A Analysis

TM would be used because this is a civil contracts dispute, so only the civil law vectors are appropriate. Because the parties have had a relationship in the past, TM might be helpful to foster some mutual understanding of each other's position (recognition). Also, the employee feels powerless, so TM empowerment might be important.

(a) Legal issues:	(b) Psycholegal issues:	(c) Intersections:
Contracts case in context of employment.	He feels frustrated, powerless, and dominated by the company.	Litigation will be costly and possibly fail, for the employee.
Contract is not in writing; plaintiff is going to have a hard time proving that his understanding was the contract of employment and thus getting his commissions.	He had no notice that his performance was unacceptable, so this decision feels arbitrary and capricious and thus he feels wronged.	Other, nonlitigative dispute resolution processes may afford him a voice and participation and equalize the power between him and the company.
Litigation will be costly and uncertain of outcome.	The company may have some good reasons for letting him go but they did not give him a chance to amend his performance before firing him, which creates tension, friction, and resentment among ex-employees.	Threat of litigation might be required to motivate company to participate in process.
Most employment is at will anyway, so he can be fired by the company for no reason at all, so he is unlikely to be able to claim he was wrongfully terminated by the company (unless it is a case of reverse discrimination, and the facts do not support this).	He will want a good reference from Company in the future, for other jobs. Needs to repair relationship as much as possible.	Any process used must give employee a chance to speak.

Skills include: the ability to conduct a mediation between the employee and the company. You may need to bring a lawsuit first to create motivation for the mediative process. Use the TM mediator skills listed in the Chapter.

Processes: The parties have a contractual misunderstanding, so that some form of mediation where each can hear the other's understanding of their contract of employment might have a healing effect and allow the employee to feel closure and emotional resolution of this event. It may also lead to a mutual compromise on the unpaid commissions, if each can understand the other's viewpoint. It appears as if there has been a communications breakdown between employer and employee over the course of the year. Utilize opportunities for empowerment and recognition in the facts as there has been a misunderstanding.

Case 13-B Analysis

This case may or may not be appropriate for TM.

(a) Legal issues:	(b) Psycholegal issues:	(c) Intersections:
Employment law Wrongful discharge At will employment means employer can fire employee for any reason or no reason at any time.	Gender issues, gender discrimination	Current lawsuit may be an indication of a life long pattern of employment, anger, honesty, and alcohol problems in this person's life.
Gender based discrimination lawsuit	Client is belligerent, angry, in anger phase of loss process over loss of job, or in denial about her alcohol problems. Client is less belligerent once faced with her dishonesty.	Current lawsuit is an opportunity for her to have a wake-up call and perhaps turn life around and resolve these issues, now.
The lawsuit has already been filed and now is in the discovery process.	Client needs a new job.	
Ethics: you have the right to withdraw from representation because she lied to you and misrepresented facts.	Possible alcohol abuse problem; client needs rehab/treatment. Client was dishonest with you about being a model employee.	Pursuing her lawsuit against the company and her ADA claim to the hilt without questioning her further, may add to her denial and avoidance of resolving her problems.
Possible future criminal problems from drinking and fighting	Client deals with problems by denial, belligerence, fighting, alcohol abuse, and anger. Anger management?	
She has substantially weakened her legal case and could easily lose the employment law case; however, she may be able to argue that they fired her in a discriminatory fashion even though she had had behavior problems on the job (for example, if they had allowed male employees with similar behavior problems more leeway before firing them.)	Maybe the company's story is accurate and your client is lying? Your client appears to have a problem with honesty, a potential alcohol abuse or dependency problem, and a problem with anger and with authority figures. All of these problems are likely to continue to cause her problems in the future with law enforcement	
You may identify that she may have a claim under the Americans with Disabilities Act if she is an alcohol abuser and identify that more legal research is necessary to determine if she can add this claim to her suit.	and with her employability, if not with her social and familial life as well. May have a problem with employment.	

(Skills and Processes omitted. Discuss.)

Case 13-C Analysis

This would require a CL hybrid, as it is a divorce case without a legal marriage. TM might be a useful secondary process or lens if CL does not work well.

(a) Legal issues:	(b) Psycholegal issues:	(c) Intersections:
No legal marriage, this is a divorce-type case without any of the legal rights or laws incident to divorce.	Resistance: Your client wants to initiate the break-up; her partner does not, so her partner may resist any attempts to reach a mutually agreed-upon resolution. The partner may even refuse to allow visitation as a threat to attempt to coerce your client to stay in the relationship.	Resistance: Unless the partner agrees to redeed the house and retitle the assets, your client will have to seek legal action to force a division of the assets (which may or may not work, re: the home)—another psycholegal soft spot.
Biological mother has full rights to the child and the nonbiological parent has no legal rights at all to visitation or custody.		
Nonbiological parent has no legal liability for child support, either.	The child is attached to your client and the child and your client both will have a psychological need to continue that relationship, but it will complicate the child's life in the future.	Also, the child is likely attached to your client and so even though she has no legal rights to continue a relationship with him, there is a psychological need perhaps to do so (and yet to do so will further complicate his life in the future, as he may end up with multiple stepparents). No legal process to award visitation to nonbiol. parent. Will be totally voluntary or contractual. Depends on good faith of mother.
There is no law relating to the division of their assets other than law relating to joint property ownership. Any agreement they reach regarding custody and visitation may not be enforceable in court, since a court will elevate the child's best interests above the duties imposed by private contract (but that isn't likely to be a problem, since your client doesn't want custody, just visitation).	Child's interests and mother's and partner's interests may diverge.	
	All the usual problems in divorce based on the grief process: denial, anger, bargaining, depression, acceptance.	
Future modifications of their proposed contract will be a problem, potentially. (Oral? In writing? Supported by new consideration? Or unenforceable?)	Social issues relating to public awareness of partners' domestic status.	
Finally, how will this proposed contract be enforced; in other words, what are the consequences of breach? (Use a liquidated damages clause?)	Social issues relating to child's social environment's awareness of child's domestic situation (stigma?).	
To divide the assets, you will need to retitle or redeed the home and other assets, which can cost money and trigger sales tax or transfer taxes.		

Skills to be used include lots of skillful questioning and empathy. The partner needs independent counsel and the child should have a guardian ad litem or other representative. Ability to refer family to the right counselor or mental health therapist to assess best course of action for child and family. Ability to assess your own ability to handle this case without overinvolvement or underinvolvement. Ability to know when to refer to another professional. Ability to draft a contract summarizing their terms.

Processes: I would likely choose some dispute resolution process that resembled CL, but without the legal force of a dissolution proceeding as the motivation for settling. TM might be a better choice. In either, you would depend on the good faith of the parties to negotiate and settle and then to abide by the terms of their settlement, and to collaborate to divide the assets in a way that minimizes financial and tax consequences. If the usual CL process would be used, one of the "hot button" issues might be visitation. Collaborative divorce might be appropriate as you may need neutral and/or partisan experts on child's issues.

Chapter 14

Vector 9 — Restorative Justice

Description

Restorative justice ("RJ") is a widespread movement in the criminal justice area that has been steadily growing since the mid-1980s.[1] RJ views crime as a "violation of people and of interpersonal relationships";[2] it is a tear in the fabric of society rather than an offense against the state. It puts the focus on the victim, wrongdoer, and society as the three main stakeholders in crime. It focuses on the harm done by crime to the victims and to the community, positing that criminal "violations create obligations" which must be put right.[3] It seeks to restore the victims, the relationship between the criminal offender and his or her community, and overall harmony. It does this not through traditional criminal adjudication and sentencing but through dialogue, negotiation, problem solving for the future, and an emphasis on the offender's acceptance of accountability to his or her victims and to the community.

The website for The Center for Restorative Justice & Peacemaking at the University of Minnesota School of Social Work explains that:

> [t]hrough restorative justice, victims, communities, and offenders are placed in active roles to work together to … Empower victims in their search of closure; Impress upon offenders the real human impact of their behavior; Promote restitution to victims and communities. Dialogue and negotiation are central to restorative justice, and problem solving for the future is seen as more important than simply establishing blame for past behavior. Balance is sought between the legitimate needs of the victim, the community, and the offender that enhances community protection, competency development in the offender, and direct accountability of the offender to the victim and victimized community.[4]

RJ emphasizes restitution and relationships between the offender, victim, and community instead of a top-down, hierarchical system focused on imposing punishment. In traditional retributive criminal justice, the goals are to punish, deter, incapacitate, rehabilitate, and obtain revenge. Sanctions focus on these goals and are imposed by a judge on the offender. Outcomes are supervised by the penal or probationary system. Victims have little or no rights. The resolution process involves an adversarial trial with full pro-

---

1. This Chapter has been adapted from Susan Daicoff, *Law as a Healing Profession: The "Comprehensive Law Movement,"* 6 Pepperdine Disp. Resol. J. 1 (2006). It also summarizes material in Howard Zehr, The Little Book of Restorative Justice (2002) [hereinafter "Zehr/Little Book"] and an excellent article by Gordon Bazemore and Curt Taylor Griffiths, describing in detail the various forms of RJ, *Conferences, Circles, Boards, & Mediations: Scouting the "New Wave" of Community Justice Decisionmaking Approaches,* 61:2 Federal Probation 25 (1997).

2. Zehr/Little Book, *supra* note 1, at 19.

3. *Id.* at 19.

4. The website is http://www.cehd.umn.edu/ssw/rjp (last visited July 11, 2010).

cedural safeguards such as due process, constitutional rights, and evidentiary rules. Statements made are limited to what is admissible and relevant. In restorative justice, the goals are to restore harmony to the community and inner harmony to the victims and offenders. Sanctions focus on reparations to the victims and community and treatment of offenders and are developed in multi-party processes, and are imposed by consensus on the offenders. Outcomes are supervised by the community or a judge. Victims have full right to participate and have a voice in the process, thus they are empowered, in this system. Statements are not limited. The process is a community-based, collaborative, non-adversarial conference with few procedural rules other than not interrupting, respect, and who speaks first.

The following table, by Howard Zehr,[5] compares RJ to traditional criminal justice, which is generally retributive in nature:

Retributive Justice	Restorative Justice
Crime is a violation of the law & state	Crime is a violation of people & of relationships
Violations create guilt	Violations create obligations
Justice requires state to determine blame and impose punishment	Justice involves victims, offenders, & community in effort to put things right
Central focus: offenders getting what they deserve	Central focus: victim's needs & offender's responsibility for repairing harm
Questions asked: a. What laws have been broken? b. Who did it? c. What do they deserve?	*Questions asked:* a. Who has been hurt? b. What are their needs? c. Whose obligations are these?

Debunking some myths perhaps, Zehr explains that RJ is not primarily focused on forgiveness or reconciliation, is not mediation, is not primarily designed to reduce recidivism (although it may have this effect), does not refer to a particular program as it has a number of forms, is appropriate for more than just minor offenses and first-time offenders, and is not new, as it is based on systems of criminal justice used by native and aboriginal people.[6] It is not necessarily the opposite of retribution, despite the simplistic comparative table, above, nor is it a replacement for the current system or for incarceration.[7]

Basic Process of RJ

In RJ, the community, victim, and offender, in a collaborative process, participate in some form of conferencing usually designed to substitute for criminal sentencing. It may be as simple as post-sentencing victim-offender mediation or as complicated as sentencing that is done in a community, "circle" conference with all parties present. Typically, the offender must either plead guilty or, at least, not dispute the fact of culpability for the crime. RJ usually relies on some sort of conference, which can be as small as a three-person mediation between the victim and the offender, a multi-person conference involving victims, victim supporters, offenders, offender supporters, legal personnel, mediators, and other family members, or as large as a community-wide circle sentenc-

---

5. Zehr/Little Book, *supra* note 1, at 21.
6. *Id.* at 8–12.
7. *Id.* at 13–14.

ing process that utilizes community or peer pressure brought to bear on the offender. The interpersonal or public pressure on the offender produced by these processes is designed to produce "therapeutic shame," which facilitates responsibility-taking, accountability, personal growth, and development in the offender designed to prevent reoffending. Extensive pre-mediation preparation of the victim and offender separately with one or more mediators is usually recommended, to ensure readiness to participate fully and appropriately in the process.

Core Sequence

In RJ, there is an exchange of feelings and the development, by consensus, of a reparations plan. Sociology professor Thomas Scheff explains that there is a "core sequence" hoped for, in RJ processes, that creates a healing cycle, as follows: (1) the victim expresses the impact of the offense upon the victim and his or her life; (2) the offender acknowledges this impact and experiences "reintegrative shame"; (3) the offender apologizes (making "symbolic reparations" to the victim); (4) the victim forgives the offender (this is not required, but when it happens, it can be healing); (5) the offender makes "material reparations" (restitution) to the victim; and, ultimately, (6) the offender is reintegrated into society.[8] Scheff explains that this reintegrative shame is a positive, healing force for the offender that allows him or her to take accountability for his or her actions and develop impetus not to reoffend.[9] In RJ, all shame connected with the crime is removed from the victim and accepted by the offender. Without the core sequence, the conference may not decrease the tension between the participants. It may leave them with a sense of arbitrariness and dissatisfaction.

Reparations can take two forms: material and symbolic. Material reparations, which can consist of monetary awards, restitution, and community service, may not differ greatly from traditional criminal court. Symbolic reparations, however, are not present in traditional justice. They can include negotiation, understanding, confession, reconciliation, and forgiveness. This requires genuine remorse and shame by the offender and forgiveness by the victim, which can lead to the reacceptance of the offender by the community.

Zehr explains the needs of the three stakeholders as follows: Victims need four things: information, truth-telling, empowerment, and restitution or vindication.[10] Offenders need accountability, encouragement for personal transformation and integration into society, and (in some cases) temporary restraint.[11] The community needs attention to its concerns as victims, the chance "to build a sense of community and mutual accountability," and encouragement to care for the welfare of their members, including victims and offenders, and promote healthy communities.[12]

Victims

In many RJ processes, the victims speak first. They are given the opportunity to express the full impact the crime has had upon their lives. They are allowed to ask questions of

---

8. Thomas J. Scheff, *Community Conferences: Shame and Anger in Therapeutic Jurisprudence,* 67 REV. JUR. U.P.R. 97, 97 (1998).

9. Scheff, *supra* note 8.

10. Zehr/Little Book, *supra* note 1, at 14–15.

11. *Id.* at 8–12.

12. *Id.* at 14–18.

the offender about the incident (Why me? Why did you do it?) and about the offender's remorse and rehabilitation (What are your plans for changing?). The victims also are given a chance to participate in holding the offender accountable for his or her actions, unlike traditional retributive justice. These features can be very satisfying for victims, give them a sense of justice, and promote their healing and closure from the incident. If the offender sincerely apologizes, the victims also receive this as symbolic reparation in addition to any material reparation the offenders make. If the victims choose, they can offer forgiveness to the offenders, which may lead to reconciliation, but forgiveness and reconciliation are not required for a successful RJ process.

Offenders

In RJ, offenders usually listen to the experiences of other parties (first, the victims; then maybe other affected persons) first, so they are able to reflect on them and understand what those experiences were like for the other parties involved. Then, they are permitted to describe their experience and tell the story of why the crime occurred and how it has affected their lives. They are permitted to disclose their post-offense rehabilitation efforts, express remorse, take responsibility for what they did, and apologize. They are also given the opportunity to make things right with the victim—to the degree possible—through some form of compensation (material reparations), that can be mutually agreed upon by the participants present in the RJ process. A plan is made, by consensus of those participating in the process, for the prevention of future occurrences and for the offender to repair the harm (to the extent possible) done to the injured parties. The community members hold the offender accountable for his or her adherence to this plan. Restitution/reparations, or compensation, can include, but is not limited to: money, community service in general, community service specific to the deed, self-education to prevent recidivism, and/or expressions of remorse (apologies, public or private).

Community

In an RJ process, the community is involved, unlike traditional criminal justice, where the community is perhaps represented by a prosecutor as the "state." In many RJ forms, concerned members of the community of the victim or offender or both are given the opportunity to meet with the individuals affected by the crime, including the victim and offender and their respective supporters, to express the impact the crime has had upon them, to learn more about the crime and its impact on the victim, and to participate in crafting a sentence for the offender.

Forms of RJ

There are many forms of RJ, such as: victim-offender mediation, family group conferences, reparative probation boards, circle sentencing, and international initiatives.[13]

---

13. The article by Gordon Bazemore and Curt Taylor Griffiths, *supra* note 1, describes these forms of RJ in great detail, with examples.

Victim Offender Mediation (VOM)

In VOM, the victim, offender, and a mediator meet in a three-party conference. It can be pre- or post-sentence. In the United States, these conferences may be held without having any effect on the criminal justice process, which occurs alongside the VOM, so to speak. The victim may speak first, or the offender may speak first, describing the offense in detail and explaining how it affected him or her. The facilitator may ask questions designed to elicit the offender to describe the consequences of the offense and how it affected him and then ask the victim how the crime affected him or her and allow the victim to ask questions of the offender. The participants then work out a settlement that is acceptable to both victim and offender.

Family Group Conference (FGC)

The process in FGCs is similar, except that the victim's supporters and the offender's supporters may also be present (friends, family, and others, such as coaches or teachers). As FGCs are often used with juvenile offenders, the facilitator may ask the offender to speak first, to avoid the offender "shutting down" in the face of extreme pressure and shame felt from hearing from the victim and his or her supporters first. The minor offender may be overwhelmed, particularly if there are a lot of adults in the conference, and may participate more fully if allowed to speak first. FGCs are appropriate in juvenile cases because they include the participation of family members, who are likely to be important in juvenile offenders' lives.

Reparative Parole/Probation Boards (RB)

Community restorative boards or RBs consist of a small group of trained citizens who conduct public, face-to-face meetings with offenders sentenced by a court to participate in this process. The board discusses with the offender the nature of the offense and its negative consequences. The board members develop a set of proposed sanctions which they discuss with the offender, until they reach agreement on specific actions the offender will take within a given time period to make reparation for the crime. The offender must document his or her progress in fulfilling the agreement. After the stipulated period of time has passed, the board submits a report to the court on the offender's compliance with the agreed-on sanctions and, then, the board's involvement with the offender ends. This process is included in RJ as it involves the community in dealing with the consequences of crime, giving the community a voice and an active participatory role. The public nature of the meetings assists in imposing reintegrative shame on the offender, also.

Circle Sentencing (CS)

CS is the RJ process with the greatest number of participants. Conferences are held in a circle. In a closely-knit community, the circle would include everyone in the community (such as in a small religious community or a tribe). Often, a traditional circle ritual and structure are employed, usually with a "talking piece," which is a token passed from person to person to indicate who has the right to speak (i.e., who has the "floor"). The circle includes the victim, the victim's supporters, the offender, the offender's supporters, and all interested community members. It can include the judge and court personnel, the prosecutor, defense counsel, and the police. One example is Figure 1, below:

Figure 1. Circle Process

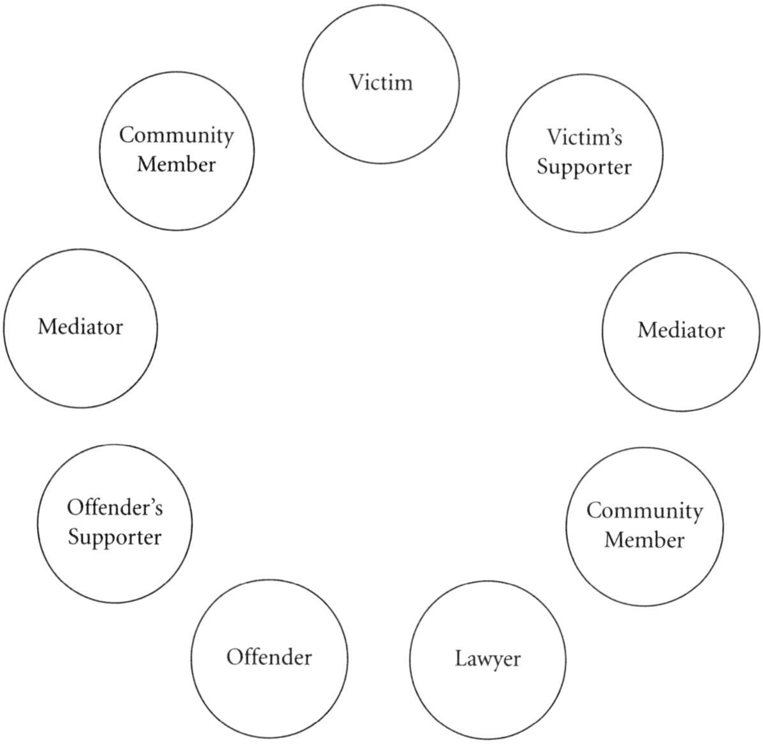

Within the circle, participants speak from the heart in a shared search for an understanding of the event and together they identify the steps necessary to assist in healing all affected parties and prevent future crimes. CS can involve a multi-step procedure that includes: (1) an application by the offender to participate in the circle process; (2) a healing circle for the victim; (3) a healing circle for the offender; (4) a sentencing circle to develop consensus on the elements of a sentencing plan; and (5) follow-up circles to monitor the progress of the offender. CS has been so satisfactory as a process that circle process has also been used in communities to handle community problems and issues, such as neighborhood crime or other conditions. For example, it might be used in a condominium homeowners' association to handle controversial systemic concerns in the condo community, or in a religious community (church or synagogue) to deal with delicate concerns of removing and replacing a community leader in the case of malfeasance.[14]

International Reconciliation Programs

RJ has been extended into the international arena in peace building efforts.[15] For example, to deal with the aftereffects of apartheid and the crimes committed in its name, the South Africa Truth & Reconciliation Commission fostered open meetings between

---

14. Credit is due to Boston mediator and collaborative lawyer David Hoffman for these ideas, personal communication in July, 2007.

15. Ellis Cose, *Learning to Heal*, Newsweek/Society (April 12, 2004), available at http://www.msnbc. msn.com/id/4660086 (last visited July 11, 2010) (adapted from ELLIS COSE, BONE TO PICK: OF FORGIVENESS, RECONCILIATION, REPARATION AND REVENGE (Simon & Schuster, 2004)).

offenders, victims, and victims' families to allow dialogue. It was intended to allow offenders to take responsibility for the crimes and victims to ask questions and receive answers, but some dissatisfaction with the process has been noted. It was an attempt at RJ but may have been (for some) an incomplete process, leaving some participants with the sense of arbitrariness, tension, and dissatisfaction Scheff mentions.[16]

In more recent years, "[i]n their quest for meaning and healing following the death of their loved ones, surviving family members of homicide victims from both criminal and political violence are seeking to meet the offenders through restorative dialogue opportunities in North America, Europe, Israel, Palestine, South Africa, and other parts of the world."[17] It is hoped that these RJ processes will bring greater healing and closure for all those affected by this violence.

Applicability

RJ can be used pre-arrest, pre-court referral, pre-sentencing, post-sentencing, or even during incarceration (some cases have held a VOM two years post-conviction). RJ is equally useful with teenage offenders and minor crimes as it is with healing victims of serious crimes, their offenders, and the communities in which they live, including murder. In petty, minor offenses, the case may be referred to RJ as a pretrial diversion. In this case, criminal charges would be dismissed after the offender's fulfillment of the restitution agreement. In serious cases, RJ may be part of a sentence that includes prison time or other punishments or may be used post-sentence. A survey published in 2000 found that "of the 116 programs that were interviewed (out of a total of 289 identified), 34 percent indicated that their primary referral was at a diversion level; 28 percent, at a post-adjudication but predisposition level; and 28 percent, at a post-disposition level of referral."[18]

RJ is seen in almost every jurisdiction in the United States, in many forms, such as: teen court, victim-offender mediation (VOM), reparative probation programs, and community parole boards. RJ is particularly popular for use in the U.S. with juvenile offenders, due to its reliance on the pressure brought to bear on the offender by peers, family, and community members and its resultant potential for rehabilitating juvenile offenders. While it can be used for sentencing of juveniles in the United States, it is not popular for sentencing of adults in the United States, most likely due to the American emphasis on constitutional rights.

For example, in the domestic violence area, restorative justice principles might be employed to alter traditional court proceedings. RJ principles might suggest that domestic violence victims should have more input into the proceedings, the state should attempt to restore victims to their former state through compensation and economic and social support, victims need varied support to become independent, offenders should be held accountable, required to make amends, required to participate in rehabilitation programs and reintegrated into the community, and the community should be more involved and

---

16. Thomas Scheff, *supra* note 8 (see above section for this idea).

17. Mark Umbreit, Betty Vos, Robert B. Coates, Elizabeth Lightfoot, *Restorative Justice in the Twenty-First Century: A Social Movement Full of Opportunities and Pitfalls,* 89 Marq. L. Rev. 251, 253–54 (2005).

18. Guidelines for Victim-Sensitive Victim-Offender Mediation: Restorative Justice Through Dialogue, April, 2000, available at http://www.ojp.usdoj.gov/ovc/publications/infores/restorative_justice/96517-gdlines_victims-sens/guide4.html (last visited July 11, 2010).

responsible for assisting the victim, the offender, and their family through the process of solving the problem.[19] These insights might be incorporated into existing court procedures and sentencing.

RJ is more widely used in Australia, Canada, and the United Kingdom, extending even to sentencing of adult offenders. Outside the American criminal justice system, RJ forms include collaborative forms of adjudication and sentencing, such as circle sentencing and family group conferences, that actually substitute for prosecution, trial, and sentencing. In other legal systems, particularly in Native American and aboriginal settings, restorative justice is used for sentencing of adult crimes in "circle sentencing conferences" used to discuss the event, air feelings, and sentence the offender via a collaborative, community-wide process including the offender, victim, their friends and families, and their surrounding communities.

Example

Victim-offender mediation is a specific, direct RJ "process." Writer Barbara Stahura relates this story of a VOM case:[20]

> One evening in July, 1998, Terri Carlson and her husband were walking home along the side of the road from the annual community festival in Byron, Minnesota, when a four-wheel-drive pickup truck going about 55 swerved, hitting and killing Terri's husband and injuring Terri. The 25-year-old driver, Eric, was a deputy county sheriff, whose blood alcohol level was 50% over the minimum for drunk driving. Yet Terri felt badly for him. She herself had occasionally driven drunk. She said, "He was only 25.... just a baby. He had lost everything he'd committed to in his profession." When he received a 44-month sentence, despite her request to give him 10 years' probation and community outreach, she felt "further violated." She packed up her three children and moved to Oregon, but upon finding out about restorative justice, she and Eric began a process designed to reconcile and resolve what had happened. It took a year of preparation and individual meetings with the mediator before they were ready to meet together with the mediator. In that meeting, "they had a warm and honest talk, even laced with laughter, and reached an agreement." Terri promised to help Eric reintegrate himself back into the Byron community. They agreed to speak jointly to schools, community groups, and the city council about how to prevent what happened. And they agreed that Eric should speak to Terri's three children about the death of their father.[21]

This is a vibrant and stirring example of restorative justice at work. In the United States, as this story illustrates, restorative justice is most often a post-sentencing process

---

19. Randall B. Fritzler & Leonore M.J. Simon, *Creating a Domestic Violence Court: Combat in the Trenches*, 37 CT. REV. 28, 35–36 (Spring, 2000) (discussing the creation of specialized domestic violence courts employing a therapeutic or restorative approach).

20. Barbara Stahura, *Trail 'Em, Nail 'Em, and Jail 'Em: Restorative Justice*, SPIRITUALITY & HEALTH 43 (Spring, 2001).

21. *Id.*

designed to bring about reconciliation between the victim, offender, and community, resolution for all, and reintegration of the offender into the community.

Advantages and Disadvantages

Despite the benefits of RJ, some point out that it may not be appropriate for all crimes. For example, it may be hard to apply in "victimless crimes," such as drug possession, unless a concerned community feels strongly impacted by the crime. It is not usable if the offender denies guilt or disputes the facts of the case. It is not appropriate if the offender is incapacitated or unable to take responsibility for his or her actions. If used without adequate pre-mediation preparation sessions, it can re-victimize the victims, by placing them in close proximity to the offender or by exposing them to a belligerent, callous, or responsibility-denying offender. Some legal systems only recognize monetary reparations, so any noneconomic reparations that are developed and agreed to may be unenforceable. Some of these concerns can be dealt with by excellent training and careful use of RJ, while some are unavoidable.

On the other hand, proponents of RJ point out that it has led to reduced recidivism (one researcher reports a 32% reduction in recidivism),[22] it prevents crime, it is less costly, and participants report 80–90% satisfaction rates with the process. Satisfaction with RJ processes is very high; Poulson reported in 2003 that RJ "outperformed court procedures on almost every variable for victims and offenders" of "judgments of fairness, accountability, satisfaction, contrition, forgiveness, emotional wellbeing, feelings of safety, increased respect, and reduced fear."[23] Confidentiality of the process can be agreed to by all participants. The victims are empowered as they are given a voice and participation in the process, consistent with procedural justice principles, which would suggest that they may be more satisfied with the fairness of the procedure, compared to traditional criminal court. Traditional criminal court can be dehumanizing and re-victimizing for victims who either are ignored or have to testify, reliving the crime in court. RJ processes (employed properly) ensure that participants participate voluntarily, are prepared via extensive pre-mediation meetings with the mediator, and are supported by the presence of their friends and family (if desired) at the conference. RJ can promote solidarity within communities and reintegrate rehabilitated offenders back into the community. Finally, high participation rates have been reported; one source states, in contrast to what was expected when RJ was first implemented in the United States, "the majority of crime victims who are presented with the opportunity for mediation and dialogue choose to engage in the process, with victim participation rates in many programs ranging from 60 to 70 percent."[24]

---

22. Barton Poulson, *A Third Voice: A Review of Empirical Research on the Psychological Outcomes of Restorative Justice*, 2003 Utah L. Rev. 167, 199 (2003) (reporting on the empirical results of seven evaluation studies of RJ and court programs from around the world; RJ outperformed court in every instance).

23. *Id.* at 167, 198.

24. Guidelines for Victim-Sensitive Victim-Offender Mediation: Restorative Justice Through Dialogue, April, 2000, available at http://www.ojp.usdoj.gov/ovc/publications/infores/restorative_justice/96517-gdlines_victims-sens/guide4.html (last visited July 11, 2010).

Practice Information

Appropriate Use

RJ is only appropriate if a confession, plea, or adjudication has occurred, first. However, since the vast majority of criminal cases are disposed of via plea, pre-trial, the opportunities for RJ are more frequent than it might immediately appear.

The parties need to be emotionally ready for an RJ process, before they meet in a conference. It may seem, at the outset of a criminal case, that they are unlikely ever to be capable of meeting face-to-face. However, the criminal court process will bring pressure to bear upon the victim, community, and the defendant as it proceeds, so that the time involved in the process may move the parties closer to the ability to conference.

Skills of The Mediator

There are excellent training materials and programs available to train as an RJ mediator (many through the University of Minnesota and/or Mark Umbreit). This small Chapter is not intended to accomplish such training; however, it attempts to mention a few specific skills the facilitator can use to encourage a constructive RJ process. For example, Thomas Scheff explains that a mediator can stop destructive anger, rage, or shame expressed by a participant, perhaps by reframing or restating a participant's statements more neutrally. Similarly, a mediator can reframe displays of aggressive emotion, such as anger and moral indignation, to be more neutral. In contrast, the mediator will want to elicit vivid expression of the painful emotions caused by the crime (usually from a victim). The mediator should patiently ask respectful questions to cut through the defensive stance of any participants. Finally, the mediator will want to watch for displays of moral or self-righteous indignation, moral superiority, and overt threats by any participant, which can impede the process.[25]

Resources

Howard Zehr, The Little Book of Restorative Justice (Good Books, 2002) (this small book, by one of the leaders in the field, gives a good overview of the various forms of and theories underlying restorative justice).

Gerry Johnstone & Daniel W. Van Ness Eds., Handbook of Restorative Justice (Willan Publishing, 2007) (this comprehensive work covers the theory, practice, applications, and social context of modern restorative justice).

Susan L. Brooks & Robert G. Madden, Relationship-Centered Lawyering: Social Science Theory for Transforming Legal Practice (Carolina Academic Press, 2010) (Chapter 2, which includes James Coben & Penelope Harley, *Intentional Con-*

---

25. Scheff, *supra* note 8, at 108.

versations about Restorative Justice, Mediation, and the Practice of Law, and John Braithwaite, *Restorative Justice and De-Professionalism*).

Mark S. Umbreit, The Handbook of Victim Offender Mediation: An Essential Guide to Practice and Research (Jossey-Bass, 2000).

Barbara Stahura, *Trail 'Em, Nail 'Em, and Jail 'Em: Restorative Justice,* Spirituality & Health, p. 43, Spring, 2001 (retrieved at http://www.spiritualityhealth.com/NMagazine/articles.php?id=668) (last visited July 11, 2010).

Gordon Bazemore & Mara Schiff, Juvenile Justice Reform and Restorative Justice: Building Theory and Policy from Practice (Willan Publishing, 2004).

Mark S. Umbreit, Betty Vos, Robert B. Coates, & Elizabeth Lightfoot, *Symposium: Restorative Justice in Action—Restorative Justice in the Twenty-First Century: A Social Movement Full of Opportunities and Pitfalls,* 89 Marquette L. Rev. 251 (Winter 2005).

Joanne Katz & Gene Bonham, Jr., *Panel Session Paper/Article—Restorative Justice in Canada and the United States: A Comparative Analysis,* J. Inst. Justice & Int'l. Stud. 187 (2006).

Thomas J. Scheff, *Community Conferences: Shame and Anger in Therapeutic Jurisprudence,* 67(1) Rev. Jur. U.P.R. 97 (1998).

Kate Paradine, *Community, Shame, and Anger: Family Group Conferences and Domestic Violence,* 67 Rev. Jur. U.P.R. 635 (1998).

Websites

http://cehd.umn.edu/ssw/rjp (last visited July 11, 2010). This is the website of the University of Minnesota—The Center for Restorative Justice.

http://www.restorativejustice.org (last visited July 11, 2010). This website is sponsored by Prison Fellowship International. The site has a diverse range of information regarding the restorative justice movement throughout the world. It also has links to other websites devoted to restorative justice.

http://www.rjmn.net (last visited July 11, 2010). This is the website of Restorative Justice Ministries Network of North America.

http://www.barjproject.org (last visited July 11, 2010).

http://www.restorejustice.com (last visited July 11, 2010). This website is aimed at offering compassion, assistance, resources and services for anyone affected by crime.

http://www.sfu.ca/crj (last visited July 11, 2010). Simon Frasier University in Canada hosts the Centre for Restorative Justice.

http://www.ojp.usdoj.gov/ovc/publications/infores/restorative_justice/welcome.html (last visited July 11, 2010). This website has 5 documents that discuss how to establish a "victim-sensitive" restorative justice program.

http://www.rjca-inc.org (last visited July 11, 2010). The Restorative Justice Community Action, Inc. is aimed at "improving neighborhood livability through restorative justice practices." The company is based in Minnesota. The website provides information on the use of restorative justice for small communities.

http://www.restorativejusticescotland.org.uk (last visited July 11, 2010). This website focuses on restorative justice practices in Scotland.

http://www.restorativejusticenow.org (last visited July 11, 2010). The National Conference on Restorative Justice is promoted on this website. The site provides in depth information on speakers and schedules.

http://www.realjustice.org (for criminal justice professionals) (last visited July 11, 2010).

http://www.restorativejustice.org.nz (The New Zealand Restorative Justice Trust) (last visited July 11, 2010).

http://www.beyondintractability.org/essay/restorative_justice (last visited July 11, 2010). This is the website for Beyond Intractability.

http://www.rjc.co.za (last visited July 11, 2010). This is the website of the Restorative Justice Centre—South Africa.

http://www.restorejustice.com (last visited July 11, 2010).

http://www.restorativejustice.org.uk (last visited July 11, 2010). This is the website of the Restorative Justice Consortium.

http://www.icjia.state.il.us/public/pdf/tiupdate/restorative.pdf (last visited July 11, 2010).

Videos

There are a number of RJ videos on Youtube; here are just two:

Mark Umbreit's Training Video: http://www.youtube.com/watch?v=IC2aBPISDno (last visited July 11, 2010).

A Healing River: http://www.youtube.com/watch?v=Nhw2llNdYeQ&feature=related (last visited July 11, 2010).

Coordination: Also read Brooks & Madden (Chapter 2, particularly p. 83–94), King (Chapters 3, 11, and p. 96–98), and Wright (p. 27–42 and 259–78).

Chapter Assignments

Exercise 14-1—Restorative Justice Discussion Questions

NOT NECESSARILY MATCHING:

Write the appropriate number(s) of all the concepts or programs that apply to each description next to the descriptions on the next pages. There can be more than one concept per description and more than one description to each concept. Some concepts may not be used at all.

CONCEPTS/PROGRAMS:

1. Reparative Probation Program
2. Circle Sentencing
3. Family Group Conference
4. Victim-Offender Mediation
5. Restorative Justice
6. Retributive (Traditional) Justice
7. Civil Dispute Mediation

DESCRIPTIONS:

_____ Makes dispositional decisions for eligible probation cases.

_____ Victims, offenders, families, police officers, lawyers, the judge, and community residents all participate in the case deliberations.

_____ Goal is to address the criminal behavior of offenders and also to consider the needs of victims and their families and the community.

_____ Offenders and victims meet with a third party to arrive at a reparative agreement, allow the victim to tell their story and get information about the offense.

_____ Decisionmaking is achieved by consensus as opposed to by a judge.

_____ Its goal is reparation of harm, reconciliation of conflict, and meeting the needs of victims, offenders, and communities.

_____ Its goals are punishment, deterrence, retribution, and rehabilitation.

_____ Decisionmaking is achieved by a trial and a decisionmaker (judge or jury).

_____ Emphasizes informality in the decisionmaking process.

_____ Emphasizes legal rules and procedures in the decisionmaking process.

_____ Is a three person process.

_____ Is a multiperson process (more than 3).

_____ Gives first priority to meeting crime victims' needs, allowing them to speak, helping them feel empowered; victims usually speak first.

_____ Recommends extensive pre-mediation preparation of the victim and the offender before a face-to-face meeting.

_____ Focuses less on victims' needs and more on offender shaming and reintegration. Offenders usually speak first.

_____ Lawyers and judges act as facilitators of community involvement and resources to the community rather than as sole decisionmakers.

_____ Judges function as sole decisionmakers.

_____ Views crime as a violation of one person by another.

_____ Views crime as a violation against the state.

_____ Focuses on establishing blame for past acts.

_____ Focuses on dialogue, negotiation, and problemsolving for the future.

_____ Focuses on improved offender competency, victim participation and services, offender accountability, and community involvement and responsibility.

_____ Emphasizes face-to-face conferences between victims and offenders.

TRUE OR FALSE:

1. Restorative justice operates in the context of the civil court system.

   T / F

2. Victim-offender mediation focuses on conflict resolution via greater understanding of each other.

   T / F

3. Restorative justice is not appropriate for use with victims of serious felonies or in serious felony cases involving harm to people.

    T / F

4. When given decisionmaking power, neighborhood residents often chose to include the most rather than the least serious offenders in community justice processes.

    T / F

5. Successful restorative justice planning requires the support and involvement of:

    a. the judiciary

    b. community leaders

    c. neighborhood activists

    d. the local plaintiff's bar

    e. all of the above

    f. none of the above

    g. a, b, and d but not c

    h. a, c, and d but not b

    i. a, b, and c, but not d

Exercise 14-2 — Victim/Offender Letters

Choose one of the hypothetical fact patterns in Exercise 14-3, below, and write a letter from the victim to the offender. Then, write an apology from the offender to the victim (review the material in Chapter 11 on apology). Finally, write the victim's response forgiving the offender. Try to fit these three letters together within one page, single-spaced, typed, total. Try to include all of the elements one would hope for, in an optimal apology-forgiveness exchange.

Exercise 14-3 — Restorative Justice Simulations

Split into several teams. Each team will be responsible for creating, devising, planning, and carrying out a restorative justice/community justice approach to a criminal offense. Each team will be given a different fact pattern. You must choose an RJ approach or process (see the Chapter for options) or creatively devise a new one that is RJ-oriented, for your problem. Then, assign roles. Plan the process (ground rules, etc.) you will use. Carry out the process in a simulation/role play.

Legal Problems for Application of Restorative Justice Processes

Instructions: (1) Break up into groups of 3 to 8 people. (2) Decide which of the following scenarios you would like to simulate as a restorative justice process. (3) Specifically, first decide which RJ process is most appropriate (FGC, CS, VOM, or some hybrid of those processes). (4) Then, assign roles within your group to the relevant players in the process. (5) Practice your simulation, with the idea that you will present a segment of the process to other groups. (6) Have one person in your group complete one "feedback sheet" for everyone in the group (see below). Feel free to revise or expand the facts, if necessary, of these scenarios, use a case in the news or a reported case, or write your own (see #6, below).

1. <u>Juvenile Sexual Battery:</u> You are a criminal defense attorney who is defending a fifteen-year-old boy who has been charged with two counts of sexual battery and one count of lewd and lascivious behavior on three two-year-old children. The boy was arrested after three children from his mother's in-home day care center claimed that they had been raped. As you routinely do in every bond hearing, you presented character witness testimony from the fifteen-year-old boy's parents and some members of their church. During the bond hearing, the boy's mother cried because she feared she had lost her only son due to what she perceived to be vicious lies. Each of the character witnesses (from the mother's church community) approached the judge and spoke with reverent praise for this fifteen-year-old boy. Each witness explained to the judge what a good boy he had always been, how he had never been in trouble before, and how he was the first to help those members in need from the church where his parents minister. Once the character witnesses and family spoke on his behalf, the court heard testimony from the victims' representative. The representative expressed how much the children's families were suffering, how the families have lost all belief in the goodness of the world, how they will never be able to overcome the violence that has changed their lives forever, and how they will never be able to trust again. Finally, the parents of the children made one plea to the court and to the fifteen-year-old boy to ask that he be tested for sexually transmitted diseases, specifically, HIV. The fifteen-year-old boy's parents immediately refused this plea, indicating that any test would have to wait until after he had been convicted. The law in the state dictates that a court can only order the testing of a sexual offender for any sexually transmitted diseases after they have been convicted of the crime charged.

2. <u>Native American Dig:</u> The University of Western Florida's Department of Archaeology is tracing and excavating an old trail used by Spanish explorers. The trail is located on state land somewhere in the panhandle of Florida. In the course of their work, the archaeologists stumble upon a large gravesite containing the remains of an early Native American tribe about which little is known, the Apalachees. The graves are particularly rich in artifacts as the Apalachees customarily buried large amounts of personal items as "grave goods" along with the deceased. The site is of great significance because it has not been plundered by grave robbers or souvenir hunters and the artifacts/remains are in a superb state of preservation. If properly excavated, it would reveal much about the culture and lives of these Native Americans, close large gaps in our historical understanding of the period, and provide a terrific learning experience for the many archaeologists who would be needed to do the work. The site also has potential to attract tourists, giving the archaeologists an opportunity to educate people on early tribal life while generating revenue for other projects. The excited archaeologists immediately applied to the state for a permit to do the excavation and began procuring the funding necessary for the work. The immediacy was necessary to protect the site from the inevitable grave-robbers and treasure-hunters that would follow once word of the find leaked out. As soon as the paperwork was filed, leaders of the modern-day Apalachee tribe filed suit seeking an injunction to stop the work. The leaders argued that any disturbance of the graves was sacrilege and would result in the deceased's spirits being forever lost. They argued that the bones of the deceased would have little overall academic value and would only wind up in shoeboxes on a university shelf or exposed to the world in sterile glass museum display cases. They also argued that any and all artifacts associated with the site were intimately related to the deceased and necessary for their continued existence in the afterlife. In addition, tribal leaders insisted that the artifacts re-

main the exclusive property of the Apalachee tribe and could not be disturbed or taken without their consent. Since the suit was filed prior to any state or federal legislation regarding historic preservation of Native American gravesites, and there were no governing treaties in effect, the judge hearing the suit ordered the state (since the University of Western Florida is a state school) and the Apalachee leaders to make their respective cases in court. Pertinent facts: Number of skeletons: 20, including several thought to be tribal leaders. The remains are the best preserved that have ever been discovered. Grave goods: Hundreds of pots, weapons, utensils, and domestic items, including several rare intact items and others never seen in a gravesite before. Area found: State-owned land away from any privately-owned property, but within relatively easy access to the interstate highway. Cost: The cost to properly excavate the site runs to $300,000, which the state intends to appropriate. The grave goods themselves are considered extremely important for their historical value. In the past, however, collectors have often paid large sums for the artifacts, whether obtained legally or illegally. There is a state statute making it a criminal offense to remove any artifacts from state land without a permit from the state.

3. <u>Three Strikes, You're Out:</u> George Lawton is a two-time convicted felon who has been rehabilitated from drug addiction for the past 10 years. While he was serving his last prison sentence, he became reformed and rehabilitated and has stayed clean and sober ever since. He has also been reunited with his girlfriend and their three children (all his). However, he has had a series of financial difficulties and this Christmas, he cut down a tree in a forest outside of town to save money and provide a Christmas tree for his children. He was arrested for trespassing and "theft" of a tree; a minor offense like this for someone with his criminal record carries with it a mandatory sentence under the state's new, mandatory sentencing laws, of six months' incarceration and loss of his civil rights, including voting. He comes to you for help with his plight. The prosecutor is a recent law school graduate whose stance is to be tough on crime; you know that she is unlikely to agree to drop the charges. The homeowner is also exasperated, as too many people have cut down her trees over the years, and she is adamant about prosecuting George.

4. <u>High School Blues:</u> The parents of a 17-year-old young man come to see you. Their son has been criminally charged with driving while intoxicated and resisting arrest. Apparently, he has been more and more depressed, alienated, and isolated since he broke his leg last fall and had to quit playing football in his senior year of high school. Last year, he was one of the better players on the high school football team and was really looking forward to a stellar last season this year. He got hurt in the first game of the season and will be unable to play for the entire school year. Having nothing in common with his old football buddies, he has spent more and more time around students who are known for drinking alcohol and getting into minor trouble at school (e.g., truancy, loitering, graffiti). Last Friday night, he got drunk all by himself, while his parents were out at a party, went out for a drive past his ex-girlfriend's house, missed a red light, and T-boned (hit) another driver at an intersection. When the police arrived, he was drunk, surly, uncooperative, and verbally insulting to the arresting officer. The person he hit was a 48-year-old convenience store clerk who was returning home to her family after finishing her shift. She has some injuries from the accident and her car was totaled. She is married, with two grown children, and takes care of her aging mother who is in poor health. Your clients (the parents) admit that they drink socially and that they have been busier this year than usual; both have professional careers and have been spending a lot of time working. They want you to handle the criminal charges against their son.

5.   10-20-Life: A father who is raising three children, ages 4, 6, and 9, on his own, feels overwhelmed by financial pressures and frustrated with his situation and challenges in general. He makes a poor choice and robs a convenience store using a gun. A struggle ensues with the store clerk and, while fighting, the gun fires, injuring the clerk. Applying the 10-20-life law, since he used a gun in the commission of a crime, he will receive at least 10 years if convicted; if he fires the gun, he receives 20 years, if he shoots someone, he receives a life sentence if convicted. If this father is convicted therefore, he receives a life sentence and his children are parentless. Suppose that the convenience store clerk is a 45-year-old divorced mother of two grown children and that she has one grandchild, age 3.

6.   Improv: Feel free to revise or expand the facts, if necessary, of the above scenarios, or write your own.

Feedback Sheet for RJ Simulations

Put the *initials* of the person displaying the concept, *EACH* time you see it, on this sheet:

"Initials"	Concept	"Initials"	Victim's Need	"Initials"	Offender's Apology
	Consequences		To express the impact the O's actions had on the V's life, including expressing the painful emotions caused in V by the event		To understand and acknowledge the impact the O's actions had on the V's life
	Apology/Remorse		To believe, have faith that the O really is sorry for what he or she did, is remorseful, regrets what happened not solely for selfish reasons		To apologize, say I'm sorry, express remorse, regret that the event happened to the V, in a sincere, non-selfish, non-self-focused manner, with O being visibly ashamed of what he or she did and not being angry, which allows V to see O as human—forges bond between V & O
	Responsibility		To have all blame shifted entirely off the V and entirely onto the O for the event		To accept responsibility for what happened, to express awareness that the event was "wrong" and that O did wrong
	Forgiveness		To forgive the O, stop being angry with O, stop lecturing O from hilltop, see the O as a fellow human being —forges bond		To receive V's forgiveness

			between V & O NOTE: relentless anger at O is moral indignation, which is unacknowledged (projected) shame		
	Understanding		To ask why, to understand more about why this happened to me May also include understanding the O as a fellow human being		Explains why the offense was done May also include understanding the V as a fellow human being
	Positive Outcome/ *Rehabilitation*		To have faith that something good can come out of this event, that the O will improve as a result		To admit that O has a problem and express O's willingness to change
	Restitution to V		To receive material restitution from the O to "make whole" the loss that arose from the event		To express willingness to make material restitution to V, outline a plan for it
	Plan for the Future		To know that this will not happen again		To describe his or her plan for changing and not recidivating
	Revenge/ Desire to Punish		(these are destructive to an RJ process)		
	Blameshifting/ No Accountability		(these are destructive to an RJ process)		
	Material Reparations				
	Reframe Destructive *Anger/Emotion*		(these are mediator moves)		
	Ask Questions		(these are mediator moves)		

Any other feedback you have for the participants:

Chapter 15

Vector 10—Problem Solving Courts: Drug Treatment Courts and Other Specialized Courts

Description

A shift parallel to collaborative law, transformative mediation, and restorative justice has occurred in the court system, mainly due to judges' interest in therapeutic jurisprudence.[1] A number of specialized, "problem solving" courts ("PSCs") have been established, based on TJ principles.[2] Their approach to judging is long-term, relational, interdisciplinary, and focused on healing. Their growth has been spurred by a joint resolution of the Conference of Chief Justices (Resolution 22) and the Conference of State Court Administrators (Resolution 4), adopted in August, 2000, that specifically encouraged the development of courts utilizing therapeutic jurisprudence principles (such as drug treatment courts), referring to them as "problem solving courts and calendars."[3] The best examples of these courts are drug treatment courts, however, there are also mental health courts, homeless courts, specialized domestic violence courts, and unified family courts, which focus on treating and resolving the interpersonal and psychological issues underlying the legal problems rather than on punishing defendants or assigning fault. Information on many of these new courts is collected at the website of the Center for Court Innovation.[4]

Innovation in court systems also includes the emergence of community courts; however, these are often viewed as a restorative justice initiative due to the participation of the community in these programs. For example, community courts are usually located in the community where the crimes occur, can involve creative partnerships with commu-

---

1. Most of this Chapter is excerpted from Susan Daicoff, *Law as a Healing Profession: The "Comprehensive Law Movement,"* 6 PEPPERDINE DISP. RESOL. L. J. 1 (2006) and Susan Daicoff, *Resolution Without Litigation: Are Courtrooms Battlegrounds For Losers?* GPSolo 44–50 (October/November 2003) (republished as a book chapter, Susan Daicoff, *The Comprehensive Law Movement: An Emerging Approach to Legal Problems,* in PETER WAHLGREN, ED., A PROACTIVE APPROACH, 49 SCANDINAVIAN STUDIES IN LAW 109–129 (2006)).

2. Bruce J. Winick, *Therapeutic Jurisprudence and Problem Solving Courts,* 30 FORDHAM URB. L.J. 1055 (2003).

3. CCJ Resolution 22, COSCA Resolution 4, http://dcpi.ncjrs.org/pdf/Chief%20Justice%20Resolution.doc (last visited July 8, 2010).

4. http://www.courtinnovation.org (last visited July 8, 2010).

nity residents, merchants, churches, and schools, can be proactive in fighting local crime, and can offer one-stop shopping for criminal defendants for rehabilitation, mental health treatment, adjudication, sentencing, and follow-up.[5]

Roger Warren presented the following helpful chart at a conference in 1998; it compares traditional adjudication with the general approach taken by these problem solving courts:

A COMPARISON OF TRANSFORMED AND TRADITIONAL COURT PROCESSES[6]

Traditional Process	Transformed Process
Dispute resolution	Problem solving dispute avoidance
Legal outcome	Therapeutic outcome
Adversarial process	Collaborative process
Claim- or case-oriented	People-oriented
Rights-based	Interest- or needs-based
Emphasis placed on adjudication	Emphasis placed on post-adjudication and alternative dispute resolution
Interpretation and application of law	Interpretation and application of social science
Judge as arbiter	Judge as coach
Backward looking	Forward looking
Precedent-based	Planning-based
Few participants and stakeholders	Wide range of participants and stakeholders
Individualistic	Interdependent
Legalistic	Common-sensical
Formal	Informal
Efficient	Effective

Drug Treatment Courts

Drug treatment courts have rapidly proliferated throughout the United States since the first one was implemented in Miami, Florida, in 1989. According to drug treatment court pioneer and proponent Judge Peggy Hora, "more than 70,000 drug court clients are being served at any given time in the United States, more than 16,200 participants graduated from drug court in 2004, and there were 2,558 total problem solving courts in the U.S."[7] as of 2007. Their success rates have drawn attention and propelled their im-

---

5. From the website of the National Center for Court Innovation (http://www.courtinnovation.org) (last visited July 8, 2010) (reporting that the first community court was the Midtown Community Court, begun in 1993 in New York City; there are others now also in the United Kingdom, South Africa, Australia, and Canada).

6. Roger K. Warren, *Reengineering the Court Process*, Madison, WI, Presentation to Great Lakes Court Summit, September 24–25, 1998.

7. Materials distributed in connection with Judge Hora's remarks made at the "Law as a Healing Profession" conference at Touro College of Law, November 4, 2007, Long Island, New York, at 1 [hereinafter Hora's Materials], *citing* "Painting the Current Picture," A National Report Card on Drug Courts and Other Problem Solving Court Programs in the United States, Vol. 1, No. 2 (May, 2005).

plementation in other jurisdictions across the country.[8] Statistics show that up to 80% of incarcerated individuals may be suffering from substance abuse.[9]

Where substance abuse is involved, courts may offer an offender a choice of traditional criminal prosecution or participation in a drug treatment court ("DTC"). The goals of drug treatment court are to reduce repeated criminal behavior, avoid the costs of incarceration, and rehabilitate the offender, thereby ultimately benefiting the community. DTCs can be implemented either pre-plea or post-plea. An offender must voluntarily enter into a formal contract that explains the conditions of DTC participation, which typically include frequent court appearances, participation in a drug rehabilitation program, close supervision, and drug screens. If the offender is a juvenile, then the offender's parents must sign the contract as well.[10]

Treatment is monitored by regular appearances before a DTC judge. Mandatory court appearances are often weekly, then fortnightly, and finally monthly. The treatment "team" usually consists of the judge, prosecutor, defense attorney, probation officer, drug treatment court coordinator, treatment provider, and community-policing officer. Typical terms of a contract include regular attendance at recovery fellowship meetings, interactions with a mentor already in the recovery program, participation in the recovery program with the mentor, compliance with routine check-ins with the DTC coordinator or case manager, random urine tests, and perfect attendance at court appearances. Hora asserts that "80% of drug treatment court participants indicate that judicial monitoring is very important to their progress."[11]

If an offender fails to comply with the terms of the contract, the offender faces a number of graduated, intermediate sanctions. Repeated failures can eventually lead to expulsion from the DTC and a return to traditional court for prosecution, trial, or sentencing (depending on whether the diversion to DTC occurred pre- or post-plea). Program completion depends on individual progress, usually between 14 and 24 months, after which a joyous "graduation ceremony" is held and the originating charges are dismissed. Offenders sometimes ask that the arresting officer be present at graduation, out of gratitude for the officer's intervention in their lives.[12]

---

8. Alex Segura, Jr., "Alumni's return shows success of drug court," South Florida Sun-Sentinel, Thursday, August 9, 2001 at 10B (noting that the Fort Lauderdale, Florida court was the third in the nation, established in 1991, after those in Miami and Las Vegas). In 2001, it was estimated that there were 660 drug courts "in 48 states, as well as the District of Columbia, Puerto Rico, Guam, a number of Native American Tribal Courts, and one federal district court, according to the Drug Courts Program Office of the U.S. Department of Justice," according to Jan Pudlow, "Palm Beach County opens its drug court," The Florida Bar News, April 15, 2001 at 14 (noting also that Miami (Dade County)'s drug court opened in 1989). Pudlow also reported a 70% success rate. *Id.*

9. Judge William G. Schma, *Alternatives for the Common Good*, 85 A.B.A. J. 103, 103 (June, 1999) (according to statistics from the National Center on Addiction and Substance Abuse at Columbia University, alcohol and drugs are implicated in 80 percent of incarcerations). On one criminal docket in Judge Schma's court, 24 out of 27 felony defendants had a history of addiction to alcohol or drugs, or mental illness or both. *Id.*

10. David Stevens Hobler, *Drug Treatment Court : The Making of Judicial Capital-Collaborative Therapeutic & Preventive Practices*, National Center for Preventive Law (2001), available at http://www.preventivelawyer.org/main/default.asp?pid=essays/hobler.htm (last visited July 8, 2010).

11. Hora's Materials, *supra* note 7, *citing* 2000 Drug Court Survey Program Operations, Services and Participant Perspectives, OJP Drug Court Clearinghouse and Technical Assistance Project, A Project of the Drug Courts Program Office, Office of Justice Programs, U.S. Department of Justice, School of Public Affairs, American University, Washington, D.C. November, 2001.

12. Hobler, *supra* note 10; *see also* National Drug Court Institute, Ethical Considerations for Judges and Attorneys in Drug Court (May, 2001), published with the cooperation of the Drug Courts Pro-

The DTC approach to adjudication modifies judicial rules, procedures, and communication postures. DTC team members attempt to collaborate with their clients to develop a flexible and realistic treatment strategy and a changed lifestyle for the client. The offender is recast into the role of a client, a term of respect and equanimity. The judge is required to have the temperament and technique to serve as a team player or coach, mediating differences, coordinating styles, and encouraging the client to recover. The judge no longer needs to referee the attorneys who collaborate for the client's benefit and accountability. The judge's role shifts from a neutral arbiter to that of the central figure in the team, a "cheerleader," and a "stern parent."[13]

The attorneys cease gamesmanship and behave like partners for a common client, tailoring remarks and input to support the client's adherence to a treatment plan. Treatment professionals report on the client's recovery progress, not the need for perfection. Emphasis is placed on positive behavior change by confirming client strengths. Sanctions for non-compliance are imposed to obtain compliance for treatment and recovery, not for punishment reasons. When intermediate sanctions are necessary, the entire team evaluates what needs immediate attention, discusses the best way to accomplish the goals, and then comes to a collaborative resolution. In the case of juvenile offenders, parents, school representatives, and concerned significant adults attend court and contribute to the solution as team members.

Some critics of DTCs charge that their reported success rates are impressive because the courts "cherry-pick" their participants, meaning they choose only those who are predisposed not to recidivate (and thus, graduate successfully without reoffending). Others note that the time spent in rehabilitative treatment, which can be in an in-patient residential program, can often exceed the amount of time one might spend incarcerated for the original criminal offense, thus they point out that the defendant's loss of liberty and freedom might be longer in DTC than in traditional criminal court. Despite these charges, the future of drug treatment courts appears sound; their reported success rates (graduation and nonrecidivism) are impressive[14] and their effect on judges' satisfaction has been remarkable.[15] Hora asserts, "in a series of surveys comparing judges working therapeutically and those working traditionally, 100% of drug treatment court judges reported being positively affected by their assignment."[16] Defense counsel has also overwhelmingly (90–97% in one study) reported satisfaction with drug treatment courts and higher job

---

gram Office of the United States Department of Justice (setting forth an interpretation of the American Bar Association Model Code of Judicial Conduct, the Model Rules of Professional Conduct, and the ABA Standards for Criminal Justice, for those attorneys and judges practicing in drug court).

13. Peggy Fulton Hora, William G. Schma, & John T. Rosenthal, *Therapeutic Jurisprudence and the Drug Treatment Court Movement: Revolutionizing the Criminal Justice System's Response to Drug Abuse and Crime in America*, 74 NOTRE DAME L. REV. 439, 477–83 (1999). One DTC judge in Georgia refers to herself as the "Velvet Hammer."

14. Jan Pudlow, "Palm Beach County opens its drug court," The Florida Bar News, April 15, 2001 at 14, reporting that, of the 100,000 drug dependent criminal offenders who have entered drug court, 70% were either still enrolled or had graduated, which was, according to Pudlow, "more than double the rate of traditional treatment programs retention rates," citing statistics from the Drug Courts Program Office of the U.S. Department of Justice. *Id.*

15. Deborah J. Chase & Peggy Fulton Hora, *The Implications of Therapeutic Jurisprudence for Judicial Satisfaction*, 37 CT. REV. 12 (2000) (reporting the results of an empirical study on the positive effects on judges of judging in problem solving courts); *see also* Peggy Fulton Hora & Deborah J. Chase, *Judicial Satisfaction When Judging in a Therapeutic Key*, 7:1 CONTEMP. ISSUES IN LAW (2003/2004).

16. Hora's Materials, *supra* note 7, at 9. *See also* Peggy Fulton Hora & Deborah J. Chase, *The Best Seat in the House: The Court Assignment and Judicial Satisfaction*, 47:2 FAMILY CT. REV. 209–238 (March, 2009).

satisfaction than when practicing traditionally, but at the same time felt that "they did not have to abandon their traditional adversarial duties."[17]

Other Problem Solving Courts

Other problem solving courts, such as mental health courts,[18] domestic violence courts, and unified family courts,[19] have developed with processes similar to the drug treatment court procedures. The establishment of these courts was spurred by the joint resolution of the Conference of Chief Justices and the Conference of State Court Administrators in 2000, which expressly encouraged courts based on therapeutic jurisprudence concepts.[20]

Four examples are as follows: Mental health court operates in Broward County under the guidance of Judge Ginger Lerner-Wren in a very therapeutic, rehabilitative manner. The Red Hook Community Court is a shining example of a community-based, problem solving court combining problem solving approaches with some restorative justice concepts. Recognizing that many of its homeless individuals were military veterans, San Diego developed a unique homeless court held outside, during a three-day community event (called "Stand Down") for military veterans. Santa Clara County in California has combined a drug treatment court with dependency cases, to rehabilitate parents who have lost custody of their minor children; they can be reunited with their children if successful in this court.

Domestic violence courts ("DVCs")[21] place the offender into a treatment program much like a DTC, but also combine the criminal domestic violence action with a civil protective order for the victim, and can address other legal needs of the family, such as those involving family law, custody, visitation, and child support. It consolidates the court interaction for the victim and family, providing one-stop shopping rather than several trips to more than one court and related offices. Overall, there appear to be mixed results. Even though the focus is on the victim, the process has been described as being time-consuming and inefficient and often not well-received by judges, prosecutors, and the existing system.[22]

---

17. Hora's Materials, *supra* note 7, *citing* Indigent Defense, Nov./Dec. 1997, at 8.

18. Justice Evelyn Lundberg Stratton, *Solutions for the Mentally Ill in the Criminal Justice System: A Symposium Introduction (National Symposium on Mental Illness and the Criminal Justice System)*, 32 Cap. U. L. Rev. 901 (2004). This entire symposium issue is devoted to articles on mental health courts.

19. Michael A. Town, *The Unified Family Court: Preventive, Therapeutic, and Restorative Justice for America's Families*, Nat'l Council Juvenile & Fam. Ct. Judges (Winter, 2002), at 14–17.

20. CCJ Resolution 22, COSCA Resolution 4, http://dcpi.ncjrs.org/pdf/Chief%20Justice%20 Resolution.doc (last visited July 8, 2010).

21. Randal B. Fritzler & Leonore M.J. Simon, *Creating a Domestic Violence Court: Combat in the Trenches*, 37 Ct. Rev. 28, 35–36 (2000) (discussing the creation of specialized domestic violence courts employing a therapeutic or restorative approach).

22. Betsy Tsai, *The Trend Toward Specialized Domestic Violence Courts: Improvements on an Effective Innovation*, 68 Fordham L. Rev. 1285 (2000).

Variety in Programs

This excerpt from the Bureau of Justice Assistance's Program Brief[23] highlights the great variance in these problem solving courts:

> ... specialized "problem solving courts" [have been] developed to address domestic violence, drug abuse, family matters, mental illness, quality-of-life crimes such as shoplifting and vandalism, and so forth.[1] Although subject matter jurisdiction varies across these problem solving courts, they all have service coordination as a core feature of their operation. Service coordination begins early in the process, often post-arrest, to determine eligibility for programs and the need for prompt, specialized services. Some problem solving courts are preadjudicatory and diversion oriented and others require a plea before a treatment plan is implemented. In either model, however, considerable service coordination has usually taken place by the time a treatment order is entered. Given their concentration on service coordination, these problem solving courts offer a starting point to explore promising court practices that integrate treatment services with judicial case processing to address the service needs of individuals in courts.
>
> This exploration was a focus of the Models of Effective Court-Based Service Delivery for Children and Their Families project. The project included field research in eight jurisdictions: Sacramento Superior and Municipal Courts in California; the Mental Health Court in Broward County, Florida; the Jefferson Family Court in Louisville, Kentucky; the Circuit Court (including its drug courts) in Kalamazoo, Michigan; the Youth Part of Manhattan's Criminal Court in New York County, New York; the Oregon Judicial Department and Integrated Family Courts in Deschutes and Jackson Counties; the Richland County Family Court in Columbia, South Carolina; and the King County Unified Family Court in Seattle, Washington. The field research was supplemented with a literature review and a telephone survey of 50 courts as a preliminary step to obtain basic information on court coordination of services.
>
> The information from the project's data collection efforts underscores that a single model of service coordination is inappropriate. Jurisdictions vary considerably in their local legal and service cultures and resources. What works for one jurisdiction may need significant modification to work in another. In recognition of this variation, the project focused not on specific models but on broader service coordination goals and strategies for achieving the goals. This approach allows each jurisdiction to assess its current service coordination needs and develop a strategy to address these needs given local jurisdiction culture and resources.

In their 2000 article, Thomas Barton and James Cooper of California Western School of Law[24] identified Navajo peacemaking circles and peer courts as similar to problem solving courts in that all three are examples of "horizontal justice." They say:

---

23. Bureau of Justice Assistance, Program Brief, *Strategies for Court Collaboration With Service Communities,* Nov. 2002, available at http://www.ncjrs.gov/html/bja/collaboration/bja.html (last visited July 11, 2010).

24. Thomas D. Barton & James M. Cooper, *Preventive Law and Creative Problem Solving: Multi-Dimensional Lawyering,* 14–19 (2000), available at http://www.preventivelawyer.org/content/pdfs/Multi_Dimensional_Lawyer.pdf (last visited April 12, 2011). Barton is the Louis & Hermione Brown Professor of Law, Director of the Louis M. Brown Program in Preventive Law, and Coordinator, National Center for Preventive Law. Cooper is the Assistant Dean for Mission Development, Center

The Navajo have, since time immemorial, used peacemaking as a means of re-solving disputes. The Navajo peacemaking program operates under the auspices of the Navajo Nation Supreme Court. Although most crimes are adjudicated in a West-ern style, some crimes are dealt with outside the Western accusatorial/blame mode.

In peacemaking, a thoughtful and attentive examination of each aspect of a given problem is provided to reach conclusions about how best to resolve the problem. The traditional concept of Navajo justice is based upon discussion, consensus, relative need, and healing.[a] The mechanism is horizontal to its core, with constituents participating in a circle and each having a right to speak their respective truths. There is no hierarchy, for no person is above another person. Navajo peacemaking pronounces no judgment or blame. Instead, it provides a framework of supportive accountability and connection. It can transform the participants involved and not just the defendant in a criminal case.

In the more vertical model of Western justice, authority is elevated to a clear de-cision maker: the judge or panel of judges, an umpire, an arbitrator. A horizontal jus-tice system, by contrast, is often portrayed as a circle. There is no judge to whom to appeal, nor is there a defendant below who is the subject of judgment. Each person on the line of a circle looks to the same center as the focus. The circle is symbolic, an unbroken celebration of unity, harmony and interconnectedness.[b]

Aboriginal cultures have dispute resolution mechanisms that are not forms of Alternative Dispute Resolution (ADR), but are "Original Dispute Resolution" (ODR). Long before the Europeans imposed their laws, there were alternative systems of problem solving and means by which a community's participants could plan for future generations. Peacemaking decentralizes power, encourages participation, and attempts to fashion solution systems that all the stakeholders can embrace. Those of us steeped in the vertical Western justice system of resolving disputes can learn much about procedures from these more organic forms of conflict management.

… Problem solving courts offer another example of how more horizontal jus-tice principles can be integrated into existing vertical judicial institutions. Drug treatment courts, for example, provide for close monitoring of and immediate response to behavior, and employ a multi-disciplinary approach to solving the problem of addiction through ongoing judicial intervention. By collaborating with community-based organizations, governmental agencies, and faith groups, the defendants enjoy an atmosphere of supportive accountability and an op-portunity for self-determination. Instead of separating constituencies, problem solving courts recognize the interconnectivity of social problems, criminal law and family dysfunction and bring together stakeholders to create solutions.

Given the increasing workload of the judiciary in the United States, it is not sur-prising that some judges' associations are increasingly supportive of more innova-tive means to deal with the pathologies of the defendants appearing before them.

. . . .

Youth Court is yet another example of a problem solving court that integrates horizontal justice principles in a preventive way. Youth Court provides nonviolent juvenile offenders an opportunity to avoid incarceration by committing to a re-habilitation program. In exchange for a guilty plea, the defendants avoid a per-

---

for Creative Problem Solving; Institute Professor; Director, Proyecto ACCESO; and Director, Chile Sum-mer Program.

manent criminal record. They must agree to have their sentences routed away from the more vertical Juvenile Court system and instead be determined by a jury of their peers—other teens. The experience is highly transformative—life-altering.

Youth Court sentencing is designed to demonstrate to the participants the interconnectivity in crime. The jury passes a sentence that includes two future jury participations (by the defendant) and a letter of apology to their victims. Other options for additional punishment and recourse are fashioned by the youth offender's peers. The defendants have two months to complete their respective sentences and are supervised by community members—parents, probation officers, law students and other volunteers. These stakeholders act as compliance monitors concerning the sentence. With such broadbased participation, Youth Court champions the value of volunteerism. Research shows that defendants are less likely to re-offend.

. . . .

Horizontal mechanisms bring together the various constituencies as stakeholders in solving a problem rather than to place blame. Often horizontal judicial mechanisms provide a forum for participants to be heard and empower them with a *voice*. These various horizontal processes are therapeutic in nature, and lead to an end of the problem, rather than result in cyclical pathological patterns. In the criminal law context, these programs are often referred to as "Restorative Justice," for they aim not simply to restore the community to its state prior to the crime, but also to restore the defendant to the community and within himself or herself.

Horizontal systems are more therapeutic, but often are also more successful in reducing crime. In seeking channels of resolution at the horizontal level, lawyers begin to recognize problems for their relational implications at many levels—the individual, institutional, corporate, regional and inter-Statal. The solutions become transformative and preventive. They look forward as well as backward.

Further, by diverting the process out of the regular criminal procedure and into an alternative regime, imaginative exercises in problem identification exercises are possible. By avoiding blame, accountability for the problem (and not merely for the effects of the problem) is recognized and behavior modification is supported.[25]

a. *See* Robert Yazzie, *Hozho Nahasdlii — We Are Now in Good Relations: Navajo Restorative Justice*, 9 St. Thomas L. Rev. 117, (1996).

b. *See* Robert Yazzie, *"Life Comes From It": Navajo Justice Concepts*, 24 N.M. L. Rev. 175 (1994).

Examples

Judge William Schma,[26] of Michigan's Ninth Judicial Circuit, provides two examples of the effectiveness of drug treatment courts and mental health courts in criminal cases involving drug addiction and mental illness, respectively:

---

25. *Id.* at 14–19.
26. Schma, *supra* note 9.

Mark, a drug addict, was arrested for selling crack cocaine. He was placed on lifetime probation but kept using. Besides facing 20 years in prison (at a cost of $20,000 to $25,000 per year), he was dying from kidney failure but could not stay clean long enough to undergo a transplant procedure. Despite these obstacles, Mark was enrolled in a drug court program. A team I supervised directed his recovery through regular court visits, treatment and case management. Now, for the first time in a life of substance abuse, Mark is clean and crime-free. And he is ready for his transplant.

. . . .

When Melvin came to court he was out of control. A paranoid schizophrenic on lifetime probation for delivery of cocaine, he had stopped taking his medication and had been arrested. As deputies led him out of the courtroom, he shouted to me, "You're a white-scum son of a bitch. You haven't heard the last of this." The exasperated probation agent was prepared to recommend prison. But when Melvin's attorney, family and probation agent agreed to cooperate, I delayed disposition of the violation. Melvin was released to the custody and supervision of family and the probation department. He resumed treatment, counseling and his medication, and he was placed on electronic monitoring. Today Melvin is stabilized and has a standing, informal visit with me every other Tuesday. The last time he brought along his toddler son and spoke enthusiastically of his hopes for the boy's future. When Melvin leaves, we shake hands.[27]

Practice Information

The best source of information on these therapeutic, problem solving courts is the website of the National Center for Court Innovation (http://www.courtinnovation.org) (last visited July 11, 2010).

One can view videos of drug court in action even on Youtube; two examples are athlete Matt Jones' initial appearance in drug court (http://www.youtube.com/watch?v =tgNhacoS1Xg&feature=related) (last visited July 11, 2010) and his successful graduation (www.youtube.com/watch?v=MToac6fkTGg) (last visited July 11, 2010).

Other illustrative videos include "Taking It to the Streets" (showing the San Diego "Stand Down" Homeless Court initiative),[28] the Santa Clara County Dependency Drug Treatment Court video,[29] and "Introducing Therapeutic Jurisprudence" (showing the mental health court in South Florida in session).[30]

---

27. *Id.*

28. The American Bar Association Commission on Homelessness and Poverty and The National Coalition For Homeless Veterans, *Homeless Court at Stand Down: A Collaborative Effort to Assist Homeless Veterans, Strengthen Communities and Maximize Court Resources,* http://www.abanet.org/homeless/ hcp_stand_down_guide.pdf (last visited July 11, 2010).

29. Superior Court of California/Packard Foundation, Legal Innovations: Dependency Drug Treatment Court, (Courter Films & Assoc. 2002), available at http://www.courterfilms.com/id2.html (last visited April 13, 2011) (showing Judge Edwards' court in action).

30. Mary Providence McGill, *Introducing TJ: Therapeutic Jurisprudence,* http://www.fanlight.com/ catalog/films/351_tj.php (last visited April 13, 2011) (showing Judge Ginger Lerner-Wren's court in action).

Resources

Peggy Fulton Hora, William G. Schma, & John T.A. Rosenthal, *Therapeutic Jurisprudence and the Drug Treatment Court Movement: Revolutionizing the Criminal Justice System's Response to Drug Abuse and Crime in America*, 74 Notre Dame L. Rev. 439 (1999).

Bruce J. Winick, *Therapeutic Jurisprudence and Problem Solving Courts*, 30 Fordham Urb. L.J. 1055, 1060 (2003).

Bruce J. Winick & David B. Wexler, Judging in a Therapeutic Key: Therapeutic Jurisprudence and the Courts (Carolina Academic Press, 2003).

Lisa Schreibersdorf, *A Public Defender in a Problem-Solving Court,* in Marjorie A. Silver, The Affective Assistance of Counsel 401 (Carolina Academic Press, 2007) (as Chapter 13).

Michael C. Dorf, *Drug Treatment Courts and Other Problem-Solving Institutions: An Idea Whose Time Is Coming,* Findlaw (Dec. 24, 2001) (available at http://writ.news.findlaw.com/dorf/20011224.html (last visited July 9, 2010)).

Barbara A. Babb, *Fashioning An Interdisciplinary Framework For Court Reform In Family Law: A Blueprint to Construct a Unified Family Court,* 71 S. Cal. L. Rev. 469 (1998).

Michael A. Town, *The Unified Family Court,* Nat'l Council Juvenile & Fam. Ct. Judges 14 (Winter 2002).

R. Boldt & J. Singer, *Juristocracy in the Trenches: Problem-Solving Judges and Therapeutic Jurisprudence in Drug Treatments Courts and Unified Family Courts.* 65(1) Maryland L. Rev. 82 (2006).

Cait Clarke & James Neuhard, *Making the Case: Therapeutic Jurisprudence and Problem Solving Practices Positively Impact Clients, Justice Systems, and the Communities They Serve,* 17 St. Thomas L. Rev. 781 (2005).

Pamela M. Casey & David B. Rottman, *Problem-Solving Courts: Models and Trends,* 26 Just. Sys. J. 35 (2005).

Websites

National Association of Drug Court Professionals: www.nadcp.org (last visited July 11, 2010).

National Center for State Courts: www.ncsconline.org/D_Research/ProblemSolving-Courts/Problem-SolvingCourts.html (last visited July 11, 2010).

Center for Court Innovation: www.courtinnovation.org (last visited July 8, 2011) and http://www.communityjustice.org (last visited July 8, 2011).

Judge Peggy Hora's site: http://www.judgehora.com/drugcourt.html (last visited July 11, 2010).

Rhode Island Judiciary: www.courts.state.ri.us/family/problem-solving.htm (last visited July 11, 2010).

Strategies for Court Collaboration with Service Communities: www.ncjrs.gov/html/bja/collaboration/bja.html (last visited July 11, 2010).

Article by Judge William Schma: http://aja.ncsc.dni.us/courtrv/cr37/cr37-1/cr9schma.pdf (last visited July 11, 2010).

COSCA/CCJ Joint Resolution: http://cosca.ncsc.dni.us/Resolutions/CourtAdmin/resolution problemsolvingcts.html (last visited July 11, 2010).

Coordination: Also read Silver (Chapter 13), King (Chapters 9–10 and 14), and Wright (p. 63–72).

Chapter Assignments

Three Integrative Cases (TJ, RJ, PSCs)

Case 15-A

The parents of a 17-year-old young man come to see you. Their son has been criminally charged with driving while intoxicated and resisting arrest. Apparently, he has been more and more depressed, alienated, and isolated since he broke his leg last fall and had to quit playing football in his senior year of high school. Last year, he was one of the better players on the high school football team and was really looking forward to a stellar last season this year. He got hurt in the first game of the season and will be unable to play for the entire school year. Having nothing in common with his old football buddies, he has spent more and more time around students who are known for drinking alcohol and getting into minor trouble at school (e.g., truancy, loitering, graffiti). Last Friday night, he got drunk all by himself, while his parents were out at a party, went out for a drive past his ex-girlfriend's house, missed a red light, and T-boned (hit) another driver at an intersection. When the police arrived, he was drunk, surly, uncooperative, and verbally insulting to the arresting officer. The person he hit was a 48-year-old convenience store clerk who was returning home to her family after finishing her shift. She has some injuries from the accident and her car was totaled. She is married, with two grown children, and takes care of her aging mother who is in poor health. Your clients (the parents) admit that they drink socially and that they have been busier this year than usual; both have professional careers and have been spending a lot of time working. They want you to handle the criminal charges against their son. How would you propose to handle this case?

Case 15-B

Your client is a twenty-year-old young man who has been arrested for burglary. He was caught inside a pharmacy after it had closed when he set off the alarm by breaking into the locked area where the controlled substances were kept. Apparently, he entered the store during normal operating hours but stayed inside the building until after everyone had left and the alarm had been set. Then, he broke into the locked area, setting off the alarm. When the police arrived, he willingly went with them. His story is that he was very tired when he entered the store. He went to the bathroom once inside, and fell asleep there. When he woke up, the store was closed and locked and he was inside. Because he could not get out, he panicked and intentionally broke into the drug cabinet in order to set off the alarm and get help to get out of the store. Another possibility is that he intentionally hid inside the store until it was closed and empty, he attempted to steal some drugs from the pharmacy, he was unable to get out of the store with the drugs, and so he gave himself up to the police when they arrived. He is currently enrolled in the local college. Both his parents are dead; he spent most of his childhood living with his aunt and older sister. He has not been in contact with his aunt or sister for about a year. He belongs to a fraternity at college but his fraternity brothers say they have not seen much of him in the last six months or so. He does not appear to have any close friends. He lives alone in a small apartment near campus. About seven months ago, his girlfriend broke up with him, leaving him broken-hearted. His grades in school are average. You believe that it is most likely that he is a drug user and drug dealer, albeit bizarre and inept in his methods of procuring drugs, and that he is a generally well-intentioned, good-hearted person who is for some reason going astray. He has no previous criminal record. The store wants to press charges against him. How do you propose to handle the case?

Case 15-C

Your client is a 26-year-old woman who was hired by a truck driving company to drive trucks cross-country. She has the appropriate professional licenses and is duly qualified to drive the trucks. She tells you that she was fired by the company because she is a "woman in a man's job" and she wants to sue the company for sex discrimination. When she initially comes to see you, she is belligerent, angry, and hostile towards the company. She insists that she was a model employee and that the company's behavior towards her was unfair and oppressive at all times. You file a lawsuit on her behalf against the company for sex discrimination. In the course of discovery, the company's attorneys depose your client. In this deposition, with you present, the company's attorneys confront your client with internal, company personnel memoranda indicating that your client had been caught drunk on the job twice, had been confronted, and had agreed to submit to whatever measures the company required of her in order to ensure that it didn't happen again. Your client had not told you of these two incidents and had, up til now, told you continually that her behavior on the job was exemplary, perfect. After the deposition is over, you talk with your client and she continues to admit that she did drink on the job and that she was still struggling with this problem. Her attitude is less belligerent, less accusatory, and less blaming than it was when you first met her. She also tells you, after the deposition, that last week she had a run-in with the local police. She got into a fight in a local bar and hit another patron. The police were called, they arrived, and they charged her with battery. How do you propose to handle the criminal charges against her?

The following are either full or summary analyses of these cases:

Case 15-A Analysis

This is a bare-bones, summary-type analysis. Applicable vectors: RJ, TJ, and DTC. Legal issues: Criminal charges relating to driving under the influence and resisting arrest. He is a juvenile. There may be civil liability also to the victim and it would involve the automobile insurance company as well, but the question is confined to the criminal charges. This is a criminal case; therefore, RJ is in order. Since this is a juvenile, it would be easy to do a family group conference or VOM or circle sentencing. DTC is also an option for nonviolent early offenders like this one if your jurisdiction's DTC allows alcohol abusers to be eligible. TJ also applies because there are things going wrong with the parents (too busy) that need intervention. The child is crying out for help or acting out because he has suffered a great loss or trauma and needs more support in order to handle it well; he does not need a criminal charge or record. He clearly needs the kind of support and intervention one gets in a DTC. However, if we can work out a restitution and rehabilitation program for him, with early intervention into his troubled life, then we can skip DTC altogether. TJ would also encourage personal responsibility-taking by this juvenile; his ability to empathize with the victim and her family would be very helpful to his development, maturity, and later life success potential.

Case 15-B Analysis

This is a much more full analysis. Vector(s): RJ, TJ, DTCs, CPS. These vectors would be chosen because this is a criminal case with some mental health or drug addiction issues. RJ is appropriate in criminal cases; TJ is appropriate when there are addictions or mental health issues; DTCs are appropriate also when there are minor crimes with underlying addiction issues.

(a) Legal issues:	(b) Nonlegal issues:	(c) Intersections:
Burglary and attempt to steal controlled substances, (criminal charges).	Possible drug abuse and addiction. Isolation socially.	Criminal disposition could take into account his social and psychological needs. This is an opportunity to improve his life.
No excuse or alibi. Record of drug abuse in past? But no criminal record; first time offender. Can ask for leniency.	Loss, depression, distraught over breakup. Bizarre behavior. Little family or friend support, but aunt, sister, and fraternity brothers exist and may be willing to help/support. First time offender. Young age, rehabilitatable. Victimless crime?	Criminal charges could be a wakeup call. Can ask for reduced sentence conditional on rehabilitation efforts, even without a DTC, see Chapters 5–8. Consider whether store owner would be motivated for VOM or disinterested.

Comprehensive law skills employed would include: empathy, open-ended questions, the ability to listen and find out why this person committed this crime, the ability to hear the implicit messages within the explicit explanation, the ability perhaps to refer the client for drug treatment and to work with a mental health professional regarding his or her recommendations for this client, and the ability to refer the client to a DTC.

Legal issues: This is a criminal case involving burglary and an attempt to steal controlled substances. Your client has a rather flimsy excuse or explanation for his behavior and if he has any drug abuse in his past, his explanation will not be credible and he will be convicted. However, because this case presents issues of mental illness, specifically, drug abuse and/or dependence, I would propose to use a combination of RJ and TJ, or a DTC, with this client. Specifically, I would look towards an RJ process of VOM or FGC (with what little family (aunt, sister) and friends he has, his fraternity brothers, him, his attorney, the prosecutor, the store's manager, store owner, etc. participating), with the goal being the rehabilitation of the client/offender and possibly also some restitution being made to the store. I would allow each person in the process an uninterrupted time to speak and include them in the decisionmaking process as to the "sentence" to be carried out by the client. Each support person would speak about the client, their experience of him, and his potential. The store people would speak about the effect of the crime on them, to shift the shame of the crime from the victim to the offender, create therapeutic shame in the offender, and thereby encourage his ability to take accountability for the crime.

This is a minor offense and his first; I would attempt to use an RJ process as a diversion from regular criminal court in an attempt to keep his record clean (e.g., withhold adjudication pending his satisfactory completion of the group's sentence). Thus, the process would be pre-plea, pre-sentencing, pre-adjudication, in the ideal setting. If he didn't comply with the "sentence" developed by the group, then a court could enforce it or he could be shunted into the traditional criminal justice system for regular adjudication. This process depends on his involvement and buy-in into the restitution/rehab/reparations plan.

The goals of the process are to create reintegrative shame in the offender designed to motivate him to change and perhaps understanding on the part of the victims. His restitutionary efforts and apology by him and forgiveness by victims, if given, would be designed to integrate him back into the community, which would be particularly appropriate given his social isolation and increasingly isolated and bizarre lifestyle.

The advantage of this process over traditional criminal court is that his underlying problem, drug abuse, and the problem underneath that (isolation, depression?) can be treated and resolved, thus greatly reducing his chances of recidivating. The traditional approach is likely to ignore his drug problem entirely, thus leading to a cycle of recidivism and progressively worsening addiction.

Alternatively, you could use straight DTC participation. DTCs might be more appropriate given that the crime victims might not be interested in participating in an RJ process. DTCs are not appropriate, though, unless he has a drug addiction, so be careful about relying on them when they aren't available. Finally, you can suggest an RJ process even if the victims are not willing to participate. Then, it would be more like an FGC, with the offender, his support people, and the legal personnel involved.

Case 15-C Analysis

In this case, TJ and DTC would be most appropriate. Because of the psychological issues (see chart below), TJ is appropriate. DTC would be appropriate if she is eligible (alcohol as her main drug, rather than a drug, might be an obstacle—it depends on your jurisdiction.)

(a) Legal issues:	(b) Psycholegal issues:	(c) Intersections:
Criminal charges from drinking and fighting. Ethics: you have the right to withdraw from representation because she lied to you and misrepresented facts.	Client is belligerent, angry, in anger phase of loss process over loss of job, or in denial about her alcohol problems. Client is less belligerent once faced with her dishonesty. Client needs a new job. Possible alcohol abuse problem; client needs rehab/treatment. Client was dishonest with you about being a model employee. Client deals with problems by denial, belligerence, fighting, alcohol abuse, and anger. Anger management? Maybe the company's story is accurate and your client is lying? Your client appears to have a problem with honesty, a potential alcohol abuse or dependency problem, and a problem with anger and with authority figures. All of these problems are likely to continue to cause her problems in the future with law enforcement and with her employability, if not with her social and familial life as well. May have a problem with employment.	Current charges may be an indication of a life long pattern of anger and alcohol problems in this person's life. Current charges are an opportunity for her to have a wake-up call and perhaps turn life around and resolve these issues, now. Aggressively defending the charges may be counter-therapeutic if it adds to her denial that she has any problems. Withdrawing from the representation may also be countertherapeutic, since you are uniquely poised to have leverage over this client to encourage her to seek help and to become more functional. She may slip through the cracks if you withdraw from representation (until her next run in with an authority.)

Comprehensive lawyer skills useful in this case include: referral to a mental health or drug rehabilitation counselor or assessor who can help with educating the client as to the extent of her problems; and creating a good, strong lawyer-client relationship through basic and advanced empathy and perhaps self-disclosure, because the client will be challenged to change, if you continue the representation, by her relationship with you as the lawyer.

I would seek to use TJ in a therapeutic fashion in order to use this legal opportunity to leverage the client into some form of evaluation of her psychological status as well as treatment designed to improve her functioning (for example, if indeed she has an alcohol dependence problem, solving that and rehabilitating her at the same time as resolving this legal problem would be a potential goal, if she agreed). Some obstacles are: that she may very well resist any kind of therapeutic goal, and deny that she has any problems. Using the "binder" approach described in Chapter 7 might be useful, to ask the court for deferred and then reduced sentencing.

The traditional legal system would assist her in this denial, since it encourages black-and-white thinking and unilateral imposition of blame. However, a TJ approach to her situation would allow her to take responsibility for her aggression.

In addition, if the nature of her underlying problem comes to light and she rehabilitates, she is in a much better position to ask for her job back or to obtain similar employment with another company. This problem provides a rare and obvious opportunity for the lawyer to intervene in a client's life in a way that could ultimately improve her life, wellbeing, and functioning, by helping her identify her problems, become motivated to get help, and ultimately resolve her internal problems as part of this legal process.

A CPS analysis may also be useful. Possible goals of the legal representation are: she wants her job back, the company wants an employee who is sober on the job, she wants to stop having alcohol-related difficulties at work and in the world, the community wants her to not assault other people, the bar probably wants her not to return (or to behave differently if she does return), she wants to continue driving trucks even if for another company. The problem is multiple and complex. One resource is that she has been caught and confronted and now her attitude is more conciliatory and less blaming. She may be becoming ready to admit she has a problem. (You may finish this, using the SOLVE process.)

In a DTC, adjudication of her criminal charges would typically be withheld, pending her successful completion of a drug rehabilitation program. She would undergo frequent (weekly, then bi-monthly, etc.) court appearances, random urine screens, and graduated sanctions for noncompliance. Ultimately, if she was noncompliant, she would be removed from the DTC and her case sent back to regular criminal court for traditional adjudication and sentencing. Successful graduation, however, would result in rehabilitation and the removal of the criminal charges against her. The DTC would assist her progress through the program via an interdisciplinary team, consisting of the DTC judge, lawyers, case managers, therapists, and others who assess her progress in the program. The great advantage is that she would not add to her criminal record and might achieve lasting rehabilitation and recovery from her mental health challenges.

Chapter 16

Capstone Chapter — Practicing Law Comprehensively

Integrating the Approaches

Practicing law comprehensively involves being facile with applying all of the vectors of the comprehensive law movement, in additional to using traditional approaches, when appropriate. One must also be able to choose when to use which vector or vectors, and how to apply them, in each case or matter. A few analogies that have been useful in learning to integrate all the vectors into the practice of law are the "toolkit" analogy, the "smorgasbord" concept, and the "soup" analogy. These are described below. Then, a template for analyzing each legal matter from a comprehensive approach is presented.[1]

The Toolkit

As mentioned in the Introduction, the vectors might be thought of as new tools to add to the lawyer's toolkit of lawyering skills and competencies. Then, when working with a particular client or matter, the lawyer would select which tools to use, as appropriate. The comprehensive law approaches can thus be of great value to the attorney seeking to add to his or her toolkit of skills, increase his or her marketability in the legal profession, and be able to offer something truly unique and "value-added" to his future clients. It has been said in the alternative dispute resolution field, "If all you have is a hammer, everything looks like a nail," meaning, if litigation is your only dispute resolution mechanism, every client's case appears to require the filing of a lawsuit. Lawyers now, however, have other options, such as mediation and other forms of alternative dispute resolution, so a lawsuit might not always be warranted. Comprehensive law expands this even further; lawyers now have many other options, such as TJ/PL approaches, holistic or CPS approaches, collaborative law, transformative mediation, restorative justice processes, and specialized problem solving courts. As these disciplines develop and grow, all attorneys may eventually need to be well-versed in their use and execution.

---

1. This Chapter is adapted and includes material from the author's manuscript of *The Future of the Legal Profession*, accepted for publication in Monash University Law Review (in press); Susan Daicoff, *Growing Pains: The Integration vs. Specialization Question For Therapeutic Jurisprudence and Other Comprehensive Law Approaches*, © Professor Susan Daicoff, reprinted with permission, originally published with Thomas Jefferson Law Review, available at 30 T. Jefferson L. Rev. 551 (2008); and Susan Daicoff, *Law as a Healing Profession: The "Comprehensive Law Movement,"* 6 Pepperdine Disp. Resol. J. 1 (2006).

The Smorgasbord

Review the "organizational chart" of the comprehensive law movement presented in Chapter 3 (reproduced below as Figure 1). In the past, lawyers and judges had only a traditional, win/lose, binary "lens" through which to view legal matters, leading only to traditional negotiation and settlement or litigation. Now, they have a panoply of "lenses" through which to view legal matters, leading to a "smorgasbord" of processes by which to resolve the matter or dispute. The lawyer can choose from among these lenses and processes, when dealing with a particular matter. For example, the lawyer might view a matter through a therapeutic lens, a preventive lens, a creative problem solving lens, a religious or spiritual lens, or with a view towards maximizing procedural justice for the parties. Once the lens has been selected (for example, therapeutic), the lawyer can then evaluate the various available processes of dispute resolution to determine which process would be most therapeutic.

"Triage," or the ability to determine which process and lens is the most appropriate for which matter, is therefore a competence that the comprehensive lawyer also must develop. See Figure 1, below:

Figure 1. "Organizational Chart" of the Movement

Lenses:	Traditional/Adversarial (win/lose—binary)		Therapeutic Jurisprudence	Holistic Justice
		Preventive Law		Religious/Spiritual
	Creative Problem Solving			Procedural Justice
Processes:	Negotiation/Settlement		Problem Solving Courts	Collaborative Law
		Evaluative Mediation		Restorative Justice
	Arbitration		Facilitative Mediation	TJ/PL
	Litigation & other judicial processes		Transformative Mediation	Preventive Law

The Soup Analogy

Purists would disagree,[2] so this next idea may be controversial, but it has been useful in teaching comprehensive law approaches to those who are reluctant to apply all of the concepts and processes in the comprehensive law movement. If one thinks of practicing

---

2. For example, I believe transformative mediator R. Baruch Bush would urge that TM be used only in its pure form and would not endorse the inclusion of TM in this "soup" approach (personal communication with Professor R. Baruch Bush, May, 2001, Cincinnati, Ohio).

or adjudicating law as if it is like "making soup," then some of the vectors might be thought of as pungent ingredients such as salt, onions, garlic, or pepper. A soup made entirely of one of these, salt, for example, might be unpalatable, but the addition of salt to a particular soup makes an enormous difference in the quality of the outcome (the soup). The soup really needs the ingredient to be "good" and it is not the same without it. For example, it is entirely possible to resolve a personal injury case without considering TJ/PL considerations (such as the relationships involved) and without an apology from the defendant (an RJ concept), thus creating a bland but edible soup. But, it is likely that the resolution of the case will be just that much better if those ideas are mixed into the lawyer's otherwise traditional approach to the case (resulting in a much better tasting soup—ensuring it will be eaten and so fulfill its purpose!). Some lawyers may never be willing to use transformative mediation in its pure form, for example, but they might see the utility of at least recognizing and providing opportunities for parties to give "recognition" to each other and to experience their own "empowerment" (as those concepts are defined by TM), in the resolution of a legal dispute.

The "Pink Sheet"

In 2007, when these ideas were taught as part of a program of the Harvard Negotiation Insight Initiative, a program of the Harvard Program on Negotiation, sponsored in part by Harvard Law School, the program faculty[3] developed a one-page "checksheet" to use when attempting to assess and evaluate a case by reference to the vectors of the comprehensive law movement. Because it was initially reproduced on pink paper, it has come to be known as the "HNII Pink Sheet." It is reproduced below, for your use in practicing law comprehensively:

Area of Inquiry	Questions To Ask Yourself:	Notes:
Intrapersonal Skills/Self:		
1. Selfawareness/ Countertransference	Visceral reactions? Triggers? Hot buttons? Reactivity? Blocks?	
2. Intrinsic Values	How does this case fit with your intrinsic values? Thinking/Feeling or Care/Justice? Can you express any in this representation?	
3. Sacred Values*	Love, Loyalty, Faith, Service, Integrity* ... which of these are involved for you?	
4. Spiritual Wisdom	Pray? Meditate? Connect? What wisdom are you given?	
5. Professional Ethical Role	Will you choose: Zealous advocate? Wise counselor? Moral lawyer? Caring lawyer?	

---

3. The program faculty were Boston collaborative lawyer, mediator, and arbitrator David Hoffman (founder of an innovative multidisciplinary collaborative law firm in Boston, see http://www.boston lawcollaborative.com/blc/people/attorneys/david-hoffman.html (last visited April 13, 2011)), former Northeastern University School of Law dean David Hall (now President of the University of the Virgin Islands), and the author.

Interpersonal Skills/ Lenses/Theories:		
6. Social science/ psychology (Therapeutic Jurisprudence)	Denial/Anger/Bargaining/Depression/ Acceptance? Family dynamics? Psychological needs of the client? Psycholegal soft spots?	
7. Procedural Justice	Voice? Participation? Dignity/respect/trust?	
8. Preventive Law	Fast forward? Rewind? Checkup? Soft spots?	
9. Holistic Justice	Apology? Moral or spiritual values? Transformative moment?	
10. Creative Problem Solving	Make problem bigger or smaller? Creative solutions? Brainstorm? Extralegal issues?	
11. Traditional Lawyering	Rights? Rule of law? Success in court?	
Dispute Resolution Skills/Processes:		
12. Transformative Mediation	Foster moral growth via empowerment and/or recognition?	
13. Collaborative Law	Family law (or civil) case? Appropriate?	
14. Restorative Justice	Criminal setting? Need for reintegrative shame, apology, forgiveness, & restitution? Useful to have a victim/offender mediation or circle process? Reconciliation, harmony?	
15. Problem Solving Courts	Is there an alternative court available (MHCt, UFCt, DVCt, DTCt)?	
16. Mediation (all forms)	Facilitative, evaluative, other forms?	
17. Traditional Nego- tiation/Settlement	When is this the best approach? Advantages to using this?	
18. Arbitration	When is this the best approach? Advantages to using this?	
19. Private Judge	Perhaps at impasse ... ?	
20. Litigation	When "indicated," if other is intractable?	

* These "sacred values" come from David Hall's excellent book, Sacred Rivers: Revitalizing the Spirituality of the Legal Profession.[4]

Return to the Paula/Castaway case presented in Chapter 7. Applying *all* of the vectors and wisdom of the comprehensive law movement to this case might yield the following analysis. Note how each lens, process, vector, or area of inquiry yields yet another layer of complexity and depth to the analysis:

---

4. DAVID HALL, THE SPIRITUAL REVITALIZATION OF THE LEGAL PROFESSION (2005).

Area of Inquiry	Questions To Ask Yourself:	Notes:
Intrapersonal work/ Self:		
1. Selfawareness/ Countertransference	Visceral reactions? Triggers? Hot buttons? Reactivity? Blocks?	Instant dislike of client, blame, or perhaps sympathy
2. Intrinsic Values	How does this case fit with your intrinsic values? Can you express any in this representation? T/F or C/J?	If you want to change people for the good, here is one with potential! Or, 50/50 blame?
3. Sacred Values	Love, Loyalty, Faith, Service, Integrity, ... which of these are involved for you?	Love? Of both sides?
4. Spiritual Wisdom	Pray? Meditate? Connect? What wisdom are you given?	Both parties appear to be at fault
5. Professional Ethical Role	Will you choose: Zealous advocate? Wise counselor? Moral lawyer? Lawyering with an ethic of care?	Does your choice here dictate your process below?
Interpersonal work/ Lenses/Theory:		
6. Social science/ psychology (Therapeutic Jurisprudence)	Denial, anger, bargaining, depression, acceptance? Family systems theory? Psychological needs of the client? Psycholegal soft spots?	Refer to a mental health therapist? This client needs to address her pattern of behavior, as does employer, old wounds may motivate behavior
7. Procedural Justice	Voice? Participation? Dignity/respect/trust?	Client may need voice, apology
8. Preventive Law	Fast forward? Rewind? Checkup? Soft spots?	Certainly change employer's policies! Implement behavior, sensitivity training
9. Holistic Justice	Apology? Moral or spiritual values? Transformative moment?	Resolving this case can be a transformative moment for both
10. Creative Problem Solving	Make problem bigger or smaller? SOLVE analysis? Brainstorm? Extralegal issues?	Does she really need more training rather than old job back?
11. Traditional Lawyering	Rights? Rule of law? Success in court?	Uncertain outcome but good enough for bringing suit and settling for some compensation
DR/Processes/Skills:		
12. Transformative Mediation	Need for moral growth via empowerment and/or recognition? Utilize TM skills in mediation?	Our client could really use empowerment, both could give recognition to the other
13. Collaborative Law	Family law (or civil) case?	Possible use? Advantages? Vo-rehab expert could provide reality checks for both.
14. Restorative Justice	Criminal setting? Need for reintegrative shame, apology, forgiveness, & restitution? Useful to have a victim/offender mediation or circle process?	Not criminal, so n/a but for the concept of apology & forgiveness and reintegration back into workplace
15. Problem Solving Courts	Is there an alternative court available (MHCt, UFCt, DVCt, DTCt)?	Not in this vignette—N/A
16. Mediation (all forms)	Facilitative, evaluative, other forms?	Advantages to using these?

17. Traditional Nego-tiation/Settlement	When is this the best approach? Advantages to using this?	(See 20, below.)
18. Arbitration	When is this the best approach? Advantages to using this?	
19. Private Judge	Perhaps at impasse … ?	
20. Litigation	When "indicated," if other is intractable?	Useful for wakeup call for employer? Useful if employer won't collaborate.

Using this checksheet, the lawyer can be sure that he or she is considering all of the lenses and processes of the comprehensive law movement, in approaching this case. The lawyer can then integrate all of these insights, ideas, and concerns into his or her approach to representing Paula in her complaint against Castaway.

Concluding Thoughts

Despite the comprehensive law movement's many successes, there are nevertheless challenges ahead. The primary challenges relate to assisting lawyers, mediators, and judges in retooling themselves to, and law students to, acquire the necessary skills for minimal levels of competence in practicing law comprehensively.

The ethics code and substantive law may also need to continue to be revised to accommodate comprehensive law approaches. Lawyers' fears about the comprehensive law movement and reluctance to employ its disciplines may need to continue to be addressed.

Integration — Convergence

One of the challenges facing the movement appears to have been resolved. This is the question whether comprehensive law approaches will exist alongside adversarial approaches or whether they will be integrated with each other. Recent authors have noted that non-adversarial justice is part of a continuum which includes adversarial justice[5] and that a "convergence" of nonadversarial approaches with adversarial approaches is occurring.[6] It is clear that what MacFarlane calls convergence,[7] here referred to as integration, is happening—that the comprehensive law movement simply adds to the lawyer's, mediator's, and judge's toolkit rather than entirely replacing the traditional adversarial systems.

Training in Comprehensive Law Skills

Next steps include training legal personnel with the required skills to practice comprehensive law well. These break down into four or so categories, as follows:

---

5. MICHAEL KING, ARIE FRIEBERG, BECKY BATAGOL, & ROSS HYAMS, NON-ADVERSARIAL JUSTICE (The Federation Press, 2009).
6. JULIE MACFARLANE, THE NEW LAWYER: HOW SETTLEMENT IS TRANSFORMING THE PRACTICE OF LAW (UBC Press, 2008).
7. *Id.*

Comprehensive Intrapersonal Skills

- Countertransference
- Boundary management
- Anger management
- Selfawareness and self-knowledge
- Reflection, mindfulness
- Paternalism and coercion checks
- Appropriate self-disclosure

Comprehensive Interpersonal Skills

- Listening
- Empathy (basic and advanced)
- Apology, forgiveness, reconciliation
- Social science knowledge (e.g., procedural justice)
- Interdisciplinary collaboration
- Rewind/fast forward
- Psycholegal soft spot identification
- Triage of cases
- Leadership
- Teambuilding
- Conflict resolution
- Problem solving

Comprehensive Dispute Resolution Skills

- Collaborative law, collaborative divorce
- Transformative mediation
- Restorative justice (circle process, VOM, FGC, etc.)
- Problem solving courts (DTCs, UFCs, etc.)

Comprehensive Judging Skills

- Triage of cases
- Interdisciplinary competence
- Collaboration
- "Tough love"

The Future

The legal profession is on the brink of wide acceptance of the importance and validity of nonadversarial approaches alongside and with traditional adversarial systems. King et al.'s idea of a "justice system," where courts are only one part of that overall system, along with many other structures and resources, makes sense.[8]

---

8. MICHAEL KING, ARIE FRIEBERG, BECKY BATAGOL, & ROSS HYAMS, NON-ADVERSARIAL JUSTICE (The Federation Press, 2009).

What is required now is more research and data on what works and how it works and the development of excellent training materials to train old and new legal personnel in how to practice, adjudicate, and mediate comprehensively—meaning, being equally proficient at adversarial and nonadversarial approaches. Law schools need to develop courses and clinics in these approaches, to balance out their usual heavy emphasis on traditional law and adversarialism.[9]

Perhaps most exciting, however, are two recent developments that have the potential to thrust the comprehensive law movement into the forefront—the current economic crisis and the rise of the Millennial generation. The economic crisis has put such intense pressure on the legal profession that it is now highly motivated to change—to find a "sustainable" form of lawyering, adjudicating, and resolving legal disputes. The Millennial generation's preference for innovation, collaboration, technology, and sustainability is also likely to propel change in the legal profession.[10] These two world events and their consequences have the potential to sound the death knell for the primacy of the adversarial system and herald the remake of the legal profession in a comprehensive way, with nonadversarial and adversarial approaches coexisting along a continuum, as equals.

Chapter Assignments

Exercise 16-1—Final Integration Cases

It is time to "put it all together," meaning develop an approach to lawyering and justice that integrates traditional law and substantive legal doctrine with the approaches of the comprehensive law movement. The cases provided in the Chapter Assignments for Chapters 8, 10, 12, 13, 14, and 15 are all useful examples for making this integration. The three cases provided in this Chapter do not neatly fit into any particular area, but can also be useful in making this integration. The final case (16-C) is particularly relevant when preparing to practice law comprehensively in complex, multi-faceted cases.[11]

The "Pink Sheet" in this Chapter can be useful when analyzing these cases; in addition, the following template may be useful when organizing your analysis:

For each case, identify:

---

9. For example, at Florida Coastal School of Law in 2010, there were approximately 30–35 trial-related courses and 5–7 alternative dispute resolution courses.

10. Howe & Strauss, Generations: The History of America's Future, 1584 to 2069 (1991); Howe & Strauss, Millennials Rising: The Next Great Generation (2000) (both books defining and establishing the existence of this generation, within generational theory). *See* Susan K. McClellan, *Externships for Millennial Generation Law Students: Bridging the Generation Gap*, 15 Clinical L. Rev. 255 (2009); Melissa H. Weresh, *I'll Start Walking Your Way, You Start Walking Mine: Sociological Perspectives on Professional Identity Development and Influence of Generational Differences*, 61 S. C. L. Rev. 337 (2009); and Melody Finnemore, *Meet the Millennials: Young Attorneys Prompt Need for Firms to Explore New Ways of Doing Business*, 66-Nov. Or. St. B. Bull. 9 (2005) (all three describing the characteristics, preferences, and needs of Millennials in the legal profession).

11. They are also sample exam questions that can be used to prepare for an examination in a comprehensive law course.

1. The vector or vectors to be used (do not attempt to apply all of the vectors, only those that are most appropriate, as lenses and/or as processes).

2. Why you chose that vector or those vectors; why they will work best in this case.

3. A brief description of the vector (philosophy and process).

4. Your case analysis, meaning the: (a) legal problems; (b) psychological and other non-legal problems; and (c) their intersections, psycholegal soft spots (see Chapter 7), or psycholegal opportunity spots.

5. The comprehensive lawyer skills you need to use in the case (interviewing, counseling, and negotiating skills discussed in Chapters 4 and 11).

6. The processes, procedures, and legal and extralegal moves you will utilize in resolving the legal matter. This means applying the chosen vector or vectors to the case, planning what you would do as an attorney, identifying what processes would be involved, and describing how those processes work.

7. The goals or outcomes you would hope for.

8. The advantages and disadvantages of your comprehensive approach as compared to a more traditional approach to this case.

Case 16-A

The father of a 20-year-old young woman comes to see you. His daughter has anorexia (the starvation eating disorder) and bulimia (the binge and purge eating disorder). She has lost over 20 pounds in the last six months, is now emaciated, weighs 79 pounds (assume this fact is true), is 5 feet 7 inches tall, was laid off from her job three months ago and has not sought employment since, and spends most of her time bingeing, purging, and exercising to maintain her abnormally low weight. She has become more and more isolated, with few friends or relationships. She lives alone in a studio apartment and sees her family only when they call or visit her. Her father wants to force his adult daughter into inpatient treatment for eating disorders. He explains that she has been hospitalized twice before, for 28 days each time, for eating disorders (once at age 16 and once at age 18). These treatment efforts were unsuccessful in the long run, although she did temporarily gain weight and develop some living skills each time. His daughter voluntarily entered inpatient treatment each of these two earlier times; this time she is unwilling to go, saying "what's the point?" The family has attempted to persuade her, with no success. She has an older brother whom she idolizes, her mother and she are somewhat estranged (due to conflict over the fact that her mother wants her to gain weight and she does not want to), and she was on the swim team in high school and maintained a good relationship with her swim coach. The law of the state in which you practice allows family members to initiate proceedings to involuntarily (i.e., against the individual's will) civilly commit individuals to inpatient or outpatient mental health treatment if the individual is "in imminent danger of harm to self or another person." The caselaw in your state has held that a person with an eating disorder can qualify for involuntary civil commitment under this statute, if their disorder has put them in danger of electrolyte imbalance (which can lead to death) or death by starvation. Her father also explains that his daughter moved out of the family home a year ago because she felt stifled at home. He and she both agree that she needs to develop more autonomy and independence. According to him, she feels like her family treats her like a child and never lets her make any decisions for herself. He also says that at the same time, she is overly dependent on him and constantly leans on him to bail her out of any difficulties, financial or otherwise, that she runs into. He would like to see her "grow up" and take responsibility for her life, but presently he is very worried about her health and feels immediate action is required. Her mother did not come to this initial client interview because she was too busy at her job. However, he confides to you that his wife is "fed up with her [the daughter's] immature behavior" and is secretly resentful of their daughter. How do you propose to handle this case?

Case 16-A Analysis

1. <u>Possible Vectors:</u> TJ, PL, TJ/PL, PJ, & CPS

2. <u>Reasons Chosen:</u> I would choose therapeutic jurisprudence for this case mostly because the daughter clearly has a mental disorder, thus psychology should be taken into account when solving this legal problem. Procedural justice also applies here since she needs a voice and participation in the matter and the decision. PL applies since her condition is chronic and longstanding and she is likely to relapse and be in this predicament again, without prevention. CPS is relevant because the problem is complex, the whole family is involved, and she has a number of extralegal needs to be considered, so the multiplicity of the problem presented suggests a CPS approach.

3. <u>Brief Definitions:</u> TJ looks at the consequences, therapeutic or counter therapeutic, of laws, legal procedures, and legal actors and reforms on the individuals involved. It does not trump legal rights, but where possible it attempts to apply and enact the law in ways that are most therapeutic for all involved. PL seeks to avoid lawsuits and proactively prevent litigation, by engaging the attorney and client in various preventive moves, such as legal audits and check-ups. It uses the rewind and fast forward techniques to assess risk of (and prevent) future litigation. The integration of TJ and PL allows for identification of "psycholegal soft spots," or areas in a legal matter where the law and psychology intersect and provide an opportunity for creative lawyering for optimal outcomes. PJ uses social science findings to enhance parties' participation in and satisfaction with legal processes, as voice, participation, and respect can be more influential to litigants' satisfaction than win/lose outcomes. CPS is devoted to "out-of-the-box," creative solutions to legal problems, realizing that problems are often mismatches of needs with the environment and that there are many ways to approach and solve legal problems.

4.   <u>Case Analysis (with Psycholegal Soft Spots):</u>

(a) Legal issues:	(b) Extralegal issues:	(c) Intersections:
Civil commitment; involuntary nature requires fulfillment of statutory requirements (danger to self or others). Not a criminal case; no tort or contract involved. Legal soft spot is whether or not her condition is severe enough that she will qualify for involuntary civil commitment.	The daughter has a mental disorder (anorexia/bulimia). The daughter feels silenced or disempowered or infantilized by the parents. The entire family is involved. She is estranged from her parents. She is no longer a minor; can make her own decisions. She needs a job, place to live, and social support. She has good relationships with her older brother and former swim coach. Mother may be uncooperative. This is the third time she has needed in-patient help. She may not trust you as a lawyer and possible authority figure. Assess how imminent any health crisis may be with her; need medical/psychological evaluation or team?	The therapeutic and nontherapeutic value of committing her should be taken into account (TJ). The daughter needs a voice and some power in the decisionmaking process (PJ). The decisional process might work best if it involves the entire family somehow. Another psycholegal soft spot is that if she is involuntarily committed against her will she may become even more estranged from her family unless she responds well to family counseling once committed so this would be considered. This is the third time so she is unlikely to go voluntarily (TJ/PL, CPS).

5.   <u>Skills:</u> family conferencing, empathy to make the daughter more at ease if you have a meeting with her and the father or a family conference. Ceding power in a group or individual setting with the daughter to increase her sense of autonomy and choice. Use Wexler/Meichenbaum & Turk's social science research on health care compliance to craft a process for designing a plan of action that she will "buy in to," using her participation, public commitment, etc. to foster buy-in.

6.   <u>Comprehensive Law Moves:</u> A family conference designed to problem solve and involve the whole family in the decisionmaking might be helpful. The goal would clearly be to convince her to go to inpatient treatment voluntarily. We would look at what was best for the parents (hospitalize her) but also whether that would be best for her overall mental health. It appears that she is dependent on her folks and needs to grow up, so I'd encourage her to have as much autonomy over the decision as possible. This will foster her sense of self and help her to grow. The family would clearly benefit from some sort of family counseling since there is an opening rift between mother and daughter. The mother needs to be brought in and involved. The family members all need time to vent, in the conference. However, ultimately, I would not allow the group to make the decision as to what to do with her if she does not willingly agree to treatment. If her condition is so severe and she is in deep denial, I would assist the father to civilly commit her as soon as possible and talk later, since her health is most important and is in danger. Perhaps there are some preventive things that can be done upon her exit from the hospital. You could have her make out a will to help convince her that she is killing herself. Note that in general, though, the TJ aspects dictate that you not simply proceed forward with involuntary civil commitment without an additional process or move, because (1) it might fail; (2) it may not afford

her the autonomy and independence she wants and may need; and (3) it does not take into account her relapsing/recidivating situation (her third time around).

7. <u>Goals:</u> The hoped-for outcome is that the daughter would enter and successfully complete mental health treatment for her eating disorder and not relapse, in the future. We would hope that she would be empowered by this process and not further driven into an infantile, dependent mode of relating to the world. We would hope that the family relationships would be preserved and that the family (including her) could come to consensus on what is needed and should be done, next, without a formal, legal compulsory process.

8. <u>Compare to Traditional Approaches:</u> A traditional approach may well simply carry out the father's wishes and proceed forward with involuntary civil commitment proceeding involving the adult daughter, without further discussion among the family members. It would ignore, perhaps, the familial relationships involved and the daughter's need for autonomy, as they are not necessarily relevant to the legal problem presented. If the commitment proceeding failed, the familial relationships and the daughter's mental health would likely suffer. If it was successful, the daughter might still resent her father's legal actions.

Case 16-B

A family comes to you for help with the father's brother, who is a 43-year-old single person living alone. The brother has been diagnosed with paranoid schizophrenia since he was 18 years old. He lived with their mother in New York City until she died three years ago. Upon her death, he moved to the city in Florida where his brother and his family live. Since her death, he has relied on the family for social and emotional support, although he has his own small apartment. The brother has been seeing an outpatient therapist and psychiatrist throughout most of his life and is currently receiving and taking psychotropic medication for his mental disorder. However, lately, the brother has been getting more and more agitated, suspicious, angry, and hostile. He has come to believe that his brother (the father in the family that came to see you) is mishandling a trust fund of money that their mother set up for him to take care of him after her death. He also believes that his brother and brother's family are secretly planning to commit him to an inpatient psychiatric institution, which he does not want. The father is worried that his brother may become violent, and is worried about the safety of himself, his wife, and their two teenaged children. The father does not have access to his brother's therapy and treatment records, due to therapist/client confidentiality, so he cannot determine whether his brother is continuing to take his medication or has stopped. He tells you that his brother is vehemently opposed to inpatient treatment and would react violently to any attempt to involuntarily civilly commit him to an inpatient psychiatric facility. The legal standard in your state for involuntary civil commitment is that the person must be imminently dangerous to self or others. The father's oldest child is currently enrolled in her sophomore year of college and is studying abnormal psychology. She has pointed out that her uncle's mental state appears to be deteriorating and is worried that he needs some kind of help. How do you propose to handle this case?

Case 16-B Analysis

1. Vector or vectors to be used: TJ with some CPS. PL.

2. Why they will work best in this case: TJ because the brother is clearly suffering from a mental disorder—schizophrenia. TJ is almost always appropriate if there is a men-

tal illness involved in one of the individuals in the case. CPS is relevant because the problem is longstanding, complex, and more than just this one episode. PL perhaps to prevent this situation from re-occurring.

3. Brief description of the vectors (see Case 16-A Analysis, above).

4. Case analysis (including psycholegal soft spots) in three columns:
    (a) legal problems; (b) psychological problems; and (c) the intersections.

(a) Legal issues:	(b) Extralegal issues:	(c) Intersections:
Involuntary civil commitment (He may fail to meet the standard of imminent dangerousness required for involuntary civil commitment and even if he does, it is only for a limited time and must be reinstated or renewed periodically—need a new hearing).	Clear mental illness, suggesting that TJ must at least be considered.

Family relational issues, suggesting that the problem be broadened past the immediate person (the brother) to encompass the family situation. | Involuntary civil commitment will further strain the family relationships and alienate the brother.

Brother may cut off all contact with family if they proceed adversarially against him. |
| Possible prevention of a tort or crime if his behavior worsens. | Family fears for its own safety.

Family has no access to medical records. | Family fears for its own safety; involuntary commitment may assist with this. |
Need for repeated commitment hearings if he does not improve.	Family manages the trust fund.	Family manages the trust fund; may consider new trustee.
No facts to indicate that he is mentally incompetent such that a guardian would be appointed (this is a legal issue to research: is he incompetent? If not, he can refuse to consent to voluntary civil commitment, he has legal rights if not incompetent.).		Want brother to agree to release medical records to family so they can monitor his health; unlikely to agree. Alternate monitor can be agreed to?
Trust fund fiduciary duties.		

5. Skills: This case would require careful mediation skills so you could mediate the family's conference with the brother, if you could get the brother to attend. All your persuasive skills would be required to get the brother to collaborate with the family on the issues, instead of filing a lawsuit to civilly commit him.

6. Processes: I would choose TJ. If my jurisdiction had a mental health court, this would be the ideal forum. However, he has not been charged with any crime or misbehavior yet (no overt act), so that that court may not be able to take jurisdiction of his case without such an act (vagrancy, loitering, assault, trespassing, etc.) In that event, the family must simply institute a petition for civil commitment to involuntarily commit him, which will create the psycholegal soft spot of further angering and alienating him. Ideally, we would want the brother to agree to get needed additional medical and psychiatric help to stabilize his condition, and we might use the threat of or the process of involuntary civil commitment as leverage to induce him to do so. The

family wants access to his medical records to ensure that he is taking his medication and getting the requisite help. The family is also going to want access to give information to his doctor and psychotherapist, in case they are unaware that his condition is deteriorating. He is unlikely to give that consent to the family, but maybe once leverage/threat of commitment process has gotten him to agree to participate, you could have a process in which each family member speaks in turn about their feelings towards the brother and his condition and their fears and then they, together with him, try to agree to some compromise. Perhaps, if he doesn't meet the standard for involuntary commitment, he might be more willing to allow them to get summary information from his doctors if they agree to let go of the purse strings and appoint a neutral trustee over his trust fund. If he is entirely intractable, then you proceed with an involuntary civil commitment proceeding, but at least you have tried mediation ahead of time and he doesn't feel blindsided by the formal proceeding (a little PJ).

7. Ideally, we would want the brother to agree to get needed additional medical and psychiatric help to stabilize his condition, and we might use the threat of or the process of involuntary civil commitment as leverage to induce him to do so.

8. The advantages of this approach over a traditional, involuntary civil commitment is, first, the involuntary approach might not work; the brother might not qualify in the state for mandatory court-ordered treatment. Even if he does, the treatment period might be very brief, thus solving the problem only for a few short days, perhaps. Second, this approach seeks to place more control in the brother's hands (which might empower him in the long run and help him take more responsibility for his condition) and preserve the family relationships in place, which will be present long after the attorney is out of the family's life. The disadvantages are that this approach might not work and the traditional, involuntary process may be the only option. (This case is loosely based on several real life situations for which solutions are very difficult to find.)

Case 16-C

This case is perhaps the most comprehensive case in this book. It should afford the best opportunity to apply a great variety of ideas, concepts, vectors, lenses, and processes of the comprehensive law movement. The case analysis is intentionally omitted.

The city of Ventana Beach, Florida (a fictional place) erected a fishing pier, which was opened to the public about 10 months ago. Last week, a 48-year-old fisherman, Frank Farmer, and a 17-year-old surfer, Keif Seyes, got into an altercation as a result of a dispute over usage of the area under the pier, as follows:

Apparently, a group of surfers was surfing on the right side (south side) of the pier, relatively close to where the fishermen were casting out their lines to catch fish. The pier charges $2 per person for visitors to the pier and $6 per person for those who want to fish from the pier. The pier is managed and operated by the City but is open to the public as long as these entrance fees are paid. The beach below is free. A free public parking lot is provided at the pier for pier-goers and beach-goers alike. In the past, surfers and fishermen have argued with each other and disagreed over who has the right to use the water under the pier. The waves are the very best for surfing right next to (practically, under) the pier, much better than anywhere else on the beach, so the surfers really enjoy and utilize the waves on both sides of the pier. Similarly, there is no other place at the beach where the fishermen can access deep water, as they can at the pier, so the fishing is best off the sides and end of the pier. As the end has limited space, the fishermen heavily use both sides of the pier.

Last week, the surfer group in the water (all of whom were 15- to 19-years-old, consisting of a few boys and one girl) began yelling obscenities at the fishermen on the pier above, who were casting their lines into the water where the surfers were surfing. The fishermen appeared to be intentionally casting the lines into the water where the surfers were sitting on their boards. The surfers, in turn, began intentionally biting the fishermen's lines, so that their rigs, bait, hooks, sinkers, etc., which can be rather expensive, were lost (dropped into the sea). More obscenities were exchanged between both groups, until one surfer challenged one fisherman, saying: "You'd better come down here and do something about it!" The fisherman then came down from the pier to where the surfer was, more expletives were exchanged, violence threatened, and ultimately Farmer, the fisherman, shoved Seyes, the surfer, who shoved Farmer in response. A short fist fight ensued. Both Farmer and Seyes have been referred to the local state attorney's office for criminal prosecution. Both are residents of Ventana Beach.

Farmer: While Farmer's anger with the surfers is characteristic of many fishermen on the pier, Farmer himself has some history with the criminal justice system, unlike most of the other fishermen on the pier. Farmer has been mostly transient, with a very flimsy permanent address (with his sister, with whom he does not always get along), since he was discharged from active duty in the Gulf War, 20 years ago. As it turns out, Farmer has been arrested four times in the last year, including several times for threatening violence. One of those arrests was for stalking a group of middle school children in an outdoor park near the beach. His most recent arrest, four months ago, was for violating the conditions of his probation by threatening to hit a store clerk with a beer bottle. He was released from custody within six weeks after that arrest. As a war veteran, Farmer might be suffering from "post-traumatic stress disorder," which could cause him to perceive situations and people as more threatening than they really are.

Frustrated with the "revolving door" of Farmer's many arrests and recidivism, the local police have contacted the state attorney's office and the judge assigned to hear his most recent case, to indicate that they will be sending police officers to the courtroom to ensure that the judge and state attorney are "fully informed" about Farmer's history. The county jail is overcrowded, which explains why Farmer and many other transients with repeat arrest records are usually quickly arraigned and released. The state attorney's office is also "swamped," which explains why it usually does not try every case brought to its doorstep. For example, arrests made on felony charges are routinely dropped to misdemeanor status and, often, the offender is given credit for time served and released after a first appearance before a judge. Farmer has been quickly released in the past, but this time the judge and state attorney's office are under pressure to "come down hard" on Farmer, as the police are tired of dealing with the frequent problems he causes.

Park & Chin: In addition, two 18-year-old friends of Seyes, Keanu Park and Ashley Chin, were so incensed by his arrest that they spray-painted words of protest on the fishing pier and attached fence, later that night. Some of the words they chose to use were four-letter obscenities/expletives. The words they spray-painted on the pier were in plain view of a church and a private elementary school, both of which are across the street from the pier. In addition, some of the paint they used drifted, due to a slight breeze, and coated the cars, windows, and outside house walls of two private homeowners whose property was next to the pier. Not only are Park and Chin facing criminal charges of criminal mischief and vandalism, but the private homeowners are threatening to bring civil actions against them for the damage done to their cars and homes.

The surfer/fishermen situation has been going on between these two groups for at least six months with frequent debates and newspaper articles, but this is the first time it has resulted in criminal actions. Describe how the attorneys for Farmer, Seyes, Park, and Chin and the prosecutors (and the judge in the matters, if appropriate) would proceed, in these civil and criminal cases, using one or more comprehensive law approaches, as appropriate.

Exercise 16-2 — Capstone Assignment

Write a one to two page typed, single-spaced paper describing five things:

1. Which vectors (if any) you plan to incorporate into your law practice?

2. Why?

3. Which vectors (can be all of them) you will not use?

4. Why?

5. How your personal approach to lawyering has changed, developed, or refined as a result of this book?

Address the following vectors: therapeutic jurisprudence, preventive law, creative problemsolving, holistic justice, procedural justice, collaborative law, transformative mediation, restorative justice, and the problem solving court movement (e.g., drug treatment courts). You may want to refer to this paper when you evaluate your work as a lawyer, judge, mediator, or other legal professional, from time to time.

Index